A QUESTION OF ARSON

COLIN O'NEILL

A Question of Arson © 2025 Colin O'Neill

All Rights Reserved. No part of this book may be reproduced in any form or by any electronic or mechanical means including information storage and retrieval systems, without permission in writing from the author. The only exception is by a reviewer, who may quote short excerpts in a review.

No generative artifical intelligence (AI) was used in the creation of this book. The author expressly prohibits the use of this publication as training data for AI technologies or large language models (LLMs) for generative purposes. The author reserves all rights to license uses of this work for generative AI training and the development of LLMs.

This book is a work of non-fiction. This publication is designed to provide accurate and authoritative information in regards to the subject matter covered. It is sold with the understanding that neither the author nor the publisher is engaged in rendering legal, investment, accounting, or other professional services. For privacy reasons, some names, locations, and dates may have been changed.

These are the memories of the author, from their perspective, and they have tried to represent events as faithfully as possible.

Printed in Australia

Cover by Melinda Childs @studioorchard

Internal design by Book Burrow www.bookburrow.com.au

First printing: April 2025

Paperback ISBN 978-1-7638-6912-7

eBook ISBN 978-1-7638-6913-4

Distributed by Lightning Source Global

 A catalogue record for this work is available from the National Library of Australia

ALSO BY COLIN O'NEILL

From Vietnam Nasho to Catching School Crooks

A Question of Arson

The April Fool's Day Lawyer

CONTENTS

Prologue	1
Defining Arson	8
Arson Investigation	16
Legislation and Procedure	30
A Question of 'Who or What Dunnit'	48
Murder Arson	71
Manslaughter or Arson Causing Death	126
Arson to Conceal Murder	162
Australia's Bushfires	193
The Churchill Arsonist	208
Firefighter or Firelighter	221
Worst of the Worst	258
Too Close to Home	288
Catching the Firebugs	326
Nursing Home Tragedy	335
Nightclub and Backpacker Hostel Fires	345
Guilty or Not Guilty?	365
A Question of Innocence	388
The Jury is Still Out	422

Epilogue	436
Glossary	441
List of Cases	468
Police Task Forces/Operations	475
Rogues Gallery	476
List of Legislation	479
References	482
Principal Reference Websites	510
About the Author	511

PROLOGUE

The destruction and often fatal consequences of fire first became apparent to me on 18 March 1968, when serving with the Australian Army in South Vietnam. Phantom American fighter–bombers were used extensively during the Vietnam War, particularly in firefights with enemy MIG fighter aircraft over the skies of Hanoi, and in dropping napalm on villages throughout the Mekong Delta. Napalm was originally used as flamethrowers to burn sections of the jungle in Vietnam and to clear out bunkers, trenches and tunnels. It was also used by the United States of America Navy riverboats on the Mekong River. In the event the flame did not kill on impact, the fire it created sucked out the air, causing its victims to suffocate.

I saw the first Phantom jet fly over the top of the village of Ngai Giao, followed by a second aircraft zeroing in and dropping its napalm canister, which tumbled head over head before hitting the ground. It appeared to be bouncing along before exploding and igniting, destroying everything in its path. The other Phantom jet followed the same trajectory and again, the canister rolled over in the air before exploding into a massive fireball, no doubt killing all those unfortunates who happened to be in the village below.

The Phantoms were then followed by two attacking Huey helicopter gunships known as "Cobras" depending on their role. A stony silence suddenly followed with no further gun fire. We immediately left the compound and headed straight towards the village to render what assistance we could. After alighting from our land rover, I slowly walked along a track that led to the smouldering ruins towards what was once a happy and vibrant local village. I was in complete shock at what had just transpired and was further impacted by what I was about to witness.

Sadly, it remains in my memories as the most unimaginable sight I could ever face. Under burnt rubble, I found what was once a much-loved home, the bodies of a family, including what appeared to be two children who had been incinerated. It was obvious there was nothing we could do for them, so we left the bodies to be recovered by their grieving family members. I then saw six Vietnamese women and a dog, raking through the charred remains. It was blatantly obvious they were in a state of shock. I suspect they had left their village at the first indication of a pending attack by the Viet Cong, only to return to discover the smouldering ruin which was once their homes and village.

I was, unfortunately, to become very accustomed to fires and arson following my appointment in 1974 as Head of School Security for the Victorian Ministry of Education. As part of my learning exercise, I undertook a five-week Investigators Course at the Victoria Police Detective Training School (DTS) in Spring Street, Melbourne. I found DTS, colloquially known as "bonehead" to be very informative, particularly in the prevention, detection and investigation of crime, as well as the apprehension of offenders and providing evidence in a court of law. The correct procedures for the collection and preservation of evidence when attending crime scenes and certainly school fires, was of valuable assistance as 'every contact leaves a trace.' This would come back to haunt me some months later.

I was obviously not paying attention in some lectures concerning crime scenes and the collecting of evidence because, not long after, I responded to a rather large school fire at Jordanville South Primary School. On arrival, the Metropolitan Fire Brigade (MFB) had extinguished the blaze so, with my offsider, we carried out a crime scene check, pending the arrival of local police. We found six cans of partly consumed beer near where the fire had started and immediately thought they could lead to fingerprints from the offenders. We carefully placed each can in an exhibit bag we now carried with us since doing our DTS course. Each beer can was picked up with a biro pen, so we would not contaminate the prints from the arsonist by leaving our fingerprints.

On the arrival of Mt Waverley CIB detectives who I knew quite well from other jobs, I told them of our find and how thankful we were to the DTS as we now knew how to store possible exhibits in an evidence bag, as 'every contact leaves a trace'. On opening the bag, our cans were happily floating around in their beer dregs because we had forgotten to empty them before putting them into the bag. One of the sayings from DTS, or should I say, Bonehead, was, 'You want to be a deetecctive but you can't even spell it.' The local CIB sergeant jokingly reminded me of that, as he watched us empty the "vital evidence" into a rubbish bin.

One of our security officers, Graeme White was certainly no bonehead though, when he attended a fire at Armadale

Primary School in the early hours one morning. The fire had been first reported to our control room by the school cleaners who arrived at around 4am to start their day's work, to find a fire burning in the administration area. They immediately contacted the MFB who attended and quelled the blaze, with damage later estimated at around $30,000. There was no sign of a forced entry so, at first glance, it appeared the fire may have been accidental, perhaps "spontaneous combustion".

Graeme, on his attendance, however, kept an open mind and on having a closer look at the fire-damaged area, he noticed what appeared to be some sort of undamaged credit card lying close by. Using two biros, he picked the item up. It was a bankcard with a person's name, with a four-pin serial number. Surely, this must belong to one of the cleaners or a teacher at the school and had been inadvertently dropped on the floor. A further examination of school records though, revealed the card belonged to a person who appeared to have no association with the school as an employee or parent of a student.

Lo and behold, Graeme then found an unlocked door leading into the administration area and, in his mind, the card had been used by this person to force the lock, by using it at an angle then sliding it down which then clicked the door open. He immediately placed the untouched card back in the same location and sealed off what now was clearly a crime scene. The arson squad attended, carried out the usual checks on the bankcard name, including fingerprinting it, to reveal a 34-year-old male from Chadstone and known to police, who was, in fact, the arsonist.

Makes my effort at Jordanville South Primary look pretty ordinary.

Unfortunately, school fires continued to rear their ugly head, as did the culprits hell bent on vandalising or taking revenge out on their school, concealing their ill-gotten crime following a burglary or, in some cases, just for the plain excitement of setting the fire and then watching it burn. If someone is going to commit a crime, especially arson, it is also advisable not to hang around and marvel at the work, because they may never know when someone might tap them on the shoulder.

This happened to one of our security officers when he attended a fire at a local high school. On arrival, he noticed a young chap in his early twenties wearing jeans with a flannel shirt and looking very pleased with himself, while watching the school burn. Our officer tapped him on the shoulder and commented, 'What a great fire!'

As the offender replied that it was indeed a superb burn, it was noted he was, shall we say, "very excited".

The crook, looking at our officer dressed in his usual scruffy, dirty, casual attire, obviously thought he was just someone passing by, so he was asked how he lit the fire. He replied that he broke into the school, gaining entry through a window and then splashed the accelerant around before setting a match to it. On enquiring where the accelerant was, he said, 'I'll show you' then led our officer to under an overpass where a five-litre plastic bottle was located. He was taken back to the fire scene and handed over to police. Believe it or not, some pyromaniacs are just plain dumb.

My luck ran out though, when at 4am one morning I was called out to Keon Park Technical School and, being a former student, I was certainly attending in a different capacity. A petrol bomb, sometimes referred to as a Molotov cocktail, had been thrown through the vice principal's window. I was able to extinguish the blaze but having suffered smoke inhalation, I ended up being treated at my not-so-favourite local hospital: Preston and Northcote Community Hospital.

A press release later stated I had been pulled unconscious from the school, but I thought that was a bit over the top. My efforts went unrewarded because the following night, the arsonist was successful in his second attempt, burning down the entire administration block and four classrooms.

Mt Waverley High School, however, was somewhat fortunate it didn't suffer the same fate as Keon Park Tech. I knew the school well from having previously arrested a crook, after my German shepherd, Edo, had chased him down as he ran away with his goodies in hand. Luckily for the school, it was the last one on our school muck up night patrol sheet before eating a well-earned breakfast at Dennys, our favourite 24-hour restaurant in Burwood. I might add that Edo, was given his name meaning Education Department Officer. Not that he knew at the time what he was being trained for.

In company with security officer, Graeme White, at about 5am, we were checking a portable building at the rear of the school when we came across a fire lit in the doorway and about to take hold. Due to carrying fire extinguishers in our security vehicle, we were able to extinguish the blaze without too much damage but little did we know at the time what was awaiting us over the next 18 months regarding school fires.

We were, however, successful in arresting two offenders for a series of deliberately lit fires at Frankston High School during 1990-1991. The arrest was as a result of an undercover operation by our security officers over a period of five months before arresting the culprits about to start another fire. Apparently, all over needing days off from school and not wanting to sit exams or complete assignments.

I, subsequently, entered the legal profession on April Fool's Day 1996, practicing mainly in the areas of crime and industrial relations over the next 25 years. I never acted for any person charged with arson but the closest I came was when I appeared for a local Mornington Shire resident charged with lighting a fire on a total fire ban day, in addition to an assault charge. Both charges carried significant penalties, including imprisonment with the charge of lighting the fire under the *Country Fire Authority Act 1958* (Vic) and the common assault charge pursuant to section 23 of the *Summary Offences Act 1966* (Vic).

My client determined that rubbish in her back yard needed to be taken care of, so she lit a fire, despite knowing it was prohibited due to the total fire ban. On arrival of the Country Fire Authority (CFA), she was not impressed and instead of putting out the flames, she squirted the CFA members, hence a charge of assault. It must have been my lucky day as my fire lady received a good behaviour bond (GBB), with a donation to the CFA.

However, given all my exposure to fires and miscreants in my early days prior to lawyering, it is now time to write about the crime of arson, initially titled "A Case of Arson". However, for reasons, which will become apparent, I changed the title as the crime of arson does in fact leave many questions, some unanswered.

I might add that what follows is not a complete and exhaustive analysis of arson and its perpetrators, as I am sure there are a number of cases that I have overlooked. However, please be warned that some of the cases I write about, particularly in respect of murder arson, are quite horrific and beyond any sort of human comprehension.

1
DEFINING ARSON

I can recall in my early school days, when studying Roman history, a reference to a 64AD emperor by the name of Nero. It seems Nero allegedly played a musical instrument while nearly most of Rome burned to the ground. It was thought Nero was responsible in that he arranged for a number of fires to be lit by drunken hooligans supposedly on the basis of wanting to rebuild Rome. On the other hand, some scholars determined the fires were not suspicious and they had emanated from a single accidental fire, then encouraged by high winds with embers starting additional fires in other houses and buildings, such fires burning for six days.

History is, however, unable to conclusively determine whether Nero 'playing his fiddle while Rome burned', was what we now term as an arsonist. Perhaps the scribes were right in that the fires were accidental and may have simply started from spontaneous combustion. A term sometimes used when arson investigators are unable to determine an exact cause and that it was probably started by self-heating from a substance with a low ignition temperature, such as straw and hay.

The definition of arson developed in English law from the late 13th century from the middle French term arsoun. It can also be traced back to the Latin word, *ársionem*, meaning "a burning". It is also translated from an old English term, baernet.

The Great Fire of London in 1666 makes interesting reading. Such fire followed the Great Plague a year before, which killed around 70,000 civilians. The fire was believed to have started in a bakery near London Bridge, in Pudding Lane. Despite best efforts of the local population and even the reigning king, using buckets filled with water, over 3,000 houses and other dwellings burned to the ground. The aftermath left only about one-fifth of London without fire damage and remarkably only six lives were lost in the inferno.

Some learned occupants did reflect, however, that the Great Fire had resulted in a much-needed city cleansing and eradicated overcrowded streets, perhaps still poisoned by remnants from the Great Plague. A rather confused fellow, by the name of Robert Hubert, put his hand up and made a number of conflicting admissions of malicious acts by burning. Perhaps we would now say arson. The king, obviously tired from firefighting, didn't muck around and old Hubert was hung from probably the only tree still left standing. It was later ascertained that this poor chap was not in England at the time of the fire.

They certainly had no hesitation in those days, sending arsonists straight to the gallows and in 1680, an English servant met the same fate. Margaret Clark was executed by hanging after setting fire to the home of her employer, allegedly after accepting a bribe as part of a so-called plot by upset Catholics, supposedly hell bent, once again, on burning London to the ground and as a misguided warning to protestants.

Arson was then loosely defined as (i) the malicious damage of property and (ii) the burning of important symbols recognised by the state. Even setting fire to a haystack was seen as a symbol of unrest. By the late 1800s the treason aspect was removed from the legal definition and was defined, much as it is today, with a number of variations as: 'the act of intentionally and unlawfully destroying or damaging the property of another by fire.'

Acts of arson, of course, not only involve deliberately setting property on fire, such as buildings, but also can involve damage by fire too. That includes motor vehicles and vegetation, such as forests, commonly referred to as wildfires or bushfires. Unfortunately, acts of arson can also result in death leading to a charge of murder or a lesser charge of manslaughter.

The alleged perpetrator, who commits an act of arson, is colloquially referred to as an arsonist. In cases of someone starting a number of deliberate fires, they are seen as a serial arsonist, when it is at least three fires, or a pyromaniac, when they simply have an attraction to lighting fires. Their handiwork is usually started with the assistance of an accelerant, such as petrol or kerosene, to ensure whatever they are intent on burning is completely destroyed.

The degree, or type of arson, by way of example in the US, can be divided into three categories: first degree arson is the burning of an occupied building; second degree arson is burning an unoccupied house or building and lastly; third degree arson is setting fire to an abandoned area, such as a forest or disused building. Penalties for such aggravated criminal acts can be as high as 25 years imprisonment and, in the case of causing death, the penalty can be a life sentence or execution.

In further defining arson, it also raises the question of, what generates such a criminal act? In other words, what is the motive behind the fire? This can be classed as either a primary or secondary reason. In other words, was setting the fire the main motive to destroy or was there a secondary reason, such as covering up another criminal act? In some instances, arson, by way of mitigation but certainly not excusable, can be carried out by a drug or alcohol affected miscreant, or somebody suffering from a mental illness, such as schizophrenia. In essence though, there are usually specific reasons why a person commits an act of arson and, in some cases, there can be a number of motives leading to a disastrous outcome.

The fire lighter may set out to simply commit an act of vandalism, such as setting fire to a school or other public building for a variety of reasons, including boredom or dissent for, perhaps, being kept in school detention. Many vandals do seem to escalate attacks on their local school by first starting off smashing a few windows, to then breaking in and graffitiing their classroom and, in a final act of intolerance, setting fire to the school building.

Arson can also result as an act of revenge based on jealousy or simply spite. It could be a means of payback or getting even for some misguided act they believe they have been subjected to. Sadly, this type of brazen conduct is often seen in unpleasant domestic and family violence situations. Some revenge-type arson extremist attacks can also, not only be targeted at an individual, but also an institution or specific group for their political, social or religious beliefs. Such firebugs go after their targets with the sole aim of causing as much disruption, confusion and certainly fear, for simply holding a belief or promoting a cause they passionately believe in.

Profit-motivated arson is a common occurrence for financial or material gain and is often referred to as an act of insurance fraud. The fraudster arsonist sets out to often benefit, usually by way of a financial windfall they are not entitled to. In some quarters, and I am not being racist, but it is sometimes called a "Jewish stocktake". While such phrase is not found in the Oxford Dictionary, it is a well-known term, despite being antisemitic. Many of these types of property insurance claims result as a consequence of an unexplained early morning fire in a building, such as a factory, shop or business.

What then follows is an insurance claim for payment for the loss of the property and its goods. Such claim is usually set a lot higher than the actual loss. The "hapless" property owner sets the insurable property on fire or arranges for a paid arsonist to do the dirty work to claim the insurance dollars. This type of arson may also be carried out by a failing business owner to cover their losses and remove themselves from any further obligations, such as mortgage or loan payments. In other situations, arson is seen as a way to eliminate competitors by burning down their premises with the hope the surviving business will profit from such fire, with increased sales.

Organised crime groups also use arson as a persuasive tool to encourage certain types of business to adhere to their rules of making blackmail payments for fear of losing their business to an arson attack. The threat could also "encourage" them to buy certain specified goods on the black market, controlled by their crime syndicate. Failing this, their shop could go up in flames.

Crime concealment is another reason arson is carried out and normally in situations to destroy incriminating evidence, such as clothing, DNA evidence, such as blood, saliva or fingerprints of the offender from an earlier crime. In some situations, such cover up can be to dispose of a murder victim's body, to prevent their identity being revealed and providing investigators with a possible valuable lead to the offender. The usual collection methods of DNA can result from items that may have been touched or worn by an individual and can include clothing, weapons and even cigarette butts, to name a few.

A concept known as "hero syndrome" can also result in a fire or series of fires, simply because the firebug wants to be recognised for reporting the event and so be seen as some sort of hero. Such grandiose delusion is often seen in firefighters or former members of a firefighting unit for which they no longer serve. In some situations, this type of offending is due to someone having an axe to grind with their superiors, or not being appreciated by their peers, so they set the fire, report it and advance their hero complex further by assisting to put the fire out.

It is not just limited to misguided firefighters, but can include police officers, security guards or night watchmen, who are known to carry out an arson attack, perhaps due to boredom on their shift. It is also not uncommon for these thrill seekers to photograph or video their handiwork to later replay their heroics.

Some thrill seekers, or firebugs, starting fires can also be driven by the sheer excitement of lighting a fire and will often remain at the scene to witness their handiwork. The term arsonist and pyromaniac can sometimes be interchangeable and confusing when considering the circumstances surrounding a fire and certainly in situations where there is more than one fire. The arsonist, of course, has a specific motive or aim in mind, however, a pyromaniac is in a realm of their own.

Initially, in the early 1800s a pyromaniac was believed to be, what was termed as, a combination of 'moral insanity and treatment', but the term now sits alongside arsonist and a common reason for starting at least more than one fire.

A pyromaniac acts on impulse or arousal in which they cannot control themselves. By starting a fire, followed by further fires, it some way releases their stress, tension and emotions. Pyromaniacs also gain immense satisfaction and gratification watching their handiwork and it is useful to quote the 2022 classification of the World Health Organisation's International Classification of Diseases (ICD) in which they characterise pyromania as:

a recurrent failure to control strong impulses to set fires, resulting in multiple acts of, or attempts at, setting fire to property or other objects, in the absence of apparent motive...There is an increasing sense of tension or affective arousal prior to instances of fire setting, persistent fascination or preoccupation with fire and related stimuli...a sense of pleasure, excitement, relief or gratification during, and immediately after, the act of setting the fire, witnessing its effects, or participating in its aftermath. [1]

In essence, a pyromaniac has no remorse and certainly no insight or concern that his or her act of setting fires may destroy property or even result in the loss of life. Pyromania is also likened to a term known as pyrophilia, meaning that the act of lighting, including the watching, of fires provides some sort of sexual gratification. It is not uncommon in these types of situations for the perpetrator to then sit back and watch their

---

[1] 11th Revision- ICD-11.

handiwork, gaining immense sexual arousal leading to relief by masturbation.

The difficulty, however, for arson investigators is trying to piece together what happened and uncover some form of evidence, which will hopefully lead to the identification of the culprit(s). Dr Edmond Locard, a pioneer in forensic science, can be attributed to the principle that a perpetrator of a crime will not only bring something into the crime scene, but leave with something from it. In other words, in any contact there will be an exchange.

While every "contact leaves a trace", arson investigation at the crime scene can be particularly difficult, as the fire, in many instances, has destroyed any evidence remaining in the rubble.

2
ARSON INVESTIGATION

The first thought an investigator may have on attending a fire is, 'Why was this fire deliberately lit?' That, of course, raises an immediate question: is the investigator not keeping an open mind? As the fire under investigation may well have been accidental. However, there is nothing wrong in initially treating all fire sites as crime scenes. I recall in my early days, in charge of School Security for the Victorian Ministry of Education, that some qualified investigators, noting I was not as well qualified, in the absence of any compelling evidence of arson, would ultimately determine, perhaps already predetermined, the school fire was accidental. They would even consider that perhaps it was "spontaneous combustion".

A more technical explanation for this type of ignition source is that it takes place due to combustible material being heated to its ignition temperature through a chemical reaction involving oxidation. I have no idea what that means, so let's try and be simple and just say, spontaneous combustion, for example, is a bushfire caused by heat from the sun, or even a lightning strike.

This is certainly no criticism of those very experienced detectives from the police arson squad, as they did have limited staffing and a number of other crime scenes to attend. What was perplexing though was, despite the school fire taking hold in the early hours of the morning in an unoccupied building, a school with a history of burglary and vandalism, the fire, in the absence of any compelling evidence, was considered as an undetermined cause or even accidental, thanks to spontaneous combustion.

Mind you, this determination may well have been right on some occasions, as such fire could have started from faulty electrical wiring or other defective equipment. Perhaps a heater was left on or some discarded cigarette butt was left smouldering for some hours before igniting into a large blaze. However, rightly or wrongly, I took the view, unless proven otherwise, any school fire was deemed suspicious.

From the outset, I would be the first to put my hand up and say I was no expert in fire investigation. I only completed and somehow passed, a very basic five-week DTS investigation course and my opening prologue typifies my first bumbling attempt to preserve a fire crime scene. There are, of course, many useful texts on fire investigation, including the *United States National Fire Protection Guide to Fire and Explosive Investigation*, which provides a very systematic explanation of carrying out such enquiries. However, I can base my knowledge and interpretation of investigating fires from many years of attending school fires and working very closely with detectives from the Victoria Police Arson Squad (now known as the Arson and Explosives Squad) and local criminal investigation units.

The role of Arson and Explosives is to primarily respond to and provide an initial investigation of suspicious deaths by fire, bombs and explosive devices and fatalities caused by bushfires. The squad also has a particular focus in targeting organised, serial or recidivist offenders.

Regardless, it is important for any arson investigator that, after the fire is extinguished, to preserve the crime scene. Note that I am still saying "crime scene" until proven otherwise. It's important to adopt a systematic process to determine the origin, meaning the ignition point, of the fire, which will then hopefully lead to a cause of the blaze. The problem is, in trying to determine the cause of the fire, much of the potential evidence has already been destroyed leaving, on some occasions, not a lot to evaluate. Hopefully, the fire scene has been properly secured and the names of any potential witnesses recorded by the first fire responders.

In many fires, including school fires, the absence of any witnesses was always a problem. It was not unusual, and I am sure this happens in any investigation, to door knock the surrounding neighbourhood, just in case a witness can provide some insight to the events that led to the fire, or any person(s) seen in the vicinity, including motor vehicle(s) leaving the scene.

In some school fires, locating witnesses was always an issue and we would always door knock the local neighbourhood, including shops. On one occasion, our investigator was informed by a local milk bar proprietor of two students coming into the shop and bragging about their exploits in starting the fire and getting days off school. This led to their arrest and subsequent conviction.

In another school fire, I decided to speak with some

students who had remained at the school after being told it had been cancelled for the day, due to the fire damage. A couple of students gave me the name of one boy who had earlier witnessed the fire being extinguished by the MFB. They stated he openly bragged about lighting the fire as he hated the school and the teachers.

This information may have been false and possibly a pay back by these two students, but on speaking with the principal, it came to light that the named student had been absent for the last two days and had previously been disciplined by the school. He ultimately confessed that he did light the fire and described in detail how he did it and why. The 14-year-old lad was subsequently charged to appear in the Children's Court at a later date but only received a "rap over the knuckles".

In the interim though, school burglaries and vandal attacks were an everyday occurrence, so at this point I needed to "think outside the square". Given that a fire in a school would often attract bystanders who'd watch the fire fighters douse the flames, I had this idea that perhaps we should video tape those observing the fire to see if anyone stood out, perhaps in unusual attire or even the same person being recorded at another school fire.

I initially would attend, as soon as possible, a school fire with a video recorder and if the fire was still in progress, record the scene and any bystanders. We would then have a look at the tape to see if we could pinpoint possible suspect(s). We tried this on a few occasions, but whilst this idea may have had some merit, it was discarded without any success. No doubt, arson investigators would look at any relevant footage nowadays as they never know what that might lead to.

Again, adopting a new investigative approach, a Richmond school fire, causing $100,000 in damage, was another one of those times where I had a "bright idea". In my discussions with the school principal following the fire, I was advised there was a rumour circulating throughout the school that the fire had been lit, once again, by a disgruntled senior student. Despite both investigating police and our further enquiries, we could not establish any possible suspects. One of our security officers was only 20 years of age but looked more like 16 and the plan was to place him in the school as a Form Six student who had just arrived from overseas. Our "covert surveillance plan" was done with the full knowledge of the principal.

This "brain wave" was based on the premise that he would attend each class, circulate and befriend other students to see if he could obtain any information which could possibly identify the culprit. It is arguable as to whether this plan fell under our charter of prevention and detection of school crime, but I thought if we could prevent any further fires, then it was part of our scope. He became a student for three weeks. I would drop him off each morning and then pick him up after school near a local tram stop. Sadly, we wasted these three weeks as no information was forthcoming, so the idea was abandoned. At least there were no more fires at the school.

Again, applying a different approach, a school in Noble Park suffered a major fire with many destroyed classrooms. I inspected the damage at the school and after discussing the way forward with members of the arson squad, we decided to try something creative in an attempt to identify the offender, or offenders. We had not gone down this path before, but it was a new addition to arson investigation and was worth a try. The school held an assembly with their teachers and 350 students where I spoke at length, appealing for any information that would lead to the identity of those responsible.

It paid off when two students came forward to inform us of their suspicions. They mentioned the bragging by another student who had told them how he had entered the school and lit the fire, all done in retaliation against his teacher and, unbelievably, the classroom piano. After making further enquiries with the principal, we were confident of a good outcome. The student was subsequently arrested, charged by detectives from the arson squad and ultimately pleaded guilty before the Children's Court. As a footnote, the school piano was destroyed, along with many other treasured items, including a student's guitar and stamp collection.

A new "initiative", for want of a better word, was also implemented by our school security team because of three major school fires over 10 weeks. We decided to install a "special hotline" to obtain any information about the school fires, which at this stage, totalled seven major events over a five-month period. The estimated damage bill was literally in the millions of dollars.

There was a press release by young journalist, Tony Wilson, to promote our "brain wave" and the number to call was 651–2627. It was emphasised that the caller did not have to leave their name and address but hopefully would provide information leading to the offenders. I had read an article at the time where a similar idea had been implemented in Albuquerque, New Mexico. Local detectives had become very frustrated with the progress, or lack of it, in a murder investigation. We knew exactly how they felt.

Although an understatement, it is fair to say our new special hotline was a complete and utter failure. All we received were crank calls, basically telling us to "get stuffed". One caller even suggested he was the 'arsonist, catch me if you can.' But then again, Crime Stoppers is now a valuable tool for investigating police in solving crimes they otherwise would struggle in identifying the culprit(s). This was once again demonstrated in the cold case arson murder of 11-year-old Arthur Haines, when he died from a house fire in 1998 after suffering severe burns.

A caller to Crime Stoppers 24 odd years later resulted in the arrest and charging of a 55-year-old male with murder and six counts of damaging property with intent to endanger life. Police will allege the accused, after a dispute with a neighbour, threw a petrol bomb into a home. The call to Crime Stoppers in New South Wales was also thanks to a $1 million reward on offer. The defendant remains in custody awaiting trial after being extradited from Queensland.

One initiative that also paid off for investigators, was identifying the alleged arsonist regarding four wildfires described as an "arson spree", set in national forests over a two-month period in July and August 2021 in California in the US. A former university professor, by the name of Gary Stephen Maynard, had investigators suspicious of his nefarious activities, courtesy of a local citizen. They obtained a warrant and then placed a tracking device in his vehicle to monitor his movements. This led to revealing that his vehicle was in the vicinity of at least two of the fires, with police finding lighters and electronic devices in it, recording him talking about lighting fires.

He was subsequently charged and indicted, by a federal grand jury, with arson in respect of the wildfires, which he initially denied lighting. Maynard, who should have known better, being a teacher in criminal justice, eventually pleaded guilty as part of a plea deal, to lighting three fires. He was facing a statutory penalty of 20 years in prison, together with a $250,000 fine on each count. He was lucky to only be sentenced to three years and three months. On release, he will be under supervision for another three years.

I am sure other investigating police would sometimes use this tool in bringing an arsonist to justice. It is exactly what police did following seven deliberately lit fires in Bega, NSW during the months of October and November 2019. Police were zoning in on the suspect and they placed a tracking device in his vehicle the day before he was arrested. He subsequently faced seven charges and was found guilty on one charge of deliberately lighting a fire and was sentenced to an intensive corrections order.

Another interesting, but certainly unusual, tool in bringing an arsonist, suspected of arson insurance fraud, to justice, was the use by Middleton detectives in the US, of data taken from a pacemaker. They discovered that the statements made by Ross Compton, were inconsistent when he said he was asleep at the time of his house being set on fire in 2016. The pacemaker data suggested otherwise, showing an increased heart rate and cardiac rhythms not only before, but during and after the fire. His lawyers argued such data was protected by doctor-patient privilege, but a judge ruled that it could be used in his pending trial. Compton died before it could be presented as part of the evidence against him, however, this unique legal situation certainly shows how technology could be used in bring an alleged arsonist to justice.

Profiling an arsonist may be of some assistance to investigators, particularly in the event where they have a suspect in mind. According to the Australian Institute of Criminology, after examining the characteristics of arsonists over many years, they determined that a typical arsonist is male, around the age of 30-40 and usually comes from a poor background. Generally, they don't assimilate very well into our community and most likely will have committed other mainly minor crimes, such as wilful damage and theft.

Nowadays, many buildings, including schools and local houses, have the benefit of closed-circuit television footage (CCTV), and we often hear of an appeal from police for any relevant footage, including from a vehicle dashcam. Arson investigators also have the ability to obtain an intercept warrant to tap a suspect's mobile phone, in addition to the investigative tool known as a "tower dump". This enables police to identify data and the location of a suspect's movements that connect to a mobile phone tower and, if in the vicinity of, or heading to any subsequent fire crime scene. Even if a mobile phone is hidden or discarded by a suspect into a river or dam, the memory data from most devices can possibly be recovered, securely embedded in what is known as the cybersphere's cloud. This is providing the phone is a late model such as a Samsung or iPhone, which are sealed airtight.

Investigators in these modern times are certainly assisted by technology, even to the degree of checking credit card usage and banking transactions. They can see if the suspect was in the vicinity of the fire by checking tolling movements and also if they purchased any items, such as possible accelerants and containers to carry the fuel. Search warrants can now be obtained to check a person's computer for internet history to see if their suspect made any relevant enquiries for the location of a victim, or perhaps even how to set a fire and cover up the crime.

Police also now have the ability to look at internet history, where specialist technicians are able to recover deleted searches, such as a suspect downloading "how to carry out an arson cover up" then erasing it. Undercover officers go to the lengths of befriending the suspect, hoping to become best mates and then obtaining a confession, or placing listening devices in a suspect's home or vehicle to hopefully record incriminating conversations.

In South Australia, police undertook "Operation Nomad". This was another initiative where known arsonists had their vehicle registration numbers uploaded to traffic cameras in prone bushfire locations, to notify law enforcement of their presence.

Another useful tool is trained technology police detection dogs, who can enter a suspect's premises to sniff out any mobile phones and even SIM cards, which have been purposefully hidden because they contain incriminating evidence. These amazing dogs are able to detect the scent of micro-thins coating, that covers computer boards, even if such items, including small SIM or memory type cards, are hidden in the walls of the suspect's premises and, would you believe, also hidden in fruit.

There are also accelerant "sniffing" detection canines, known as arson dogs, which are specially trained animals that can detect and locate the use of accelerant that has started a fire. These accelerants include not only petrol, but the use of kerosene, diesel and lighter fluids. Their training can take anywhere up to two years, before they are used in service. These animals are so highly trained they can even differentiate between the use of accelerants and other scents typically found at a fire scene, such as burnt plastic or wood. The US Bureau of Alcohol, Tobacco, Firearms and Explosives (ATF), also uses these dogs to identify odours emanating from an explosion.

The use of and advancements in DNA technology is certainly another tool that assists crime scene investigators. Something as innocuous as a piece of chewing gum, spat onto the ground by a homicide suspect under police surveillance, was able to be matched to DNA swabs taken from a victim's body. This led to his subsequent arrest some 40 years later, resulting in a conviction for first degree murder in March 2024.

DNA taken from a crime scene has now been further advanced in assisting investigators, when identifying a suspect, by the use of forensic genetic genealogical analysis. It involves a DNA swab obtained from a crime scene and then comparing it to literally millions of DNA samples, not just from law enforcement criminal databases, but also from DNA samples lodged with public ancestry databases such as Ancestry DNA, a subsidiary of Ancestry LLC.

These databases are commonly used by donor conceived persons to trace, for example, their biological siblings. By 2020, Ancestry announced it had at least 18 million DNA kits purchased by customers and in excess of 10 billion digitised records. One can imagine such technology being used by investigators in respect of a cold case arson murder, leading to the identity of the perpetrator.

The much-publicised arrest of the Golden State Killer, Joseph James De Angelo, who committed at least 13 murders across California over a 12-year period from 1974, was thanks to DNA evidence identifying him through forensic genetic genealogy (FCG). This technology is also known as long-range familial DNA searching and can assist investigators in identifying family member matches as far back to third and fourth cousins, in the event no match is detected on existing criminal DNA databases.

Such DNA breakthroughs recently assisted Australian Police with an unsolved 1993 cold case, when DNA from a crime scene was compared to other samples of relatives on a database as far back as 1810. This is a giant leap forward as an investigative tool, given that the National Criminal Database in Australia normally could only identify close family match ups.

Another investigative advancement to assist law enforcement bodies, such as the US Federal Bureau of Investigation (FBI), is facial recognition technology, which is capable of matching a human face when compared to a digital image or a video frame against a plethora of faces from a data base. The US, at present, has one of the most capable and largest face recognition systems, with a total of around 117 million adult citizens on its database, largely obtained from drivers' licences.

The FBI also has in place, in its early stages, what is known as "Next Generation Identification". This project will see the expansion capabilities of fingerprint identification from criminal databases, which will include identification, not just from fingerprints taken from a crime scene, but also from eye irises, palms and face identification.

Apart for the various investigative tools now available, determining the origin of the fire is, of course, critical and where possible, investigators take samples, tag and properly bag separately any potential evidence, such as any incendiary devices. Fire investigators may also sketch the fire scene and the point and source of ignition and take copious photographs and video of the origin point and the fire path, together with any valuable evidence and subsequent damage. In ascertaining the point of origin, it is important to obtain from the first responders: the type, volume and colour of the flames and smoke and, in particular, the direction it took.

It should also be noted what was observed on first attending the fire scene and, certainly in school and building fires, the investigator would always want to know if there was any evidence of a forced entry, fresh graffiti and open or smashed windows. Of course, anything else that stood out or was considered unusual, such as internal lights left on, leading to the origin of the fire, which would assist in determining it was deliberately lit. In the case of school fires, previous acts of vandalism and burglary and, of course, arson attacks were very relevant in determining the possible reason for the fire and that it was indeed suspicious.

In properly examining a fire's origin, cause and development can, at times, be rather confusing. Thankfully, developments since 1992 saw a more scientific analysis being applied. The US-based National Fire Protection Association (NFPA), released such guidelines to assist in fire and explosive investigations and one critical and new phenomenon that certainly gained some traction was what is known as "flashover". This occurs from a combination of factors, such as char patterns, smoke damage and potential ignition sources, providing an insight into reconstructing the fire dynamics, in order to identify critical aspects during its development. It can, however, mimic a fire started deliberately, with similar post-burn fire patterns resembling those from an arson fire, but the new concept of flashover, in a number of cases, resulted in guilty verdicts, against the alleged perpetrators, being overturned.

Another crucial investigation technique to assist investigators to determine if an accelerant was used to start a fire, is what is known as a chromatogram test. This is used by chemists when analysing the debris from a fire scene, by comparing, what is known as, gas chromatography for evidence of known flammable liquids. Such a test, in some cases, particularly in the US similar to the flashover exoneration, would also see arson murder convictions set aside.

Ascertaining a possible motive would subsequently follow if arson was confirmed. Investigators would then speak with the owners of the damaged complex, to ascertain if there was any possible motive of why their premises were torched. This would also include whether they had been subjected to any threats or unreasonable demands that may assist the arson investigator in targeting and further investigating a possible suspect, hopefully leading to the identity of the arsonist. Another potential line of enquiry may also include whether the fire is linked to some type of insurance fraud.

It is certainly not uncommon for arson investigators to not hand over the fire crime scene for some time, as they have to make sure all bases have been covered, all potential evidence has been collected and such evidence, after being tagged and bagged, is dealt with in a proper chain of custody to avoid any contamination. The problem is, whilst arson in Australia can cost anything up to $1.6 billion annually, it is a difficult crime to investigate, particularly in trying to prove intent. Given that, many fires are still deemed as either cause unknown or accidental.

In summary, my take on arson investigation is by no means exhaustive, but it goes without saying a proper reconstruction of all events, including up to, during and after the fire, is critical. Hopefully, such a thorough and systematic approach will eventually lead to criminal charges, with the alleged miscreant(s) having their day in court and being held responsible for their actions. In other words, follow the evidence as you may never know where it might lead you.

3
LEGISLATION AND PROCEDURE

Australian law and its legal system can be traced back to English law. Following the landing of the initial British settlers at Sydney Cove in 1788, we slowly set up our own legislation by Acts of Parliament and legal principles with our common law, as developed by the judiciary on a case-to-case basis. However, English law still played an important role and obviously had a guiding influence on our system of justice and its legal principles, known as an adversarial system of justice.

This means that a court is solely impartial, presiding over the prosecution and defence as compared to what is known as an inquisitorial system of justice, prevalent in France and Italy, whereby the court is closely aligned to investigating the facts of the case matter before it.

Initially, under British law, arson was classified with the usual definition of the unlawful destruction or burning of a building by fire. Such English and Welsh terminology, as a common law offence, was replaced by the *Criminal Damage Act 1971*. If the damage or destruction is caused by fire, a charge of arson will follow, including a fire caused without intent but by reckless and malicious indifference. The maximum sentence in the United Kingdom is life imprisonment being applied in the most exceptional cases.

In the US, the offence of arson is generally considered a felony and is treated as a violent crime, due to the outcome of destruction and sometimes death, being legislated by both Federal and State laws. The severity of the offence of arson varies with first degree arson as the most serious. This is the setting of a fire to an occupied structure and would normally result in a term of imprisonment from as little as two years to a maximum of life in jail, but penalties vary by state and can also include a heavy fine.

First degree arson is also known as aggravated arson, in that the defendant maliciously and intentionally set fire or caused an explosion that resulted in the risk of the loss of lives and/or for financial gain. Second degree arson is classified as burning an unoccupied structure and some states have further lesser degrees of arson in situations where there was no intent to start a fire, but where the offender was negligent.

In Australia, the laws pertaining to arson, intentionally and maliciously destroying property by fire, varies as indictable offences between the states and territories, noting there is also a Commonwealth offence in respect to damage to property and, although not specifically referred to, also covers arson resulting in damage to, or the destruction of, property belonging to a Commonwealth entity.[2]

---

2   *Criminal Code Act* 1995(Cth)- section 132.8A.

However, in each Australian state and territory jurisdiction, it is an offence to start a fire that destroys or damages property, including endangering life or resulting in injury. In the event of any death, this could also result in a charge of murder, or the lesser charge of manslaughter, or arson causing death.

In the Australian Capital Territory, the offence of arson is set out in section 404 of *Criminal Code 2002* (ACT) with conviction resulting in imprisonment of 15 years and the *Crimes Act 1900* (ACT) under section 117(1), carries a penalty of 25 years imprisonment for intent to endanger the life of another. The *Criminal Code Act 1983* (NT) provides, for those charged with arson offences in the Northern Territory (NT), penalties up to and including a life sentence (see sections 243-245 of the Act).

The offence of arson in Queensland is legislated under section 461 of the *Criminal Code Act 1899* (Qld) and if you are convicted of wilfully (meaning intentionally and recklessly) and unlawfully setting fire to a building or structure, including starting a bushfire, you can be sentenced to life imprisonment. Tasmanian arson legislation is courtesy of sections 268-269 of the *Criminal Code Act 1924* (Tas), which prohibits any person from unlawfully setting fire to public or private property, which includes, not only building structures, but a vegetation stack, fuel source or forest, with a term of imprisonment of up to 21 years. Specific provision is made under section 269A of the Criminal Code Act for intentionally injuring a person or their property by fire.

In NSW, under sections 195-199 of the *Crimes Act 1900* (NSW), it is an offence to damage property by fire or explosion, including with intent to injure a person or endanger life, or for financial gain. It can carry penalties ranging from five years to 25 years imprisonment. The offence of causing a bushfire, intentionally and recklessly, is dealt with under section 203E of the Crimes Act with a maximum term of imprisonment up to 21 years, while a lesser charge of setting a fire or allowing a fire to escape, is covered under section 100 (1) of the *Rural Fires Act 1997* (NSW). This might apply, for example, in a situation where a more serious charge under the Crimes Act could not be substantiated. The penalty under the Rural Fires Act can be a fine or five years imprisonment, or both.

In South Australia, section 85 of the *Criminal Law Consolidation Act* 1935 (SA) governs offences of arson and property damage, including to a motor vehicle, either by fire or explosives with a separate offence for starting a bushfire, including setting fire to vegetation (section 85B), all carrying a maximum penalty of a life sentence. In addition, application can be made by police under section 99L of the *Criminal Procedure Act 1921* (SA) for a person, deemed to be a risk of lighting further bushfires, to be ordered to wear an electronic monitoring device, as well as reporting to police as considered necessary. The court must, under section 127 of the *Sentencing Act 2017* (SA), make an order for restitution to the victim by way of compensation.

Western Australia carries a similar maximum life sentence under section 444 of the *Criminal Code Compilation Act 1913* (WA) for damage to or destroying a property by fire, being increased from 14 years imprisonment to life, courtesy of the *Arson Legislation Amendment Act 2009* (WA), in addition to an offence of arson legislated by the *Bush Fires Act 1954* (WA). Under section 32 of the Bush Fires Act, there is a maximum penalty of imprisonment for 20 years if you light, or attempt to light, a fire that is likely to injure a person or damage property.

Section 30 of the Bush Fires Act also makes it an offence if you dispose of a cigarette, or similar item, during a prohibited period in a situation where a bush fire could start, carrying a penalty of a $5,000 fine.

The common law crime of arson was removed in Victoria by section 3 of the *Crimes (Criminal Damage) Act 1978* (Vic). Arson, involving setting fire to a property resulting in harm and malicious destruction, is now legislated by section 197 of the *Crimes Act 1958* (Vic), and includes: setting a fire causing criminal damage (197(1)); endanger the life of another (197(2)) and with a view to gain, such as in an insurance fraud (197(3)). A crime of arson in Victoria, as in other states and territories, is rightly considered a major crime and can lead to a sentence maximum on conviction of up to level 4 imprisonment of 15 years (sections 197 (7) (Crimes Act)). A convicted high-risk arsonist can also be fitted with a GPS tracking device on release from prison under the *Corrections Act 1986* (Vic) and under section 6B of the *Sentencing Act 1991*(Vic) deemed as a serious arson offender.

Victora also has a specific and separate section regarding arson causing death under section 197A of the Crimes Act, which also carries a maximum penalty of 25 years incarceration. Intention to cause death is not a necessary element for the offence to be committed. It is, of course, still considered to be a significant offence which was determined as a new category of offences and introduced in 1997 as an amendment, courtesy of the Sentencing Act. Section 201A of the Crimes Act also covers bushfires that were started both intentionally and recklessly with a maximum prison term of up to 15 years on being found guilty.

In Australia and other Commonwealth countries, under

an adversarial system of justice in which the court is primarily the impartial referee between the prosecution and defence, you must plead either guilty or not guilty and face a jury of 12 ordinary members of the community to determine your fate beyond reasonable doubt. Such system of justice is dated as far back as the Magna Carta, which is Latin for "Great Charter of Freedoms", of June 1215 that provided for no one, not even the King of England, being above the law. It provided for a process of protection from unlawful imprisonment and a swift and impartial judicial process.

There is available, in the event of pleading guilty, a process of plea bargaining which means lawyers for the defendant can negotiate with the prosecution. For example: 'My client will plead guilty to manslaughter and arson but not murder and arson.'

If the lesser charge is accepted, the guilty plea will then result in a reduced or more lenient sentence.

What also is available, for example in the Magistrates Court of Victoria, is what is known as a sentence indication, without any formal plea being entered.[3] It only applies to summary and indictable offences, triable summarily, and once a magistrate gives an indication what sentence would be imposed, the defendant, in consultation with lawyers, will then determine whether to accept same and proceed by way of a guilty plea, or failing that, to a contested hearing. Offenders pleading guilty also have the benefit of a sentence reduction courtesy of section 6AAA of the Sentencing Act, as the court on sentencing will indicate what higher sentence would have been imposed, but for the plea of guilty.

In the event of a not guilty plea to a serious indictable

---

[3] *Criminal Procedure Act 2009* (Vic)-section 60.

offence in Australia, the first step before a trial by jury, or judge alone if agreed to, is what is known as a filing hearing. This process establishes a timetable for an exchange of particulars to be relied on by the prosecution and defence, before proceeding to an administrative committal mention with the defence receiving a hand up brief by the prosecution. This brief contains all witness statements and exhibits to be relied on.

A committal hearing then takes place before a magistrate who determines if there is sufficient evidence that will support a conviction for the offence(s) as charged and whether the matter should proceed to trial in a higher court. In Victoria, that is either the County or Supreme Court. If the defence chooses to test the evidence to be relied on, in proving guilt beyond reasonable doubt, the prosecution will call its witnesses to give oral evidence in chief, or by simply adopting the contents of their sworn statement, then being subject to cross-examination by the defence.

The defence can, of course, call its own witnesses, but that would be unusual as the main aim in such proceedings is to test the prosecution's evidence. In cases such as murder and/or manslaughter, a defendant may choose to "fast track" the matter without a committal hearing by electing to stand trial[4]. In that event, any alibi defence must be served on the Director of Public Prosecutions (DPP) within 14 days.[5]

The presiding magistrate then must determine if there is sufficient evidence to commit the accused to stand trial or, if there is not, dismiss the charge(s) as laid. Alternatively, if the defence concedes that the evidence contained in the hand up brief is sufficient for the matter to proceed to a higher court,

---

[4] Ibid-section 143.

[5] Ibid-section 190.

then it can be procedurally dealt with by way of a hand–up committal procedure and usually occurs when a defendant intends to plead guilty. The committal procedure may vary slightly in our states and territories but will be governed by appropriate legislation.[6]

The US has a similar procedure, but it is known as a probable cause or preliminary hearing, in order to determine whether there is sufficient evidence as charged and to proceed to trial. If, in the event the accused is held in custody, in most jurisdictions the hearing must take place within 14 days and if on bail, within 21 days. In the event the judge determines there is probable cause, then the matter will proceed to trial. Some states also have what is known as a grand jury as against a preliminary hearing, but they are usually held without involvement of the defendant and if they consider, as part of the investigation, there is sufficient evidence to lay criminal charges, then an indictment or presentment against the accused person will be filed and served. The concept of a grand jury actually emanated during the Middle Ages and not only are they held in the US, but also Liberia.

Japan has a three-tiered court system, with a single judge presiding over minor crimes in a summary court, similar to a magistrate in Australia, while a district court can also have a single judge and a three-judge panel type system to hear more serious cases with heavy statutory penalties. A three-judge system also applies in cases such as homicide and arson of inhabited buildings, but there is also what is known as a "saiban-in judicial panel". This is where six people are chosen at random from an electoral roll, similar to a jury system. One

---

[6] In Victoria, it is governed under sections 95-100 of the Criminal Procedure Act.

difference is, not only do they determine the facts, together with three judges, they also deliver sentencing as part of the judicial panel.[7] This type of citizen participation in the more serious cases has also been adopted in France and Germany and in these two countries, unlike Japan, legal interpretation rests with not only the judges, but also the panel of citizens.

In Australia, there is also an option available with a judge-alone trial, where the judge has a role, also as the jury, on deciding the guilt or innocence of the accused. Normally, both the accused and prosecutor must agree and it is important the accused has received legal advice on the process and possible implications of a judge-alone trial. In the event the prosecution doesn't agree, it may still proceed if it is determined to be in the interests of justice.[8]

The US has a comparable option, but it is known as a bench trial and, like Australia, one of the main considerations in seeking a judge alone without a jury, or in some jurisdictions, three sitting judges, can be influenced by the complexity of or the publicity surrounding the case. A judge may well be better equipped to take all that into account. The other overriding thinking is, of course, a jury's decision-making can, at times, be rather unpredictable, particularly in cases where the evidence is largely circumstantial.

There is also what is known in some overseas jurisdictions as an inquisitorial system of justice, in which the court and, sometimes even part of the court, is actively involved in the investigation of the facts of the case. The aim is then to settle

---

[7]   see *Act on Criminal Trials with Participation of Saiban*-in-Act No 63 of 2004.

[8]   see for example sections 132–133 of the *Criminal Procedure Act 1986* (NSW) and *Brown v DPP* (NSW) [2018] NSWCCA 94.

each matter courtesy of, not only the extensive investigation by the judge, but then coupled with a further examination of all the evidence. The inquisitorial system is prevalent in a number of European countries such as France, Germany, Italy and Austria. Several Latin American countries have also adopted such a system for use in their legal proceedings.

Of course, under Australia's adversarial system of justice, any person charged with the criminal offence of arson is deemed innocent until proven guilty. Such presumption of innocence is set out by way of example in Article 14 of the *International Covenant on Civil and Political Rights* adopted in 1966 which states:

Everyone charged with a criminal offence shall have the right to be presumed innocent until proven guilty according to law.

It is up to the prosecution to prove guilt beyond reasonable doubt and generally, in proving guilty as charged, requires a number of elements in order to reach that threshold. In simple terms, the first element of proof is that the defendant, being the person accused of the crime of arson, is actually the one who was involved in carrying out the crime. It then follows that such property damaged by the starting of that fire was the property of another, unless of course, such property belonged to the accused, as in cases of insurance fraud motive.

However, there is no burden on the prosecution to prove any motive and the guilt of the accused rests with the jury to reach a unanimous verdict beyond reasonable doubt. If there is, on the other hand, any reasonable doubt, then the accused must be found not guilty.

Circumstantial evidence can play a crucial role in criminal

cases, including arson, which can allow a jury to draw certain inferences to find the accused guilty beyond reasonable doubt. For example, this could include a motive for setting the fire, to cover up another crime, such as burglary or a homicide. This leads to it being demonstrated beyond reasonable doubt that the person charged before the court had sufficient *mens rea* (intent) to destroy or cause damage to the property. Such intent can also be shown by proving facts surrounding the planning or premeditation involved prior to carrying out the guilty act (actus reus) and that there was absolutely no legal basis or grounds to justify the conduct of the accused.

The defendant may have a legitimate excuse for starting a fire, which is often referred to as a statutory defence, in that they had a lawful right with or without authority to set such a fire.[9] It could also be argued, in defence to a charge of arson, that the perpetrator was under or subjected to duress, it was done by way of necessity, or the fire was an accident and not deliberate. In other words, it was started unintentionally without malice.

Some defendants, probably on the recommendation of their lawyer, often engage the services of a fire investigation expert in order to demonstrate they are not guilty. Perhaps they are hoping such expert report will suggest a possible other cause, such as faulty wiring, or gaps and errors in the prosecution's case. This, of course, would create problems in reaching a conclusion beyond reasonable doubt. Apart from pleading by way of mitigation, such as insanity or under the influence of drugs or alcohol, quite often a person accused of such a serious crime presents an alibi where the fire could not have been started by them as they were nowhere near the scene at the time.

---

9   see for example in Victoria lawful excuse as per section 201(2(a)(b) of the Crimes Act.

Following a not guilty plea, a jury is then empanelled and, depending on the complexity of the charge of arson and any other related indictable offences, a jury of 12 is normally appointed. The process of jury selection varies in each jurisdiction, but those named for jury service are chosen by random computer selection from the electoral roll. A Notice to Prospective Juror is then sent to the selected person, which includes a questionnaire and any reason why they should be excluded from selection.

If accepted for jury duty, an attendance summons is then sent out and, before a final jury is appointed by way of empanelment, a process known as a "voir dire" is then conducted. This is a French term meaning "to speak the truth". This involves nominated questions by the prosecution, defence and even the judge to the potential jurors concerning their background and any potential conflict of interest or bias they may have. A selected jury is then empanelled and sworn in prior to the commencement of the trial.

Such a jury selection process is one of many checks and balances that will take place during a criminal trial. This is in order to make sure the accused receives a fair trial. This includes evidence to be put before a jury that may cause an unfair bias. This occurs in the absence of the jury and after arguments are presented by both the prosecution and defence, the presiding judge will then determine whether such evidence will be admissible.

In the event the trial is expected to take many weeks due the number of witnesses and complexity of the evidence, 14 to even 18 jurors may be empanelled, but of course, that is entirely at the discretion of the presiding judge. This then allows replacements in the event any juror becomes unavailable, such as in the case of illness. If more than 12 are selected and then not needed, they will be discharged by way of a ballot system at the end of the trial and, following the judge's charge, before the jury considers its verdict.

There is also what is often called a preliminary hearing or a pre-trial, which may include a question of law, or if, in fact, a certain piece of evidence is allowed, such as hearsay or if it was unlawfully obtained. Such a process is also called a voir dire. This provides discretion for a judge or magistrate to determine and make a ruling on whether the prosecution or defence have satisfied the court on its merit and to ensure a fair trial.[10]

After the accused enters the plea of not guilty, a brief summary of the matter is then provided by the judge and an explanation that the prosecution must prove the charge(s) as laid, beyond reasonable doubt. This will then be followed by the crown prosecutor and defence counsel delivering their opening summation and what evidence they will be presenting before the jury, noting the defence can stay mute as they don't have to prove anything as the onus of guilt is up to the prosecution. Such prosecution evidence will include experts and other witnesses and exhibits, usually in the form of photographs and documents, which will then be formally tendered to the court.

Following the completion of all evidence, both the prosecution and defence will then make closing submissions to the jury: the prosecution on why they say the accused is guilty beyond reasonable doubt and the defence, summarising why the jury should find the accused not guilty. This will then be followed by the judge giving what is termed "the charge" to the jury, summarising the evidence and arguments from both the prosecution and defence and then providing instructions,

---

10   also see section 189 of the *Evidence Act 1995* (Cth).

explaining the legal issues and applying the relevant legal principles. The jury will then retire to consider its verdict.

In Australia, an accused charged with a criminal offence can only be found, either guilty or not guilty by way of a unanimous verdict. In other words, a jury of 12 requires a verdict agreed to by all the jurors. If all the jurors don't reach a unanimous verdict and, even if only one juror disagrees, it will be a "hung jury" and a retrial could be ordered. A reasonable time is allocated for a jury to reach a unanimous verdict, which is usually determined by the judge.

If, for example, after at least eight hours or even longer, sometimes weeks, a unanimous verdict has not been reached, the presiding judge must be satisfied such a verdict will not be possible if given additional time, then a majority verdict may be directed by the judge meaning 11 out of 12 jurors must agree to the guilt of the accused.[11] If a person is charged under Commonwealth legislation, then a majority verdict is not permissible.

Criminal trials by judge-only are also possible, but they do not happen on a regular basis and are not available in all Australian states and territories. If provided for under relevant legislation, both the prosecution and defence must agree and, in the absence of consent by either party, application can be made to the trial judge for an order to be made, provided such order is in the interest of justice. One important caveat though, if the defendant doesn't agree, then such trial by judge sitting alone is not permissible. Such judge-alone trials may be considered more appropriate in cases where the accused has a high profile, or so well-known a fair trial by jury may be

---

11   see for example section 55-*Jury Act 1977* (NSW).

deemed inappropriate as the jury may well not be impartial or could be persuaded by publicity surrounding the accused.

If, in the event, the person charged is ultimately convicted of arson by way of a guilty plea, the court must take into account such plea, for example, in Victoria under section 6AAA of the Sentencing Act when handing down the sentence. The common expression used by the presiding judicial officer is, 'If it was not for the plea of guilty, I would have imposed a sentence of…', which of course is higher than the one determined. In Victoria, cases of arson exceeding $100,000 are tried by judge and jury in the County Court and under $100,000 by the Magistrates Court.

On being found guilty, a presiding Magistrate, County, or Supreme Court judge, in more serious cases such as murder and manslaughter involving arson, would then take into account a number of factors in determining an appropriate and just sentence. There are several principal considerations that guide the courts in order to ensure overall fairness and justice, not only for the defendant being sentenced, but also the protection of the community from further offending. These principal factors include proportionality in sentencing, in that the punishment must be in keeping with the gravity of the offending and to ensure parity with comparable sentences.

Denunciation of the conduct must also be seen in condemning what has been committed and deterrence, both in respect of the offender and of others who may contemplate committing such similar offending. The bottom line is, what is known as parsimony in sentencing, is any sentence imposed should not be more severe than necessary to achieve the overall purposes of sentencing and proportionate to the gravity of the offending.

Other sentencing factors would include the offender's age and any prior criminal history, motive, the risk of injury to another, the spread of the fire, including financial damage, and the degree of prior planning. Lawyers for the defendant may submit psychological reports and references to good character by way of mitigation in the sentence. The degree of remorse will also play a part as well as the prospect of rehabilitation of the offender, including assisting them in reintegrating back into society. A question of rehabilitation, as we have seen in the juvenile justice system, plays a big part and in some ways is given precedence, time and time again, over other sentencing factors.

In some situations, a defence of mental impairment may be submitted with legislation, acknowledging that in the event a person is mentally impaired, they do not have the capacity to be held criminally responsible for their conduct. Such a defence, however, does not include such impairment arising from alcohol or drug factors. In the event the accused is found not guilty due to a mental impairment, a supervision order may be ordered or, in the event the person is not considered a danger to either the community or even themselves, they can be released on an unconditional basis. This would apply only in the most exceptional circumstances and need to be supported by expert medical evidence.[12]

Any person convicted of a criminal offence also has the right to lodge an appeal. For example, following a conviction in the Supreme Court of Victoria, an appeal must be filed within 28 days from the sentence date. Any appeal outside the 28-day window can still be lodged, provided there is a reason why such

---

[12] see for example the *Crimes (Mental Impairment and Unfitness to be Tried) Act 1997* (Vic).

appeal is filed out of time. The Victorian Court of Appeal will then consider if the appeal will be allowed and such various grounds are set out in the Criminal Procedure Act.

In respect of the person convicted, such appeal can include, against the sentence being manifestly excessive or by the Crown as an inadequate sentence, or the jury verdict was unreasonable given the evidence placed before it. Other grounds may include there was a substantial miscarriage of justice, based on a procedural error of law or irregularity during the course of the trial.

In the event the appeal is successful, the accused, on a manifestly excessive ground, could, in fact, receive a more comparable sentence or, if by the Crown, increased. If successful on the other grounds, they could be acquitted if the court determines the jury verdict was so unreasonable as to not be supported or based on the evidence before it and any new trial would be a waste of time. Alternatively, a new trial may be ordered but the bottom line really is, in a situation where the Court of Appeal must decide, whether any error or procedural irregularity would have made any difference to the jury verdict.

This is often referred to in Australian jurisdictions as the "proviso" which allows a Court of Appeal to dismiss the appeal, even in situations where there has been some sort of error, but there was no substantial miscarriage of justice. The final say, however, is reserved for the High Court of Australia, meaning that any court decision can ultimately finish up in the High Court. However, very few cases are granted such special leave to appeal.

The US has a similar procedure for criminal appeals and many of its jurisdictions give rise to two types. One is a direct appeal to a higher court of appeal, either following a state or federal court trial. If the conviction arises from a state court, the defendant may first appeal the decision to an intermediate-level state appellate court and then, if unsuccessful, to the state's highest court. For those convicted in a federal trial court, there is also a federal appellate court with a last resort appeal in the US Supreme Court.

The other is known as collateral appeal, which is a last resort after all else has failed, seeking post-conviction sentence discretion and can even include grounds such as poor and ineffective defence representation, or new evidence being found that clearly demonstrates the innocence of the convicted person.

Arson of any description, whether it be damage to property, arson causing loss of life or bushfires deliberately lit, have their own set of unique facts and can prove very challenging for, not only the victims and their loved ones, but the first responders and team of investigators. Many cases, however, remain unsolved as it is often difficult to first, determine what started the fire and, if indeed it was arson, let alone bringing the person or persons responsible before the court to prove guilt beyond reasonable doubt.

4
A QUESTION OF 'WHO OR WHAT DUNNIT'

The term "whodunnit" derives from a type of detective fiction novel and involves a game for a reader or players, assisted by clues to second guess, or perhaps get it right to who committed the crime, following a process of deduction. Such a game is under the auspice of one of the main players who acts as the sleuth, or perhaps the bumbling over-the-top amateur detective to solve the puzzle of whodunnit.

One such paradigm game, played by a husband-and-wife team on a supposedly happy and romantic St Valentines Day in 1998, celebrated at a local resort at St Michaels, Los Angeles in the US, actually ended with a real-life tragedy, or more to the point, murder and arson. The grief-stricken wife, Kimberley Hricko, perhaps encouraged by the whodunnit murder mystery plot, allegedly poisoned her unsuspecting husband, Stephen, then set him on fire, most likely to cover up her earlier plot, hoping all evidence would be destroyed. Unfortunately for Kimberely, on speaking with police, it was obvious her alibi simply didn't stack up. She said that following an argument with her now deceased husband, she walked away to get some fresh air and on returning, after supposedly getting lost, she found their resort room, and Stephen, on fire.

The only problem for Kimberley was the subsequent autopsy, which indicated Stephen was dead well before the fire engulfed the room, leading the prosecutor at trial to submit the type and quantity of poison found in her husband. It just so happens, as an aside, the fictional murder mystery plot they both previously participated in, was the murder of a groom by poison at his wedding reception and most likely committed by his former betrothed, but now, grieving wife. It also came to light during the trial that Kimberley, who just happened to work at a local hospital, had previously bragged to one and all that she had big plans for Stephen, which involved poisoning him and then disposing of his remains by setting fire to curtains with the help of a cigar, perhaps as a way to celebrate.

Indeed, it also came out, the author of the murder mystery, the now accused had participated in, had also formed the view that it was all very suspicious. That opinion, however, was not part of any evidence. The jury of Kimberley's peers felt the same and she was convicted of first-degree murder and arson. Despite her subsequent appeal, all to no avail, on spurious grounds that somehow, the evidence did not legally support a conviction of murder and arson and the coroner was incorrect with his evidence of probable poisoning, Kimberely remains behind bars for the term of her natural life.[13]

Church fires are a continual reminder that even places

---

[13]   *Hricko v State of Maryland* 134 Md. App. 218 (2000).

of worship are not protected from those individuals or groups who, based on some sort of anti-religious ideology, or for some other spurious reasons, take out their frustrations and burn these holy places to the ground. Was this what happened in the 1863 Church of the Company fire in the city of Santiago, Chile, or was the fire ignition simply accidental? An estimated 2,500 churchgoers died in the blaze on what was supposed to be a joyous celebration known as the Feast of the Immaculate Conception, with only about 50 churchgoers being rescued.

Early indications suggested the fire was caused by a faulty gas lamp, but the problem with that was the church was not fitted out with gas. The next nominated cause of ignition was that a strong wind, gusting through the church doors, blew over an oil lamp and presumably set fire to coverings adorning the church walls. Some said, it was a candle on fire, not an oil lamp.

The aftermath must have been horrendous as the majority of those lost in the fire were burned beyond recognition and were buried in a mass grave. The fact the fire started within the church while it was occupied, with one worshipper trying to smother the burning candle, (or was it an oil lamp?) probably gives credence to the fire had started accidentally. Then again, with three possible scenarios, gas lamp, oil lamp or candle, who knows how it started.

The Great Chicago Fire of 8 October 1871 in the US, in which almost 17,500 buildings were destroyed, left over 100,000 local residents homeless, also saw the deaths of around 300 people. There were certainly hot and windy weather conditions over a long period prior to the fire, but its origin left two possible scenarios. The first being, the fire was believed to have started in a barn near an alleyway with a cow supposedly knocking over a lantern. Alternatively, it wasn't the cow, but a gang of gamblers who were responsible causing the lantern to be the culprit. On the same day, there was also a large forest fire in Peshtigo, Wisconsin, about 145 miles from Chicago. On this occasion, the villain allegedly slashed and then burnt embers, resulting in at least 1,500 killed and could have been as high as 2,500. However, the plot thickens as to "who or whatdunnit" in respect of both fires, as a theory evolved that these fires were due to fragments from a comet known as Biela.

The Winecoff Hotel fire on 7 December 1946 in Atalanta, US, killed 119 patrons including the hotel's original proprietors, with many unable to escape through the building's single stairway. The fire started around 3.15 am in the morning and the question remained of whether it was arson, or the original theory of a discarded cigarette butt. A book, "The Winecoff Fire: The Untold Story of America's Deadliest Hotel Fire" published in 1993, suggested it may have been carried out by an upset patron, but to this day, the cause is still listed as "unknown".

Was it also a similar case of who or whatdunnit in the Warrenton nursing home fire in Missouri, US on 17 February 1957 in which 72 infirm residents perished, with about the same number lucky to escape the fire? Given that the blaze started around 2.40pm in the afternoon in a first-floor linen cupboard, while most of the residents were at an in-house church service singing, 'What a Friend We Have in Jesus', you would think that fire investigators could possibly come to the conclusion it was accidental.

On the other hand, how could a fire start on its own without some sort of human help? Unless, of course, it was spontaneous combustion. The building went up in flames with nurses evacuating many of the residents, but unfortunately, those who were locked in their room and some even secured to a bed, due to their health issues, would perish with no way of escaping. Victim identification also became a problem as the roof collapsed, but it was later determined that 46 of the victims were male and the balance of 26 were female.

The cause of the fire ranged from accidental, given that the complex was over 50 years old, no doubt with possible faulty electrical wiring, or alternatively it could have been due to a faulty heating system that kept the residents comfortable during freezing temperatures. However, Missouri Police came to a view that it could have been deliberately lit. This considered opinion gained more weight when further enquiries revealed that a relative of the manager of the home, was in charge of a similar facility, being the Cedar Grove Nursing Home in Hillside, Missouri, in which 20 people died in 1952 from a fire. In the end, the cause of the Warrenton nursing home fire was officially listed as undetermined or a case of who or whatdunnit.

The case of the incineration of the Steiglitz Coffee Palace in country Victoria, Australia in September 1895 suggests that perhaps the prosecution did get it wrong regarding who committed the crime of arson. The problem in those days was, arson was a capital crime and if you do the crime, you won't do the time, because it carried a sentence of death on conviction. In this case, the alleged perpetrators, Joseph Gill, who leased the palace and his mother-in-law, Ella Hicksh, were sentenced to death, but remarkably the chief prosecutor appealed for their release, expressing grave concerns as to their guilt, based on possible false evidence and perhaps they were mistaken in identity of who actually started the fire.

Was it Joseph or was it Ella, or were they both innocent? This was despite the chief prosecutor initially arguing before the court they were both in on it for the insurance payment. What followed was, perhaps two innocent people initially sentenced to death, escaping proper justice, with Joseph serving less than three years, whilst his mum-in-law was out in four. To this day, the question still remains, who was responsible? Or, like similar fires at the same coffee palace, perhaps it was accidental.

Much like the Steiglitz Coffee Palace, many fires and their origins remain unsolved or were, perhaps, accidental, such as the Our Lady of The Angels school fire in Chicago in 1958. The fire was believed to have started in a cardboard bin and burnt for over 30 minutes before the school could be evacuated. Sadly, 92 students and three nuns lost their lives and, whilst some discarded burnt matches were later found by investigators, no one was ever charged, despite some suggestions a 13-year-old student, with a prior history of setting fires, may have been responsible.

Another US school fire in 1908 in Collingwood, Ohio resulted in the deaths of 172 students and one other person who tried in vain to rescue those trapped. Like many similar building structure fires, there was a suggestion that perhaps the fire started accidentally. The local coroner formed the view the subsequent tragic outcome with the large loss of life was due to "conditions" and perhaps even materials, giving rise to a spontaneous fire. The memorial plaque, since erected in 2003, states the fire was of "unknown origin".

Unsolved murders, as a consequence of a fire and most likely deliberately lit as a means to cover up a previous crime by destroying any evidence, was also a point of contention following the 1929 inferno in the small rural outlet in Himatangi, New Zealand. To this day it remains somewhat perplexing as to what actually happened, following the discovery of eight victims' burnt bodies, one of which was Thomas Wright, with evidence of shotgun pellets to the back of his head. It was first thought Wright started the fire after killing his wife and four children, together with two other adults before turning the shotgun on himself. In other words, it was suggested it was a murder/suicide.

However, it remained unsolved, with a possible further explanation that Wright himself was the target and the killer then had no choice but to murder all witnesses, then set the fire to destroy any credible evidence. One possible suspect, convicted of a similar murder by arson, was questioned, but alas nothing could connect him to the crime scene, leaving another case of whodunnit.

There was also a possible suspect in the 1973 Upstairs Lounge arson in New Orleans in the US in which 32 people perished. The fire occurred in a well-known gay bar and was initially believed to have been started by a gay man by the name of Roger Dale Nunez, who suffered from a psychiatric disorder. However, he was never charged and committed suicide in 1974, perhaps taking his guilt or, then again, his innocence, to the grave.

It was certainly a question of who did it and why, following a massive blaze in a US Los Angeles library in April 1986, destroying 400,000 books and damaging a further 700,000. All up, the damage was estimated to be in the order of $22 million, which by today's estimates exceeds $50 million in US currency. Not only were books lost or damaged, but the fire also destroyed valuable records and artifacts, including car manuals of every make and model and is still considered the largest library fire in US history.

Was there a motive behind it and, if so, who lit it? Or

was it an accident? The problem is, like many of the who or whatdunnit fires, we may never know. Arson was suspected and in February 1987, actor, Harry Peak, was taken into custody but released three days later due to insufficient evidence. He initially said he started the fire but then denied any involvement. However, Peak strangely gave a total of seven different alibis of his whereabouts on the day of the huge blaze. He went to his grave in 1993, perhaps taking secrets with him, but he did successfully sue the City of LA prior to his death for false imprisonment, slander and emotional stress.

The Ghost Ship warehouse fire around 11.30pm on 2 December 2016 in Oakland, California, US, raised a number of questions to its origin. Was it a possible electrical fault? Was it caused by spontaneous combustion? Did it emanate from the building next door? Was it insurance arson or an act of pyromania, or perhaps the easy way out, simply put it down as cause unknown? The principal lessee, by the name of Derek Almena, who had the control and right to sublease the building, was also using the complex as an entertainment venue, albeit illegally.

On the night of the fire, he was conducting a music concert for the 80-100 attendees, when a series of fire explosions erupted, resulting in the deaths of 36 victims, many of whom were found huddled together, dying from smoke inhalation. The victims struggled to escape from the inferno as the building was littered with obstacles, such as furniture, pianos and even mannequins, all providing a combustible fuel load. The building did not have fire alarms, let alone sprinklers, fitted so any early warning of what was about to engulf the patrons, didn't happen.

The initial investigation into the cause of the fire

first suggested that it was an electrical fault, as a building maintenance report stating it required some attention, had been made some months earlier. This notification from the owners of the building was ignored by Almena on execution of the lease. Then it was considered that perhaps the fire was due to a faulty refrigerator. Once again, investigators from the Bureau of Alcohol, Tobacco, Firearms and Explosives (ATF) rejected this assertion, but did not rule out, at this point, possible other electrical faults for the fire. Lawyers acting for Almena, after he was charged, along with one of his employees, with 36 counts of the felony, involuntary manslaughter, then originally suggested that the fire originated from a building adjacent to the leased warehouse, so he could not be held accountable for criminal negligence.

Involuntary manslaughter, under US law, is defined as either stemming from recklessness or criminal negligence, resulting in unintentional death. It is different to the usual forms of homicide as it does not rely on any act that is either deliberate or premeditated. Almena's lawyers ran an argument that it was indeed arson and produced an eyewitness who detailed a conversation she allegedly overheard from a cohort of unidentified males bragging about their exploits in lighting the fire. This claim was rejected by one of the principal investigators saying, on the one hand, they could find no evidence of arson, yet alternatively, the source of the fire was not established due to its intensity.

The question was, notwithstanding the charges in which Almena would plead no contest and was sentenced to 12 years imprisonment, the fire origin still remained undetermined. His employee was, however, finally acquitted on all charges, with the City of Oakland paying out compensation in the order of $33 million. The owner of the building was not criminally charged and invoked the fifth amendment right to remain silent on the ground of self-incrimination. He was, however, sued and entered into bankruptcy, advising in the court petition that all assets would be liquidated in order to compensate survivors and families to the sum of $11.8 million.

It also wasn't originally a case of whodunnit after an Alabama, US pastor and his wife, allegedly assisted by an acquaintance, set fire to their church, albeit a building owned by them but used by their local brethren. It was alleged that "Mrs and Mrs Pastor" set the fire in order to make an insurance claim and I don't think, if successful, any payout monies would have been put into the donation plate. The fire was set on January 2019 and saw them charged with first degree insurance fraud, second degree arson, together with criminal conspiracy.

However, lo and behold, it did become a whodunnit case after the pastor died apparently from a heart attack the night before he was due to appear in court. Charges against his wife and the other accused were then subsequently discontinued, as prosecutors against the, now absent, pastor considered they did not have sufficient evidence to proceed. The withdrawal of the charges was, however, on the basis of "without prejudice", meaning it may well not be a whodunnit as the prosecution could still file indictments, if and when, more evidence became available.

Tokyo's red-light district saw an explosion and fire burn for over five hours in a complex known as Myojo 56 in September 2001, believed to be a haven for gambling and tied up with organised crime. A total of 44 people died in the blaze and arson was always considered to be the cause, but again, no arrests were ever made. However, some two years later, the building's owners were convicted of criminal negligence for various breaches of the fire code regulations, receiving suspended prison sentences.

The Salvation Army's William Booth Memorial Home in Melbourne, Australia was a refuge for both destitute individuals and those suffering from alcoholism. On 13 August 1966, a fire swept through the multi-storey building, resulting in 30 male residents, who could not escape from their locked rooms, perishing in the blaze with around 150 others lucky to escape. You would think that, given it housed residents who obviously had a number of varying mental issues and sadly referred to by some as "nobodies", investigators would understandably consider the fire must have been deliberately lit, perhaps as payback for some perceived wrong. It appears though, that one of the residents knocked over an illegal portable heater, which smouldered for some time before exploding into a fireball when his room door was opened. In 2016, a memorial plaque was placed at the former home site commemorating those who were lost in the fire.

A similar fire at the NSW Sydney Savoy Hotel in 1975, resulted in 15 persons being burnt to death. This time, however, a local well-known convicted thief and arsonist, by the name of Roger Lyttle, was initially sentenced to life imprisonment, which was subsequently reduced on appeal with a non-parole period of 28 years. It, however, came to light that an Australian hotelier, amongst other things, by the name of Abe "Mr Sin" Saffron was the owner of the hotel.

It was later alleged that perhaps the affable Abe had also been involved in another seven fires, including one in the building next door to the Savoy, originally known as the Pink Panther Strip joint. This 1989 fire in the now renamed,

Downunder Hostel, resulted in the death of six people and, guess what, Saffron also owned this establishment. He, of course, denied any involvement.

Interesting that a fire took place some 10 years earlier in 1979 at Luna Park in Sydney, when its ghost train somehow caught fire, with a so-called police investigator, being a not-so-well credentialed detective sergeant, sometimes called "Mr Fixit", stating within hours of the fire being extinguished, it was all due to an electrical fault. How he could determine that so quickly, I have no idea. Sadly, the fire not only destroyed the train ride but killed seven people, including six children. The origin of the fire was never determined, with criticism levelled at both the police and the coronial investigation. There were suggestions the investigating police's view, that it was accidental, just didn't stack up. In 2007, the niece of Saffron alleged that Uncle Abe was the instigator and apparently according to her, his plans were to gain control of the lease connected to Luna Park, but she later recanted this allegation.

In 2021, Australian Broadcasting Commission (ABC) journalist, Caro Meldrum-Hanna, in an excellent investigative series program, not only alleged that Saffron was involved in the Luna Park fire, but perhaps acted in concert with others, including a well-known local, eminent politician and a former High Court justice. According to the ABC's compelling version of events, Saffron was the main man and arranged for his criminal bikie associates to set the fire, again supporting the "taking control of the lease" scenario, but a 1987 State Government inquiry came to the conclusion that Abe had no links to any such lease.

A now retired NSW detective senior sergeant of police however, supported the view that Saffron was definitely involved in the fire. Abe, who died in 2006, with only a conviction for tax evasion, went to his grave again denying any involvement and taking his secrets with him. Perhaps, he may have been greeted by the big fella in the sky with, 'Mr Saffron, I need to have a word with you.'

Luna Park seemed to attract firebugs as, at St Kilda in Melbourne, Victoria in 1981, it was the subject of an arson attack with its aptly titled, "Shoot Em Up Gallery", being destroyed and again the culprits escaping the claws of justice. Another fire close by in St Kilda saw the St Mortiz Ice Rink go up in flames in 1982. The place was known for its attraction to young lovers skating around arm in arm. Perhaps this fire was started by a spurned lover, but we will never know.

The site of St Kilda's famous Bojangles nightclub was also set on fire on a number of occasions with well-known criminal identity, Mark "Chopper" Read, being one of its infamous guests enjoying a drink or three, no doubt while dancing the night away, even though he was missing half an ear. Before it became a nightclub, its prime position housed the St Kilda Sea Baths which, according to some, went up in flames in 1926, due to "spontaneous combustibles".

I am not sure what the attraction is to St Kilda, but the Palace Nightclub was also destroyed by fire in 2007, although on this occasion, police investigators determined that it was definitely deliberately lit but still remains unsolved with the perpetrator never being held to account. Interesting though, this fire was only four weeks after its tenants were told to leave, following a much hard fought and lengthy court battle with the state government, so the question remains as to who the culprit was.

At least the St Kilda Pier kiosk arsonist, Mike Lee Smith,

was arrested following a fire in 2003, resulting in $750,000 damage. He was sentenced to a term of imprisonment for a minimum of 15 months. The fire was originally determined by investigators to be started from an electrical fault, but Smith was the one whodunnit, confessing that he heard a voice in his head demanding he set fire to buildings.

The suburb of Port Melbourne, which is only a short distance from St Kilda, certainly lost a piece of its history when the former Port Theatre went up in flames on 30 August 2015. The two-storey building, which now housed three different businesses, including a massage parlour, was attended to by around 80 firefighters in order to bring it under control. As far as I am aware, the cause was never determined, but it certainly wasn't the first time this integral part of the locals' entertainment location was hit by fire. At least the blaze in 1924 was a cause of whatdunnit, with the fire igniting in an operating projector while the audience was watching the film, "The Governor's Lady". Everyone evacuated safely from the theatre, with one patron suffering a broken leg in the mad rush to get out.

Melbourne restaurants also couldn't escape the public spotlight, not just for the quality of the dishes they served or, in some cases, perhaps not so great quality cuisines, but also for unsolved fires. The Victorian, Eltham Barrel Restaurant, was more likely renowned, not for its fine dining, but its distinct shape and if ever filled with water, had the capacity to hold approximately eight million litres. It certainly had to be doused with water by local CFA trucks after a fire started around 7.30 pm on Sunday, 4 June 1989. The fire fighters took six hours to bring the blaze under control and, initially, its cause, for want of a better explanation, was put down as "mysterious".

The destroyed building had the pleasure of the attendance

of State Coroner, Hal Hallenstein, who's function was to oversee and co-ordinate coronial services in our state. As coroner, he has the power to not only investigate deaths but conduct an independent investigation into any fire in the public interest, how it happened and make recommendations to prevent similar fires, which was the reason for him visiting the scene.[14]

Although the fire started in the early hours of the evening and, as there were rumours circulating in the local community that the business was suffering from poor sales, which was vehemently denied by the restaurant owners, consideration was given to the fire being carried out by a professional-for-hire arsonist, meaning an insurance fraud. However, as an arsonist for hire usually strikes in the early hours of the morning to avoid detection, coupled with the restaurant being the target of burglaries over the preceding months, that motive was definitely ruled out.

Police also released a description of a male, aged in his late 30s with a receding hair line, who was seen loitering near the restaurant just prior to the fire. A reward of $25,000 was offered by the Insurance Council of Australia leading to the conviction of the arsonist, but as far as I am aware, no one was ever charged. As an aside and with tongue in cheek, the owner of the now demolished Barrel restaurant was a recently retired Collingwood AFL footballer, so perhaps the perpetrator was a disgruntled footy club fan, giving their lack of premierships.

The Swagman Restaurant, situated in Ferntree Gully, was a well-established and much enjoyed meeting place, not just for Victorian diners enjoying its fabulous smorgasbords, but overseas tourists partaking in the cabaret shows. Unfortunately, the restaurant went up in flames around 4.30am on 27 May

---

[14] Division 2-Investigation of Fires-*Coroners Act 2008* (Vic).

1991, not only destroying its kitchen but the whole complex. The question was now, how the fire started and given this blaze was in the early hours of the morning, arson was clearly in the frame.

Obviously, the insurer thought it was an arson fraud, refusing to pay out to the restaurant owners their insurance claim to the sum of $7 million, leaving them with no choice but to sue in the Supreme Court of Victoria to recover their loss. Counsel for the insurer didn't mess around, saying that the insurance claim was nothing but a fraud, suggesting the restaurant owners conspired to commit arson.

The Swagman owners totally refuted the accusations and, lo and behold, reached a confidential settlement with the insurance company in October 1992. So, the question of whodunnit was left up in the air but raised further enquiries when the same owners were again sued, but this time by their bank, alleging arson fraud. The outcome of that litigation was never made public and, who knows, there may well also have been a commercial settlement between the parties. It was, of course, with some interest that the restaurant was never rebuilt, the land being sold by its owners. Funny enough, it was later replaced by a stylish nightclub under the sole management of one of the former Swagman owners.

Following the 1991 Swagman fire, another restaurant suffered the same fate in December 1991. The restaurant, known as the Efficient Ships in Toorak, was totally destroyed by fire, with the body of a family friend of the owners being found in the kitchen in the aftermath. Investigators formed the view that the deceased, who had left the restaurant about 2am, but then returned some three hours later and splashed petrol around the building, lost his life after setting the fire.

You would think the question of whodunnit was not an issue, but police were not convinced he acted on his own. In late 2019, the Victoria Police Arson and Investigation Squad were contacted by a person who allegedly knew who else was involved and the motive behind the fire. The case of who conspired with the arson victim, to this day, remains unsolved.

It was not a case of whodunnit following a major fire at the Melbourne Fifteen restaurant on the night of 5 June 2008, which also caused major damage to two adjacent businesses. Initial police investigations determined that its general manager, Kevin Stralow, who had only been employed for few months prior to the fire, had a habit of not banking the restaurant's takings and when asked by management why, he would just make up lame excuses. It was also uncovered that he was a regular player of poker machines and, indeed, known as somewhat of a "high roller" at one particular gambling venue.

Following the fire, he initially used that as an excuse for the loss of $12,000 of takings, which he said was kept under his desk in an expendable file waiting to be banked. When questioned by police about his movements on the night of the fire, he stated he had gone home early and then stayed at his girlfriend's place for the remainder of that night.

However, the problem for Stralow was that CCTV detected him entering the restaurant around 7.18 pm and 15 minutes after he had left, it went up in flames. His excuse then to police was he had only returned to the restaurant to quickly check his emails and continued to deny any involvement in the arson. It was later established by the business owners that around $23,000 was unaccounted for in restaurant takings and, by this stage, police had no doubt as to whodunnit, charging Stralow with 16 counts of theft and one of arson.

He pleaded "not guilty", all to no avail, after a jury in April 2011 found him guilty on all counts, leaving no doubt that the fire was started by Stralow to cover up his thieving of the takings to feed his gambling habit. He was sentenced to two years and six months in prison and the restaurant, which was owned by renowned chef, Jamie Oliver, as a part of his foundation to assist disadvantaged youth, never really recovered and closed in 2012.

One restaurant fire certainly became a whatdunnit, when the 25-year-old heritage Stokehouse restaurant in St Kilda went up in flames late one evening in January 2014. The blaze was so intense the building had to be demolished the following day due to safety concerns. If the complex had been closed and not occupied at the time of the fire, then perhaps it may have been a case of not whatdunnit, but whodunnit. But in respect to this fire, it was still occupied by staff and their patrons when the fire began in the kitchen, with everyone quickly leaving the burning building. An examination of what was left of the kitchen and evidence from staff, determined that what caused the fire was fat build up in a kitchen griddle and rotisserie

As Head of School Security for the Victorian Ministry of Education, I attended many school fires which were clearly arson, but the perpetrators, on some occasions, were never determined. Case in point was a fire at the Forest Hill Secondary College's Blackburn Campus, with two LTC wings, being the northwest and southwest wings, set on fire and completely destroyed. I was working a night shift in the early hours of Monday, 7 October 1991, when the call for 'any units in the vicinity of' came over our radio network at 0223 hours.

Being only 10 minutes from the campus, I was flashed speeding through a red light but arrived to witness both wings burning furiously. Leaving my dog in the vehicle, because the flames would be intense, I could hear the MFB in the distance. I checked the school grounds, hoping to find our arsonist watching intently, but all to no avail as the building went up in flames. The MFB extinguished the fire after a solid one-hour battle but all that was left was a smouldering ruin.

The intense fire and the publicity given to, not only this fire, but our previous 17 fires for the year, resulted in our State Coroner, Hal Hallenstein, attending next morning. Mr Hallenstein had previously attended at private school arson attacks, but this was the first occasion he would attend any of our fires as part of his coronial role. I subsequently spent most of the morning with Mr Hallenstein going over the fire scene and found him to be very easy to talk with, not that he smiled much.

Then again, given the nature of his charter, which would not be an enviable task, I can understand why. We were never able to locate the offenders for this fire, so once again, we have a question remaining of whodunnit? The only positive outcome was I was able to get out of the red-light camera fine.

Now, you would like to think that the rich and famous would not be linked to an arson whodunnit, but this is what happened in an exclusive suburb, often referred to as billionaires row, in Point Piper, NSW. On one early, hazy morning in November 2008, a multistorey mansion was subjected to a firebombing, courtesy of a Molotov cocktail. This was followed some six days later by exactly the same incendiary-type of device setting alight another home, but in a less fashionable street some blocks away. The question remained, what was this all about and were the fires connected? It seems they were, as the property owners and a developer, by the name of Ron

Medich, were in some sort of dispute over monies owed by one owner of a now damaged home.

So, the obvious answer was to sort out the dispute, by setting the fires and surely, they will see some sense. A person by the name of Michael McGurk, had been appointed by Medich as trustee to recover monies owed and, at first glance, one of his debt collection methods was to intimidate the debtor by setting his house on fire.

McGurk was charged in early 2009 by police with two counts of arson, together with lesser charges of intent to injure the homeowners and assault. The DPP subsequently withdrew all charges against McGurk, putting the question of whodunnit clearly back in the frame of police. However, some months later in September 2009, the crime of arson would pale into insignificance as Medich, after having a falling out with McGurk, paid $500,000 to send his now former trustee to his grave with a bullet to the back of his head.

Medich, on being sentenced in 2018 for the murder, was told by Justice Geoffrey Bellew that it was obvious he had a deep-seated hatred of McGurk as a motive for the murder, despite Medich continuing to plead his innocence. A subsequent 2021 appeal by Medich over his sentence of a maximum of 39 years jail was dismissed, meaning he will be nearly 100 years old before becoming eligible for parole.[15]

It still remains a question though as to whodunnit regarding the arson attacks.

The same can also be said over the dilemma of who was the firelighter, although it was initially thought to be a firefighter in the small town of Middleton in Tasmania, when the rural fire station went up in flames. Two separate fires were lit in

---

15   *Medich v R* [2021] NSWCCA 36.

July 2017, with the second fire destroying the station, along with two fire trucks, at an estimated damage bill of around $1 million. Police initially charged one of the brigade's volunteers with attempted arson and arson, for which he vehemently denied any involvement and continued to maintain his innocence. Well, it certainly became a question of whodunnit, as the DPP withdrew all charges against this now suspended fire volunteer. The fire station has since been rebuilt, but I am not sure whether the suspension was ever lifted.

I have left the last question of whodunnit, to perhaps the most intriguing but sad 1945 case of the Sodder children. It certainly wasn't a happy Christmas for their family as, in the early morning hours just before Santa arrived, their family home in the small coal mining town of Fayetteville, West Virginia, US, went up in flames. The parents, along with four of their children, escaped from the intense blaze, but sadly their five remaining children were trapped.

Or were they?

It was assumed, as they watched the fire destroy the house, that the five youngsters were trapped inside with the blaze so intense, the father's attempts to save his kids was fruitless. His endeavours were not helped by the fact he could not find a ladder, which somehow had disappeared, nor would his coal truck start so he could climb on it to enter the second floor of the house where the children were. The problem, of course, at this point was where was the ladder? It was in its usual location the day before and the truck was previously working without any mechanical issues. The other problem facing the Sodder family was the local fire brigade was nowhere to be seen, apparently over a lack of crew to immediately attend the unfolding emergency.

The question for investigators was, of course, where the remains of the five children were. Initially, firefighters said they had found no evidence of any remains, but it was later revealed, albeit with a question mark, that they found their burnt remains but didn't tell the parents for fear of causing them further grief. The next contradictory account was that the fire was so intense, it was much like a cremation, therefore, leaving no credible evidence of any charred remains.

The problem with this conclusion was many of the household items were still either intact, or only mildly damaged by the flames, so it could not have been that intense. The local coroner was convinced, in any event, that the children perished and were cremated in the intense heat, quickly coming to such a conclusion some five days later, issuing death certificates for each of them, stating they died by fire or suffocation. Many decades later though, at the request of the family, the cremation theory was totally rejected by a local crematorium.

A subsequent examination of the fire scene next morning suggested that the blaze may have emanated from a fuse box located in the family study. This was confirmed by Mrs Sodder, who stated that she was first made aware of the fire seeing flames coming from this part of the house. This accidental cause theory, however, started to unravel, with one witness allegedly telling police that when he drove past the house just before it was set alight, he observed some person setting it on fire.

It poses the question of its credibility. Why didn't he stop or at least report it to police? Perhaps it was arson as Mr Sodder had supposedly made some derogatory remark about the leader of Italy, then received a warning from some unidentified individual that, 'The house would go up in smoke.'

A further alleged threat was later revealed and believed

to come from an insurance salesperson, after Mr Sodder supposedly rejected the purchase of life insurance for his children. It was also determined by investigators that their telephone line had been cut on Christmas Eve, which led to the arrest of a local for theft from the Sodder garage and wilful damage. All very suspicious, but he vehemently denied any involvement in the house fire.

The Sodder family was, however, not convinced their children had perished and even engaged a local private eye to see what he could unravel of their whereabouts. They also offered a reward, together with putting up a billboard, seeking information on what happened to their children. All to no avail, despite a number of alleged sightings all over the US and even as far as Mexico. Many decades later, another theory emerged from withing the local community that the Sodder children had, in fact, been kidnapped by the Sicilian Mafia and taken to live in Italy, supposedly over a failed extortion threat involving their father.

Sadly, the five children were never located and perhaps they did perish in the fire, given that their father had stored a number of 55-gallon drums of petrol under the house for use in his coal trucking business. Then again, did they die by cremation? As to how the fire started, perhaps we will never know if it was a whodunnit or simply accidental.

There will always remain a question for investigators of not what, but whodunnit and, as we know, there are individuals out there deliberately setting these fires, using arson to carry out a murder, or indeed to conceal and destroy any evidence from the crime scene of such a dastardly deed. This makes it very difficult for investigators to identify the culprit, sometimes leaving the crime unsolved.

5
MURDER ARSON

The perplexing case of Daniel Dougherty, at first glance, or then again, maybe at third glance seeing his case, was subjected to three separate trials and left me wondering. Should it be included in the previous chapter as a question of perhaps whodunnit? Or even in my later chapter "Guilty or Not Guilty", but then again, he was eventually found guilty of the August 1985 murder arson of his two sons. It certainly begs the question though, whether this fire involved a high degree of planning and was premeditated. Was it simply carried out as an act of revenge or was he indeed innocent?

His two sons were only aged four and three and lived together, quite happily, with their father and his girlfriend, who also had a young child. Dougherty was arrested by police in 1999, which was almost 14 years after the Philadelphia house fire in the US, when the mother of their deceased children told police he had, in fact, confessed to her that he was responsible for their deaths. His only admission to police and the jury trial though, was that he indeed was responsible for the deaths of his children, not because of any murder arson, but when he woke up in the downstairs lounge room, surrounded by smoke and flames, he didn't try and save them. He was adamant his first instinct was to quickly leave the burning house and, with the help of a garden hose, try and extinguish the blaze. In the meantime, the two boys, who were upstairs asleep in their bedroom, would perish.

At his first trial in 2000, with Dougherty maintaining his innocence, the prosecution-led evidence, said he was a jilted lover and acted out of revenge against both his ex-wife and girlfriend by starting three separate fires in the home of the girlfriend, who was not present at the time but was about to bring to an end their relationship. His defence counsel wasn't much help during the trial, as he accepted, without challenge, the prosecution's witness forensic evidence that Dougherty was responsible for the three fires, which would later provide Dougherty with a successful appeal for a new trial. A jury of his peers at the first trial would find Dougherty guilty of arson. Regarding the capital murder charges, he was sentenced to death, which was affirmed in 2004 by the Pennsylvania Supreme Court.[16]

In 2005, Dougherty filed with the US Supreme Court, a writ of certiorari, seeking an order for the original sentencing court to deliver up its findings to a higher court in order for the case to be reviewed, was rejected. In 2012, a retrial was ordered, based on the lack of adequate legal representation in the first trial. Dougherty was once again found guilty, but his death sentence was commuted to life imprisonment.

In 2014 on appeal, a new and now third trial was ordered,

---

16   *Commonwealth of Pennsylvania v Daniel Dougherty* [J-39-2003].

this time on the successful ground that he again had been unfairly convicted. This was thanks to the judge allowing the first trial witness testimony by the original arson investigator, who gave supposed scientific evidence of three separate fires, to be admitted as "read into evidence" as he was unable to attend in person. This, in effect, meant he couldn't be properly cross-examined because, the defence can't put questions to a witness who does not appear. In other words, they couldn't question the evidence of a piece of paper.

Dougherty was then offered a plea deal which he refused and, given the time already served, if accepted, he may well have been eligible for parole. In March 2019, Doughty once again went before a jury pleading his innocence and, after a deliberation of some two days, you guessed it, he was found guilty again. This was despite the defence again providing expert evidence from two renowned arson investigators, who told the court their separate reviews of the initial arson investigation led them to the considered opinion there was no evidence to suggest arson and that it was started by what became known as "flashover".

This meant it was a simultaneous ignition that, in turn, mimicked arson as they could not find any evidence of a deliberately lit fire. They were quite adamant the original 1985 fire investigation was with the use of what could only be described as, 'Outdated and discarded fire investigation techniques.'

On that basis, it was argued the cause of the fire should simply be put down as "undetermined", which was supported by another expert witness who disputed the three separate fires theory saying, when a fire envelopes a room, burn patterns will be lost.

The prosecution, of course, disagreed saying there had been little change over the decades, if any, in the scientific way investigators conducted their examination of a fire scene, but still portrayed the fire as an act of revenge against his then girlfriend. The defence, on the other hand, all to no avail, in their final summary to the jury submitted that no one had witnessed Dougherty light the fire. No one had heard of or gave evidence against him talking about his plans to burn the house down; he had no grievance against his children who he loved dearly and, of course, the point of origin of the fire was in dispute.

The trial Judge had the final say, however, in that his conduct was:

despicable…pure revenge against a girlfriend and a wife…you don't burn your own children to death…

He sentenced Dougherty to two consecutive terms of life imprisonment for arson and second-degree murder.

It is difficult to imagine the grief and despair for any family losing a child, let alone any family member in a murder arson, but how could they possibly cope losing eight loved ones from the same family. Shahid Mohammed obviously had no compassion, let alone any regret, for his victims when he set fire to a family home in Huddersfield, a town in West Yorkshire, England, in the early hours of 12 May 2002. Mohammed was somewhat aggrieved with the family, all over his sister having a relationship with a man who was friends with them.

Along with three of his acquaintances and as the family of eleven slept, which included five children, the perpetrators first checked that all the house lights were off and everyone was asleep, knowing that when the staircase caught fire, all those upstairs in the house would be unable to escape. They then used a number of petrol bombs, weighted with metal to ensure they would smash through the double-glazed house windows, together with accelerant, which they poured into a letter slit in the front door, which led into the hallway at the bottom of the stairs, to set the home on fire.

Seven family members, which included all the children, one only six-months old, perished as the fire completely took hold. The children's grandmother later succumbed to her injuries after jumping through a first-floor window trying to escape. Three other family members would survive, but only after suffering from severe burns and smoke inhalation. Somehow, the 19-year-old Mohammed was allowed bail after being interviewed by police some hours after the fire, making a "no comment" record of interview.

It would take 17 years, after he fled to Pakistan and married, having children of his own, after lengthy extradition proceedings, which commenced in early 2015, so another three years before he would face the Leeds Crown Court for sentencing. In his absence, in 2003, three of his accomplices faced court with Shahid Iqbal being convicted of eight counts of murder and sentenced to life with a minimum of 22 years. Shakiel Shazard and Nazar Hussain were jailed for 18 years for manslaughter.

Mohammed finally faced justice in 2019 before a jury with him pleading not guilty on the basis that he was not involved in setting fire to the home as he only went there as the lookout, thinking the plan was to set fire to a family car. The prosecution-led evidence, which included a witness saying he had observed the four men, wearing some sort of latex gloves, running away from the burning home, with one having a big smile on his face as they left in a vehicle. Defence counsel for Mohammed in final submissions would say to the jury, 'Was he part of a plan to kill or cause really serious harm? Or was he, as the defence said, "…caught up in events that spiralled out of control".'

The jury had no problem though in finding him guilty and Mohammed was initially sentenced on eight counts of murder to life imprisonment, with a minimum of 23 years with a determinate fixed length of time sentence of 14 years for the offence of arson. On appeal by the Crown as to the sentence being manifestly inadequate, the minimum jail time was increased by a further three years to 27 years by the Court of Appeal.[17]

Following the successful appeal, the Solicitor General for England and Wales said:

Eight innocent lives were lost, including five small children under 13, in an utterly odious and wicked attack perpetuated because of a personal dispute. The offender then extended the pain and suffering of the victims' relatives by fleeing the jurisdiction and avoiding justice for many years…

There was certainly no issue in determining the actions and guilt of sadistic killer, David Warwick Hopkins, following his "unspeakable act" as described by Her Honour on sentencing him in October 2011 to a minimum of 30 years in prison. Hopkins was in a volatile de facto relationship with his victim, Nicole Millar, but through no fault of her own making, he set

---

[17] *The Queen and Shahid Mohammed*—In the Court of Appeal (Criminal Division) [2020] FWCA Crim 766.

her on fire in early June 2010 at a petrol station in Bayswater, Victoria.

Hopkins, not long after he put some fuel in the vehicle, then placed the petrol nozzle inside the car and splashed his victim before stabbing her in the upper body. This was then followed by him using a cigarette lighter to set alight the accelerant, with the vehicle, including his victim, being engulfed in flames. Somehow, she was able to remove herself from the vehicle in a desperate bid to escape, despite burning all over and screaming in unrelenting agony.

He was arrested by police at a nearby church and taken to hospital with burns and a self-inflicted stab wound. His innocent victim died in hospital later that evening with full thickness burns to over 90 per cent of her body. In hospital, she was placed in an induced coma to alleviate the immense pain and, as she was put under, she pleaded with nursing staff to not let her die. Unfortunately, this 42-year-old woman passed away, leaving behind three much-loved children with the youngest only 15 years of age.

Hopkins pleaded guilty before Her Honour Justice King in the Supreme Court of Victoria and on 19 October 2011 was sentenced to life imprisonment, with a minimum of 30 years before being eligible for parole. He did, however, try to alter his plea of guilty, prior to sentencing, to not guilty based on a mental impairment allegedly due to a drug-induced psychosis, such application being refused by the court. The learned judge had the unfortunate task of having to view the CCTV footage of the arson murder and, in regard to this horrific act, said:

For a period of three minutes and 21 seconds (the victim) sits on the forecourt of the garage burning from head to toe. It is beyond human comprehension that this is a person that is on fire and burning to death...Not only have you doused her in petrol and set her on fire, you then take even more horrific action, in that you prevented any person coming to her assistance or aid. People are ringing triple 000... also to get to her to try and extinguish the flames... But anyone who came towards approaching her was told by you, 'fuck off, I'm going to kill you'...Whilst you were preventing all of these people...you made comments to her...walking up close...ensuring that she could hear you... 'burn bitch burn, I hope you die, burn let her burn-hurry up and burn...[18]

Her Honour, on sentencing, took into account Hopkins' plea of guilty and that around the time of his inexplicable act of murder had consumed a large number of assorted illegal drugs, noting he also had a history of excessive drinking. The expert psychological report submitted to the court determined that he was mentally stable, but his mental state was obviously affected by drugs and alcohol, with the latter being described by Hopkins as being a "happy drunk".

Her Honour accepted that while Hopkins may have had some regret over his actions, he ostensibly failed to demonstrate that he was truly remorseful and a minimum of 30 years in prison was certainly warranted. As aptly put by Her Honour that:

This case is in the category of the worst type of murder and should attract the maximum sentence that parliament has legislated for this offence...[19]

---

18   *R v Hopkins* [2011] VSC 517–para 17.
19   Ibid- para 53.

Hopkins subsequently sought, by way of an application for extension of time, to lodge an appeal against sentence, based on the head sentence or non-parole period being manifestly excessive, such application being refused. Justice Redlich of the Court of Appeal, at the time, made it plainly clear the untold suffering of such victims when he said:

It would be a futile exercise to attempt to imagine a death that more appals the conscience than death by burning. It is a form of death likely, in common knowledge, to be accompanied by extreme pain...[It has been] aptly described...as a form of death so brutal as to be beyond the understanding of most civilised human beings... [20]

A former girlfriend of Craig Anthony Leonard, was fortunate to escape his murderous intent when he set fire to her Queensland Sunshine Coast house early on the Sunday morning of 17 April 2011. Unfortunately, her current boyfriend and her auntie, who was also asleep in the house at the time, were not so lucky, being burnt to death. Leonard was not only annoyed she had the audacity to break up with him some eight months earlier, but how dare she start up a new relationship.

A few weeks earlier before the fire, Leonard sent his ex a sexually explicit picture of her saying that if she didn't pay an alleged debt, he would post the picture on the internet. He then followed up a week before setting the fire with text messages accusing her of having a venereal disease, that she was riddled with cancer and in graphic terms, suggested she needed an operation.

Just prior to setting the fire, he ascertained she was in

---

20   *Hopkins v The Queen* [2015] VSCA 174–para 28.

the house asleep with her boyfriend, so a jealous Leonard, carrying petrol in a drunken and drug affected rage, set fire to a mattress in a downstairs room. His ex-girlfriend woke up with her feet on fire and was lucky to escape the burning inferno by jumping off a top-level veranda badly breaking her back, but her boyfriend and aunt were not so lucky. The boyfriend's remains were found on the bathroom floor with the deceased auntie also being badly burned. DNA tests were required in order to positively identify her.

Leonard was interviewed by police the following day in the presence of his father but denied he had anything to do with the fire. He gave some sceptical version that he was on the road around the time of the fire, driving to see his father, as he was concerned for his welfare, as his mother had recently died. After a break of around 45 minutes and a so-called private, but unrecorded, conversation between police and their suspect, the interview recommenced and he admitted taking the petrol to his former girlfriend's house and setting fire to a mattress, but only as a means to frighten her and, as put in his words to police, 'Fuck her up financially.'

The break, followed by the second recorded interview, would later become the subject of a pre-trial appeal as to the admissibility of the evidence, where it was argued, unsuccessfully, that the prosecution would be unable to prove Leonard made his admission voluntarily.

In allowing the evidence of the conversation and subsequent admission to be used at trial, Justice James Douglas did comment that:

> ...to resolve the issues of what was said in this 'brief chat' between Detective Ford and the defendant illustrates how

> *desirable it is for conversations between police and suspects to be recorded fully. Where portable recorders are readily available there is every reason to use them, even in a brief break in a more formal interview. Nonetheless, I am satisfied in this case that no threat, promise, or inducement was held out to the defendant to make this confession.*[21]

On Tuesday, 19 February 2013, Leonard pleaded guilty to two counts of murder and one count of arson and causing grievous bodily harm to his ex-girlfriend. In a late plea for mercy, he spoke to the court saying his conduct was uncharacteristic and that he was very sorry for his victims' families. His Honour, Justice Douglas said whilst there was evidence to indicate the conduct of Leonard was fuelled by alcohol, it was nothing but a stupid act and even that understates the severe effect of what he did. This jealous revenge double murderer and arsonist was sentenced to a maximum term of life imprisonment, with a minimum non-parole period of 20 years.

Evidence that more needs to be done regarding these sorts of tragic domestic violence acts was again very apparent in the sad and shocking murder of Hannah Clarke and her three children at Camp Hill, Queensland on 19 February 2020. Hannah was fatally set on fire, as were her children, by her estranged husband, Rowan Baxter. He had a chequered history of all types of controlling behaviour during their relationship, including being the named respondent in a domestic violence order (DVO).[22]

The DVO was initially made after he kidnapped one of his children. It was then varied some weeks before the fatal

---

21 *R v Craig Anthony Leonard* QSCPR 4; [2012] QSC 425–para 58.

22 *Domestic and Family Violence Protection Act 2012* (Qld).

incident, allowing Baxter unrestricted contact with his children. This access was then revoked by police in early February 2020, leading to his rampage which also included Baxter stabbing himself to death shortly after the murder of his estranged family.

Hannah's family set up the foundation known as "Small Steps 4 Hannah" in recognition of her and her children with the aim to HALT (named in memory of H(Hannah), A (Aaliyah), I (Laianah), T (Trey) (the names of the children)), incidents of family violence and trauma in Australia. The foundation provides short term quality crisis accommodation for affected family members to escape and be safely housed from the perpetrators committing violent and abusive behaviour.

A domestic violence survivors refuge named "Hannah's Sanctuary" was subsequently opened in May 2023 in honour of Hannah and her children and is now one of nine much needed safe house facilities in Brisbane. The Queensland government, also in their commitment to end coercive control in domestic violence situations, enacted specific legislation in a further effort to prevent such terrible acts.[23]

Another murder arson that can also be placed in the worst of the worst category was the ghastly burning to death of local lawyer, Katie Foreman in Wollongong, south of Sydney, NSW. Her bedroom was set alight in the early hours on the morning of 27 October 2011, while she was no doubt asleep, being woken up by a horrendous fire. Following an examination of the fire scene, it became evident she had been murdered, after crime scene investigators found evidence of petrol spread about inside the house and then ignited. They would also find a key to

---

23 *Domestic and Family Violence Protection (Combating Coercive Control) and Other Legislation Amendment Act 2023* (Qld).

the home lying out on a roadway nearby as there was nothing to suggest the house had been forcibly entered.

Police were also advised by the fire brigade that when they arrived at the home around 2.35am and after extinguishing the blaze, found the charred remains of Ms Foreman in the upstairs landing next to her bedroom. It was clearly apparent that she had tried to escape the inferno before becoming overcome, with a subsequent autopsy disclosing she had inhaled soot and smoke from the fire. An examination of what remained of her badly burnt clothing would also conform that petrol had been used by whoever started the fire.

Given that her death was clearly a case of murder arson, police would keep an open mind and look at everything that could possibly lead to an arrest. The first thing that had to be established though was what was the motive for her death and their first point of call would be to look at her "nearest and dearest", then work from there. A person of interest was Bradley Max Rawlinson, after police determined he had been in a relationship with Ms Foreman from time to time, over a period of some four years.

He had even hosted a dinner party some months earlier to celebrate her birthday, so they interviewed him the same day of the fire. Rawlinson denied to police, at their first interview, any knowledge of the fire and did not confirm with them that he had, in fact, been in a relationship with Ms Foreman. He did admit he had been in contact with her some days prior to the fire, including sending her a text message, but denied any knowledge or involvement in what had fatally transpired earlier that morning.

There were, however, a number of inconsistencies and gaps in the story Rawlinson was telling police. He had omitted to tell them he was having an affair with a person by the name of Wendy Anne Evans, who had three children and also had been an acquaintance of the deceased. Police quickly put in place electronic surveillance and would also look at a large quantity of mobile phone and SMS records over the next few weeks. They soon uncovered what was clearly a motive where Rawlinson and Evans wanted Ms Mahoney out of the way so they could go on and live happily ever after. An incriminating text message between Rawlinson and Evans before the murder arson, confirmed this when Evans said:

I hate it when you leave, with him replying, *Yeah, so do I but just keep thinking one more week. Then she is gone and we are away from her.*

Police would also determine the involvement of two others, namely a Michelle Sharon Proud and her then de facto partner, Bernard Justin Spicer. Police would later allege that Rawlinson, via Proud, who also happened to be a friend of Evans, paid Spicer the sum of $3,000 to carry out effectively what was a "contract killing". Indeed, telephone records indicated a copious amount of back-and-forth communication between the four suspects during October 2011, including on the day of the fire.

One call involved Evans and Proud discussing who they could get to bash the now deceased, with Spicer later confirming he was prepared to do their bidding. Rawlinson would then carry out a withdrawal of cash the day before the fire, including further withdrawals in November 2011, which were then passed onto Spicer in payment for his handiwork.

By the middle of November 2011, the police net was tightening, with Rawlinson again being interviewed by police where he said he had not spoken with Evans for at least the last six months. On leaving the police station, he immediately made contact with Evans and they met at a Telstra shop over concerns about their now deleted incriminating text messages, particular those the day before and after the fire. They were incorrectly advised by a Telstra employee that if they had been deleted, they could not be retrieved. How wrong was that advice? They would ultimately find out and pay the price.

Evans was interviewed by police the day after Rawlinson and she did not reveal that she was in any sort of relationship with him, saying further she had no knowledge or was in anyway involved in the house fire and certainly had not spoken with him since that fatal day. Evans would also give police a false alibi of her movements on the night of the fire.

Detectives then contacted Rawlinson on 19 December 2011 and advised they again wanted to speak with him, particularly regarding a number of concerns and inconsistencies about Evans. A police intercept also recorded the following conversation together with other further incriminating discussions between Rawlinson and Evans, who were now in obvious panic mode:

Rawlinson: We cannot be seen to have been together because they'll put the two of us together, as the two that did it. We cannot say that we've been together. I don't know what to do.
Evans: Fuckin' hell
Rawlinson: I'm fucked; my life is over.
Evans: If you go, I've got to go with you.

It was readily apparent that their lives as they knew them, would soon come to an end as Spicer was also being secretly listened to and recorded by police, including from a covert listening device installed in his home. These conversations would also show how callous Spicer was, as all he seemed concerned about was, he had not yet received payment in full as part of the murder arson contract. On 21 December 2011, a mere 55 days after the death of Ms Maloney, all four were arrested and charged with murder as part of a joint criminal enterprise, which carries a maximum sentence of life imprisonment.

Evans would ultimately plead guilty, while Rawlinson and Proud would plead not guilty, to no avail, being subsequently found guilty following a jury trial. Spicer pleaded not guilty in a separate trial, but a jury would also find him guilty. In sentencing Evans on 28 July 2014 to a term of imprisonment of 24 years, with a non-parole period of 18 years, Judge Ian Harrison said regarding the murderous role she played in company with Spicer that:

At about 2.20am, Ms Evans and Mr Spicer entered the deceased's home using the keys provided by Mr Rawlinson. Mr Spicer carried a firelighter and the bucket that he had earlier filled with petrol. Ms Evans and Mr Spicer walked up the stairs in the deceased's house. Mr Spicer handed the firelighter to Ms Evans, which Mr Spicer had wrapped in a petrol-soaked cloth...Mr Spicer said, 'Light it now.' Ms Evans lit the firelighter and threw it into the bathroom. Mr Spicer retrieved it from the bathroom and threw it into the deceased's bedroom. The petrol ignited immediately. They ran from the house. Fire consumed the bedroom within a very short time. Whilst fleeing from the house, Ms Evans dropped the two house keys[24]

---

24   *R v Evans; R v Rawlinson; R v Proud* [2014] NSWSC 979-paras 38-39.

In sentencing Evans, the Court took into account that she had no prior criminal record; her offending was a gross anomaly; she had good prospects for rehabilitation and that her conduct was certainly completely out of character. His Honour would then go on to say, in regards to Evans, despite finding a consistency with an intention to kill, that:

> *I consider that the need for specific deterrence is small. The same cannot be said for whatever sentence Ms Evans receives, ought to say about the terrible nature of her crime and the consequences for anyone committing a similar crime. I remain even now completely puzzled about why the deceased was killed. She did nothing to anyone that set her apart from any but the most saintly and pious among us...[25]*

Regarding the sentence of Evans and given that she pleaded guilty to such an horrendous crime, she was allowed a discount on the overall sentence of 25 per cent, meaning she will serve at least 18 years before being eligible for consideration of parole. His Honour then turned to Rawlinson, who had steadfastly maintained his innocence throughout the trial but did offer to plead guilty to the lesser charge of manslaughter, which was rejected.

He exercised his right to silence during the trial, which, of course, was his choice to do so, and His Honour then referred to the police record of interview, which, to put bluntly, he found quite bizarre. Rawlinson tried to convince police that Ms Maloney had threatened to kill one of his children on at least 50 separate occasions, so he arranged for her to be bashed, but he didn't mean for them to murder her.

---

25   Ibid-para 126.

On finding Rawlinson was also part of a joint criminal enterprise, His Honour then said:

At all times, before and after the murder, Mr Rawlinson sought to distance himself from the killing. However, he paid for the killing to be carried out. Notwithstanding that, he falsely portrayed himself as the deceased's grief-stricken partner and actively sought to suggest false probabilities about how and why she may have been killed. [26].

Counsel for Rawlinson tried to convince the court, in mitigation against sentence, that his client was a person of good character, was likely not to re-offend and he had good prospects for rehabilitation. His Honour wasn't convinced with those submissions, finding that Rawlinson was involved in the crime that involved detailed planning, that he was the principal coordinator and, indeed, was the driving influence, delegating the dastardly deed to others. Whilst Rawlinson was diagnosed with a depressive illness, His Honour noted that it had not interfered in any way with his day to day living.

The sentence imposed, taking in all the relevant circumstances, resulted in Rawlinson being jailed for a total of 36 years and he would not be eligible for parole until the expiration of 27 years, which means his first chance of release will not be until 20 December 2038. By then, he will only be 69 years old and, if eligible for parole, will still have some time to enjoy life, which was not the outcome for Ms Maloney, who was only 31 years old when she died.

Proud was next in line for sentencing and the court had no hesitation in determining that she was a willing and

---

[26] Ibid- para 135.

eager player in what transpired. His Honour summed up her involvement perfectly when he said:

> *Ms Proud was approached by Ms Evans to engage her then partner, Mr Spicer, in the criminal enterprise. She was the link or connection between Ms Evans and Mr Spicer in the payment of money and in encouraging Mr Spicer to participate in the commission of the offence. Ms Proud later showed no remorse concerning what had occurred...[27]...at all times sought to distance herself from any involvement in the crime. However, she was part of an agreement to cause grievous bodily harm to the deceased...[28]*

Proud, to her credit, for want of a better word, did give evidence at the trial waving her right to remain silent and during the sentencing phase did express regret of what had transpired, which was rejected by the court. His Honour did, however, accept that her role in the joint criminal enterprise, unlike the other three offenders, was entirely passive and that she was not directly involved in the events that led to the murder. Proud was sentenced to a term of imprisonment of 20 years, with a non-parole period of 14 years. It was noted in the media that when Evans and Proud were led out of the courtroom in handcuffs to begin their sentence, they were in tears, most likely for themselves and not the deceased.

Contract killer, Spicer, proceeded by way of a separate trial and despite his plea of innocence, a jury would also find him guilty beyond reasonable doubt. This denial was despite Spicer,

---

27 Ibid-para 173.

28 Ibid-para 174.

during a police record of interview, after being told Proud admitted to being involved in the murder arson, saying:

This is fucking bullshit man. It wasn't supposed to happen.

He then provided a very detailed account of his participation, including that when he purchased the petrol, all he believed was going to happen would be the burning of the deceased's motor vehicle. That, of course, all changed with Spicer then telling police, as he had already accepted the dastardly deed money so, what choice did he have but to go through with the murder? Later, he maintained he didn't know she was home at the time and he was just a follower.

The covert listening devices were his further undoing and on 15 May 2015, he appeared before His Honour Justice Ian Harrison for sentencing. Given that Spicer had a criminal record, including convictions for serious violent offending, there was little his defence could offer in mitigation for sentencing, other than, supposedly, he felt shattered when he found out the next day that Ms Maloney had died from incineration.

His Honour, on sentencing Spicer to a term of imprisonment of 32 years, which was four years less than ringleader Rawlinson and that he could apply for parole after serving 24 years, summed it up perfectly, stating:

The deceased died in circumstances that were particularly callous and brutal. Her death was undeserved, avoidable and pointless. Mr Spicer permitted himself, for a pathetic reward, to become the instrument of others... The deceased was obviously an energetic and talented lawyer, a loving daughter and a well-loved personality. The community in general and the deceased

> *relatives, friends and professional colleagues, in particular, are the worse for her death.*[29]

His Honour, in an unusual mention, and I think it should be often said in many difficult cases, shared his immense gratitude for the efforts of NSW Police. He, quite rightly, deemed the untiring work of the investigators, who had the difficult and unfortunate task of trying to identify the perpetrators, as truly remarkable. This relenting pursuit included not only the electric surveillance, but literally scores of interviews with potential witnesses, together with technical experts, in order to provide a very comprehensive brief of evidence that could be presented to the jury. It goes without saying, the general public, at times simply forget, or indeed, don't want to know, what is involved in any police investigation and the tireless hours put in to bring those responsible before a court of law.

New Zealand Police are also very persistent, leaving no stone unturned in finally bringing Lynne Maree Martin to justice some 10 years after she murdered her elderly father, by torching his family home in Te Karaka, burning him alive. Her father, due to his health issues which rendered him basically immobile, was often looked after by his son, John. Just after midnight of 25 January 2013, he told John, as he was putting him to bed before leaving, of a disturbing phone call he had received from Martin earlier that day.

Soon after John left, Martin went to the house with her father asleep after he'd taken a sleeping pill and by leaving cooking oil burning on the stove, she set the fire that killed him. John, on being told the family home had been destroyed

---

[29] *R v Spicer* [2015] NSWSC 519-para 93.

and his father had perished, immediately told police of his suspicions that he believed his sister was responsible.

The initial investigation by police was not going to be easy, as mere suspicion would not be enough, so they carried out what can only be described as a diligent, although time-consuming, investigation. They uncovered that Martin, on leaving the family home when she was 16, went to Australia to live in the city of Orange, which is about 250 kilometres from Sydney. During that time, she just happened to be convicted of arson in May 1999 when she set fire to her partner's two vehicles, all over a dispute over money.

On returning to New Zealand, she racked up further appearances in court including, in 2009, her third drink driving conviction and in 2010, she was convicted of 22 charges of obtaining financial advantage by deception. This offending occurred while she was working as a therapist in a nursing home, taking money from an elderly woman who suffered from advanced Alzheimer's. Martin was lucky not to be sent to jail, being ordered to serve 300 hours of community work and to pay restitution to the elderly woman of $11,298.90, with the sentencing judge describing her conduct as 'low-down, deceitful, deliberate and pre-mediated.'

The issue for police still, was to try and prove the arson and death of her father was pre-planned by Martin. To that aim, over the next three years, police would conduct two separate operations, including an undercover officer befriending Martin by using the name of "Millie Tait". It took a total of 157 days for covert Millie to obtain a somewhat guarded confession from Martin, who spoke about how to set fire to a house and destroy all the evidence.

Martin would also say that, 'arson is the easiest thing in

the world and very hard to prove', further elaborating that all was needed was cooking fat heating on a stove. At this point, the cause of the fire had not been definitely established, so police obtained some further expert evidence as to whether the house fire could have been started by the cooking fat method. It was no surprise it was confirmed as most likely.

In Martin's further conversations with undercover operative Millie, she also said that when committing arson, don't take a mobile phone and certainly don't leave any fingerprints. Well, Martin should have listened to what she preached as, while she vehemently denied being anywhere near her father's house on the night of the fire and his death, her mobile phone data told otherwise. Tower records confirmed she was in the vicinity around that time for some two hours. In addition, police placed listening devices in her home and bugs on her phone and, by the time they had finished, had a total of around 22,000 separate recordings, which included some incriminating evidence.

In particular, while Martin and her husband were watching a 2020 crime cold-case TV podcast, which just happened to be about her father's murder arson, she was bugged at various points making comments. When the program mentioned the phone call her father received from her the day before the fire, Martin is heard saying, 'There was nothing, there was no malice in it, no nothing, he was in good spirits.' This obviously confirmed what her brother had told police about the phone call that had worried her father. When asked by her husband if she had tormented her father, Martin responded by saying:

Oh fuck, I was always having a go at the cunt, but I can't say that.

At this point, Martin knew police had evidence from her mobile phone that she had been in the vicinity, by the time the crime podcast finished. She said to her husband:

They can put me down there, but it doesn't prove I went to Whatatutu (the father's house). It doesn't prove I set the house on fire.

Unfortunately for Martin, she was wrong, because the Crown proved their case before a jury beyond reasonable doubt, including a motive that Martin was bankrupt and murdered her father so she would get a substantial inheritance from his will. Not only did the evidence from the undercover police officer and all the listening device conversations bring her undone, but the prosecution was able to lead evidence of her Australian arson conviction as proof of her propensity to commit similar type offences.

Such disclosure is normally considered prejudicial and is only allowed in certain situations and with leave of the court. The argument by the prosecution was, she had in fact committed the offending in order to resolve her financial problems, assisted by anger and an alcohol dependence. Her defence counsel, of course, opposed the application, which went all the way to the High Court in August 2023, but was upheld.

The jury would hear all the evidence, sitting for 12 days, which included a total of around 50 witnesses, not only from her brother, but also her husband. The defence, as is their right, led no evidence and maintained Martin was innocent, but the jury thought otherwise, taking just over two hours to find her guilty on 22 November 2023. Martin was remanded in custody, but was found dead, most likely by suicide, in her cell the following day before being transferred to prison. Sadly, all this case does is once again highlight the devastating impact of arson and the consequences it has on the lives of the families left behind.

It's hard to fathom, once again, what the motive was, other than perhaps just sheer family violence, following the burning to death of 45-year-old Darren Reid in the Bendigo suburb of Long Gully, Victoria, by his long-term wife and mother of their five children, Kate Marie Stone. To make matters even more appalling, Stone said her husband was set alight around 11.20 pm on 18 December 2016, when three intruders entered their home and then allegedly poured petrol over both of them and ignited them with a cigarette lighter.

Stone named the three men, telling all and sundry who would listen, her version of events. The three men were arrested by police, held in custody and interviewed. Stone had a few problems though when she made a detailed, signed nine-page statement to police two days after the fire and following her partner's death, after he sustained 95 per cent burns to his body, including his airways. His injuries were certainly horrific. He was found conscious in a bathtub, but in agony and eventually he was air lifted to the Alfred Hospital in Melbourne, He was placed in an induced coma and died on the afternoon of 19 December 2016.

Put simply, the fact Stone denied any involvement in what took place just simply didn't stack up. The first issue was, the three named suspects had rock solid alibis, with one even being held in police custody at the time they were supposed to be involved in the murder and arson. Further, DNA evidence taken from a paint thinner tin, that contained highly flammable liquid, identified as enamel thinner, used to set Reid on fire, did not have any trace to the alleged three intruders.

What it did show on the tin though, was the DNA of Stone and a crime scene investigation confirmed it was fluid from this tin and not petrol, that had been used to ignite the fire. Her account of being doused in petrol was totally inconsistent with what actually took place, as Stone only suffered minor burns and not from petrol. In addition, there was simply no evidence in any event on her clothes that she had been exposed to any sort of flammable substance. It was also evident the location of the seat of the fire was inconsistent with what Stone had told police.

Police would also obtain incriminating witness statements, including from a neighbour who spoke to Stone a few days after the horrific fire, enquiring how she was, with Stone replying with words to the effect, 'I'm fine, I did it, I killed him.'

Other neighbours would also say that during the three months prior to the fire, they would often hear Stone and Reid arguing and, on that fatal day, such sounds were consistent with, not only a loud argument, but what appeared to be followed by them engaged in a physical fight. Notably, this loud argument then suddenly stopped and the next they heard, sometime later, was the sound of an ambulance.

Reid's grieving mother would also provide evidence that her son told her, only a month earlier, about Stone chasing him down a street holding a knife. He had said, 'I'm really scared mum, I'm in fear of my life'.

His stepmother also would give evidence at trial that, on the day of the fire, he said he was leaving Stone and asked could he stay at her house that night.

Stone maintained her innocence, still blaming the three alleged intruders during a further lengthy police record of interview on 4 January 2017. All to no avail though, with

Stone being charged with the vicious murder of Reid and on 20 November 2018, after a four-week jury trial, she was found guilty of the murder. The jury was satisfied, beyond any reasonable doubt, she was the culprit. The jury totally rejected the version of events proffered by Stone, and also a dying declaration from Reid as he was being rushed to hospital in an ambulance, when he said to a police officer he was set on fire by an unknown male. They also rejected the evidence of her two daughters, who supported their mother's story, of intruders setting the fire.

What they didn't dismiss though was evidence from the 16-year-old daughter, who told police she witnessed her father, engulfed in flames, running and jumping into a bath filled with water, telling her he was going to die.

It was abundantly clear the jury accepted the totality of the incriminating evidence before them, completely dismissing the false account of intruders being responsible. Further, the jury, on rejecting the version put by Stone, was clearly entitled to come to the conclusion she had concocted such blatant lies, in a feeble attempt to ensure any suspicion was deflected away from her. They also reached a reasonable inference that Stone had indeed persuaded her daughters to stick to the intruder story, which left them in no doubt as to what really happened and that she was solely responsible for the murder of Reid.

Stone appeared for sentencing on 12 July 2019 before Justice Taylor in the criminal division of the Supreme Court of Victoria sitting at Bendigo. The victim impact statements, once again, would tell of the unbelievable grief suffered by the victim's loved ones, with the mother of Reid and his siblings all speaking about now living a shattered life and the unbearable grief in having to bury him, knowing what he once looked like and now completely unrecognisable, with his burnt and badly disfigured remains.

The judge certainly didn't hold back in reference to the gravity of the offending, saying:

The manner in which you murdered Mr Reid was vicious. You knowingly poured a highly flammable liquid on Mr Reid. You could not have been ignorant of the unbelievable terror and pain you would unleash upon him the moment you ignited the fuel...[30]

After scant submissions by counsel of the personal circumstances of Stone, Her Honour would conclude further:

Your actions were despicable. For no obvious reason, you ended the life of the man you say you loved, in an excruciating manner, making him suffer unimaginable pain and fixing him with the belief he would die. You did so in the sanctity of the family home and while two of his children were close by. You invented a patently false story and perpetrated it as far and wide as possible, thereby ensnaring three innocent men in a murder investigation.[31]

With no disrespect to counsel for Stone and, perhaps he didn't have a lot to work with, but no evidence was submitted to try and place Stone in a better light. Her Honour, quite rightly, mentioned that no character references were tendered. The sessions with a psychologist, that Stone undertook in prison, apparently being depressed, were not explained and there were

---

30   *R v Stone* [2019] VSC 452-para 30.

31   Ibid- para 43.

no submissions made for the custody and care of any of her children.

Stone showed no remorse and continued to maintain her innocence, but the judge noted her high degree of moral culpability, given that her offending could only be placed in the top range of the murder scale. Stone, quite rightly, was sentenced to a maximum term of 34 years imprisonment, with a minimum 28 years before being eligible for parole and taking into account the 919 days served on remand, meaning, when eligible for release, she will be around 67 years of age.

It was no surprise that, as Stone was led away from court in handcuffs, she told waiting media that she was, 'innocent, I never murdered my husband, I loved him too much,' with one of her daughter's continuing to profess she was not guilty of the murder.

It was no surprise either, when Stone lodged an appeal against her conviction, asking whether a guilty verdict was reasonably open to the jury and, amongst other things, was it appropriate for the judge to find the dubious statements of Stone as lies? In a lengthy summation and reasoning of the appeal grounds, it was also no surprise that the Court of Appeal, on 24 June 2021, refused the application for leave to appeal.[32]

Another love triangle, for want of a better description, resulted in the death by murder arson in March 2017 of three victims: squatters living in a derelict factory in the Melbourne western suburb of Footscray. Darren Clover, at 52 years old at the time of the fire, had earlier, around 2013, met up with Tanya Burmeister, who was 32 years of age when she died. Tanya had a 15-year-old daughter, who would squat with her mother from time to time and would also lose her life. It's fair

---

[32] *Stone v The Queen* [2021] VSCA 186.

to say that both Clover and Tanya had some issues during their tenuous relationship and not just with each other, both being unemployed, on social security benefits and long-term drug abusers.

Clover had a long history of criminal offending, dating back as early as 1982, including imprisonment for unlawful assault and affray, drug trafficking and had been subject to community-based orders, good behaviour bonds and suspended sentences. His offending certainly wasn't helped by his heroin addiction and he was often seen begging around Melbourne's CBD. Clover, from his own admissions, said he loved Tanya madly and wanted to marry her at some stage. A person, by the name of David Griffiths, also had some affection for Tanya and eventually they got together as a couple from time to time, much to the disdain of Clover.

In October 2016, David and Tanya made a complaint to police that Clover had threatened to set the derelict factory, they called home, on fire. By February 2017, Tanya had severed the relationship with Clover and shacked up with David. To say Clover was very annoyed, is an understatement, particularly after he was falsely accused of committing an indecent assault on Tanya's daughter, including taking intimate photos of her. Clover continued to make threats against the couple, yelling abuse and saying he was going to assault them.

Unfortunately, Clover went further than just "bashing and smashing" them, as heard by one witness. Two days before the fire, he purchased some petrol and by placing fuel, from a red container, around the door of the factory, he set it alight around 11.20 pm on the night of 1 March 2017. Clover well knew that Tanya and David were inside the building, but it would later emerge in court that he was not aware her daughter was also present. Not that that doesn't make him recklessly culpable for her death.

Clover then walked away from the early stages of the fire, but a resident, who lived adjacent to the factory, did observe a male walking down into a nearby laneway. CCTV footage would later identify Clover at a number of different locations in the vicinity of the factory, before and after the fire. Another witness also heard screaming and crying out for help coming from inside the, now burning, building as it exploded into a fireball.

Firefighters, who arrived within a matter of minutes, found the factory entrance still chained and the red container half full of petrol, but also the three deceased victims lying near the door. An examination of the bodies would reveal they died from thermal burns, together with smoke inhalation, clearly as result of the fire started by Clover. Crime scene investigators determined that an accelerant was used and petrol had been spread out around the doorstep and then ignited flammable materials nearby. It was now a question for the investigators to follow the evidence and, within a matter of hours after the fire, they arrested Clover in the Melbourne CBD as he was carrying out his usual begging, obviously without any concern for what he had done earlier that morning.

He verily denied, during the record of interview, that he was in anyway involved in making any threats and setting the fire, however, he did go into some detail about the love of his life leaving him for David. Clover also mentioned that he was very cross over being accused of paedophilia and taking explicit photos of Tanya's young daughter. He then gave, what can only be described as, a bizarre account of leaving the red container of fuel outside the factory alcove on the night of the fire, under some suggestion of a pre-arrangement with David. It was no surprise that Clover was charged with three counts of murder and remanded in custody.

It was subsequently agreed with Crown prosecutors, after a contested committal hearing, that the murders were not carried out with prior intent, on the basis he would plead to three counts of reckless murder. In other words, Clover agreed that his conduct did create a significant risk of grievous bodily harm to a victim, in this case, the death of three victims, with what amounts to reckless indifference by continuing to proceed with the criminal act, regardless of the consequences.

Clover appeared for sentencing in the Supreme Court of Victoria on 25 February 2019 before Her Honour, Justice Jane Dixon, who noted that his early plea meant there would be no need for a contested trial, which would have brought untold grief to his victims' families and friends, but also further expressed his lack of remorse during the police record of interview. Her Honour also accepted that while there may have not been any meticulous planning, despite the threats he had made in the months leading up to the fire, his anger took over and, with obvious reckless intent, he lit the fire knowing it would most likely cause untold serious injury to his ex-lover, Tanya and also David. It was accepted he was totally unaware, however, that her daughter was also present and would lose her life, alongside her mother.

On sentencing Clover, as a serious violent offender, to a total effective prison term of 30 years, with a fixed non-parole period of 24 years, Her Honour took into account that no submissions had been made by the Crown seeking a life sentence and that Clover was entitled to a "utilitarian discount" for his pleas of guilty, meaning a lesser sentence, because he contributed to the efficiency of our criminal justice system and that he exhibited psychological disorders.

In arriving at a just and appropriate sentence, in respect to the overall criminality resulting in the deaths of three innocent victims, Judge Dixon also took into account Clover' age and said:

> *Your present age and the lengths of sentences (I have) imposed for murder, mean that you will be quite old before being eligible for consideration for release on parole or that you may even die in prison. Your age is a relevant factor…along with prospects of rehabilitation after a lengthy term of imprisonment…avoiding a crushing sentence that would deprive you of any realistic prospect of useful life after release…[33]*

Clover was afforded the usual section 6AAA sentencing discount under the *Sentencing Act 1991* (Vic), meaning if he had not pleaded guilty, he would have been sentenced to a further six years at the top with a bottom of an additional seven years. He was 54 years of age at the time his prison sentence was imposed meaning, if he is eligible for release after serving the minimum before he can apply, he will be 78 years old, if indeed he lives that long.

Another vengeful, jilted lover was Ashley Martin who, after buying what can only be described as a murder briefcase, which included, not only a hunting knife but a 20-litre jerrycan full of petrol, he drove to his former girlfriend's home in Kirton, Lincolnshire, UK. He had only one thought in mind and that was to murder her, after she had parted company with him in

---

[33] *DPP v Darren Clover* [2019] VSC 123-para 87.

December 2018. In his view, 'If I can't have you, then no one can.'

His premeditated plan was to first stab her to death and then set fire to the house with him inside.

In the early hours of New Year's Day of 2019, he went to her house to find his ex and her new boyfriend. Martin took his revenge out on both, stabbing the boyfriend in the heart and then causing a massive fireball explosion with windows being blown out, resulting in the deaths of not only his two victims, but himself. A subsequent post-mortem would reveal they all died of smoke inhalation, but with one body also having a deep and life-threatening wound to the heart. Police would later find a death note at the home of Martin which said, 'Fuck that bitch,' adding that if he survived, he would have been charged with two counts of murder.

Any human being with an ounce of compassion must have some difficulty in trying to comprehend how anyone could murder another human being by setting them on fire, then watch them die in untold agony. One cannot imagine such an excruciating and terror-filled painful death, but that is also what happened to victim Wade Still, when he was set alight in a disused quarry near Newcastle, NSW on the night of 20 August 2018, not once, but twice.

Two offenders were responsible, namely Troy Lee McCosker and his then, partner-in-crime and friend, a Mr Stone, who was given this pseudonym for turning Crown's evidence against his now former friend. Mind you, Stone was, however, identified in the media by his proper name prior to his conviction and sentence. For obvious reasons, I will refer to him under his veiled identity.

It appears that Still was known to both Stone and

McCosker with Stone saying there was no animosity between them, regardless of the fact that Still stole items belonging to McCosker and assaulting him for good measure during a "run in" (carrying out a home invasion), with McCosker returning the compliment and also bashing Still senseless. Things may well have come to a head when Still discovered McCosker was having an affair with his de facto partner while he was in jail. He was released in early July 2018, with Still then stealing a bag belonging to McCosker, some three days before he was murdered.

It was alleged Stone then said to another mate that Still needed to be "knocked", as he didn't want McCosker blaming him for the theft committed by Still. Stone then arranged to meet Still, under the guise of helping him with a car float that he needed in respect of a vehicle he was purchasing. He also arranged for Still to buy some petrol for his unregistered and uninsured motor bike, which he did not want to be seen in by police at any service station as it didn't have any lights.

They both rode on the bike with Still as pillion passenger and carrying the fuel, when they stopped near a quarry to refill the vehicle as it had run out of petrol. According to the version offered by Stone, they both then consumed some Xanax tablets, but things then turned very badly for Still. When Stone kicked the petrol, now in a bucket, at him, somehow Still, on Stone's initial version, was then "accidentally set on fire", and engulfed in flames. Stone then left on the bike, hearing Still screaming in pain and made contact with McCosker from near the quarry, telling him, 'I think Wade's in a bad way, I've got go back there.'

Both Stone and McCosker returned, after purchasing more petrol, to see Still lying on the ground. It was at this point Stone decided to, either call an ambulance, or, as he would later tell police in a record of interview, 'We've got to finish this prick off.'

Finish him off, he certainly did, as Stone spread petrol either over or around Still and, on seeing him being consumed by flames, they both left the scene, no doubt in a hurry. They discarded the fuel container, but it would later be found by police on the side of a road.

A short time later, a taxi driver saw what he first thought was a grass fire, but then realised a person was involved, so he called for an ambulance. This call would later be played to the jury in the trial of McCosker and they would hear Still screaming and wailing in obvious pain in the background and saying, 'I'm dying I'm dying.'

Ambulance and fire brigade attended the scene and, prior to being medevac'd by chopper to hospital, Still said to one fire officer, 'Stone poured petrol over me.'

This dying declaration was crucial and would be used in court against Stone, if needed, noting such evidence is not hearsay if it was made in the belief of impending or certain death.[34] Still, sadly, did not survive on the way to hospital and an autopsy would later determine that he had died from deep burns to over 90 per cent of his body.

Stone was interviewed by police the next day after the fire, being 21 August 2018, where he said that all he did was drive Still to the quarry in order to meet another person and then left. At his own request, many months later, on 26 June 2019 he voluntarily attended at a local police station and confessed with a truthful version of what happened. He, of course, agreed to turn Crown witness against Mc Cosker, who had already been identified and charged by police in August 2018, on the basis

---

34 see for example *R v Golightly* 17 WAR 401.

he would receive some sentencing discount for his disclosures and for agreeing to give evidence for the prosecution.

Stone pleaded guilty to murder before the Supreme Court of NSW being sentenced on 6 October 2020 to 23 years and four months and would not be eligible to apply for parole until he had served 17 years and six months. The penalty for murder, like other states and territories, is life imprisonment and in NSW the standard non-parole period is 20 years. Given that he would give evidence against McCosker in a later trial and, also taking into his early plea of guilty, at first glance his sentence for murder might seem rather harsh compared to today's sentencing regime, where criminals seem to escape time and time again from any sort of proper punitive punishment.

His Honour, Justice Hulme, notwithstanding he was unable to come to any determination of motive, had no hesitation in putting into perspective the final act by Stone setting fire to Still, noting he was set alight on two occasions. He noted that it was deliberate and certainly with one aim and that was to ensure Still died. Stone also had a significant criminal history, including periods of imprisonment, but His Honour accepted that Stone was, belatedly, quite remorseful.

However, in terms of realising this is not a harsh sentence, the following comment by the judge really puts it in a proper perspective, saying:

Death in the way it came to Mr Still must have involved an extreme level of terror and excruciating pain. He was first engulfed in flames at about midnight. The offender (Stone) returned to finish him about an hour later. Mr Still remained alive for a further two hours before succumbing to his terrible

> *injures. He died because of an objectively sadistic and callous act in one of the worst ways imaginable.*[35]

Stone, noting again that is not his real name, will be eligible to apply for parole on 20 February 2036 when he will only be 53 years old. In the interim, he has time to think about his actions on that fateful night and what really was his motive, if indeed there was one. Stone will also recognise that he was only afforded a 10 per cent sentence reduction for his assistance in turning Crown witness against Mc Cosker and 25 per cent for his guilty plea.

Mc Cosker pleaded "not guilty" to the charge of murder before a jury in October 2020, but no such luck, being found guilty. He appeared before Justice Hulme for sentencing on 16 December 2020, following the jury's guilty verdict. His defence counsel made much of the fact that he was not the one that poured and ignited the petrol and that he had no motive to kill Still.

His Honour was having none of that, saying:

> *It was the offender (McCosker) who had the motive to cause harm to Mr Still, not Mr Stone. Mr Stone presented the offender with a way to vent his animosity towards Mr Still. The offender seized the opportunity and used Mr Stone as the means of achieving a result that met his satisfaction...*[36]

His Honour had no hesitation in determining that both McCosker and Stone had every intention to murder Still and that the offender now before him, despite not being involved

---

35 *R v Stone* [2020] NSWSC 1485-para 41).

36 *R v McCosker* [2020] NSW SC 1822-para 34.

in carrying out the earlier burning, was more than aware of the initial injuries inflicted from the lighting of the petrol by Stone. McCosker then became a party in having more petrol spilt near or over Still in order to, *'finish him off...'*[37]

McCosker, now aged 51, also had an extensive criminal record dating back nearly 20 years, including house breaking and seeing the inside of a prison cell. He also had a penchant for carrying illegal weapons and only weeks before the murder, he was placed on a good behaviour bond for carrying a prohibited weapon.

McCosker showed absolutely no remorse and was found to have little, if any, prospects for rehabilitation. He will certainly be an old man when, and if, he is ultimately released from prison around 2045. He will have served 27 years before being eligible for parole, noting all up, his effective total prison sentence was 36 years, dated from his time in custody, following his arrest on 22 August 2018. In effect, on paper, he received the same sentence as Stone for their joint criminal enterprise, minus, of course, Stone's entitlement to the total sentencing discount.

Japan and other industrialised countries, such as parts of the US, are the only two G7 nations that impose a sentence of capital punishment. In Japan, this is particularly the case when in such situations the murder involves more than one victim. In that respect, they do not treat murderers lightly and, in the absence of mental impairment, meaning the offender cannot be held criminally responsible, a sentence to death can be handed down. Japan certainly doesn't muck around as, for example, in 2018, they executed by hanging a total of 13 members of the doomsday cult known as "Aum Shinrikyo" founded by Shako

---

[37] Ibid-para 40.

Asahara, which was responsible for the March 1995 murder rampage carried out on Tokyo's subway.

This domestic terrorist attack, using a sarin nerve gas, killed 13 people, with more than 1,000 seriously injured. Such gas was also identified as the primary cause of Gulf War syndrome, affecting numerous soldiers who served in the 1991 Gulf War, when the nerve gas was released into the air after stockpiles of Iraqi chemical weapons were bombed.

Human rights groups have been very critical of Japan's death sentence policy, even alleging that many of those sentenced to death did not know of their impending execution until the early morning on the day it was to be carried out. I suspect some victims' families could argue the same thing though, as their loved ones, on many occasions, would not have been aware of their impending death. By December 2023, there were a total of 107 people waiting in a special death row prison for their execution.

On 25 January 2024, they could add one more to the death row list with Shinji Aoba, sentenced to death. Aoba was responsible for the 18 July 2019 arson attack carried out on the animation studio building in Kyoto, Japan, which resulted in the death of 36 people and injuring scores of other victims, including the perpetrator. Aoba, allegedly over some grudge that his work had been plagiarised by the studio, entered the building with petrol carried on a trolley, then poured the accelerant around and over some of his victims before igniting it.

The fire set off an explosion with many killed trying to escape and Aoba also seriously injured, arrested by police running away from the inferno. He would spend 10 months in hospital, recovering from burns to 90 per cent of his body, but his victims were not so lucky, with many burnt beyond recognition and only DNA testing leading to their identity, others dying from carbon monoxide poisoning.

Aoba's lawyers tried to convince the court their client was mentally unfit to the point of being insane and therefore was not guilty, but the trial judge ruled that the offender could differentiate between right and wrong at the time of the murder arson. Prosecutors, in calling for the death penalty, submitted that Aoba was indeed mentally competent, with the sentencing judge even saying that the attacks were predetermined, to the degree that Aoba had looked up previous cases of arson as part of his planning. Aoba, in front of a packed courtroom with many of the victims' loved ones crying, said, 'I didn't think so many people would die and now I think I went too far.'

Well, he certainly did go too far and now he sits on death row awaiting his fate.

It's hard to imagine what the victims' families must go through with the loss of a loved one, but how could they have possibly coped following the loss of five much-loved family members? This is what happened in a fatal fire in August 2020 that rocked the local Green Valley Ranch community in Denver, Colorado, US. The three offenders, carrying accelerant, were first observed on CCTV footage wearing hoodies and masks in the backyard of the home, where members of three Senegalese immigrant families lived.

They set the house on fire, killing a mother and her six-month-old baby and the mother's young brother and his wife, together with their 22-month-old toddler. Other members escaped by jumping from an upstairs window. Police and fire responders would find the five victims burnt to death, with one officer later breaking down, describing how he kicked in the door of the burning home to first find a small's child's badly burnt body near the doorway, then a deceased mother with her arms wrapped around her six- month-old baby.

The police investigation would take some five months of studious and dedicated detection methods, including reviewing surveillance footage from nearby petrol stations, followed by around 23 search warrants, all to no avail. At one point, they had exhausted all leads without identifying any suspects. They then carried out a Geo-Fence warrant, namely a Google keyword search, often described as a "digital dragnet", that literally searches billions of transmission data from cell phones, tablets, desktop computers and even devices, such as pacemakers, hearing aids and smartwatches.

Such an investigative tool is issued by a court by way of a search warrant, to allow law enforcement bodies to search database services such as Google Chrome and Google Maps to locate all active mobile devices and transmissions within a particular designated area. This then also allows information to be obtained and assessed under warrant from such databases, which collects historical geolocation data from personal users. Of course, the Fourth Amendment to the US Constitution protects individuals from unreasonable searches and warrants requiring them to be exact as to what and for whom they apply. On that basis, many lawyers and academics believe the use of a Geo-Fence-type warrant also often referred to as a "reverse Google keyboard warrant", is illegal under the Fourth Amendment.

This perceived warrant illegality would later become a point of contention, when investigators believed the suspects first observed on the CCTV footage would have no doubt planned what they wanted to carry out and would have searched for directions to the house in order to set it on fire. They hit the jackpot after they asked Google to release the name of the person, or persons, who had searched for the address within 15 days leading up to the fire. The search revealed five google accounts, with three young suspects then identified from additional warrants for their cell phone and social medial usage. This was followed by charges of first-degree murder, attempted murder, arson and burglary.

Kevin Bui was the one identified from the Google data address search. He told investigators he had been robbed a month before the fire when trying to purchase a gun and that his phone, money and shoes were stolen. Bui then used an app to track his stolen phone, but the problem was it led him, together with Gavin Seymour and Dillon Siebert, to the wrong house as it was not the home of who they believed were responsible for the theft.

Bui would then say he and Seymour only found out their mistake the next day, hearing about the fire and its named victims by a news report, which Bui admitted to was as a result of their planned handiwork. All the victims were a case of mistaken identity. Rather than come forward to police about their involvement, Bui and Seymour then went camping without any concern of what had transpired on that fateful night.

During a 2023 petition for a review and show cause hearing, lawyers for Seymour raised the issue of the Google warrant being illegal under the Fourth Amendment and attempted to have it thrown out. Regardless, the Supreme Court of Colorado rejected any suggestion that the warrant lacked unconstitutional grounds, such as probable cause and particularity, concluding that law enforcement obtained and executed the warrant in good faith. On that basis, the court ruled that such evidence should not be suppressed under the exclusory rule.[38]

The first to face court for sentencing was 17-year-old Siebert, being 14 years old at the time of committing the crime, who pleaded guilty to second degree murder. He was sentenced in December 2023 to three years in a juvenile court and a further seven years under their Youthful Offender System, meaning he will serve 10 years before being released. The court accepted his young age at the time of the offending and, to a degree, his lesser involvement in the planning and execution of the crime.

Seymour, who was 16 years of age at the time, also pleaded guilty to second degree murder and was given the possible maximum sentence of 40 years imprisonment by the Denver District Court, together with five years of mandatory parole on release. Of course, his lawyers argued that he should be given another chance, his young age, immaturity and good rehabilitation prospects.

It was also pointed out he had no prior criminal history, but the final word is left to one law enforcement detective, saying:

We see death every day…usually learn to live with it…This case I am going to take with me forever…This is by far the worst and most senseless murder I have ever investigated…I can't think of anyone that is more deserving of a maximum sentence. Five people died, two babies. Their families are completely broken.

As for Bui, he faced over 60 charges, including first degree murder and attempted murder with extreme indifference,

---

38 see further *People v Seymour* Oct 16, 2023, CO 53(Colo 2023).

burglary and assault with a deadly weapon, for which he has pleaded not guilty. The charge relating to extreme indifference is different, in the US, from other forms of murder as it is a category of homicide that involves knowingly causing the death of another person, in this case five deaths, under circumstances that show a complete disregard for human life. It carries a life sentence or the death penalty.

In a plea deal, Bui agreed to plead guilty to two counts of second-degree arson in exchange for the remaining 60 counts being dismissed. He was sentenced to 30 years consecutively on each count, meaning a total of 60 years behind bars in the Colorado Department of Corrections State Prison.

A sentence for murder arson, carried out in the early hours of 20 November 2020 in Nottingham, England, on the face of it seemed to have some parity, given the loss of life. But then again, how can you say that life imprisonment with a minimum of 44 years imprisonment is in any way a just and proper sentence, for the taking of the life of a young mother and her two daughters, aged three and one, all dying from smoke inhalation? Thirty-three-year-old Jamie Edwin Barrow, after consuming copious amounts of alcohol, took petrol from his motor bike and, by using a cigarette lighter to ignite a tissue, while wearing blue medical gloves, poured it through the front door letterbox of the family who lived next door to him.

He then gleefully sat back and watched the fireball spreading to the upstairs living area, before taking his pet dog for a walk. He even had the audacity, on returning from the walk, to gather with neighbours outside what remained of the home, then later telephoned the local council wanting compensation for the loss of some of his belongings due to smoke from the fire.

Police made door-to-door enquiries and soon arrested

Barrow. He was charged with three counts of murder, but the other terrible fact associated with his despicable crime, was there appeared to be no motive for why he set the fire. At the jury trial, for which he first agreed to plead to manslaughter, which was rejected, prosecutors initially considered he may well have had some grievance against the victim, despite him denying he knew the mother was home with her children, when he set the fire.

This so-called motive may have stemmed from his annoyance they were leaving bags of rubbish outside his home in an alleyway. A mental examination, as part of the sentencing process, unsurprisingly found he had a personality disorder, was in a state of mental distress and that he could not explain why he lit the fire, other than he found it "cathartic", meaning it gave him some sort of psychological relief. Despite his defence counsel saying Barrow, who had previous convictions and was sorry for what had happened, Justice Tipples on sentencing said:

I do not accept you have shown any genuine remorse for what you have done…you knew they were all home, asleep and you knew they had no chance whatsoever…Seconds after you lit the fire you heard the fire alarm go off. You did nothing. Seconds after that you heard…screaming…you did nothing…It is only you who knows why you did this…[39]

One arsonist who will not ever be released from prison is Hakeem Kigundi, being sentenced to a whole life order for murdering two people after setting fire to a block of flats. In the

---

[39] *Regina v Jamie Edwin Barrow*-In the Crown Court at Nottingham, Friday, 7 July 2023-sentencing remarks.

UK justice system, a whole life order is exactly that, meaning the perpetrator will spend the rest of their life in prison as there is no minimum term and certainly no chance of parole. It is the most severe punishment that can be imposed and usually reserved for the more serious of crimes, such as terrorism and, like in the case of Kigundi, multiple murders.

In the early hours of the morning of 15 December 2021, apparently annoyed with his neighbours who complained about his anti-social type of behaviour and then being served with an eviction notice, he set fire to their block of flats by pouring petrol over the ground floor and then watched it go up in flames as he sat in his car laughing. His petrol attack was premeditated and, no doubt, he had set out to cause as much mayhem and death as possible. It was lucky that only two residents lost their life, with two others suffering severe injuries after they jumped from the burning building.

Prior to his revenge attack, he purchased petrol and fuel containers from a local garage and recorded in his diary:

All the actions I am about to take are warranted, believe me. Only cure for a cunt who's persistent is death and I am going to give them that.

Kigundi had no choice but to plead guilty to two counts of murder, two counts of causing grievous bodily harm and one count of arson with intent to endanger life. He now joins more than 70 other prisoners in UK jails who are also serving whole life sentences.

Another murderer, who certainly won't see the light of day other than from his jail cell, is 80-year-old pensioner, David Clarke. In September 2023 in Swansea, Wales, he bashed his elderly wife with a hammer a number of times, then set her on fire, after dousing her in petrol, while she sat in their car, with witnesses describing seeing a "ball of flames". A council worker told police he heard her screaming and tried to save both of them, but Clarke pushed him away and then drove off in the burning car before crashing into a hedge. Mrs Clarke would survive for a further two days in hospital before succumbing to her injuries but was able to say, 'My husband did this,' noting he only suffered minor burns.

Clarke and his now deceased wife had four children and had been married for some 50 years, but according to their son, had always argued with Clarke being somewhat violent towards their mother, but he thought they had now both mellowed. This murder arson was pre-planned with Clarke first sending a text message to his children professing his love and then driving his unsuspecting wife, on the pretext of going to a local beach, to carry out his dastardly deed.

It was later revealed in court that the apparent motive appeared to be over Clarke confessing he had an affair some years earlier and had arranged a trip to Australia to see the woman again. Understandably, Mrs Clarke was not happy and they had begun to argue, but this was certainly no excuse in any way for Clarke to murder her. Clarke was sentenced to life behind bars with a non-parole minimum of 21 years and eight months, meaning he will be at least 101 years of age, if he survives that long, before even contemplating applying for release.

However, was the minimum sentence handed down acceptable following the murder of 27-year-old Kelly Wilkinson in Queensland, Australia in April 2021? Given that the perpetrator will unfortunately get to see the light of day when he is released from prison. Her estranged husband, Brian Earl Johnston, somehow escaped a prison sentence of life imprisonment with a lengthy non-parole period, despite killing his wife by first stabbing her a number of times, then to ensure she died a horrible death, doused her in petrol and set her on fire.

To make this even more graphic, he wore a black mask and carried a duffle bag and some accelerant. He performed this despicable act in front of their three young children with them screaming out, *'Daddy put Mummy in the fire.'*

It seems his premeditated motivation was for two possible reasons in his deluded mind: one being to prevent her from testifying against him in respect of allegations of physical, emotional and sexual abuse, including rape. Johnston was then released on bail by police, leaving Kelly with no choice but to take out a temporary protection order a month before she died and police, within two days of her murder, admitting they failed to protect her. His other reason may well have been that he wanted her dead, as he no longer had any control over her and she simply wanted him out of her life.

Johnston faced the Honourable Justice Applegarth for sentencing in the Supreme Court of Queensland on 13 March 2024, in respect of a charge of murder and a breach of the temporary protection order, for which he pleaded guilty. As aptly put by His Honour on whatever Johnston's deluded beliefs were, there was no doubt he acted with sheer intent to end the life of Kelly and that:

Kelly Wilkinson was not yours to control. You ignored her dignity and her autonomy. You violated her security in breach of a court order for her protection. You brutally killed her in a sustained attack with knives and burnt her to death. You did this with your children able to witness this extreme violence. They will carry that trauma and that knowledge into their adult lives. They are three of your many victims.[40]

Johnston, at first glance, didn't seem to have lot in his favour in mitigation against his sentence. But he did plead guilty, despite such plea coming at a late stage of the proceedings after being committed to stand trial, was a former US marine, having served in Iraq and was now diagnosed with ADHD and depression. He did suffer self-inflicted severe burns himself at the time of the offending, which he extinguished by jumping into the house pool holding the knife he had used, but he got to live a lot longer than Kelly did. Johnston asked for his expression of remorse to be read out in court, but understandably, his victim's family and friends didn't want to hear any such supposed regret coming from him.

In respect of the parole eligibility date, the issue for the judge was whether 20 years as a minimum, before being eligible for parole, in view of all the circumstances, was appropriate, regardless of the fact he would be sentenced to a maximum of life imprisonment. Given all the factors surrounding the commission of this horrific crime and taking into account what is also known as the Bugmy principles, if it had not been for the Crown pointing out two matters in mitigation against sentence, His Honour would have imprisoned Johnston to more than a 20-year minimum in recognition of the '...*enormity and brutality of your crime.*'[41]

Johnston escaped a longer parole period as the Court took

---

40   *R v Brian Earl Johnston* [2024] QSC 36–para 20.

41   Ibid-para 41.

into account his plea of guilty and, at the committal stage, his instructions that he did not want his children cross-examined. The 20-year minimum was not opposed by the Crown, meaning if he is eligible for parole and with time served of three years on remand, he will be released in April 2041 at 55 years of age.

It should be noted, release is not automatic, as the parole board will take into account whether he deserves the privilege of parole, his genuine remorse, whether he has been rehabilitated and, of course, if such release is in the interests of the community at large. In the interim, Johnston still faces a charge of rape and maintains his innocence.

It was certainly a sad day for the family of Kelly and her many friends, with her sister understandably shattered saying:

Pure evil decision to destroy my sister's body…You have robbed me of a normal life with my baby sister, my confidant and my best friend…You have caused me and everyone around me a lifetime of immeasurable pain and suffering.

Police also alleged Johnston was assisted by a good mate that they said drove him to the home of Kelly and, along the way, stopping to fill up the can of petrol. His co-accused was also charged with murder and the issue for the jury was whether this person knew of, or reasonably suspected, what Johnston was about to carry out. He, of course, vehemently denied any knowledge and his plea of not guilty included giving evidence before the jury, ably assisted by testimony from Johnston, saying, at the time, he was just a "scared kid", despite being 26 years old, and all he did was to drive Johnston past the house and then returned and dropped him off.

Despite the jury hearing he had "admitted" in a record of

interview that he was aware Johnston planned to first tie Kelly up and then set her on fire, which he denied, the jury would deliberate for six hours on 13 September 2024, acquitting him of both murder and manslaughter. The good mate of Johnston was then released from custody, after being held on remand, awaiting trial for over three years.

The only solace the Kelly family hopefully might get is from the outcome of the internal review undertaken by Queensland Police Ethical Standards. This was part of a coronial inquiry, given their systematic failures once again, as in the murder of Hannah Clarke, and now in the death of Kelly. One of the key elements looked at, was why Johnston was released on bail only a matter of days before Kelly was murdered and after she had made numerous complaints to police over concerns for her safety.

One police officer was subsequently disciplined and ordered to undertake professional development, while two further operational directions were issued to all police reminding them of the requirements relating to bail decisions in instances of domestic violence. One can only hope that we will not see another terrible outcome regarding a domestic violence victim, but sadly that is unlikely.

Despite a maximum sentence of life imprisonment, following a conviction for murder by arson, unfortunately, in Australia, as we have seen, there have been some individuals who have not been subject to the full force of the law, given the low minimum parole periods. There has also been a number of other offenders only convicted for manslaughter, which, for example in Victoria under its *Crimes Act* 1958(Vic) (Crimes Act), now carries a maximum sentence of 25 years, with arson causing death also subject to a maximum of 25 years imprisonment. Prior to 10 June 2020, the punishment for manslaughter in Victoria was 20 years, but was amended to increase the penalty to 25 years.[42]

There is a subtle difference between murder, which is the wilful and intentional killing of another person, including acting with reckless indifference, as against manslaughter, with the latter defined as, 'the crime of killing a person when the killer did not intend to do it or cannot be held responsible for their actions.'[43]

In other words, was there any intent to set the fire to cause harm or death to the victim? If not, depending on the circumstances, it is manslaughter. For example, was it manslaughter by an unlawful and dangerous act, was it criminally negligent, with the conduct of the perpetrator showing a high disregard for life and safety?

There is a charge for arson causing death in Victoria, which is defined as a person who intentionally and deliberately carries out an act of arson, as defined under section 197 of the Crimes Act to a property or building, which results in another person losing their life.[44]

It goes without saying, the two limbs that must be proved by the Crown beyond reasonable doubt is that the accused deliberately destroyed or damaged a property by fire and secondly, that the fire resulted in death.

The question of an appropriate penalty and whether the offender should have been convicted of murder by arson and not manslaughter, let alone arson causing death, does however

---

42   *Crimes Amendment (Manslaughter and Related Offences Act 2020* (Vic).

43   Cambridge Dictionary.

44   see section 197A of the Crimes Act.

raise its ugly head and poses an interesting dilemma for our legal system for the basic fundamentals of sentencing. These guiding principles must ensure the sentence consequences of the offending are indeed proportionate to the crime committed and, at the same time, provide and maintain a degree of fairness, consistency and justice being seen to be done.

In many instances, the sentencing court will take into account the Bugmy and Verdins principles. In respect of Bugmy, the High Court of Australia acknowledged that the effects of profound childhood deprivation would, in turn, make the offender's moral culpability less than what it would have been if raised in a normal upbringing. Such deprivation may stem from being brought up in an environment of which alcohol and violence played a major part.

This exposure may then explain, to a degree, the offender's responses, when, for example, becoming frustrated and unable to control their natural impulses and therefore, these must be taken into account in the application of sentencing principles. This was despite a dissenting opinion from one of the justices in that it should be looked at on a case-by-case basis.[45]

As to the Verdins principle, the Victorian Court of Appeal found that an offender's impaired mental functioning may well be a relevant factor to be taken into consideration for a lesser sentence. For example, any impairment of their mental functioning can demonstrate a very real connection with the offence committed and a more severe sentence may have a further impact on such mental illness. In that event, the

---

45   see *Bugmy v The Queen* [2013] HCA 37.

sentence imposed should be moderated in respect of the need for a general and specific deterrence.[46]

It will become very apparent in respect of a number of arson cases involving a death, how frequently, particularly based on the Bugmy and Verdins principles, an offender's reduced moral culpability, supported by expert psychiatric assessment, will be a mitigating factor in any sentence handed down.

It then poses the statement that 'justice must not only be done, but must also be seen to be done,': a famous century-old legal precedent laid down by the Lord Chief Justice of England.

---

[46] see further *R v Verdins & Ors* [2007] VSCA 102; (2007) 16 VR 269)- also see *DPP v O'Neill* [2015] VSCA 325 as to the scope and limitation of such principles.

6
MANSLAUGHTER OR ARSON CAUSING DEATH

Involuntary manslaughter is when a death results from an act that was unlawful and dangerous. Or was the accused criminally negligent and in total disregard for the safety of the victim? If it was deemed to be criminally negligent, as opposed to an unlawful and dangerous act, there is a legal argument that moral culpability is less and, as such, should be taken into account on sentencing in mitigation. Voluntary manslaughter is defined as a criminal act carried out as a result of reacting to being provoked, in cases where it can be shown the accused had an abnormality of mind, or carried out in an act of self-defence, albeit excessive.

Regardless of whether it was deemed voluntary or involuntary manslaughter, the penalty, for example, in most states and territories in Australia, is a maximum of up to 25 years imprisonment. Noting that a verdict of manslaughter by an unlawful and dangerous act will normally see a heavier sentence, as against manslaughter by criminal negligence which is at the lower end of the sentencing scale but, of course, is dependent on the facts of each case. In Victoria, voluntary manslaughter was deemed the most serious but no longer exists following the abolition of provocation as a partial defence to murder. Prior to 2005, provocation could be used to reduce a conviction of murder to one of manslaughter.

In November 2000, a jury sitting in the Supreme Court of NSW was left to determine whether the accused, Shane Eugene Olig, was guilty of murder or manslaughter. In respect to the charge of murder, for which Olig pleaded not guilty, the question for the jury was, did Olig intentionally set out to kill the victim, on the basis that he knew of that probability with reckless indifference and that the deliberately lit fire would cause death or serious injury? Alternatively, was it manslaughter by criminal negligence being carried out, without intention to kill or cause serious bodily harm and was only an unlawful and dangerous act, which then resulted in death?

The Crown's case was that on Saturday, 24 July 1999, Olig, who was now no longer in a relationship with the victim, Annette, was angry with her over a number of matters, including her relationship with another man. Olig went to her house with a can of petrol and set it on fire, leaving very quickly after making attempts to save the victim. She would later be found in the kitchen of her home and an autopsy determined that she died from smoke inhalation. Olig, on leaving the burning home, was heard calling out, 'Annette you bitch,' then telephoning another, now Crown witness, and said words sounding very upset to the effect that:

> *I have done it this time…I put fuel down the hallway and lit it…tell me she is okay? If she isn't, I'll kill myself.*

On the basis of that last comment, you may well think that perhaps he didn't mean to cause any serious harm. However, that became an issue for the jury when another witness stated that some months earlier, Olig had said he was considering murdering her by burning the house down and would then plead diminished responsibility to avoid life in prison. In effect, he seemed to think by pleading this as a potential defence, he would not be held completely liable for what had happened as he was mentally impaired at the time.

Olig would make a number of statements to police admitting he had lit the fire, even saying, 'I put the fuel down the hallway and lit it,' followed by, to another investigating police officer:

> *She wasn't supposed to die…I went in there with petrol and I was playing with it and said…Annette, I will burn this whole house down…I lit up a cigarette and it caught on fire all down and it just went…She bolted…before I could get to the front door the smoke had just gone straight up with the house and everything.*

Olig then gave a different version to a psychiatrist saying he splashed a can of petrol on the floor and, on being taunted by Annette, he then threw a cigarette on it in an attempt to frighten her. On being driven back by the fire, he still tried to save her. These versions all then changed at the trial with Olig then saying the deceased took the jerry can, splashed the accelerant on the floor and something went flying over it and then it caught on fire. The jury total rejected his latest version of events but acquitted him of murder, finding him guilty of manslaughter. In other words, he never intended to kill her or cause serious injury or think that she might die in the fire.

His Honour, on sentencing 36-year-old Olig on 21 December 2000 for manslaughter, taking into account there were no special circumstances applicable to depart from the statutory requirement for sentencing and the non-parole period, had some significant concerns for any genuine remorse. His dishonest evidence at trial, clearly showed any lack of such contrition. As for the sorrow and anguish displayed by Olig, on learning of her death, the judge, whilst accepting that to a point, also commented that it was done with a sense of self-justification. The question of domestic violence also came into the court's consideration, saying that such factors point to the importance of a general sentencing deterrence, particularly in situations when a victim had died, notwithstanding such death was not intended.

Olig had no significant criminal convictions; his upbringing was difficult as he was sexually abused by a relative and his IQ was somewhat limited. He did, however, maintain steady employment and the court was assisted by a character reference from his employer. The sentencing judge, in trying to remain objective and dispassionate and weighing up all the relevant factors, noting manslaughter carries a maximum term of 25 years imprisonment, sentenced Olig to a maximum of 12 years, with an eight-year non-parole period. This meant that Olig, taking into account time served in custody on remand, would have been eligible for release in 2007.[47]

---

[47] *Regina v Olig* [2000] NSWSC 1246-also see *R v Olig* [2002] NSWCCA 249, noting such appeal against conviction and sentence was dismissed.

Let's have a look then at the case of Duan Tich Huynh, who was presented before a jury on a charge of murder where he deliberately set his former wife on fire on 22 July 2000, resulting in her death from thermal burns. Following a trial that lasted nearly three weeks, he was found not guilty of murder, but guilty of manslaughter, as the jury were not satisfied that he had any intention to kill her or cause grievous bodily harm.

In sentencing Huynh on 21 November 2003, Justice Kirby was left to first to determine whether the actions of the defendant were either an unlawful and dangerous act or criminal negligence, a better analysis of his conduct, that gave rise to the verdict of involuntary manslaughter. Justice Kirby, following the jury verdict, would first consider a summary of the facts if, indeed, the actions of Huynh were criminally negligent, then sentence him accordingly.

The relationship between Huynh and his wife fell apart after he was told by her that their son who was born in June 1999 was not his, confirmed by DNA testing, resulting in their marriage being dissolved. It's fair to say that Huynh still loved his ex-wife and their son and he was able to convince her to return to Australia from Vietnam and live in a separate flat so he could visit the much-loved child, despite knowing he was not the father. On the afternoon of 22 July 2002 during a visit, he had an argument with his ex-wife when he splashed some methylated sprits around the kitchen of her Cabramatta home in Sydney's west, with some falling on her clothes. He then lit a cigarette lighter and bent down, with the fumes emanating from the spilt liquid igniting.

Both Huynh and his ex-wife suffered burns and, after he extinguished minor burns to his hands and arms, he tried to help his screaming ex-wife, whose upper body was on fire.

With the help of neighbours, they poured water over her, all to no avail as she died from the injuries.

When interviewed by police, Huynh could offer no explanation of why he lit the cigarette lighter, knowing there was flammable liquid all over the kitchen floor, other than he was angry. He verily denied he set out to harm his ex-wife. His defence counsel submitted that such irrational conduct happens too often when people are angry, but without any particular purpose in mind. In essence, it was further submitted that his conduct, at best, could be seen as a build-up of his continuing frustration over arguments with his now deceased ex-wife.

Justice Kirby, on balancing all the facts, came to the view that Huynh did not intend in any way to cause harm to the deceased and said:

It is plain that he loved her and wished to be reunited...as a family...I accept the flame spread very quickly. I accept that Mr Huynh did not foresee that they would spread to that part of the kitchen where (Mrs Huynh) was standing and envelope her.[48]

His Honour, on the one hand, said there seemed no plausible explanation as to why he acted in the way he did:

He ignited the lighter. He then maintained pressure on the spring-loaded mechanism as he bent down towards the floor, which he knew was covered with methylated spirits. What he may not have recognised is that fumes hover above the liquid and that the fumes ignite, not the liquid. I think it is likely he intended to scare the deceased and that, to his surprise and

---

48   *R v Huynh* [2003] NSWSC 1066-para 16.

> *horror, the fire exploded, enveloping him and thereafter rapidly spreading to the deceased.*[49]

On that basis, the culpability of Huynh meant he would be sentenced on a charge of involuntary manslaughter by criminal negligence, not by an unlawful and dangerous act. The court would also take into account his excellent prospects for rehabilitation, that it was unlikely he would reoffend and any mitigation in leniency to sentence was even supported by the victim's family. The welfare of their young son was of paramount importance and any lengthy sentence would impose hardship as, in effect, there was no other family member to take care of him in the long term.

This hardship, by way of mitigation was, therefore, deemed and accepted by the court to fall under special circumstances for the relevant minimum and maximum sentence, noting that whilst the act, as notably gross negligence, it was not premeditated. Huynh was sentenced to six years imprisonment with a non-parole period of three years and six months and with time served in custody on remand, he was eligible for release on parole on 21 January 2006.

Perhaps then, the burning to death of an elderly quadriplegic man by his estranged wife would result in a more significant penalty, yet, given all the circumstances, was the sentence still at the lower end of punishment? Grace Soon was initially charged with murder for which she pleaded not guilty, but guilty to manslaughter, which was accepted by the Crown. It was recognised that her culpability was substantially impaired leading up to and when, on 4 September 2006, she set fire to his residence in Daceyville, part of Sydney's south-east, killing her husband, Stephen Chin.

---

[49] Ibid-para 19.

Soon, at the time of the offending, was 70 years of age and for some 10 years had lived separately from her husband and they were in the throes of a property settlement dispute. He lived alone in a semi-detached cottage and became a paraplegic in 1999 when he broke his neck, apparently as result of a fall. Stephen required nearly full-time care with his carer's last task ensuring he was safely in bed that night, before leaving.

About 6am on the fateful morning, Soon went to his cottage and used an accelerant, first setting fire to the front fence and then throwing the remainder of the petrol in a can through the bedroom window. Stephen would later be found deceased in his bed, with a postmortem determining he had died from burns. The fire and soot inhalation in his body meant he was still alive at the time of the fire. In her first interview with police, it was apparent to a point that Soon had a few issues as, when asked by police for her date of birth, she said, 'Twenty something.'

It's fair to say that on further questioning, her responses were either vague or she would give approximates to dates.

However, as later acknowledged by the sentencing judge, the police records of interview did somewhat display her ability to verbally joust with police. In addition, Soon also, at various times, exercised her right to make no comment and depending on the question, declined to give any answer.

On being shown CCTV footage of her leaving a local Big W store carrying petrol cans, Soon suggested it was not her and even rejected a copy of the relevant receipt of the purchase, continuing to deny any involvement in the death. Soon certainly came across as being very competent, even to a degree of refusing to voluntary supply her fingerprints, not agreeing to DNA or a photograph and when asked whether she would participate in a line up, she refused which was her right.

Any suggestion of Soon being inept in anyway was, however, further demonstrated by her realisation that it was not in her best interests to continue with any sort of denial, given the incriminating evidence police had placed before her. Soon then, attempted to negotiate with detectives and asked what would happen if she confessed, being advised she would still be charged. Soon then wanted to cancel the first record of interview, which was refused and the following exchange took place:

> *Police: Were you involved in Stephen's murder?*
> *Soon: Yes.*
> *Police: What happened?*
> *Soon: (after pausing for a while) There are two tins of petrol, I take one tin and pour petrol on the wooden fence at the front. I forget what it's called and I light it with a match, and the other one I threw inside his bedroom window.*
> *Police: Why did you do that?*
> *Soon: He is coming after my property; I worked so hard to save my money and now he is coming after my property.*

After agreeing to a further interview, she then elaborated on how the fire was started, saying it was set by using a newspaper. After again being asked why she did it, Soon went into some detail about the dispute over the property settlement, Stephen wanting a divorce and that he never supported her, even giving her a venereal disease at one stage, allegedly after using all his money on sex workers. When asked by police about the lack of Stephen's mobility, Soon confirmed she knew he could only move around in a wheelchair.

The sentencing judge, on 20 June 2008 in the Supreme

Court of NSW came to the view, the sole motive of Soon to eliminate Stephen, was the possibility that she would have to share her assets with him as part of any divorce settlement and any other excuse was plainly misguided. Soon had a number of factors in her favour, including the guilty plea, her age, making it more onerous in prison, a low risk of reoffending with an unblemished record up until now, her apparent forgetfulness when examined by different medical practitioners, even to a point she claimed she knew nothing about killing Stephen and didn't know what the word "guilty" meant.

Soon, on the other hand, would further provide a number of inconsistencies when further examined, prevaricating from buying the petrol to kill weeds, then saying she had no idea why she was in prison. This led to one expert psychiatric report indicating that 'her mood was more depressed than angry at the time she committed the offence,' but coming to the conclusion Soon had a defence, albeit partial, of a significant impairment by an abnormality of mind.

On passing sentence and accepting that the impairment of Soon was indeed substantial, as supported by the psychiatric evidence, Justice Michael Grove said:

> *The objective seriousness of the killing, perpetrated by you, remains and your responsibility for it is not extinguished. On any view, killing by fire a person, who you knew had no capacity to self-mobilise from bed, was a monstrous act. To do so, motivated by an obsession with ownership of property, does little to diminish that quality.*[50]

However, the learned judge, faced with a reduced level of

---

50 *R v Soon* [2008] NSWSC 622-para 41.

impairment to Soon's capacity for judgment, noted she was also entitled to the benefit of a number of mitigating factors when passing sentence. To that aim, Soon was sentenced to nine years with a non-parole period of five years and six months. I will let you be the judge as to the severity, or lack of, in respect of the sentence, taking into account, of course, the suffering of Stephen, who had no possible means of escape from the fire that engulfed him.

It is hard to imagine how three so-called human beings could literally escape a life sentence without parole, after setting fire to a family home resulting in the death of six children. It then becomes more horrendous when those children, aged between 5 and 13, who all died from smoke inhalation, were from the same shared family, with their father, Mick Philpott, responsible for their deaths.

Around 4am on 11 May 2012, with all the children asleep, Philpott, along with his now wife, Mairead Duffy, and an individual by the name of Paul Mosley, decided to set fire to their home in Osmaston, a suburb of Derby in England. This was supposedly over a pending custody hearing dispute that Philpott had with a former lover and mother of some of his children.

It seems, Phillpott came to the view that if they set the fire, he could try and frame the mother and also be seen as some sort of hero dousing the flames and saving the children. He would definitely be awarded sole custody of all six of his kids.

The house certainly went up in flames with neighbours observing Philpott desperately trying to smash the windows, as he tried to rescue the screaming children trapped inside. Sadly, after fire crews doused the flames, they would find five of the children deceased with the older boy dying in hospital some days later. Police then interviewed both Philpott and Duffy, who said they were both asleep in the house when they first observed it was on fire. It was obvious the fire had spread very quickly and, as the upstairs doors leading to each bedroom had been left open, it was understandable the children would have been overcome by smoke.

Three days after the fire, on 14 May 2012, police determined that petrol had been used to start the blaze and initially arrested the ex-lover of Philpott and her brother-in-law as suspects, on suspicion of murder. In the interim, Philpott and Duffy held a news conference describing with great anguish the events surrounding the fire. However, their account was starting to raise some red flags with police, as was the criminal record of Philpott, which included a conviction for attempted murder of a former girlfriend whom he stabbed some 13 times.

The two initial suspects were released without charge and police bugged the hotel room where Philpott and Duffy were staying. The covert recordings would reveal they had indeed been involved in the fire with Mosley, the latter being a friend who was also involved in a sexual threesome with them. On 30 May 2012, Philpott and Duffy were charged with murder and, after the clothes of Mosley were also found to contain traces of petrol, he was also charged with the same offence.

Following a jury trial in April 2013, 56-year-old Philpott was unanimously found guilty on six counts of manslaughter and sentenced to life imprisonment, with a minimum term of 15 years. The trial judge agreed that Philpott had not intended to kill his children or indeed, that they should suffer any serious harm, but also said:

What you did intend, plainly, was to subject your children to a terrifying ordeal. They were to be woken from their beds in the middle of the night with their home on fire so you could rescue them and be the hero. Their terror was the price they were going to pay for your callous selfishness...mercifully their deaths were swift and, it would seem, without pain...

As to the plan Philpott put together on the eve of the custody battle, the judge said further:

It was a wicked and dangerous plan...and you put it into effect with the assistance of your two co-defendants. You poured petrol on the floor. Paul Mosley was responsible for removing the containers from your home. You set light to it....

However, on the character of Philpott, Her Honour certainly didn't mince words when she said:

You are a disturbingly dangerous man. Your guiding principle is, what Mick Philpott wants, he gets. You have no moral compass. I have no hesitation in concluding that these six offences are so serious and the danger you pose is so great that the only proper sentence is one of life imprisonment and that is the sentence I impose on you.

Despite the fact Philpott only received a minimum of 15 years before being eligible for parole, that does not mean he will be released when he is 71 years of age. Given his track record with previous convictions for domestic violence and the circumstances surrounding his latest incarceration, I suggest he may well have some trouble convincing any parole board he is now rehabilitated and no danger to the public.

His wife, Duffy, and their friend, Mosley, were both sentenced to 17 years and must serve at least half of their sentence before being eligible for release. Duffy was released on licence in 2020, which means in the UK effectively the same as parole, but they must adhere to a strict set of rules for the balance of their sentence. As for Mosley, he was also released on licence in May 2021, after serving half his sentence, but was soon back inside for breach of the conditions applying to his release.[51]

The question of intent, or lack of, again came to the aid of a Geelong, Victorian woman who set her husband alight after she doused him in petrol, before igniting a cigarette lighter near him. In what was described as a "cataclysmic fireball", he was burnt to death as he lay screaming in the front garden of their home. Angela Surtees had been in a relationship with her 36-year-old husband, Daniel Surtees, for some 10 years and they were married in 2017.

At first glance, they seemed a happy family with two young children, but underneath, their life together was described by some as volatile with Daniel bordering on alcoholism. In addition, he was charged with assaulting his wife just prior to their marriage, for which he was not convicted but had to complete a Men's Behavioural Change Program. Surtees wasn't without her own issues, later described by members of her family as on the same aggravated level as Daniel, with her mother even saying she gave as good as she got in their tit-for-tat relationship.

Their volatile relationship reached a pinnacle with a tragic outcome on the evening of 25 January 2020, following an on-going argument between the pair with the drunk Daniel

---

[51] Also see section 19AP-*Crimes Act 1914* (Cth).

increasingly taunting Surtees. While their children were watching television in another room, Surtees, now totally sick of Daniel and his continual aggressive behaviour, with the help of a container full of petrol poured it over him as he sat in an armchair. He then made an effort to lunge at her but she threatened him with a burning cigarette, so he sat back in his chair. He was then engulfed in flames as the cigarette was very close to him. Surtees immediately telephoned for an ambulance saying to the operator it was all an accident and that the petrol ignited when he lit a cigarette.

Daniel would succumb to his injuries and died the following morning from deep thermal burns to more than 80 per cent of his body. In the interim, Angela would tell all and sundry, varying accounts of what had transpired. In her first police record of interview on 26 January 2020, her version of events included splashing the petrol over him and, as Daniel came towards her, she flicked the lighter and he caught fire, it being an alleged accident.

Surtees was subsequently charged with murder, still maintaining it was all an accident, but declined, as was her right, to a police request to take part in a re-enactment. Following, no doubt, lengthy negotiations between her lawyers and the Crown, they were able to reach a plea agreement on the basis of manslaughter by an unlawful and dangerous act. This meant that intent was removed from the equation, but this intimidatory, unlawful assault, resulting in death, was not just a mere accident, even being described by the sentencing judge as a serious case of family violence in order to terrify Daniel. Notwithstanding, he died.

Surtees appeared before Justice Andrew Tinney in the Supreme Court of Victoria on 11 March 2022, for sentencing in respect of her plea of guilty to manslaughter. His Honour referred to, with some concern, the number of versions given by Angela, including the false account she provided to psychologist Professor James Ogloff, regarding the events surrounding the death of her husband. Despite these somewhat clashing accounts of what happened, it was noted that at no time did she mention in any aspect that she was terrified or even frighted of her husband before she committed the crime.

In essence, what she tried to do was make an attempt to portray herself as favourably as possible and deflect blame, suggesting Daniel splashed the petrol over himself and then lit the fire. The learned judge also rejected any suggestion of assault, or even an attempted assault, on her by Daniel. For all intents and purposes, she was simply "egged" on by him. This, in turn, led to her losing control, with His Honour saying:

> *You lost your temper and allowed yourself to do something extraordinary…You obtained a jerry can, deliberately poured a good deal of petrol over Daniel and then lit a cigarette lighter. You took a number of deliberate steps in a very dangerous and outrageous direction, without ever stopping in your tracks to ponder whether you should continue in pursuit of the shocking and life-threatening design you had…fixed on.*[52]

It was accepted, however, by the court in some mitigation against the offending, was her plea of guilty and that she had been in custody for just over two years. Such delay being brought before the court was thanks to the COVID-19 pandemic. Regarding the virus, the court made particular mention that personal visits were suspended from March 2020 and, in

---

52   *The Queen v Angela Surtees* [2022] VSC 124–para 82.

effect, Victorian prisoners were subject to stringent lockdown procedures, which meant they didn't spend the usual accepted amount of time outside their cells. In other words, her time in custody on remand was, to a degree, more burdensome and, given this, the court took that into account in of the sentence to be imposed.[53]

His Honour was somewhat hesitant to accept her remorse in the essence that:

You seemingly have been slow to fully accept that you and you alone are responsible for Daniel's death…[54]

Taking all relevant factors into account, including that Surtees will be without her young children for some time, having no prior convictions and, according to Professor Ogloff, had very good prospects for rehabilitation, a sentence was imposed of 12 years imprisonment with a non-parole period to be served of eight years.

Despite the judge correctly concluding the crime committed by Surtees was at the higher end range of manslaughter, an appeal was lodged on the basis that the sentence imposed was manifestly excessive. In the appeal, in February 2023, her lawyer relied on other cases of manslaughter, but not those of causing death by fire as they were extremely rare, submitting that sentences of 12 years or more all related to much more serious offending.

For example, one of six cases relied on was where a husband was convicted of manslaughter due to the death of his wife, whose body was located some eight months later. Despite

---

53   Ibid-para 122.
54   Ibid-para 101.

refusing to reveal why she was killed and maintaining ongoing lies and deception for nearly three years and even being a pallbearer at her funeral, he was only sentenced to nine years with a six-year minimum, after pleading guilty to the lesser charge of manslaughter. On appeal by the Crown, he was resentenced and even that was not really justice being seen to be done, with his overall sentence only increased by four years. [55]

In other words, the sentence imposed on Surtees in the first instance by Justice Tinney exceeded the applicable range open to him regarding the crime of manslaughter, noting at the time of the offence, the maximum sentence was 20 years imprisonment. However, on the basis of overruling the original sentence, the Court of Appeal imposed a term of 10 years and six months and reduced the non-parole period by one year to seven years, meaning Surtees will be eligible for release in 2027.[56]

I will let you be the judge again on the appropriateness of a sentence for another case of death by fire, leading to a charge and conviction for manslaughter.

Jennifer Louise Hay pleaded guilty where on 25 February 2019 she unlawfully killed Kyli Green, contrary to section 18(1)(b) of the NSW *Crimes Act* 1900 (count 1) and to a further charge of recklessly destroying a property under section 195(1)(b) (count 2). Despite count one having a maximum of 25 years imprisonment and count two of 10 years, Hay somehow was treated leniently, being sentenced on 13 December 2021 in the District Court of NSW to an aggregate sentence of 10 years and three months, with a non-parole period of six years and 10 months.

The circumstances leading to the death of the 36-year-

---

55   *DPP v Borce Ristevski* [2019] VSCA 287.

56   *Angela Surtees v The King* [2023] VSCA 42.

old victim were again, quite horrific, yet the court didn't seem to acknowledge the loss of life, worthy only of a short period in jail, subject to parole. It becomes more puzzling when the motive for the death was all over Hay being evicted from her accommodation, after she became somewhat difficult to live with for the two tenants. Indeed, she was first invited into the home after she told the sister of the victim she had nowhere to live, so they happily invited her to stay with them. Sadly, the victim had lived a difficult life, suffering from physical ailments, which included extreme obesity and asthma and she was subject to a torrent of abuse from Hay.

Following the eviction, in the early hours of the morning around 6am, Hay returned to the Wagga Wagga premises and, using a cigarette lighter, set fire to a two-seater couch located on the front porch. The victim, being limited in movement due to her disability, could not escape the inferno, despite the best efforts of her sister and local neighbours. She was later found lying face down inside the house in a dressing gown, with the fire causing her horrible death, contributed to by her physical incapacity. Two days after the fire, police interviewed Hay, followed by a further interview, where they seized a number of items, which included her footwear and clothing.

Ticking all the boxes while gathering sufficient evidence to charge Hay, police took out a mobile telephone intercept warrant, together with other electronic surveillance. They were also able to locate CCTV footage, showing their now firm "person of interest", walking towards the unit around 6am on the morning of the fire. Hay was arrested and charged on 21 May 2020 after invoking her right to silence, making a "no comment" record of interview.

Hay, on pleading guilty to counts one and two, before District

Court Justice Lerve and, despite her conduct being criminally unlawful and dangerous, the learned judge accepted the intention, albeit based on revenge, being one of a number of factors that determined the overall seriousness, was to only set fire to the couch and not the house. The Crown, however, pointed out to His Honour, which he accepted to a point, that indeed the couch was set on fire, but it was in very close proximity to the house and Hay well knew that one of the now deceased occupants suffered from a physical disability and a lack of mobility.

The Crown also submitted that Hay well knew the occupants would have been asleep, given the early hour of the morning the fire was set, but conceded and, in the Judge's view such concession was appropriate, that overall, the offence was not based on any pre-planned criminal endeavour.

In determining the appropriate sentence by taking all the relevant factors into account, including in the Surtees case, the usual COVID-19 sentencing considerations, His Honour determined the offending fell slightly above the mid-range of seriousness, with the Crown conceding that the principles set out in Bugmy came into play. This was mitigated from such factors, submitted before the court, from expert reports that Hay was herself suffering from a number of health issues, including having a complex borderline personality and PTSD after her partner was killed in a car crash some years earlier.

Indeed, in making some general remarks and to provide an overall understanding of sentencing principles[57], His Honour effectively concluded with what must be taken into account by saying:

> *The purposes of punishment, namely: (a) to ensure that the offender is adequately punished for the offence, (b) to prevent*

---

57   *Crimes (Sentencing Procedure) Act 1999* (NSW).

crime by deterring the offender and other persons from committing similar offences, (c) to protect the community from the offender, (d) to promote the rehabilitation of the offender, (e) to make the offender accountable for his or her actions, (f) to denounce the conduct of the offender and (g) to recognise the harm done to the victim of the crime and the community. [58]

In an analysis of the above two cases of manslaughter and given all the circumstances leading to and surrounding the horrible deaths of two innocent victims, it remains, in my view, somewhat perplexing, notwithstanding any acceptance of the Bugmy and Verdins principles applying to sentencing. Even when taking into account in further mitigation of the sentence, the effect on prisoners because of the COVID-19 pandemic, that Surtees and Hay received sentences with a bare minimum before parole of around seven years, which can, in no way, be seen as them being adequately punished for their crime.

You may well disagree with my considered opinion, but let's look at other cases which involves sentencing not for murder, not for manslaughter, but for the crime of arson causing death, which was legislated in Victoria in 1997.[59]

The essential elements of such a crime include the offence of arson, as set out under the Crimes Act, which is committed intentionally to damage or cause destruction to property by fire and the act of the accused must have resulted in a death. It is not necessary for the prosecution to prove beyond reasonable doubt that the accused intended, in other words, acted with predetermined malice, to cause such a death. All that is required to be proved is the accused was of a fit mental state to carry out

---

58   *R v Hay* [2021] NSWDC 669–para 90.

59   *Crimes Act 1958* (Vic)-section 197A.

the offence of arson and that such act resulted in death, which carries a maximum penalty of 25 years imprisonment.

Two bodies were found in a Ballarat property in country Victoria, following a fire at their rental property that occurred on 17 October 2002. It was determined by police that the fire was an act of revenge carried out by Luthanuel Alex Joshua Chambers, when he entered the property of his former housemate in the early hours of the morning. After placing photographs on the lounge room floor, he poured about a half a cup of kerosene over them and started a fire using a cigarette lighter.

The act of revenge carried about by Chambers, who was intoxicated at the time, was apparently over first not paying due rent when he was boarding at the house, followed by him forcibly entering the property some two weeks before the fateful fire, causing some minor damage. It seems then that one of the victims who died in the fire, had previously set fire to some of Chambers' belongings, including his suitcase, in retaliation.

Chambers would later tell an acquaintance that he set fire to the house because his stuff had been burnt. On being interviewed by police, Chambers maintained he did not know that anyone was present in the house, claiming he had knocked on the front door and, when no one answered, entered the house through a back door. He also claimed he looked into one of the bedrooms and saw no one sleeping but did see a doona "clumped up". Then, for some reason, he turned off the power to the house. He would then leave the residence with the photos burning and in his police record of interview when asked what extent of damage did he hope to achieve, Chambers said:

The carpet burnt and stuff like that and the photos burnt, smoke to make it smell…

Chambers did more damage than that though, with the two deceased later being found covered in soot. The cause of death was later determined as smoke inhalation, dying from carbon monoxide poisoning. Chambers, on pleading guilty to two counts of arson causing death, was then sentenced by Justice Coldrey in the Supreme Court of Victoria on 19 December 2003, noting that this was the first time a person had been before the court on a charge of arson causing death since it was legislated in 1997.

His Honour took into account that whilst there was a need for a specific general deterrence for this sort of crime, he accepted that Chambers had experienced significant traumas in his life and, at the time of the offending, his borderline personality disorder may, in some way, explain his conduct and to a degree, the motivation behind his criminal act. The question of personal and general deterrence and his borderline personality disorder would later become a successful point of contention in an appeal against the sentence.

Following Chambers being sentenced, on two counts of arson causing death, to 12 years, with a minimum of eight years imprisonment before being eligible for parole,[60] he was granted leave to appeal under section 582 of the Crimes Act on four grounds, in that the sentence was manifestly excessive and including:

(3) The judge erred in failing to moderate the weight to be given to general deterrence on account of the appellant's (Chambers) borderline personality disorder. [61]

The Court of Appeal rejected two of the grounds for

---

[60] *R v Chambers* [2003] VSC 506.

[61] *R v Chambers* [2005] VSCA 34-para 3.

appeal, but did accept that the initial sentence imposed was manifestly excessive and, as submitted by Counsel for Chambers and supported by expert psychological evidence that:

> ...*this disorder meant the appellant was not an appropriate vehicle for the full weight of general deterrence in the sense that he was not able to make calm and rational choices about his conduct in the situation and would be regarded by the general community as a person whose offending arose substantially from his disability.* [62]

As a consequence of their Honours finding that the judge, in the first instance, made an error and with no disrespect to him, they said, 'No account was taken of the appellant's borderline personality disorder in the consideration of general deterrence.'[63]

On that basis, Chambers was resentenced to an effective term of 10 years imprisonment, with a non-parole period of six years and six months.

Despite the loss on this occasion, of two innocent lives and, while I accept that Chambers was obviously not a well man, a sentence for arson causing death does carry a maximum sentence of 25 years imprisonment. Yet, we see once again, a jail term just shy of a minimum of seven years being imposed. It, therefore, must beg the question, how can this be seen by the community as fulfilling the purposes of punishment?

The reckless conduct of John Robert Bennett, not once, but on three separate occasions, was indeed fortunate, certainly not for his victim who died in one of his deliberately lit fires,

---

62   Ibid-para 25.

63   Ibid-para 32.

that more innocent victims didn't suffer the same fate. Bennett obviously had an attraction to lighting fires, as well as the occasional odd drink of alcohol or three to help him on his way, with his first effort, setting fire to his aunt's house on 24 November 2001, where he was living at the time.

The family were asleep, which he well knew, but Bennett still placed inflammable material near a heater which then ignited, with him asleep in his car in an adjacent garage. Fortunately, one of the children woke up to the flames and smoke and everyone was safely evacuated with the fire extinguished by the local CFA. Bennett, of course, told police he had no knowledge of the fire as he was soundly asleep in his car.

A victim in his next fire would not be so lucky as, in the early hours of the morning on Friday, 1 March 2002, when he was residing at a hotel in the Victorian county town of Sale, he entered a bedroom of another guest. As his victim slept, a drunk Bennett lit a candle on the sofa next to his bed and, once again, flammable material burst into flames after he left the room. He then had the audacity, first to put on an act over his distress of what had happened, followed by a willingness to help firefighters extinguish the blaze.

The victim would die from extensive burns to his body, combined with high and lethal blood concentration levels of carbon monoxide and hydrogen cyanide poisoning emanating from the fire. Once again, Bennett would tell investigators he knew nothing about the blaze and no doubt using the, "I was asleep at the time", excuse.

He was at it again, this time seven months down the track, setting fire to a mattress and bedding with a cigarette lighter in an unoccupied bedroom after he was told to leave a party, no doubt, due to his drunken behaviour. Fortunately, the occupants were warned of the fire, thanks to a smoke detector alarm. On seeing smoke, they were able to escape.

Bennett again denied any involvement and, by this stage, police were at their wits end trying to establish who was responsible for the suspicious fires, given the crime scenes didn't reveal any evidence and the fact no accelerant had been used. Investigators obviously came to the view that as Bennett just happened to be at each of the three fires, they needed to have a very close look at him.

So close that they put in place, in late October 2002, a covert police operation with an undercover officer becoming very friendly with Bennett and no doubt joining him for the usual Friday night drinks. They became such good mates that Bennett even made admissions about what he had been up to, resulting in his arrest on 12 December 2002. He obviously lawyered up, as was his right, and made a no-comment record of interview.

It didn't matter though, as police had enough evidence charging Bennett with one count of murder, arson causing death and two counts of reckless conduct endangering life. The latter under section 22 of the Crimes Act, which alone carries a maximum penalty of 10 years imprisonment.

Bennett, after being committed to stand trial in the Supreme Court of Victoria and no doubt following negotiations with the DPP agreeing to withdraw the charge of murder, pleaded guilty to arson causing death and the two counts under section 22. On sentencing on 4 June 2004, over the three separate fires, one of which resulted in death, His Honour accepted that 23-year-old Bennett, who only had minor prior convictions but certainly a problem with alcohol, did not have any intention to kill and was simply reckless, but he knew exactly what he was doing.

Indeed, in that regard, the court heard he told the undercover operative that, 'It was like I was oblivious to the fact that something might happen.'

Well, something did happen and an innocent life was lost and Bennett was lucky, as were the victims, that more lives were not lost, not only in the hotel fire, but the other two separate fires.

This of course was recognised by His Honour when he said in respect of the principles of sentencing:

> *General deterrence is relevant as these offences are most serious and there is a terrible potential in fire. Whatever your underlying problem is, Mr Bennett, or problems, specific deterrence is especially relevant in your case. There were three separate fires committed over 11 months, the last after you had previously caused the death of another human being. Reformation(sic) also is centrally relevant…as there are three counts, I bear in mind, of course, the principle of totality.* [64]

In criminal law, the principle of totality requires that when a court imposes multiple imprisonment sentences, the total sentence should not exceed the maximum sentence in respect of the most serious offence. In this instance, the maximum sentence was 25 years imprisonment for arson causing death. So, on the basis of such principle, Bennett was sentenced to 10 years on count one for arson causing death and the two remaining counts of reckless conduct endangering life, a total of 10 years. However, by taking into account sentences to be served concurrently and cumulative, this meant, all up, Bennett received a maximum of 12 years, with an eight year non–parole period. [65]

---

[64] *DPP v Bennett* [2004] VSC 207-para 44.

[65] Ibid-paras 45-51.

This was the second sentence imposed, relevant to section 197A under the Crimes Act charge for arson causing death. As we saw in Chambers, the non-parole period was just under seven years and now with Bennett, all he gets is a minimum of eight years. Even taking into account the principle of totality, in Bennett's case, we have an offender who sets three fires, which could have resulted in more than one death. He had no motive, other than he was drunk and no psychological reports were tendered in evidence as part of the mitigation against sentence process under the Bugmy and Verdins principles. Yet he got off with a minimal sentence and I am sure his victim's family and friends were left with no comfort as Bennett was led out of the court in handcuffs.

To make matters worse, he only did the bare eight years, which included taking into account the 541 days he had spent in custody on remand and, after being paroled, he headed back to his hometown in Tasmania. Didn't take long though before he was sentenced to 16 months for numerous offences of dishonesty, including burglary, but luckily no fires causing death. He must have some sort of endearing demeanour, despite now suffering from substance abuse and not just alcohol, as he was paroled after eight months. They did have some reservations in agreeing to letting him out when the parole board said:

> *Despite concerns held by Community Corrections regarding the applicant's high risk of offending, due to lack of therapeutic intervention while in custody, the Board is of the view that appropriate therapeutic support and intervention can be accessed by the applicant in the community through the structure and conditions proved by a parole order.*[66]

[66] *In the matter of an application for parole by John Robert Bennett*–Department of Justice–Parole Board 15 January 2021.

One of the parole conditions was that he had to be assessed for a mental health plan and also undergo psychological counselling. All we can hope, though, is he does get the help he needs as we don't want another repeat of his serious offending resulting in the loss of life. However, Bennett is back in jail, being sentenced in July 2023 by the Launceston Magistrates Court to 20 months, again for dishonesty offences, this time involving a crime spree at Bunnings.

Was the sentence then for David John Campbell, who set a fire in September 2013 that killed his estranged wife, her new partner and their pet dog, also seen as justice being served? His initial relationship with his former wife was interrupted on a regular basis by them both having drug and alcohol issues, leading to instances of family violence. Indeed, over a 15-year period, from 1995, there were a total of 13 family violence orders with Campbell being the respondent on 11 separate occasions, convicted for breaches and contravention of such orders.

In August 2013, his wife finally left him for another man going to live in his Victoria Deer Park unit and, for all intents and purposes, it was all over as far as the marriage was concerned. However, Campbell believed there was no one home after being told by a female acquaintance his estranged wife had left the unit and her new relationship for good, following a domestic incident. With her now ex-partner seen asleep at the Footscray Mall, Campbell went to the unit at around 12.40 am on Friday, 20 September 2013.

Using a cigarette lighter, he set fire to a curtain through a broken window and then left the burning premises and telephoned the same female acquaintance on two separate occasions telling her, 'I torched the place,' or words to that effect. On receiving the calls, she knew exactly what he was talking about and would later make a statement to police about what Campbell had told her. The MFB on receiving earlier notifications of the fire had attended to find the unit completely gutted, with two victims and their pet dead in the master bedroom.

For some unexplained reason, Campbell wasn't interviewed by police for more than a year until 9 October 2014, where he faced some very lengthy questioning in a record of interview. He first denied any involvement and stated he had been working on the night of the fire. When confronted with the telephone calls he made just after the fire, including the statement police had now obtained of his alleged involvement, which also confirmed he genuinely was under the belief no one was home at the time, he readily confessed.

He told police his motive behind destroying what he thought was an empty unit, was that his estranged wife would somehow now come back and live with him. In any event, he wanted to pay back the unit owner who he thought had allegedly assaulted her.

On 1 April 2015, Campbell pleaded guilty in the Supreme Court of Victoria before His Honour, Lex Lasry, to two counts of arson causing death. His Honour first commented that Campbell lit the fire after some four to five hours had passed, after being told no one was home at the unit, but he failed to check in any event if it was indeed unoccupied. However, for sentencing purposes, the court accepted his offending was carried out with a genuine belief that it was empty and his only intent was to destroy the property.

Campbell had an extensive criminal history dating back to 1987, including making a threat to kill his then wife. His Honour, however, took into account the early guilty plea and that Campbell was remorseful, notwithstanding there was certainly a degree of thought behind his actions in setting the fire.

One point of contention that did arise was the submissions by his counsel that Campbell had cooperated with police, urging His Honour to also take this into account. However, Justice Lasry, quite rightly, said that in the first instance there was a significant delay from the fire and the police interview, meaning Campbell made no attempt, in the first instance, to go to police and tell them what had happened.

In addition, when first confronted with the allegations, he denied any involvement and it wasn't until around 900 questions and answers later, in the record of interview, that he finally confessed. A psychological report was tendered to the court and, apart from Campbell still having an ongoing drug issue and now needing ongoing support for the state of depression he was suffering from due to his reckless conduct, there was no evidence his mental state had any connection to his carrying out of the offences.

The court, once again, made the point that the offence of arson causing death carried a maximum penalty of 25 years imprisonment, which at the time was five years more than for manslaughter and the need for a general and specific deterrence was very relevant in this case, noting the Bugmy and Verdins principles were not relied on in mitigation as to sentence.

On that basis, Campbell was sentenced as a serious arson offender with a total effective prison sentence of 13 years, with a non–parole period set at 10 years. The usual 6AAA of the *Sentencing Act 1991*(Vic) was declared, noting the guilty plea saved Campbell from a total effective sentence of 16 years, with a minimum of 13 years.

Arguably, in the matter of Campbell, justice was served, to a point. But was this the case for an arsonist who killed a three-week-old baby and her doting parents? On the night of Tuesday, 2 December 2020, a gentlemen engaged the services of a sex worker by the name of Jenny Hayes. He arranged to meet her at a friend's Point Cook townhouse under some agreement with the owners to use a downstairs bedroom from time to time. After Hayes provided the sexual services, things turned ugly when she refused his second request for sex.

An argument then developed, over money for her services being taken from her purse, with Hayes becoming very annoyed, to say the least. The not-so-satisfied client left the townhouse with Hayes taking a photo on her mobile phone of his number plate, followed by a text alleging he had raped her. Hayes then followed up with another text message around 2.50 a.m. saying:

And I'm setting your house on fire right now.

She certainly did set it on fire by using a cigarette lighter to ignite a mattress in two to three separate places. Hayes then left the townhouse and took a photo of it on fire and sent a further text message to him saying, 'Your house is on fire,' accompanied by the photos of the now burning premises. Firefighters would later find the bodies of the parents and their three-week-old baby, who all died from carbon monoxide poisoning. The total building damage was estimated in the order of $1.2 million, with the fire spreading to two adjacent townhouses.

Hayes realised she had done something, in her words, "pretty stupid", telling another client what had happened. Later, she said in a text message, 'A client took all my money, so I burnt his house down,' also further confirming she had set the mattress on fire by using a jetty lighter. Hayes was arrested by police on the morning of the fire, Wednesday, 3 December 2020 and was initially charged with three counts of murder, with the alternative charge of arson causing death.

On the way to the station, police covertly recorded a lengthy conversation they had with Hayes of her anguish when told that three people had died in the fire. Her hysterical crying and the disbelief at the loss of life was also apparent during her formal record of interview.

Following a committal mention and the not-so persuasive and unimpressive evidence of Hayes' client at a preliminary hearing, in which he alleged she knew there were people sleeping upstairs when he told her to keep her voice down, the Crown withdrew the murder charges. They, in turn, accepted Hayes' plea of guilty to three counts of arson causing death, rejecting any suggestion she was aware of the presence of others in the townhouse. This was despite this no longer credible witness, not being subject to any cross examination of Hayes allegedly having knowledge that the town house was occupied.

Hayes' version, on the other hand, was that she had told police and also her friends that she was asked to be quiet, but only because there were nosey neighbours. She then lied in her record of interview telling police her male client was inside the bedroom when she lit the fire and that he had, in fact, thrown cardboard on the bed. The Crown, however, accepted they would be able to prove beyond reasonable doubt that Hayes had the requisite knowledge she did indeed know there were other people in residence at the time.

On sentencing, on 11 November 2022 in the Supreme Court of Victoria, Her Honour Justice Hollingworth said:

> *At the time of setting fire to the mattress, you may not have thought about the possibility, or likelihood, of the fire spreading and destroying the rest of the house. By the time you left the scene, there were substantial flames visible from out on the street and it should have been apparent that the fire might get out of control.*[67]

The problem, of course, was and, as rightly pointed out by the court, Hayes lit the fire in the early hours during a week, that she well knew other people would be residing and most likely asleep in neighbouring houses. When she drove away, seeing the fire take hold, she made no effort to contact emergency services. All Hayes did was take photos and send text messages. She must have known the fire could get out of control, yet she didn't care. It was only after the event and, on learning of the death of three family members, that she became:

> *...genuinely and immediately remorseful upon learning that people had been killed as a result of (her) actions.*[68]

Submissions by her counsel, supported by expert evidence, painted a very bleak picture of 48-year-old Hayes, in that she had a very difficult childhood, was physically and sexually abused in her younger years and began sex work at the young age of 16. She also had a young son suffering from a number of disabilities and that she had been using drugs since her teenage years and was prone to self-harm and suicidal ideation. Counsel was able to successfully argue that the Bugmy and Verdins

---

67   *DPP v Hayes* [2022] VSC 679-para 37.

68   Ibid- para 33.

principles must be taken into account, to further reduce her moral culpability and the sentence to be imposed by the court.

Victim impact statements were very confronting, in particular for the family of the young parents who died at the ages of only 28 and 19. The young baby's grandfather died some four months after he lost, not only his grandchild, but his dearly loved son. As put in a family victim impact statement, he had been slowly dying ever since the deaths of his loved ones in the tragic fire. An immediate neighbour also told the court of their harrowing experience being woken up with their five-month-old baby, fleeing the home to escape the fire and losing most of their treasured belongings, which were also destroyed.

On balance and taking into account the early guilty plea of Hayes, acceptance of the Bugmy and Verdins principles, COVID-related hardship while on remand and that Hayes will most likely continue to serve her time in protective custody, given the death of a young baby, one would hope for a tangible sentence. I think its first fair to state the anguish of the victims' family as they left the Supreme Court in disbelief following sentencing.

Statements such as:

We feel absolutely devastated. We feel no justice has been done. I know nothing will bring them back, but I just can't believe the sentence we've got now. We don't get closure on this. We get three life sentences.

Hayes will get some closure though as she will be eligible for parole by 2028. In other words, out in six years, taking into account time served on remand of 709 days. Hayes was sentenced as a serious offender but only to a maximum of 13 years but becomes eligible for parole after only eight years. Just as well Hayes pleaded guilty as she would have been jailed for a total of 17 years with a minimum of 12, but even that can't be seen as justice being served. What makes it even more appalling is that the young baby who died, thanks to the handiwork of Hayes, would have been starting grade two when Hayes might be released.

The deliberate setting of fires has the potential to not only cause significant damage, but the loss of life of victims, whether it be as a weapon to cause the death intentionally, or as we have seen, in situations where a charge of manslaughter or arson causing death will follow. Arson has also been used in situations to destroy a crime scene and any incriminating evidence, hoping to increase the likelihood of the initial crime, namely murder, to remain unsolved.

7
ARSON TO CONCEAL MURDER

In the early hours of 13 July 2003, after stabbing his wife of 31 years in the left side of her chest and penetrating her lung, Richard James Watson, obviously not satisfied she was dead, then strangled her. Perhaps, in order to cover up his crime of murder, Watson then splashed kerosene and other accelerants throughout their home and over his deceased wife, a motor vehicle and a mobile touring bus and then set them on fire.

To further hide his brazen and deadly crime, resulting in the death of his wife, Watson feigned unconsciousness in the backyard of the burning home, even to the degree that a firefighter performed cardiopulmonary resuscitation (CPR), which resulted in Watson then pretending to have fits and seizures. On being taken to the Bendigo hospital in Victoria, he carried on with his charade, telling police he had been bashed and rendered senseless by unknown intruders.

Watson had a number of problems, though, trying to hide his blatant murder. For a start, the subsequent autopsy determined his wife was already dead before any fire. In addition, Watson was known to be in significant financial difficulty, being unemployed for some two years prior to the fire and had obtained a replacement valuation on the now destroyed house some 12 months earlier. All up, he received nearly $188,000 from the insurer after the fire for the loss of the house and contents and two vehicles.

Watson would then change his story about the so-called intruders, blaming his two brothers-in-law and a police officer, while continuing to maintain his innocence. Two witnesses would then come forward and say his wife had told them some four weeks before her death, that she did not want to accompany Watson on a trip he was planning in their mobile bus and wanted to move back to NSW. Watson would then be formally interviewed by police and spent two days in custody, before he was released, in order to make further enquiries.

It was not until 29 January 2008 that police charged Watson with the murder of his wife and three counts of arson regarding the house, the motor vehicle and the touring bus. Watson maintained his innocence but was committed for trial in July 2008 and was found guilty by a jury on all counts in April 2009. He appeared before Justice Whelan for sentencing on 24 June 2009 facing a maximum penalty of life imprisonment for murder and for the crime of arson, a maximum 15-year prison sentence. In any sentencing procedure, a judge must be satisfied, beyond reasonable doubt, of any matters adverse to the accused and those factors that go in favour of the accused, are then accepted on the balance of probabilities.

Regarding what happened in the lead up to the fateful

crime, the judge was satisfied beyond reasonable doubt that Watson set out with the clear intention to burn his house down, together with the vehicles, in order to make an insurance claim, even to a degree where he removed some items, most likely of sentimental value, before setting the fire.

Regarding his intention to kill his wife, Justice Whelan was somewhat nonplussed about Watson's motivation saying:

At some point you formed the intention to kill you wife, Anne. I cannot determine when that was or why you formed that intent. Perhaps she interfered in your plan to burn down the house. Perhaps she was intending to leave you and return to Sydney. Only you know why you chose to kill your wife of 31 years. I make no finding as to your motivation save that, because of the arsons and the murder occurred at about the same time, I am satisfied that there was some connection between them. [69]

Watson, from the commission of the crime, right to the end of the trial and during sentencing, continued to maintain his innocence and at no stage demonstrated any remorse whatsoever, aggravated by his charade and ongoing false story and accusations. His Honour did take into account, in favour of Watson, no prior convictions and the nine glowing character references tendered on his behalf, which were mitigated against, when considering a total of seven victim impact statements, parts of which were referred to during sentencing.[70]

In balancing the age and poor health of Watson, given he was now 62 years old, suffering from type 2 diabetes and neuralgia, it was accepted by the court that imprisonment

---

69   *R v Watson* [2009] VSC 261–para 16.

70   Ibid-paras 32-39.

would be somewhat of a greater burden. It was further suggested by counsel for Watson, given his age, the sentence should be moderated to at least give him a chance, albeit small, of returning to a meaningful life on release. It goes without saying, of course, that he certainly didn't give his wife the same consideration.

Justice Whelan made a salient point though:

Age, whether young or old, is always a factor relevant to the exercising of the sentencing discretion…but those of advancing years who commit serious crimes cannot expect to escape appropriate punishment by reason of that factor alone.[71]

Taking all relevant matters into account, noting the court did accept that in view of the advancing age of Watson, the sentencing factor for specific deterrence and prospects for rehabilitation were a lesser issue. Watson was sentenced as a serious arson offender and ordered to serve a total effective sentence of 22 years imprisonment, with a non-parole period of 17 years and seven months. It should be noted, for the murder of his wife, his prison sentence was 20 years, which meant the cumulative maximum sentence for the three counts of arson was only two years. Watson will be nearly 80 years old when he is eligible to apply for release.

The question remains though, was this a case of an arson murder cover up? Did Watson set the fire trying to cover up the murder of his wife? Did she simply get in the way, so he murdered her in any event and then went on his planned venture to burn down the house to claim insurance money? I will let you be the judge in that respect.

---

71   Ibid-para 44.

An attempt to cover up a murder by arson was certainly very evident regarding a house fire in Albury, NSW in September 2004. What made it even more pathetic was the murderer, James Harry Barton, tried to claim he was acting in self-defence and had been subjected to threats from his victim. This was despite the fact that he couldn't explain how the fire started, which killed his alleged aggressor and his 4-year-old daughter, with another child fortunately surviving the blaze with burns to his face and hands.

The victim was not without his fault though, having a significant criminal record and known to traffic in drugs as well as having a reputation for somewhat violent behaviour. He had, in fact, been blackmailing Barton for a number of years and, it is fair to say, he was somewhat scared of the standover tactics.

On the evening of 3 September 2004, their relationship came to a sudden and violent end over an argument to do with the purchase of a vehicle to be paid for by Barton. It was obvious he didn't accept what was being proposed, so Barton shot the victim in the head. To make matters worse, Barton returned to the deceased's house the following day, in order to conceal the murder. He gave the victim's two children some methadone to make them drowsy and then set fire to the house. His intention was to, not only destroy any evidence of the murder, but also for the children to perish and hopefully, in his mind, the house fire would then be deemed an accident and sadly the whole family had perished.

It didn't quite work out that way though, with an autopsy determining that the male victim had indeed been shot, with Barton admitting to police he was present but acted in self-defence. Of course, he told police he had absolutely no idea how the fire started and it was indeed thanks to him that he assisted one of the children from escaping the blaze, forgetting, of course, that he caused the death of two victims.

Barton was charged with two counts of murder and attempted murder and, after a lengthy jury trial, which included the jurors seeking clarification from His Honour on the issue of provocation, he was convicted of manslaughter in respect of the child's father, the murder of the child that died and attempted murder of the surviving child. Barton admitted he shot the father in the back of the head, using a bullet fired from an unregistered rifle, but maintained he had clearly acted in self-defence, not that he could argue that regarding the young child that also perished. This issue, in any event, as to provocation was left to the jury to determine and in the circumstances, they were not convinced of the charge of murder, finding it was manslaughter.

At sentencing, before Justice Buddin on 29 June 2007, His Honour determined that in the circumstances, the act of manslaughter could not be considered as excessive self-defence, but the requisite standard of provocation had been met, given that Barton had been blackmailed over many years by the deceased. On that basis, Barton, on the count of manslaughter was sentenced to a fixed term of five years imprisonment. For the murder of the child, the judge declined to impose a life sentence, but ordered he serve 37 years with a non-parole period of 30 years and for the attempted murder, a fixed term of 13 years.

This meant that Barton was sentenced to a total effective maximum sentence of 42 years, with an overall non-parole period of 35 years. At last, it goes without saying, that a proper and just sentence was handed down, given the horrific circumstances, particularly in respect of the poor four-year-old child that lost her life. Barton will not be eligible for parole until 12 September 2039, if he survives that long, noting that his time in prison will most likely be served in protective custody. He will be 82 years of age if released on parole or 89 if he serves the total term of imprisonment.[72]

A minimum sentence of 20 years before being eligible for parole, regarding the murder of a 41-year-old mother of six children and then setting her body on fire in a failed cover up attempt, however, did provide some comfort to the victim's grieving family. This was despite Con Vlahos repeatedly stabbing the woman, followed by stomping on her head in his flat in Preston, Victoria on 8 October 2011.

To make matters worse, after holding a knife to the throat of her 11-year-old son, the young child witnessed the death of his mother. Vlahos then set fire to her body to conceal the murder and left on foot with the body still burning. He later stole a motor vehicle nearby in an attempt to get away from the crime scene.

A post-mortem would later reveal that the badly burnt mother died as a result of five stab wounds, causing substantial blood loss and was deceased before her body was set alight. This blatant murder and attempt to conceal the crime was witnessed by the victim's partner, who had tried to intervene, even having boiling water thrown over him and the victim before she was stabbed. He would later give incriminating evidence in the trial of Vlahos, who had pleaded not guilty to murder, arson and a threat to kill, but guilty to the theft and attempted theft of a motor vehicle.

Vlahos, who was now 41 years of age, appeared before

---

[72] *R v Barton* [2007] NSWSC 651)-also see *Barton v Regina* [2009] NSWCCA 164, noting his appeal against sentence was dismissed.

Justice Lex Lasry in the Supreme Court of Victoria for sentencing as a serious violent offender on 12 April 2013, after being found guilty by a jury on all counts, despite his not guilty charade and his trial evidence that lacked any credibility. His Honour could not find any rational explanation of the motive for this despicable crime, other than a mistaken accusation by Vlahos that his victim had stolen his drugs. Such belief was totally out of proportion to what took place and, of course, to make matters worse, the murder was carried out in front of the victim's child.

Vlahos showed no remorse whatsoever and his lengthy criminal history, which began around 1987, included breaches of a suspended sentence and intervention order taken out by his own family. I would have thought that overall, he would have copped a heavier penalty, than just a bare minimum of 20 years, with a total effective maximum sentence of 26 years. Alas, it was not to be, as His Honour, although reflecting that the offending was indeed serious, said it appeared to be spontaneous and most likely as a result of the cocaine consumed by the parties just prior to the murder.[73]

It was later reported in the media, as Vlahos was led out the court in handcuffs to be taken back to prison, the victim's family members left with a smile on their faces and happy with the term imposed as, in their view, justice has been served and 'we can finally move on'.

It can't get any more horrific though, in the case of a headless burning dismembered torso found dumped by the side of a road near Gympie, Queensland in September 2013. The body was not only missing a head, but also hands and legs and it would take forensic police some 10 months to identify

---

73   *The Queen v Vlahos* [2013] VSC 171.

the burnt remains of George Gerbic. Naturally, they focussed on his family members, leading them to his de facto partner, Lindy Yvonne Williams, discovering that she had been telling family and friends during this period that Gerbic was absent overseas. She was found to be using his phone and personal email address.

Williams would initially tell police in a record of interview that Gerbic hit his head on a kitchen benchtop in their Sunshine Coast home, after slipping on blood, due to a laceration from her arm. Williams then said she had acted in self-defence when Gerbic allegedly attacked her with the steak knife during an argument, so she also hit him over the head with a bar stool.

Her story then becomes even more murkier, with Williams stating in a police video recorded re-enactment at the house in July 2014, that she locked herself in a bedroom and next morning found him lying dead on the kitchen floor. After leaving the house, Williams then said she returned some days later to find his body missing its head, legs and hands which were wrapped in plastic in the bathroom. Williams denied that it was her that had cut him up and said:

I just picked up the stool, trying to get him off me. I had a whole lot of blood here. He slips and then falls back. I don't know where he hit his head but I heard a bang.

Willams accompanied police into the garage and, although maintaining her self-defence motive, finally admitted to wrapping up and dumping the body some 80 kilometres from their home saying:

I tried to pick it up with just the plastic, but I couldn't…because it was heavy and that's when I got the tarp and rope and after I dragged it out.

William pleaded guilty to interfering with a corpse and dumping the torso, including setting the fire near a grassy road area, but not guilty to murder, which went before a jury in the Supreme Court of Queensland in July 2018. The Crown alleged that Williams dismembered the body of Gerbic with an electric saw she had purchased from Bunnings some 10 days after his death. It was further submitted that Williams was in no state of panic as she set about her so-called elaborate cover up, given the charade she had also carried on with to all and sundry that Gerbic was alive and well, travelling overseas.

The Crown prosecutor, in referring to Williams as, 'cold, manipulative and deceptive,' summed it up perfectly stating in a final jury submission that:

The inescapable conclusion from all of that, the thing that has finally caught up with Lindy Williams is that she killed her partner.

Defence counsel for Williams totally agreed with the Crown's submissions and, in fact, rubbished his client's earlier varying accounts to police and, at trial with her, even saying a friend had interfered with the body of Gerbic, but regardless, she acted in self-defence. Yes, his client did kill Gerbic; yes, she cut up his body the best she could with a saw; yes, she disposed of it on the side of the road and finally, yes, she did lie, but that didn't make her a murderer. According to her counsel, the death of Gerbic was a terrible accident and most likely caused by Williams defending herself. She was a domestic violence victim and not just on this one occasion. She panicked and then put together a string of lies to try and cover up what had happened.

In his words in a final submission, counsel said:

It is a huge leap of faith to say that she intended to kill him, or at least do grievous bodily harm... Why? Why would she? That's where it doesn't make sense in the Crown's version and Lindy's does make sense. That something happened at a flashpoint...

With respect to learned counsel, how does that explain why his client set fire to the remains? This was, no doubt, a misguided and fruitless attempt to try and cover up the fact he had been murdered. And what happened to the head, hands and legs? Perhaps, if Williams had admitted the cutting up of the body and setting it on fire was all in a state of panic and to bring some comfort to her victim's family, she would have revealed what had happened to the severed remains.

At least, Gerbic could have been buried with some dignity. But alas, even to this day, his severed remains have never been located, nor has his cause of death ever been determined.

Well, the jury certainly didn't accept such an implausible explanation, that Williams acted in self-defence and that the dismembering of the body and then setting it on fire was in a state of panic. They found Williams guilty of murder and she was sentenced by Justice Flanagan to life imprisonment with a minimum of 20 years. Williams will be eligible for parole in 2034 when she will be 76 years of age. In October 2023, she applied for early release which was refused by the parole board. Williams was faced with legislation in Queensland, like some other states, of a No Body, No Parole law, which also includes body remains.[74]

---

74   *Corrective Services Act* 2006(Qld)-section 193A.

It was reported in the media that Williams, now being referred to as the "Black Widow" supposedly made a chilling, but desperate jailhouse confession in which she detailed how she killed, dismembered and then dumped the torso of Gerbic, but failed to convince the parole board for her early release, most likely under an exceptional circumstances application.[75]

It remains to be seen if these so-called admissions will bring some closure to the family of Gerbic and whether she did, in fact, reveal the location of the remainder of his body parts.

The family of a prominent Melbourne interior decorator, who was also murdered by his partner, were totally broken with the meagre sentence handed down to Michael Anthony O'Neill (no relation, I might add), and understandably so, in that respect. The build-up before the death of 53-year-old Stuart Rattle on 4 December 2013, saw the couple both working very hard in their interior design business and the restoration of a property in Daylesford, Victoria. They had, for all intents and purposes, both been in a loving and business relationship for some 16 years.

However, it would later be revealed that Stuart, who had a dominant and controlling personality, would often complain to many of their friends about his life partner being lazy, even to a degree of calling him a parasite and that their sexual relationship left a lot to be desired. In essence, O'Neill was treated like he was the office boy and not the life partner and it was apparent in the lead up to the murder and arson, that tensions between the couple were simmering and would eventually erupt.

Well, the tensions did reach boiling point when O'Neill, in a fit of rage, hit Stuart over the head with a frying pan after

---

[75] Ibid-section 176.

being called a "frigid bitch", for refusing to again have sex with him, after being intimate the night before. O'Neill then picked up a dog lead and strangled him until he died. It was later revealed in court that as he was being strangled, Stuart said, 'Michael, don't do this.'

O'Neill then placed the lifeless but bleeding body in a furniture bag and laid him out on their bed.

A few days later, after noticing blood all over the bed, O'Neill then put Stuart in another furniture bag. O'Neill continued on with a charade for the time being, telling their friends and business acquaintances that Stuart was not well, even on some occasions by making calls and sending text messages pretending he was his dead partner. Such a guise even included O'Neill continuing to set a table for dinner for both of them, laying out two plates of food and talking to the body of Stuart as he consumed a glass of wine.

This pretence came to end on the night of Sunday, 8 December 2013, when he placed a burning candle next to curtains in their Malvern apartment bedroom that contained the body. He then left, under the pretext that he went to a local service station to buy some sweets. When he returned to their apartment, it was well alight with emergency services in attendance, who discovered the badly burnt body of Stuart covered in a plastic substance.

As there was no accelerant used in the fire and the burn patterns and charring pointed to candlesticks, it was initially deemed as accidental. O'Neill provided a sworn statement to police supporting the accidental cause, telling them he left to get some sweets while Stuart was asleep and the fire obviously started while he was absent. O'Neill then continued grieving over the death, being comforted by family and friends and even organising the funeral, knowing of course, it was him who had killed Stuart.

It was only a matter of time before his charade would be unravelled and that is what happened when an autopsy revealed there was no soot present in Stuart's lungs or airways. In addition, his body showed signs of decomposition, which indicated he had been dead for some time before the fire and that he also had skull fractures, obviously as result of being hit over the head with the frying pan.

Homicide detectives arrested O'Neill on Wednesday, 11 December 2013 and, after being told of the autopsy results and still initially trying to continue with the same false version of what had transpired, he finally admitted to killing Stuart. O'Neill would go on to say to police he lit the fire in an effort to make the death of Stuart more dignified, in that he died accidentally, a supposition that the sentencing judge would later accept as not an unreasonable possibility.

In the Supreme Court of Victoria on 11 February 2015, O'Neill appeared before Justice Hollingworth to plead guilty to murder and arson and where their complex relationship would unravel. Her Honour would also accept that O'Neill committed the murder in the heat of the moment. Expert evidence from a psychologist would reveal that O'Neill suffered from a dependant, narcissistic personality disorder and had self-harmed while on remand in custody.

Based on the Verdins principle, Her Honour accepted that the impaired mental functioning of O'Neill was a relevant factor to be taken into consideration for a lesser sentence, as it played some role in his offending. It then followed that it reduced his moral culpability and moderated it to a degree the need for a general and specific deterrence when sentenced.

Taking these factors into account and, in particular, the history of their relationship and the fragile psychological state of O'Neill, Justice Hollingworth was also not satisfied beyond reasonable doubt that she should treat the setting of the fire as an aggravating feature of the murder. Further, it was apparent that O'Neill was indeed genuinely remorseful and would continue to suffer from grief, that he had made a full confession to police, even to a degree that he disclosed certain evidential factors to them which went against him and were not known to the investigators at the time. His early plea of guilty meant he was entitled to a discount on sentence as there was now no need for what would have been a very traumatic trial.

Justice Hollingworth sentenced O'Neill to 17 years for the murder, two years on the charge of arson and ordered that one year on the arson count be served cumulatively making a total of 18 years, with a non-parole period of 13 years.[76]

Understandably, the family and friends of Stuart were totally shattered with the meagre sentence imposed as they lost a much loved and talented man. The other aggravating feature for them is that O'Neill will be eligible for release when he is around 60 years of age and will get to continue on with his life.

On Friday 11 April 2014, Colin Orman Thomas attended at Dandenong Police station following a fire in the early hours of the previous morning, in which a 49-year-old man, known as George, was found dead in his East Malvern home, being a suburb about 11 kilometres from the Melbourne CBD. According to Thomas, he did belt George within an inch of his life but didn't kill him. It was not him that set the fire, it was not an accident, it was, in fact, George who decided to end it

---

76 *DPP v O'Neill* [2015] VSC 25.

all by then taking his own life and what better way to do it, but setting himself on fire?

Part of the elaborate hoax, which is a bit different to the usual murder then arson cover up, went along the following lines in the police record of interview:

George regained consciousness and was helped to a chair by me. He was limp but responsive…George was looking pretty pissed off and acting aggressively…he was threatening me in both English and Greek…He then said, 'I am happy to pour petrol and take you and Heke with me right here and now.'… He picked up a jerry can and poured petrol from it…I picked up Heke and dragged him out…last thing I saw was George with a lighter…an explosion occurred as I was pushing the flyscreen screen and we were both blown out into the yard.

Thomas and his poker playing mate, Heke, who was present when this all allegedly happened, both suffered moderate burns. Now, Thomas had a couple of problems with this not-so-elaborate disguise in that he admitted to bashing George prior to the fire some 20-30 times but, lo and behold, the autopsy revealed George was indeed dead before the fire, so obviously he couldn't have started it. He had blunt injuries to his head, neck, face and torso and had, in fact, died from bleeding on the brain.

Thomas pleaded not guilty to both murder and arson and the jury had to determine (a) whether he intended to kill or cause serious injury to George and (b) the factual proposition that, in some way, his death resulted from the explosion and not the injuries inflicted on him by the accused, Thomas.

A jury had no hesitation in finding him guilty of both

charges, with 33-year-old Thomas appearing before Justice Jack Forrest for sentencing in the Supreme Court of Victoria on 29 January 2016. His Honour did indeed give Thomas some credit for his utilitarian approach to the criminal trial regarding his account that the death was not of his doing. This was taking into account his cooperation and admissions of the bashing of George, of course somewhat then clouded by his elaborate story of what had eventuated, which the Crown had no problem proving to the jury, it was just plain rubbish.

If Thomas had any remorse, Justice Forrest was of the view it was moderate and ambivalent at best and said:

> *There is the utilitarian benefit of you admitting your role in the assault to the police at the first available opportunity. It was open to you to take a variety of courses to complicate the investigation, but you made admissions and a number of those admissions were relied upon by the prosecutor to prove the case of murder. Of course, that needs to be balanced by the lies that you told the police about events after George was rendered unconscious.*[77]

To a degree, it was balanced against his self-serving fabrication that he was not responsible for the death of George, which emanated from a dispute Thomas had with him over some reluctance to reveal the name of a mutual acquaintance, who allegedly had a sexual dalliance with the former partner of Thomas. Luckily for Thomas, the Crown did not allege that the unprovoked vicious bashing he inflicted on George was not with the intent to kill him, but only to cause him serious injury but, of course, he died. Taking that into account, His Honour

---

[77] *DPP v Thomas* [2016] VSC 8-para 28.

accepted submissions from both sides that the offending, albeit murder, fell into the middle but lower end range of serious offending.

Thomas had a number of prior convictions including for assault, affray, attempted robbery and had served time in prison, so he was certainly no "clean skin", so rehabilitation was going to be an issue. Indeed, while on remand awaiting trial in this matter, he assaulted another prisoner, so he clearly had an anger management problem and a personality disorder, which was supported by a psychological report tendered to the court.

Thomas was sentenced to a total of 26 years and six months and it was further directed by His Honour that a minimum of 16 years and six months imprisonment must be served before being eligible for parole, noting he had already served 428 days of pre-sentence detention on remand. Despite being sentenced to, what I would describe as, a somewhat lenient lengthy period of imprisonment for murder and arson, His Honour still summed up succinctly the Thomas' offence when he said:

> *You murdered a helpless and innocent man. When George did not give you the answer you wanted, you "snapped" and erupted into a violent rage beating him repeatedly. Such lack of control cannot be tolerated…In time, and with treatment, you may learn to deal with stressful situations and conflict without resorting to aggression.* [78]

Despite murder carrying a maximum life sentence then coupled with a conviction for arson, as we have seen time and time again, Australian courts, shall we say, are somewhat lenient when it comes to imposing a maximum and minimum sentence.

---

78   Ibid-para 47.

Interesting though, while Switzerland also has a maximum life sentence, according to Article 64 of the *Swiss Criminal Code* 1942, the practical application for serious criminal offending, such as murder, also allows for conditional release following a specified period of incarceration. In other words, while a Swiss court does have the ability to impose a life sentence for murder, the term "life", also does not for one moment mean the convicted offender will spend the rest of their days locked up.

Case in point was the sentencing of Thomas Nick, who was dubbed the "Beast of Rupperswil", when in December 2015 he entered a Swiss family home, posing as a school psychologist and, after tying up three teenagers, he forced the 48-year-old mother to accompany him to a local bank to withdraw money. On returning to the house, he then raped one of her young sons, followed by slashing the throats of the mother, her two teenage boys and a girlfriend of the older son. He completed his ghastly crime by setting the house on fire, for firefighters to find the victims dead and murdered, prior to the arson cover up.

It's fair to say, these terrible murders sparked a massive man hunt for the perpetrator, even with a £75,000 reward on offer leading to his capture and conviction. Some five months later, his DNA, along with his fingerprints, led to his arrest and subsequent detailed confession, with Nick telling police that following the gruesome murder, he thought nothing of it, taking his mother and dogs for a walk, before going to a restaurant in Zurich for some fine dining. The use of phone records was also believed to have tracked him to the location of the house, together with an internet search history also playing a part in determining him as a suspect.

On searching his home, police found further incriminating evidence with child pornography, cable ties, adhesive tape and even an old Swiss army pistol, combined with rope handcuffs stuffed in a ruck sack. It was obvious Nick was not just satisfied with his first murder spree and most likely had other victims in his sights, with the names of 11 young boys scribbled in a notebook.

Nick was convicted of murder and related offences, including kidnapping, sexual assault and arson. On being found guilty, he was sentenced in March 2018 to life imprisonment, but this doesn't mean this beast of a person will spend his life behind bars.

This was despite the sentencing court President, Daniel Auschbach, saying that Nick:

> *...acted in a primitive, cold-blooded manner, showed no capacity for empathy and was extremely egoistic... The danger of a repeat offence is high, he committed a textbook crime, and acted in an utterly ruthless manner... What he did was simply grotesque. He was fully aware of his actions and it was a deliberate act...*

As is usual in Switzerland and even other German speaking countries, offenders sentenced to an indefinite term of imprisonment and, in his case, a maximum life sentence, it seems Nick, in line with common practice, can indeed apply for a conditional release, which means usually after serving anything as low as 10 to 15 years. However, in the case of Nick, in December 2018, an application, by way of an appeal by Crown prosecutors to have him ruled ineligible for parole, was dismissed by a higher Swiss court, despite the initial sentencing judge saying his chances of repeating such crimes was very high.

This means, in the case of this murderer, he could be

considered for release after serving say around 20 years, or even less. Let's hope though, he does spend the rest of his life where he belongs: in a prison cell. A final point, in respect of sentencing principles in Switzerland, it has been said that when compared to other countries, Swiss judges are somewhat lenient as their approach is apparently towards the lower bottom end of the sentencing range.

If indeed, they are at the lower end of the sentencing scale, then perhaps Victorian Courts are also at the same bottom end range when it comes to sentencing serious criminal offenders. Another example may well have been in respect of Stuart Matthew McKnight, who was initially charged with murder and arson in May 2016. After assaulting his elderly neighbour, he burnt down his house with the badly injured victim still inside. I will let you be the judge on whether the eventual prison sentence was lenient after reading the circumstances that resulted in death and an attempt of arson cover up.

The problem for the Crown in the case against McKnight at trial, to prove murder was going to be very difficult. This was despite the victim still being alive after being rescued by firefighters and succumbing to his injuries in hospital some three days later, which included blunt force trauma to the head, combined with the effects of the fire.

The issue the prosecution now had was to try and prove the evidence of murder beyond reasonable doubt regarding what did take place in the home, which led to the death of 79-year-old Graham Stevenson. The dilemma for the jury was going to be the events on the night of 19 May 2016, as the Crown's case was circumstantial. So, was it murder or was it manslaughter? McKnight pleaded not guilty to murder and arson.

Proving the charge of arson was not going to be an issue,

given the evidence of flammable liquid detected on both McKnight's clothes and shoes. In respect of the charge of murder, the initial, but questionable, evidence put forward by the Crown to the jury was that on the evening of Thursday 19 May 2016, an alcohol-affected McKnight found himself in an argument with his elderly neighbour. This occurred after he drunkenly mistook an accidental and innocent physical contact from Stevenson as sexual flirtation, while he was fixing a pantry door for him.

The immediate response from McKnight was to first punch the unsuspecting Stevenson, breaking his nose. Stevenson then picked up a carving fork off a nearby kitchen bench to protect himself. After grappling with each other, McKnight hit his victim over the head with a piece of wood and then impaled the fork into his chest. Believing Stevenson was dead, McKnight, now in panic mode, cowardly sought to conceal his crime by setting the house on fire by using a can of petrol. He splashed the accelerant around the house but, according to the Crown and most likely based on the postmortem examination, no petrol was splashed on Stevenson.

An eyewitness, relied on by the Crown, would give not so credible evidence at the trial, that McKnight was then seen running from the burning house. It was further established that firefighters found the still barely alive Stevenson, with one saying he had been "beaten up" and with a very odd and highly agitated McKnight carrying on and pretending to try and enter the smouldering house. He then tried to gain entry on more than one occasion into the back of the ambulance, where paramedics were treating Stevenson.

He then told them blatant lies, that the victim was a sex offender and suicidal. When questioned about what he was doing at the house before the fire, he responded he was simply using a computer and of all things, collecting flowers from the garden. His odd behaviour, combined with blood on his shoes and smelling of petrol, led police to immediately arrest him.

In the early hours of the next morning, he was interviewed by police and the only real admission he made was, he was at the house earlier that day and on no other occasion, except returning when the house was on fire, denying any involvement in what had taken place. At a further interview the same day, he came up with a concocted scenario in that Stevenson asked him to come over and help remove a damaged pantry door. After attending to that, McKnight left but later could smell something and on hearing someone yelling, went over to the house and, on finding nothing, left.

A DNA analysis of the crime scene established strong evidence linking blood from Stevenson on the shoes of McKnight, with fingernail scrapings taken from the deceased victim, showing further incriminating evidence that they belonged to McKnight. Not surprisingly, he was charged with murder and arson and subsequently committed to stand trial in the Supreme Court of Victoria.

Given the plethora of what appeared to be damning evidence linking McKnight to, not only the assault on Stevenson, such as the fingernail scapings and blood spots, together with the accelerant on his clothes and shoes, the Crown prosecutor still considered what actually took place inside the home was circumstantial. This was even despite the blunt force trauma to the victim's head, the carving fork impaled in his chest and evidence of the effect to his body from the fire.

Regardless of the substantial amount of evidence being presented to the jury over a number of days and, following a short adjournment to consider their possible discharge for reasons which were not disclosed, the prosecutor obviously took a deep breath and, with "cap in hand", entered into negotiations with the defence.

One of the problems considered was that the evidence given by the so-called eyewitness, who allegedly saw McKnight running away from the house on fire, left a lot to be desired. In addition, McKnight's DNA was excluded from the handle of the carving fork, so it was arguable he had a defence to all the charges he was currently on trial for. On that basis, it was agreed that McKnight would plead guilty to manslaughter and arson, as there was no possibility it could be proved beyond reasonable doubt that McKnight intentionally murdered the victim.

In other words, it was agreed that McKnight may have carried out an unlawful and dangerous act, albeit voluntary and deliberately, resulting in the death of Stevenson. As a consequence, the jury was discharged and a new indictment was served on McKnight for manslaughter and arson with a plea of guilty.

On 22 December 2017, McKnight appeared before Justice Croucher for sentencing and, in referring to one victim impact statement, it was readily apparent the ongoing trauma inflicted on the victim's family. The son of Stevenson was a surgeon and, as he said, even his medical training had not prepared him when he saw his father in hospital as he lay dying. He could not recognise him. Other family members also made it very apparent the trauma and grief they were all experiencing, following the circumstances surrounding what had taken place and the death of their much-loved family figure. His Honour indeed referred to these statements when he said:

> *These victim impact statements are powerful, eloquent and moving documents. In so far as is permissible to do so, I have regard to their contents in considering sentence, particularly on the manslaughter.* [79]

Before turning to the mitigating factors, His Honour would take into account, in which McKnight was entitled to rely on, the sentencing statistics that were of some guidance to the court regarding what should be imposed on the defendant. The learned judge specifically referred to the average prison sentence for manslaughter for the period 2011-12 to 2015-16, which showed two to 12 years, with a non-parole period ranging from nine months to nine years. The maximum penalty, at this point, for manslaughter was a maximum of 20 years imprisonment, but now set at 25 years.[80]

In applicable circumstances, a non-parole period of 10 years must be imposed[81] unless a special reason applies, such as a mental illness or an intellectual disability.[82] For arson, the maximum sentence for the period 2011-12 to 2015-16 was as low as three months to just over four years, despite a maximum penalty of 15 years imprisonment.[83]

Whilst every case turns on their own facts, including regarding mitigation, given that is what had been imposed in Victorian courts for similar offending, the chances of McKnight receiving a substantial term of imprisonment was starting to appear very unlikely. The court, quite rightly, highlighted the

---

79 *The Queen v McKnight* [2017] VSC 782-para 25.
80 see section 5 of the *Crimes Act 1958* (Vic).
81 *Sentencing Act 1991*(Vic)-section 11.
82 see further section 10A of the Sentencing Act.
83 section 197(1), 6 & 7 of the Crimes Act.

serious features of the case, notably McKnight bashed the victim for a spurious reason, then hit him over the head with a piece of wood and, to make matters even worse, impaled a carving fork into his chest, the latter being overlooked by His Honour.[84]

The gravity of the offending included, it took place in the home of the elderly Stevenson and believing he was already dead, the judge took into account, whilst it was a callous and cruel act, nonetheless, McKnight acted out of panic by setting the fire to cover up his criminal act.

A number of factors in favour of McKnight were then considered, even the fact the bashing, although quite brutal, was deemed to be only of a short duration and, indeed, was spontaneous and not planned. It was agreed by His Honour, however, that this was a very serious case example, giving rise to manslaughter and he said:

> *…well above the mid-range of gravity…there is no escaping the fact that this was an extreme and brutal response with tragic consequences and which involved a very high level of culpability[85]…an aggravating feature of the manslaughter that the house and body were burnt in an attempt to cover up that crime…[86]*

In my view, the agonising death of Stevenson, at this point, still seems to have been largely overlooked, noting he suffered serious head injuries, a puncture wound to his chest, carbon monoxide poisoning and agonisingly, full thickness burns to

---

84 *Queen v McKnight* [2017] VSC 782-para 31.

85 Ibid-para 41.

86 Ibid- para 45.

his body. The fact he survived for another three days before succumbing to his injuries, is remarkable although sad, noting his daughter-in-law held his hand when he took his last breath.

As they must do, the court took into account a number of mitigating factors in favour of the 47-year-old McKnight, noting his heavy drinking was due to a spinal injury, he suffered from depression and he had other ongoing health issues. His guilty plea, despite coming somewhat late, was also taken into account with His Honour stating, given the problems the prosecution had regarding the questionable eyewitness testimony and the lack of the carving fork DNA, Mc Knight had forgone, in any event, the possibility of an acquittal on the more serious charges of murder and arson.

While his plea may have determined an early resolution and facilitated the course of justice, no doubt, the jury would have found him guilty, perhaps not to murder, but certainly manslaughter and arson, but then again, we will never know. McKnight did show a limited degree of remorse, writing a letter of apology, albeit a paltry 23 words and, whilst on remand in prison, he supposedly used his time very well taking up a position as head billet.

His prospects for rehabilitation were only listed as fair, but with a low risk of reoffending. This was despite McKnight having, shall we say, a rather extensive criminal history. As the judge said, '(It) makes for depressing reading.'[87]

From his early twenties, McKnight had convictions for assaults, breach of intervention orders and driving offences, community corrections orders and suspended prison sentences, including spending short periods behind bars.

Despite his poor criminal past, the judge took the view

---

87 Ibid-para 55.

that, on the one hand, given McKnight has had a serious and continuing problem with drinking, with periods of abstinence, combined with anger management and violence issues, he said:

Despite the disturbing nature of the crime and his prior convictions, I still consider it unlikely that Mr McKnight would act in such an unlawful, violent and dangerous way again.[88]

His Honour then took into account the common law principle of parsimony, in that a court cannot apply a sentence that is more severe than that which is required to achieve the purpose for which the sentence is imposed. No doubt, the previous sentencing statistics also came into play, given that McKnight was sentenced to 11 years for the manslaughter and five years for the arson, with two years to be served cumulatively, meaning all up, his effective term of imprisonment was 13 years, with a non-parole period of 10 years.

It was noted by the judge that if McKnight had not pleaded guilty, he would have determined there was no remorse whatsoever and his prospects for rehabilitation were poor. However, if he had pleaded not guilty, under section 6AAA of the Sentencing Act, His Honour would have imposed a total effective sentence of imprisonment of around 16 years, with a non-parole period of 13 years. That well may have been considered a more appropriate sentence given all the circumstances.

What saved McKnight from a lengthier prison sentence was, despite the bashing and stabbing of Stevenson, followed by the arson cover up attempt, leaving him to suffer further, he was only sentenced on the lesser charge of manslaughter and arson,

---

[88] Ibid-para 84.

thanks to his plea of guilty. The fact he left his elderly victim to die, although thinking he was already dead, to then suffer from burns as he lay in his burning house, leaves no sympathy, in my view, for McKnight. Surely, a harsher sentence should have been imposed, but then again, the jury is still out in that regard.

One accused person, who may well not escape the wrath of the justice system if found guilty, is Victor Serriteno, a resident of Vacaville, California in the US. In August 2020, a massive wildfire in Northern California which resulted in the death of two people in their homes, one who was 82 years of age, was allegedly started intentionally by Serriteno in order to cover up an earlier murder. It would be alleged, he set the young woman's murdered body on fire in the wildland areas of Solano and Napa counties, with the arson then developing into one of the largest wildfires in Californian history.

The young woman's motor vehicle was located some two days after her first date with Serriteno, which was arranged using an online dating app. She was never to be seen again. Her body was only discovered when, after being reported missing, police used cell phone records and other relevant data to start a grid search, leading to her remains. Police arrested Serriteno a month later in September 2020, charging him with first degree murder and following a further extensive 8-month investigation, he was also charged with an additional two counts of arson related murder committed during a state of emergency.

Serriteno is facing the prospect of either a death sentence or life imprisonment without parole if convicted, as the charges have now been elevated to special circumstances. This means, in the US justice system, situations where criminal activities are carried out with high and total disregard to the community and life, it can be determined as a special circumstance, meaning if convicted, a more severe punishment. If provided for by state legislation, this can result in being sentenced to death.

Serriteno maintains his presumption of innocence and, in a preliminary hearing held in August 2024, the evidence continued to mount up. Such a hearing in the US is similar to a committal hearing, where the prosecution leads enough probable evidence for the matter to proceed to trial. The evidence included packages of tape found in his house, similar to what was found in the deceased victim's mouth. We, of course, wait with interest for the outcome of any jury trial.

While the term "wildfire" is sometimes referred to in Australian vocabulary, it really is just in US lexicon. A bushfire is seen as an uncontrolled fire in bushland and normally used in Australian terminology, even from as far back as the 19th century. In fact, according to University of Queensland Emeritus, Professor Roly Sussex, it was used as early as 1847 by explorer, Ludwig Leichhardt, as he trekked across the Australian landscape and noted bushfires in his journal as he penned his adventures.

Australian bushfires have, unfortunately, also resulted in the loss of life of many people, including livestock and native animals, together with the destruction of property. Many of our bushfires follow as a consequence of strong winds, with trees crashing down onto power lines, high temperatures with low humidity and even dry lightning igniting blazes, where there is thunderstorm electrical activity but little to no rain, not helped by persistent droughts.

One of the other difficulties still faced is, despite many fires started as a consequence of such extreme weather conditions, there are a number of individuals out in the community setting them without any regard for the devastating consequences.

This has not only seen the death of innocent victims, but total devastation of livestock and property.

8
AUSTRALIA'S BUSHFIRES

Bushfires in Australia are a fact of life, burning in grass and scrublands, volatile forests and countryside, with the eastern part of our vast lands deemed to be a region prone to significant events. The bushfire season typically runs from December through to May but, of course, can occur at any time depending on extreme weather conditions. These fires have resulted in the death of an estimated 800 people over the past 170 years.

One such deadly fire started on Friday, 13 January 1939 in Victoria. It was the most ferocious, with other fires in NSW and the ACT, which burned for the next seven days, urged on by high temperatures with low humidity and encouraged by strong velocity and northerly winds. "Black Friday" resulted in an estimated 4.9 million acres of land being razed in Victoria alone, with 71 people perishing as a consequence of a number of towns completely destroyed, with around 1300 homes and other buildings and property burnt to the ground or badly damaged. These fires were so intense that New Zealand residents some 2,800 kilometres from the fire zone reported ash falling from their skies.

The report of the 1939 Royal Commission set out its investigation into "The Causes and Measures Taken to Prevent the Bush Fires of January 1939 and to Protect Life and Property". The commission was also tasked to determine what actions and measures needed to be taken to prevent similar bushfires. This investigation was led by Judge Leonard Stratton and sometimes referred to as the Stratton Inquiry, ultimately finding that the fires were due to accidental causes, not just limited to careless burning by campers but also negligent farmers and operators of a local sawmill and certainly assisted by extreme weather conditions.

Often deemed in history as one of the worst bushfires ever in Australia, it was aptly put by Stratton that the majority of the fires were but by the 'hand of man'. Whilst negligent campers and farmers played a role, one can also conclude there were evil hands at play, not that that was ever determined. The commission, however, summed up such tragic events succinctly with the following vivid description:

It appeared that the whole state was alight. At midday, in many places, it was dark as night. Men carrying hurricane lamps, worked to make safe their families and belongings. Travellers on the highways were trapped by blazes or fallen trees and perished…Where the fire was most intense, the soil was burnt to such a depth…may be many years before it shall have been restored…

The commission made a number of recommendations, particularly in respect of future safety preventative measures and most notably involving the clearing of land by burning off and the safe operation of sawmills. It was also strongly recommended that road and forest fire breaks be carried out, much like we see today, for example, with such controlled planned fire burn offs by the CFA and under the control of Forest Fire Management Victoria.

Local farmers and graziers now can only carry out a burn off under permit and we have in place total fire ban days, where any sort of open fire is totally prohibited. Interesting, the commission also recommended the use of the Royal Australian Air Force (RAAF), to carry out observant patrols and, little did they know, now we have such air patrols and also aircraft being used as waterbombers to douse bushfires.

Despite the recommendations of the commission, they were put on hold due the start of the Second World War the same year, so it was not until the 1943-44 bushfires, largely in Victora, that finally led to some proper co-ordination of statewide firefighting. It was hard enough for our civilian population, as it was after four years of war, with many men and women posted overseas as part of the Australian Military Forces (AMF), which would have included many firefighting volunteers and personnel. Those remaining at home were also subject to much hardship, with the rationing of day-to-day basic needs not helped by a labour shortage, while at the same time worrying about their loved ones serving our country.

The summer of 1943-44 brought with it, once again, extreme drought with less than 50 millimetres of rain, about a third of what would normally occur. This resulted in major bushfires all over Victoria, with the loss of 51 lives and in excess of one million hectares burnt and 650 properties either destroyed or badly damaged. The fires spread from the border of

South Australia to Central Victoria and as far wide and down to the Mornington Peninsula, destroying caravans, and even to the Gippsland Region. The usual large number of civilian and army volunteers, although somewhat reduced due to overseas military service, fought the fires but, hampered by lack of water pressure, making their fire hoses basically useless.

Australian Prime Minister, John Curtin, provided a Commonwealth grant of 200,000 pounds and even the racing fraternity got behind an appeal for the local Bayside victims, naming a race called the "Beaumaris Handicap", won by a horse ridden by famous and legendary jockey, Scobie Breasley. He would also win the Caulfield Cup four years in a row from 1942 and again in 1952. The fires in the bayside area saw many people camped on the surrounding beaches, accompanied by their pets, at the height of the fire threat. Once again, a royal commission into the fires was led by Judge Stratton which established in 1945, the CFA as the coordinating entity for areas outside the jurisdiction of the MFB.

Another black day occurred, this time in Tasmania on 7 February 1967 and was colloquially known as "Black Tuesday", with nearly 1300 homes and buildings destroyed as the fire reached the outskirts of Hobart, a death toll of 62 local residents in a single day, with around 900 suffering from non-fatal injuries, but with 7,000 left homeless. The total damage was estimated then to be in the order of $40 million, which by today's monetary standards is massive.

Farm animals didn't escape, with literally thousands lost in the fires. Again, this inferno was assisted by an overbearing heatwave but also deliberate back-burning was a predominate cause. No doubt, arsonists were also at play as reports came out that of the 110 separate fires, only 22 could be considered as accidental but no one was ever charged with arson-related offences.

Late spring and the summer of 1974-75 saw massive bushfires in 15 per cent of the landmass in Australia, from the NT and as far across as WA. Loss of life was six people with 50,000 head of livestock and around 10,0000 kilometres of fencing and crops being consumed by fire. According to the Australian Bureau of Statistics (ABS), the main cause, particularly in Central Australia, was not, this time, below average drought and rainfall as experienced in the previous two years, but exceptional and certainly above heavy average rainfall, which in turn provided fuel for the fires due to overgrown grassland and forests.

On Wednesday, 16 February 1983, again fuelled by extreme weather conditions, with 22 days of total fire bans and a massive dust storm leading into this terrible day, with gale force winds changing direction and record high temperatures, saw nearly 3,200 fires with untold destruction across South Australia and Victoria. It certainly was a black day, but this time it was to be referred to as "Ash Wednesday" also known as a Christian holy day.

South Australia lost 28 of its citizens, which included three firefighters, with nearly 600 homes and buildings destroyed. Victoria also did not escape a heavy toll with 2,000 homes and buildings either gutted or damaged and 8,000 people evacuated. Loss of life was high with 47 dying in Victoria, including 11 CFA members who died sheltering in their trucks. Overall, it was estimated 350,000 livestock were killed or had to be put down.

A total of $176 million was paid out in insurance claims. Again, extreme drought, giving rise to extremely combustible scrub and bush and tree branches falling on power lines, was listed as the main causes for the fires. There was, of course, suspicions that a number of the fires had been deliberately lit. A subsequent CFA study of 32 civilians who died on that fateful day, found such deaths were largely due to insufficient and early warnings and sadly, the victims most likely had not put in place an effective strategy to survive.

It was also determined by police victim identification personnel that some poor souls had perished in or alongside their vehicle trying to escape the oncoming flames, but the intense heat vaporised the petrol, causing the engine to stall, or they had stopped driving because of thick smoke providing zero visibility.

Unfortunately, Santa Claus was not the only arrival in NSW and the ACT during a Christmas period, when over 100 fires that started on 24 December 2001 and continued to burn for the next 23 days. The Black Christmas bushfires burnt through nearly 750,000 hectares of land, destroyed or damaged nearly 600 homes and buildings, not to mention the loss of hundreds of motor vehicles and 7,000 in livestock. Thankfully, no one was killed or seriously injured, but the overall damage bill was put at $70 million, with firefighting costs in excess of $100 million.

The ACT was again not left untouched with Canberra experiencing destructive fires surrounding its capital and in rural errors, causing an estimated damage bill topping $700 million. These fires on 18 January 2003 saw four people die with numerous injured, together with the loss of over 500 properties. A state of emergency was declared as the firestorm approached, again fuelled by extreme drought. It was so intense, some years later, academics referred to it as a "fire tornado".

The main cause was attributed to dry lightning starting fires in surrounding national parks, which merged some 10 days later into a massive blaze. It was later determined by the ACT's coroner that the government's Emergency Services Bureau had not only failed in their initial response but were also negligent in providing early warnings to the public. What followed in response was the introduction of the *Emergencies Act 2004* (ACT), which also established a combined tactical operational body known as the Emergency Services Agency.

Unfortunately, Victoria was also to experience similar types of fire tornadoes over extremely hot days towards the end of January 2009, giving rise to tinder dry bushfire conditions. On the morning of Saturday 7 February 2009, the state was engulfed by fire with over 400 separate blazes. It was certainly a "Black Saturday" with the fires burning well into March 2009. There was the loss of 173 people, which included 119 found dead inside their property, and the complete destruction of over 3,500 homes and buildings.

The fires raged all over the state, including and not limited to, as far away as Beechworth to Kinglake, Marysville, the Dandenong Ranges to the Bunyip State Park, through to Wilson Promontory and across to the Central Gippsland region. Other country regions, such as Horsham and Coleraine, were not left untouched. It was the same for Bendigo, burning through from Long Gully to Eaglehawk.

In April 2009, the Victorian Government determined that a royal commission was needed, which would be chaired by The Hon. Bernard Teague AO, eminent judge of the Victorian Supreme Court. The charter was to carry out a lengthy investigation of what started the bushfires, in order to determine what exactly had occurred, taking evidence from

100 lay witnesses. Its overall aim, at the conclusion of their deliberations, was to make recommendations and ensure lessons could be learnt, 'for minimising the prospect of a tragedy of this scale ever happening again.'[89]

It was determined, of the 12 select fires investigated by the royal commission, six were due to faulty power lines, lightning strikes in extreme weather and bushfire conditions, also helped by machinery malfunctions, whilst the balance were all deemed to be deliberately lit. In respect of bushfires igniting as a result of faulty or fallen power lines, the royal commission recommended that:

> *The State…take such steps as may be required to…the progressive replacement of SWER (single-wire earth return) power lines in Victoria with aerial bundled cable…underground cabling or other technology that delivers greatly reduced bushfire risk… replacement program should be completed in the areas of highest bushfire risk within 10 years…*[90]

There was, ultimately, a multi-million dollar settlement in a 2014 class action claim lodged in the Supreme Court of Victoria against an electricity company's negligence, over failing to install a proper conductor on a power line, creating the ignition of the fire in Kilmore East, which then headed across to the Kinglake area. The successful legal proceedings relied on the investigation and report of the Royal Commission, which had formed the view that the faulty power line was the cause of this particular disastrous fire.

---

[89] Preface-Final Report -2009 Victorian Bushfires Royal Commission, July 2010.

[90] Ibid-recommendation 27.

Victoria Police were actively involved with assisting firefighters, to the safe evacuation of residents and, unfortunately, victim identification. Two victims were well respected television newsreader and compere, Brian Naylor and his wife, Moiree, who both died when the Kinglake fire engulfed their property. Sadly, a year earlier, they also lost their son, who was killed in a light plane crash in the same area.

In well-deserved recognition of Brian, he was posthumously inducted into the TV Week Logies Hall of Fame in 2010. Another two victims, who lived in a mud brick house in Kinglake, were British actor, Reg Evans, who had made many appearances in numerous Australian television dramas such as Homicide and Division 4 and his partner, Angela Brunton.

Subsequent enquiries by police task forces would also determine that the cause of some blazes was at the hands of arsonists. A number of overt actions were taken, including visible patrols by police to deter and detect any would-be firebugs and to stop looting by unscrupulous individuals preying on the misfortune of the fire victims. It was, in fact, reported on an ABC news broadcast that residents in Kinglake had put up a sign in the town that spelt it out in no uncertain terms, "Looters will be Shot". This followed such an inexcusable act when looters ransacked a victim's house at Heathcote Junction, not long after a body had been removed.

Given that some of the fires were believed to have been deliberately lit, Victoria Police Chief Commissioner, Christine Nixon, took the unusual step of stating that all fire scenes were to be considered a crime scene, until proven otherwise. This would allow the extensive gathering of evidence, that may or may not lead to what started the fires and, if deliberate, the identity of the culprit, or culprits. While 'every contact does leave a trace', the difficulty in examining a fire scene is that there is not a lot left to provide an important clue.

However, following an exhaustive task force investigation over some 12 months into the Bendigo fires, in which 60-odd houses were gutted in their western suburbs, with damage also to farmland and machinery estimated to be $24 million, and despite the initial assumption that suggested perhaps a discarded cigarette butt was the culprit, police made a breakthrough. Two local youths were arrested and charged with arson causing death plus a plethora of 135 other related charges, which included lighting a fire on the day of a total fire ban.

In November 2011, the two defendants were found to be unfit to stand trial on the account of mild to moderate intellectual disabilities. Understandably, this caused the loved ones of a Long Gully arson victim to be concerned that, not only was no-one now being held to account, but it would only be a matter of time before such a tragic fire would again take place.

Police also arrested two men acting suspiciously and believed to be involved in the fires around Yea and Seymour, but they were never charged. A 40-year-old resident from Narre Warren North was, however, proceeded against for using a power tool on a total fire ban day, which, it was alleged, started a grassfire destroying two homes. Subsequent investigations surrounding the suspicious fires in Churchill in Central Gippsland resulted in charges being laid against a local resident, which included arson causing death and intentionally lighting a bushfire.

In the final report of the royal commission, it was evident that the approach to bushfires would now take a significant and different path, compared to just focusing on emergency response and investigation of the fire's origin to identify those responsible. The focus of Victoria Police would now be more preventative as against detection after the event, with the establishment of a statewide operations response unit. With around 230 officers, its designated tasks are to concentrate around periods of extreme bushfire risk and prone areas.

This would include visible police presence during times of typical high bushfire weather conditions to not only detect potential fires in their early stages, but also any misguided individuals with intent to start a fire. This in turn would hopefully lead to a reduction of at least arson as a cause of a bushfire.

The royal commission succinctly set out such a preventative approach by Victoria Police which stated that they would:

...pursue a coordinated approach to arson prevention...a research program aimed at refining arson prevention and detection strategies...comprehensive training, periodic evaluation of arson prevention strategies...a requirement that all fire-prone police service areas have arson prevention plans and programs according to their level of risk.[91]

In addition, the royal commission encouraged, not only the Commonwealth Government, but all states and territories to continue to undertake a national plan of action to reduce bushfire arson, with ongoing data collection to ensure a best practice approach.[92]

The Victorian Government would also go on to enact

---

91 Ibid- recommendation 35.

92 Ibid- recommendation 36.

and update regulations for buildings, together with exhaustive guidelines of strict standards for the type of constructions now required and not just in bushfire prone areas. It was to be known as a "bushfire attack assessment".

All these measures would hopefully reduce the casualties and damage caused by such raging bushfires. The royal commission estimated, on a conversative basis, a total loss of $4.4 billion, noting it considered the:

protection of human life and the safety of communities as the highest priority for bushfire policy.[93]

Unfortunately, the Black Saturday bushfires were then followed by a black summer during 2019-20, emanating from fires in Queensland around June 2019 and due to untenable dry weather conditions. Hundreds of fires then tore through our states and territories. Even Tasmania was not left unscathed during the period from December 2019 through to May 2020.

Over 243,000 square kilometres were ravaged and, when converted to hectares in just NSW alone, it was estimated to be in the order of 5.5 million, which, according to the Commonwealth Scientific and Industrial Research Organisation, exceeded the area burnt out in the 1983 and 2009 bushfires. There was an estimated 9,500 homes and buildings destroyed or severely damaged during this black summer and alarmingly 34 people died as direct result of the fires, with a staggering 445 dying from associated causes including smoke inhalation.

A royal commission was again put in place, this time by the Morrison-led Federal Government, with its report

---

93   Ibid-summary.

making 81 recommendations.[94] One of the recommendations was suggesting that all governments undertake more cultural burning in consultation with First Nations peoples and fire agencies. Such burn-offs would incorporate traditional Aboriginal land practice initiatives to, not only limit fire hazards, but also protect our native wildlife.

The state governments of NSW and Victoria also carried out independent reviews, mainly to revisit the likely causes of the fires and what needed to be done, not just in the detection of arsonists, but what better preventative measures were further needed. The NSW State Coroner, Teresa O'Sullivan, also conducted, as part of a coronial inquiry following the loss of 25 lives in that state alone, numerous hearings throughout the state, making a number of recommendations in the 734-page report released in March 2024, mainly directed at the NSW Rural Fire Service (RFS).

In calling for significant change as a result of the unprecedented 2019-20 bushfires, Coroner O'Sullivan recommended that new rules be adopted for firefighting aircraft in order to provide a better and effective response to bushfires and the existing alert systems, which were in desperate need of an overhaul, to be replaced with more accurate and timely community communication in times of danger. The report also addressed various causes of the bushfires, notably the usual arson, power lines, lighting strikes and out of control back burning operations.[95]

Once again, it was determined that the bushfires largely

---

[94] The Royal Commission into National Natural Disaster Arrangements Report-28 October 2020.

[95] See Inquests and Inquiries into the 2019/2020 NSW Bushfire Season-Volume 2–Decision of State Coroner O'Sullivan, March 2024.

emanated from timber dry conditions urged on by dry lightning and high temperatures. Climate change, as a crisis factor, once again reared its ugly head, but there were a number of critics in opposition citing arson as the main contributing factor with arrest numbers varying from around 180 individuals, down to as little as 30, charged overall with various related offences. The consensus view was based on data released by the Australian Institute of Criminology that on a balance of probabilities, bushfires in Australia are as a result of human intervention, either intentionally or accidental.

Deliberately lit fires fell in the range of around 13%, but a staggering 37% were deemed as suspicious, in other words, most likely intentional. Human involvement in starting accidental fires also consisted of discarding cigarette butts, negligent burning off, embers from campfires, the usual faulty power lines and mention was made of faulty electric fences and sparks in the countryside from railway trains as also contributing to non-suspicious fires. The balance, in the order of 15%, was due to extreme weather conditions with poor hazard reduction, fuelled on by lightning strikes.

Such extreme weather conditions, as we've moved into 2025 have led to scientists identifying a specific weather phenomenon, aptly titled "hydroclimatic whiplash". It now plays a significant role in deadly bushfires, as the local regional environment changes dramatically. Thanks to on-going rapid swings from wet to dry weather, with temperatures continuing to rise due to climate change, for which global temperature data indicates that 2024 was the hottest on record since 1850, coupled with extreme rainfalls, this has led to severe droughts, with some being described as a "megadrought". Ferocious winds only add to the problem, as evidenced in the fires that engulfed parts of Los Angeles in the US in January 2025.

The consequences of hydroclimatic whiplash means we will continue to see more intense and frequent bushfires, as we witness an increasing and volatile change in our climate. Hopefully, we can address and limit this type of extreme weather event by reducing greenhouse gas emissions, together with properly overseeing the management of vegetation. Regardless, there will have to be other solutions to reduce its effect or we will continue to see more devastating bushfires with properties destroyed and lives lost.

One such solution, albeit somewhat expensive, was a property dubbed "last house standing". Despite being consumed in the LA wildfires, which saw literally thousands of other structures reduced to nothing but ashes, this property survived with minimal damage. This was credited to the type of construction, initially designed to allow it to survive earthquakes. It consisted of stucco and stone with a fireproof roof, according to its owner. Perhaps we will see more of this type of house built in our bushfire prone areas in the future.

The problem still, of course, is that bushfire arson is a fact of life and what motivates such individuals to cause mayhem and death, such as the Black Saturday Churchill arsonist, takes some delving into.

9
THE CHURCHILL ARSONIST

The township of Churchill, situated in Central Gippsland in Victoria, is around 160 kilometres from Melbourne and within 11 kilometres of Morwell. The town's name acknowledges and honours Sir Winston Leonard Spencer Churchill, the cigar smoking World War Two Prime Minister of the United Kingdom, who also served another term from 1951 to 1955. There is a monument reflecting his cigar in the main town centre, often referred to as the "Big Cigar". The town was initially developed from 1965 and its main shopping centre opened some two years later, with the majority of the town's housing being built by the then Housing Commission of Victoria, supposedly to accommodate workers from the Hazelwood Power Station.

At approximately 1.30pm on Saturday, 7 February 2009 (Black Saturday), a fire ignited and was helped by extreme hot weather conditions and powerful winds which began south of the main town centre in a eucalyptus plantation. A further fire was started in close proximity to the first fire and, by late afternoon, it had gained traction heading towards the Gippsland towns of Yarram and Woodside, near the south coastline.

The fire also threatened the Loy Yang Power Station and by Monday, 9 February 2009 was still burning largely unchecked. The fire front was 15 kilometres and even though it was called the "Churchill fire", it still threatened other townships, including Traralgon South. It, overall, involved the Latrobe Valley through to the Strzelecki Ranges.

Some intermittent rain and resultant cooler temperatures eased the fire but it still caused total damage engulfing some 36,0000 hectares and destroying, in its path, 156 houses and a community hall with 11 people killed. The agony suffered by the victims is hard to describe, with some dying from asphyxiation, whilst another lost his life trapped in his vehicle, with his son also dying nearby in his abandoned vehicle.

Two brothers, who were experienced firefighters, perished defending their parents' home in Hazelwood South, with a wind change giving them no chance of survival from the fire front. Another victim was found deceased alongside a pet dog after driving into a creek bed, obviously in an attempt to escape the ferocious fire. Another four victims perished, including a family of three, found dead under their house in a concrete garage. Others were lucky to escape seeking shelter in a local creek until the fire front had passed.

Investigators, including from the Department of Sustainability and Environment (DSE), had now determined, after examining the fire scene in Glendonald road, there was evidence of two deliberately lit fires. This was despite the overall mass destruction of plantations and forests, but with the help of photographic evidence, they zeroed in on a small area where it was determined that two small, but separate, fires had been lit close to the intersection of Glendonald road and Jelleff's outlet and within a short distance of each other.

An odd character, for want of a better description, by the name of Brendan James Sokaluk, being a 38-year-old unemployed Churchill resident on a disability pension, with no prior convictions, came to the early notice of investigating police by chance when speaking with a number of local residents. It seemed that on the day of the fire, he was acting, not only in strange manner, but rather suspiciously, particularly when investigators were advised by a farmer who lived not far from Glendonald road, that he had seen the car, belonging to Sokaluk, parked on a strange angle near the location of the fire and around the time it had started. This witness also received a message from Sokaluk, played to police, where the now suspect said his vehicle had broken down and confirmed he had left it in Glendonald road.

Another witness also put Sokaluk close to the fire at around the same time and he also told her that he 'hoped his car didn't go up in flames', as it was left in close proximity to the fire. It also came to light, for want of a better description, another witness observed Sokaluk in his vehicle checking out the aftermath of a fire that occurred in the same location prior to this Black Saturday disaster. There had also been a local rumour going around that where 'there is smoke and fire', there is also Sokaluk in close vicinity.

At this point and not believing their luck, expecting to take literally weeks, if not months, identifying the perpetrator, police were becoming very interested in the activities of Sokaluk. Their suspicions were further enhanced when, on checking emergency services Triple 0 calls on the day of the fire, they found their suspect had, in fact, made a call at 1.32 pm reporting the fire and saying, 'it's getting big', which was only a couple of minutes after the fire was believed to have started. This meant, of course, that he must have been very close to the fire's origin.

It was now time to knock on his door and introduce themselves as detectives from the Victoria Police Arson and Explosives Squad. Sokaluk would have been given his rights when taken into custody for questioning and cautioned in the usual manner, 'We must inform you that you do not have to say or do anything, but anything you do say or do may be given in evidence against you.'

Sokaluk, of course, had the common law legal principle of a right to remain silent, including a refusal to give evidence at trial and could have refused to answer questions put to him. As a general rule, a court cannot place any adverse inference on such right to silence. Now Sokaluk, being the chatty chap he was, even before he was formally interviewed over 12 and 13 February 2009, voluntarily gave police his version of events on the day in question and said:

want to tell you...regard the fire stuff...I was smoking in the car when I was driving...you can go bitumen road or the gravel...I go the gravel road...I was smoking, a bit fell down... so I grab a bit of paper...flick it out sort of thing...it must've have ignited...went up this track...top of this was rubbish... the car wasn't working too well...then I noticed there was a fire and I panicked...called 000...just tried to get away as quick as possible, just panicked. [96]

---

[96] *R v Sokaluk* [2012] VSC 167-para 19.

The formal police record of interview was conducted over two days with an independent third person present, which he was entitled to, but most likely police were being very careful at how they conducted the interview, given there may have been some concerns about his mental state. This became more obvious to police when they asked Sokaluk if he knew what a legal practitioner was. He simply replied, 'A doctor?' His limited mental capacity became more obvious when asked his full name he could not remember what his middle name was, other than 'J'.

I think, if indeed he had first obtained legal advice, which police told him of that right in the formal caution, his lawyers would have most likely advised him in the formal record of interview to say, 'on legal advice, I make no comment,' to each question put by police. At some stage, police would have given up and stopped the record of interview, following such a response to each of their questions. This would mean they would have to prove their case in the absence of any admissions, largely on circumstantial evidence and including witness accounts of his actions putting him at the scene of the fire ignition. In other words, it would have made the prosecution's case, in proving his guilt beyond reasonable doubt, a lot more difficult.

In any event, the formal record of interview went along similar lines to his initial voluntary statement, except for one glaring, differing version. He initially said, in both the earlier voluntary statement and in the formal record of interview, that when he put the cigarette ash in the paper, it ignited when it fell on the floor so he 'squished it out'. This was followed then by:

I threw the paper on the road out of the car window close to trees on the edge of the plantation, where it ignited. Then he kept on driving.

Sokaluk again agreed that he did call 000 at 1.32pm to report the fire on the right-hand side of Glendonald road and then his car broke down, further stating, 'I did a bad thing and I'm scared, shit scared.'[97]

However, when questioned further by police as to what he lit the paper with, Sokaluk changed his version of events:

Q. How did you scrunch the paper up?
A. I did it real quick. I just grabbed the paper, grabbed it…I wanted to get it out the car.
Q. What did you light it with?
A. Cigarette lighter.
Q. A handheld one?
a. Yeah, cause I don't have one in the car.

Sokaluk now introduces a handheld cigarette lighter into the equation, which was used to light the paper.[98]

So, in his first explanation, it's the cigarette ash in the paper which is thrown out the window and starts the blaze, but then as a further excuse, for want of a better word, he now states:

…it wasn't the cigarette ash that burnt the paper as I lit the paper with a cigarette lighter.

The jury perhaps is still out on that differing version of

---

97   Ibid- para 12.

98   Ibid-para 24 and:[5].

events, but if you had no intent and it was caused by ash igniting the paper, you might accept that his reckless indifference simply caused the blaze. However, it seems that he knew exactly what he was doing and, given the ash didn't light the paper, if indeed there was ever any cigarette ash, his actions made sure the plantation was deliberately set on fire. Alternatively, perhaps he was confused about the question and thought it related to the lighting of his cigarette, not the paper, but the paper was obviously burning when it was thrown from his vehicle.

It didn't matter, in any event, as Justice Coghlan said in his opening sentencing remarks:

I am satisfied beyond reasonable doubt, for the purposes of sentencing, that you intentionally lit the fire, intending to set fire to eucalyptus plantations...I am also satisfied that you lit the fire at two distinct places at or near the intersection...[99] [and]...that you knew your actions would cause damage to the plantation...that you did intend to kill anyone.[100]

In His Honour's overall sentencing summary, mention was also made that after his car had broken down and he was evacuated from the Glendonald Road area, he telephoned his father to tell him what had happened and that he only drove to their area to 'avoid the heat and visit Peter', his mate. This was despite his father advising him earlier that day not to travel to the hills, due to the extreme hot weather conditions.[101]

Regardless, intent is not a necessary element to prove beyond reasonable doubt with arson causing death. The jury,

---

99   Ibid-para 5.

100 Ibid-para 7.

101 Ibid-para 8 & 9.

after listening to evidence and final submissions from the prosecution and defence counsel over three weeks, rejected his explanation of what had happened, found Sokaluk guilty of 10 counts of arson causing death, which carries a maximum penalty of 25 years imprisonment. Justice Coghlan deemed Sokaluk as a serious arson offender, that he was remorseful and took into account his reduced moral culpability by accepting, on a balance of probabilities, in applying the Verdins principles.

Indeed, the expert evidence of his intellectual disability demonstrated a reasonably mild degree diagnosis of autism spectrum disorder. On that basis, he sentenced Sokaluk on 27 April 2012 to an effective maximum prison term of 17 years and nine months, with a non-parole period of 14 years with 1041 days already served at sentencing.[102]

The DPP subsequently appealed the sentence on the grounds of being manifestly inadequate, citing the learned judge had placed too much emphasis on the intellectual disability of Sokaluk, that the sentence imposed did not give sufficient weight to the protection of the community, which in turn, cancelled out any mental health factor in mitigation against the sentence. On that basis, the DPP was seeking on appeal a sentence in the order of 24-26 years.[103]

Interesting though and again emphasising that intent is not a necessary element to prove beyond reasonable doubt arson causing death, the DPP, in its appeal submissions, said:

In his interview, the respondent said that he accidentally started the fire when part of the cigarette he was smoking in his

---

[102] Ibid- paras 70-75.

[103] *DPP v Brendan James Sokaluk* [2013] VSCA 48.

car fell to the floor. He said that he used a paper serviette to pick it up and threw it out of the car window, where it ignited...[104]

I am somewhat surprised that the DPP then made no submission about the use of the cigarette lighter and perhaps that was just an oversight, but in some way, if it was included, the term "accidentally started the fire" could perhaps give way to "intentionally started the fire". Simply put and based on the formal record of interview, Sokaluk knew exactly what he was doing when he lit the fires in two distinct areas, although it was never submitted by the Crown that he actually drove to the plantation area with the sole intent of lighting the two fires.

The fact he lit the two separate fires intentionally and, as also confirmed by Justice Coghlan in his sentencing summary, it begs the question once again, how the DPP in their submission could possibly only refer to the part of the formal interview that the fire was lit accidentally. Regardless, the Court of Criminal Appeal, in dismissing the appeal of sentence, stated that Justice Coghlan did not err in the reasonable exercise of his sentencing discretion.

It now remained as to the motive behind the lighting of the fires by Sokaluk, if indeed there was any motive, but on the basis that the events on Black Saturday were certainly no accident. On one interpretation of the facts, was his moral culpability reduced to such a degree due to his intellectual disability? That was accepted by His Honour as a mitigating factor. This was coupled with having absolutely no idea what was evident to all and sundry, perhaps except to him: the results of lighting the two fires and the massive damage and deaths it would cause.

---

104   Ibid-para 10.

However, as aptly put by Justice Coghlan when sentencing Sokaluk in the 2012 trial, he stated:

This was a very hot day, perhaps our hottest day after a week of very hot weather. There had been a very long drought and the amount of dried material in the plantation was obvious. You had, in the past, at least some rudimentary training in the CFA and you must have known of the risk.[105]

Sokaluk was a former volunteer member of the CFA in 1987 and he may indeed have had some morbid attraction to setting fires and watching them burn. Perhaps he fitted the criteria set to be considered a pyromaniac or was there simply no motive? This may not be helped by his intellectual disability and so isolated from society, his actions were a cry for help. It is, therefore, useful to look at his life history to ascertain if any possible motive lies hidden beneath.

At the time of sentencing, Sokaluk was a single man of 42 years of age, born in Seymour, Victoria and then moved to live in Churchill. He attended a special school and was described as being a bit of a disturbed loner, constantly teased and bullied by his peers. He gained employment for some 18 years as a gardener at the Monash University Churchill Campus but was not held in high esteem by his co-workers.

In 2006, after taking stress leave, he ceased working and qualified for a disability pension. Whilst he was often described as a bit odd, his social skills, to a degree, were adequate but his verbal and writing skills fell into a very low IQ level. He subsequently took up casual employment delivering local newspapers and would often be seen on his delivery rounds, pushing a pram with his beloved pet in tow.

---

105   *R v Sokaluk* [2012] VSC 167-para 38.

He couldn't manage his own finances and was largely dependent on his parents for financial support, the cleaning of his house and also cooking his meals. However, despite his lack of normal range of domestic, social and intellectual skills, he was still able to complete and file an insurance claim the following morning after his vehicle was destroyed in the Black Saturday fire.

It was also common knowledge, as reported by his neighbours, that he would always be working in his shed listening to tapes of "Bob the Builder" and "Thomas the Tank Engine". His strange behaviour was also complimented by hiding in his back yard peering over the fence and, according to one neighbour, ducking out of sight when seen. He would also often light fires in the yard. He was observed late on the afternoon of Black Saturday, watching his handiwork from the rooftop of his house.

His attraction to fires seems to have stemmed from his early school days, with one school student saying Sokaluk was fascinated with fire and was believed to have also lit one in a park and once again using a cigarette lighter. This apparent attraction perhaps did lead to him to joining the local CFA, but his tenure lasted less than a year, with a family friend in her statement to police saying he had a passion for the fire trucks and craved the attention, bordering on hero syndrome.

Interestingly though, Justice Coghlan even commented on sentencing, that after Sokaluk had taken refuge from the fire front, he assisted a local family in fighting the fire[106] and further that:

I suspect your time in the CFA many years ago was also difficult.[107]

---
106   Ibid- para 11.
107   Ibid-para 38.

Indeed, one CFA member commented to investigating police that when Sokaluk first attempted to join their unit, they reported his strange demeanour to police, concerned about his fascination with fires. Perhaps his anger over his short time with the CFA led to him telling all and sundry who started the fire, even sending an email to Crime Stoppers, which was later discovered by police on his computer, reporting that he had observed a DSE firefighter in a four-wheel drive vehicle lighting the fire at Glendonald Road. His Honour said further that this false report was apparently made so he wouldn't get blamed for lighting the fire.[108]

A court expert witness opinion evidence from Professor James Ogloff was tendered by the Crown on the impaired mental functioning of Sokaluk and also whether he was indeed fit to stand trial. In his report, Professor Ogloff stated, due to his denial that he had in fact committed the offences, noting the report was written prior to the County Court trial, it was not possible to determine any possible motivation, but that he does meet a diagnosis of autism spectrum disorder, with an impoverished level of intellectual functioning.

Professor Ogloff, however, further went on to say as referred to by the Court of Appeal:

…it is my opinion that Mr Sokaluk does not meet the criteria for a diagnosis of pyromania…while Mr Sokaluk does have several characteristics associated with firesetters, there are a number of important criteria lacking (e.g. the abuse of substances, general criminal offending, antisociality)…it is likely that his motivation was either expressive (as a result of his social inadequacy) or instrumental (to achieve a particular extrinsic goal).[109]

---

108   Ibid-paras 15-17.

109   *DPP v Brendan James Sokaluk* [2013] VSCA 48- para 20.

It is somewhat difficult to exactly determine what motivated Sokaluk and what his particular goal was, which was impeded by his intellectual disability, noting it was accepted that he never meant to kill anyone and he still maintains it was simply an accident. However, did he light the two separate fires so he could then report them and be looked upon as some sort of hero? Was his goal in lighting the fires simply because he wanted to help put them out or was he just fascinated with fire and watching his handiwork?

Did his volunteering with the CFA, which ended abruptly after less than one year, mean he held a grudge and this was all about pay back? Albeit many years later, noting his efforts to "dob in" a DSE firefighter, albeit to cover his tracks. If all these possible reasons of motivation are then taken into account, perhaps he falls under the phenomenon known as "firefighter arson".

Sokaluk was eligible for parole in June 2023 but was not released at the time, allegedly due to a paperwork issue. He was subsequently released after serving 15 years, in late April 2024, under strict parole conditions, including he remains in secure accommodation at least 80 kilometres from Churchill. His release, understandably, was met with some disdain from the local Churchill community, noting he still has a house there with family members still in residence, albeit his mother changed her surname for obvious reasons.

No doubt, Sokaluk will be closely monitored by police and, all going well, we won't hear from him again.

10
FIREFIGHTER OR FIRELIGHTER

The final report of the 2009 Victorian Bushfires Royal Commission, although determining that, 'the overall majority of firefighters do not have fire setting propensities,' their research suggested that there were a small number of firefighters who had such a tendency to intentionally set fires. For example, the royal commission referred to statistics from the NSW Police Strike Force Tronto, who after investigating 1600 suspicious fires, determined that eleven RFS volunteer firefighters were responsible and, subsequently, charged with various counts of arson.

The royal commission also obtained a report from eminent Professor James Ogloff of Monash University and Director of Psychological Services at the Victorian Institute of Forensic Mental Health. The learned professor, whilst identifying several "red flags" that could assist in detecting firefighters attracted to intentionally setting fires, considered, in any event, that they were a select group of offenders functioning at a higher level of intelligence than other arsonists.

This, of course to a degree, eliminated Churchill arsonist, Brendan Sokaluk, in the realm of firefighter arsonist, but Professor Ogloff was of the opinion that one of the indicators to identify such a person, was they would often be the first to respond to a fire even in situations when they had not been notified to attend as a responding unit. It was also considered that a firefighter arsonist had an uncanny ability to separately locate and report a fire that other members of the local community had not seen, combined with the expertise to somehow to know the fire's initial point of ignition.

The royal commission concluded that all firefighting agencies should continue to review and have in place proper screening procedures and to identify any criminal history of firefighters, including applicants, together with proper testing processes to assess and identify any psychological or behavioural issues which might render their suitability to become a member as inappropriate.[110]

Whilst firefighter arsonists are generally classified in a disproportionate number when compared to the usual type of arsonist, the term or motive known as hero syndrome can be one factor leading to the setting of a fire. In these types of situations, the fire is first lit and then reported by the perpetrator who follows up by responding and, in some situations, is first on the scene and proceeds to assist in extinguishing the blaze.

Such a "hero" is then recognised by others, particularly firefighter colleagues, as a hero or somewhat of a legend. Other

---

[110] Final Report of the 2009 Victorian Bushfires Royal Commission- Para 5.2.3.

motives can also come into play, such as boredom, perhaps sitting around in the fire station with not much to do, or excitement bordering on pyromania. There are also situations where the firefighter, now turned arsonist, is totally annoyed for whatever reason, with either his colleagues or his unit and then lights the fire as a means of payback or some sort of revenge.

These types of firefighters', now turned firelighters, motives have however, on the odd occasion, led to investigators completely ignoring obvious evidence that the fire may have been accidental. Such investigators must keep an open mind, other than simply forming the belief it is arson, until proven otherwise. Case in point was the investigation into the Marysville fire in country Victoria, which occurred on Saturday, 7 February 2009, claiming 40 lives and destroying, not only the town's main street, but around 400 buildings and houses.

For reasons only known to police and, without any physical evidence, they focused their attention, for some two-odd years, on a well-known and respected elderly local volunteer firefighter by the name of Ron 'Ronnie' Philpott. He had diligently served his community for some 50 years including as captain of the CFA Murrindindi unit since 2002. He was first brought to the attention of police as a possible suspect by SP Ausnet employees. They had attended to a reported power fault where the blaze was believed to have started at the Murrindindi Mill and told police of their suspicions.

This was despite reports of loud explosions and what was heard as "metal on metal", meaning most likely an electrical fault, just prior to the fire first being reported, which was attended by Ron, who lived about a kilometre from the mill.

Contrary to obviously a probable electrical fault, police zeroed in, without any evidence, but perhaps looked at the scenario of Ron first reporting and attending at the fire, so he must have started it. He was subsequently interviewed by police on a number of occasions and this was despite what appeared to be overwhelming evidence from witnesses of the electrical fault. This included technical evidence and photographs from an expert of frayed power lines that most likely had clashed. There was even one local resident who tried to tell police, when attending the mill fire, he drove across power lines that apparently had fallen down from a nearby paddock power pole.

These reports were rejected outright by police, saying they had absolutely no basis whatsoever and, in the middle of February 2009, further stated in support of their arson belief, 'This was a deliberate attempt to create a bushfire on a massive scale.'

The statement was then followed by a further press release in April 2009 with the Assistant Commissioner for Crime stating, they nearly had their man as the gap was closing, obviously referring to innocent Ron.

It was alleged by police that on interviewing him, there were a number of inconsistencies in his answers to questions put, that understandably, he put it down to being somewhat stressed, given he was being accused of some wrongdoing. He subsequently took a lie detector test, not at the instigation of police, but, of all places, on Channel Nine's, "A Current Affair" program. Now you would think that if Ron had anything to hide and he didn't, why would he go to this degree and subject himself to such public scrutiny but he did, noting his appearance and polygraph test was inconclusive and blamed solely by the interviewer on his nervousness and inability to sit still.

Victoria Police finally discontinued their investigation and rightly so, in respect of the much-loved Ron Philpott, with police citing that their exhaustive criminal investigation was over. They, believe it or not, were now engaging independent consultants to re-evaluate the original substantive theory that the ignition point of the fire was probably caused by faulty and clashing power lines.

Unfortunately, Ron passed away in September 2018 and went to his grave without any apology from police, but with all and sundry knowing the unfounded accusations and criticisms simply had no basis, whatsoever. May he now rest in peace.

Similar initial accusations also occurred in October 2002, following a disastrous fire at Abernethy in the NSW Hunter Valley region. A total of 13 homes were destroyed with the loss of life of one local, who was engulfed by fire when trapped in his motor vehicle. There was some suggestion of foul play by an investigator attached to the RFS, who admitted, on questioning before the NSW Independent Commission Against Corruption (ICAC), that he had informed a local resident who lost his home in the fire that there was most likely a cover up, but he had not played any part, a comment he later recanted. This fire had started only two kilometres from the Central Cessnock RFS fire station and within minutes of two fire trucks manned by volunteers departing for a training day.

A subsequent coronial inquest determined it was a deliberate case of arson, with an accelerant being used but exonerating any involvement or cover up involving the RFS trainees. One possible suspect that was investigated for this fire, which still remains unsolved despite a significant reward, was Cessnock RFS volunteer firefighter, Brendan Hokin.

Hokin had been charged with lighting a bushfire some four days before the fatal Abernethy fire, which he denied any involvement in and was supported by an alibi. Hokin did admit, however, to starting an earlier fire in Pokolbin, NSW, for which he was sentenced to 12 months imprisonment, with a non-parole period of only four months. In trying to establish his motive for lighting this fire, given he had been a volunteer for over six years and was seen by some as a hero after attending literally many hundreds of fires during that period, it begs the question, was he attracted to fire? Perhaps he was bored, or was he seeking further accolades from his peers, based on a hero type motive?

Surprisingly, it was none of the above and, for all intents and purposes, he probably does not fit into the designated classification of a firefighter arsonist, other than he was a firefighter and he did intentionally light a fire, but without any motive. His defence counsel, on his guilty plea, submitted to the court a psychological report that suggested his conduct was nothing more than a "cry for help" and that he was very remorseful.

It seems, at the time of setting the fire, he was suffering from depression, possibly stemming from being unemployed and fearing a relationship breakdown. Other factors in his favour, which perhaps supports the diagnosis of a cry for help, is that the fire was easily seen and he made no attempt to avoid detection, maybe wanting to be caught.

The firefighter turned firelighter hero syndrome was very obvious regarding the Black Christmas arsonist, Peter Burgess. He was a volunteer with the NSW RFS and he lit many of the fires that caused untold misery, particularly throughout the state from Christmas Eve 2001, starting in the Blue Mountains and fanned by strong winds. Burgess, on being arrested by police after they traced the calls to emergency services back to his mobile phone, said he was inspired by the heroics of the New

York firefighters, watching them rescue victims from the World Trade Centre, following the events, where terrorists hijacked two planes and crashed them into the buildings, now known as 9/11, in September 2001.

He wanted to be just like them and police considered he may have also been inspired by the Stalag 17 war movie. He had used the same method starting the fires as in the film, by crushing matchheads, placing them in a filtered cigarette and watching it slowly ignite in the bush undergrowth.

He was hoping his hero status, after he often first telephoned 000 then arrived at the fire scene proudly wearing his RFS uniform and assisted in extinguishing the blaze, would elevate him to a full-time career with the NSW Fire Brigade. One problem Burgess did have for an excuse was, one of his fires had been lit by him prior to 9/11, when he set a blaze near his home in Albury, NSW in January 2001. Burgess was certainly no hero though and was sentenced to a term of imprisonment of two years in June 2001, following a plea of guilty to lighting 25 fires.

Whilst some arsonists, on the odd occasion, may have no real motive for lighting a fire, the same cannot be said for volunteer firefighter, Jarred Brewer. He was a member of the Victorian Darraweit Guim CFA and it seems he became rather annoyed with his volunteer colleagues and abused them when he was denied access to a fire truck so he could assist in extinguishing a reported fire. On sentencing in the County Court of Victoria to three counts of intentionally causing a bushfire between November 2008 to January 2009, together with 16 counts of improper use of emergency services, the court was told the three fires, fortunately, did not result in any major damage.

Brewer also said to police they were simply backburns, so new members could get to ride on the fire trucks, including him. However, in respect of one fire at Mount Disappointment in November 2008, Brewer also made a number of calls to emergency services over two hours after starting this fire. His penchant for making Triple 0 calls also extended to other numerous occasions when he would report fires that did not exist, apparently on the basis, this would stretch emergency resources and result in his brigade being called out, with him on board. He even made a false emergency call on Christmas day, reporting that his tree, lined with presents from Santa Claus, had caught alight from, all things, a roast left in the oven.

So, it's obvious that Brewer had a few mental problems, apart from, on the one hand, being annoyed with his firefighter colleagues over being denied access to a unit truck and, on the other hand, he seemed to have an attraction to attending and fighting fires, including those that didn't exist. Apart from that, based on submissions to the court, he was of low intelligence and had an attraction to fire trucks which he got a thrill riding in.

Unfortunately for Brewer, his low intellectual capacity also assisted investigating police in finally determining that he was responsible. This was assisted by CCTV footage of him purchasing incriminating products, including a barbeque gas lighter and a box of fire starters, which he then left behind at one of his fires, along with his fingerprints. In addition, the use of his mobile phone, to report to Triple 0 the ambiguous fires, was also traced back to him, despite him removing his SIM card, apparently thinking the calls could not be traced. Brewer was sentenced to just under three years in a youth training centre.

Brewer's penchant for riding in fire trucks pales into insignificance compared to the perilous conduct of Nicholas Archer, sentenced in the County Court of Victoria by His Honour, Judge Smallwood, on 11 October 2016 to 14 years imprisonment, following his guilty plea to 12 counts of arson and other charges, including reckless endangerment and sabotage.

Archer can only be classified as a firebug and a dangerous one at that. He was also a Victorian CFA volunteer and his arson spree commenced in November 2009, when he set fire to the Newport Steam Rail Museum, apparently after being told he was not old enough to work there. Archer then contacted security in order to report the fire which caused $36,000 in damage.

His attraction to lighting fires and causing other mayhem continued over the next six years with around $4 million in damage, including a fire at the Melbourne Rail network and even derailing a train at the Hurstbridge rail station. On 16 June 2015, he ventured from his home, which was only a short distance from his local CFA station at Clonbinane and set fire to its communications room. He waited for the fire to properly ignite and then drove a truck from the station and telephoned Triple 0, to first report the building on fire and then assist other CFA volunteers in extinguishing the blaze. The overall damage was in the order of $600,000, but the CFA, being unaware of him as the culprit, lauded him as some sort of hero in trying to save the building, even sending out a newsletter to that effect.

His hero status, not just in his own eyes, was also perhaps illustrated further when during his offending, he would drive around town in a Toyota Landcruiser displaying registration plates CFA 4x4 with a CFA sticker, a yellow revolving light and a number of aerials as if to say, 'Look at me, look at me. I am a CFA firefighter.'

He would drive this vehicle to fires he lit, including one in a national park in December 2015, followed by other fires on total fire ban days in January and February 2016, knowing that he would also be called out with his unit to attend.

So, was his motive simply based on hero syndrome? Or were there other underlying reasons why he set out on such a maniacal spree, lighting fires unchecked and causing untold other damage? It did come to light during sentencing that he well knew his spate of fires would, in any event, result in him being called out to respond. This would be with either his CFA unit or as a member of Metro's disaster recovery team, where he worked. He enjoyed not only being on a fire truck but also getting to use a hose.

His excuse, however, for lighting one of the fires at the Newport Rail Steam Club was as a consequence of him being allegedly sexually assaulted. This was accepted by Justice Smallwood but not to the reason for lighting all the fires. There was a suggestion that after the Hurstbridge station damage, he tried to commit suicide.

Psychological and psychiatric reports, submitted on behalf of Archer, further indicated that neither alcohol nor drugs played any part in his offending, but there was also evidence of unrelated depression prior to carrying out the crimes and that he had an anxious personality disorder coupled with social phobia. Not surprisingly, what was also revealed in an expert report was Archer also had a penchant to collect firefighting photographs, together with associated memorabilia, apart from also suffering from anxiety and mood swings coupled with bouts of self-gratification.

One of the expert reports determined that Archer struggled to identify such a mood swing prior to setting a fire, but it was somewhat telling that he told a psychologist he wanted to be seen by his CFA colleagues as more than capable. His Honour rejected any notion of what could be considered as self-justification, which he described as bordering on vague.

Justice Smallwood took into account, the prosecution's case against Archer was largely based on self-admissions, including re-enactments of his crimes with police, noting that thankfully the last escapade on 13 February 2016, when in company with a co-accused, set fire to car tyres at the rear of a factory in Yarraville. They were pulled over by police, on seeing their vehicle in close proximity.

When asked by police about the tyre fire, Archer confessed straight up and said:

We started it, there no point in denying it. I used some firelighter liquid gel…it was my idea. A silly idea.

A subsequent search of his home under warrant by police located flammables, sparklers and fire extinguishers and again Archer made admissions saying:

I don't know why I keeping lighting fires. Why I do these things.

On sentencing, His Honour left no stone unturned to the extreme conduct of Archer and his avoiding detection over a number of years when he said:

I can safely say I believe that, in many years as a criminal lawyer and as a judge, I do not think I have seen a rampage from an adult approaching what you did over that period of time. [111]

The judge, although determining a lesser period for parole of nine years to what normally would be imposed, was still concerned to the risk of Archer re-offending on release, stating:

The risk of you re-offending again, I have no idea... The best I can do in this situation...for extremely serious offending, is to give you an opportunity for parole at a significantly earlier time...I am not in a position at this time, on the materials before me, and I doubt very much whether either the psychiatrist or the psychologist, to make a determination as to what the risks of you, if you become depressed or alienated or suffered grievances against somebody, would not resort to very similar offending. There has to be a risk involved in that and I am just unable to quantify... [112]

It is obvious that Archer has a few issues with his mental health, but I think it is fair to say that on his release, the community will still feel somewhat concerned this "wannabe firefighting hero", who well knew what he was doing, will reoffend. Maybe then, he will once again be brought before the court and perhaps this time sentenced as a serious arson offender.

From one extreme to another and this one-time volunteer, but a very disgruntled one at that, was hell bent on pay back to get even with his CFA colleagues. It seems that Andrew Robert Briggs lit his first fire about four weeks after he got his nose out

---

111 *DPP v Nicholas Archer* [2016] VCC 1522-para 13.

112 Ibid-para 135.

of joint. In other words, he was "pissed off", simply because his CFA unit didn't include him in a response to an extensive bushfire in February 2013. Luckily, the fire he lit in March 2013 was only minor, but he then lit a further four fires in late 2014 near the township of Great Western in Victoria, situated about 225 kilometres from Melbourne. Again, fortunately, only causing minor damage.

The 49-year-old Briggs was a clean skin with no criminal record and was first interviewed by police after the March 2013 fire, which was started about 1.5 kilometres from his home. Police observed Briggs checking out, what they didn't know at the time was, his handiwork and on being seen by both police and the CFA, he quickly left the scene. Investigators then found near this fire a quantity of paper, together with an IGA supermarket receipt, would you believe, in the name of Briggs.

For some unknown reason, he was not interviewed by police until April 2014 when he denied any involvement, but he did confirm he was very annoyed with his Great Western Brigade for not being allowed to attend the February 2013 bushfire. Despite physical evidence possibly connecting Briggs to the March 2013 fire, he was not charged by police and some months later in November 2014, he drove to the east of Great Western and set another fire which, thankfully, only destroyed a small area of bushland.

However, once again, he left behind some incriminating evidence, namely tyre marks which were later confirmed to be from his vehicle. He continued on his merry way and lit two more fires on 14 December 2014 in a dry creek bed, but this time police were closing in on their suspect, with his vehicle being recorded by Department of Environment and Primary Industry cameras set up near the fire scene.

Investigators, however, took a further cautious approach, obviously wanting more concrete evidence, so they placed a tracking device on his vehicle. On 19 December 2014, on his way to work, he lit another fire with the help of a candle and cigarette lighter, which caused damage to ten acres of vegetation. He was arrested the same day and a search of his motor vehicle located a number of firelighters, including packets of matches, together with a large quantity of toilet paper and newspapers. Briggs readily made a number of admissions to police, again confirming his grudge towards his local CFA members, that he was very angry and trying to "piss off" the fire brigade members who had giving him a hard time.

Briggs appeared in the County Court of Victoria before His Honour, Judge Taft, for sentencing on 19 October 2016, where he pleaded guilty to four counts of having recklessly caused a bushfire, together with a further charge of possessing items for the purpose of destroying or damaging property. A psychological report was tendered to the court where Professor Ogloff commented on the motivation of Briggs to set these fires:

...lit the fire at times when he had been angry and seeking revenge for his perceived slights by others... setting fires became a way of overcoming feelings of anger and resentment... thinking about planning, carrying out actions toward and ultimately successfully setting the fires, gave him a sense of power and control... Setting fires was the one thing in his life that he controlled and mastered...[113]

His Honour, on sentencing Briggs to only nine months

---

113   *DPP v Andrew Robert Briggs* [2016] VCC 1557–paras 32 and 33.

imprisonment and on release to a three-year CCO, took into account he had no prior convictions, that he was certainly no pyromaniac and, as supported by Professor Ogloff, only posed a medium risk propensity to reoffend on release. It is, of course, hoped that this get even, now ex firefighter, will learn by his mistakes and correct his ways and that he does compensate the CFA to the sum of $40,000 in restitution as ordered by the court. [114]

Whilst Briggs was certainly not good at covering his tracks and avoiding detection after setting the fires, His Honour still ordered a forensic sample by way of buccal swab be taken, [115] to ensure, at the very least, his DNA remains on record, just in case.

One volunteer firefighter, by the name of Alex Gordon Noble, was deemed to fit the definition of pyromaniac, after lighting a total of 15 separate fires during 2012 and 2013, including one which destroyed an historic house in Lake Macquarie, NSW. He first commenced his arson spree in 2012 going undetected and then during his increasing reign of terror, his deliberately lit fires also burnt around 3,000 hectares of land endangering the community and also destroyed the Big Prawn service station situated on the Pacific Highway at Crangan Bay in 2013. After starting his fires, he would then report the blaze and attend to put the fire out while wearing his RFS unform. He subsequently came to the attention of police by his consistent quick responses to the fires to douse the flames.

There was no doubt his fires were carefully planned and orchestrated, initially telling police it was also about wanting to gain experience in fighting fires, so he could hopefully one

---

114 Ibid-para 56.

115 Ibid-para 55.

day become a full-time professional firefighter. His reasoning though, started to fall apart when it was discovered on his Facebook account, images depicting fires with scorching flames. A psychiatric report subsequently determined he was, in fact, fascinated by fire and clearly fitted the category of a pyromaniac.

He was initially sentenced in the Newcastle Local Court in 2014 to two years jail and in 2016 by the District Court to a total of eight years in jail, with a non-parole period of five years. The court noted, although he had expressed genuine sorrow for his actions, his conduct was pure recklessness causing substantial damage.

Another firefighter, who lit two separate fires and would then report them, so he could quickly attend at his local fire station in order to be sent out to fight the blaze, was a 20-year-old volunteer by the name of Keegan Danielz. He became qualified as a wildlife firefighter after joining his local CFA Brigade at Silvan, Victoria in July 2013. He readily became experienced in fighting fires and yet, for some stupid reason, later described by him to police as a "brain fart", as he was in "a shit of a mood", he lit two separate fires, some 200 metres apart in the Dandenong Ranges on Saturday, 21 March 2015 when fire restrictions were in place.

His efforts first began to unravel when police ascertained that Danielz was the first person to report the fire to his CFA colleagues wanting, in his vernacular, 'A code 1 response,' which was then followed by other witnesses in the area telephoning emergency services.

Danielz rushed to his brigade station, being the first to arrive and attended with other volunteers to help extinguish the blaze. Police interviewed him some days later, possibly under the pretence that they wanted to examine the footage of his attendance fighting the fire, taken from his helmet camera. It showed he even suggested at the time that the fire was deliberately lit.

He was asked to provide an explanation of where he was prior to the fire being reported and he lied, telling police he was with a mate in Lilydale, enjoying a Big Mac at McDonald's, when they first saw smoke coming from the fire in question. His story was corroborated by his mate who knew it was false. In any event, he later recanted his statement, but it all came to an abrupt end when police viewed the CCTV footage from McDonald's at the time they were supposed to be eating their meal. Lo and behold, they did not appear.

Danielz was subsequently arrested and quickly made admissions at getting his so-called witness to lie for him, while he was lighting the first fire on 21 March 2015 with a lighted match thrown from his car window, but he emphatically denied lighting the second fire. He showed some remorse for his conduct, although he described in detail to police that he felt bouts of loneliness and that 'the CFA was like a family to him.'

His Honour, Chief Justice Kidd, on sentencing Danielz in the County Court of Victoria with his plea of guilty to two charges of recklessly causing a bushfire and a charge of perjury, was concerned with his denial in lighting the second fire and said further:

You have never given an account of lighting the second fire... denied lighting the second fire...all I have is a bare plea of guilty...charge two...the fact you never offered any explanation for the second fire is troubling...[116]

---
116   *DPP v Keegan Danielz* [2015] VCC 1506-para 29.

His Honour ordered Danielz to serve 15 months in a youth detention centre with the usual forensic sample order, after taking into account his plea of guilty. He had no prior convictions and, apart from him lighting two separate fires causing only minimal damage, he was generally of good character with prospects for rehabilitation. He was addressing some obvious psychological issues, with the court accepting that the Verdins principles applied. His Honour, however, did comment on the fact as a member of the CFA, this made his conduct more serious and certainly displayed an abuse of his membership. [117]

Surprisingly, his defence counsel initially submitted to the court that, given his client participated in helping his CFA colleagues fight the fire, somehow this mitigated his offending. Such tenuous submission was rightly rejected by His Honour.[118] It seems the only motive in this case can be put down to the fact that Danielz just simply wanted to join his CFA mates in fighting his two deliberately lit fires.

A cry for help or simply wanting to be involved in helping his firefighting brigade members was apparently what motivated Stephen Kenneth Johnson of the Donnybrook State Emergency Service (SES) and local bushfire brigade in Argyle, WA. He lit three separate bushfires in December 2015 requiring, for one of the fires, the attendance of aerial water bombers to extinguish the blaze at an estimated cost in excess of $500,000. Johnson displayed the usual characteristics of first lighting the fire and then waiting to be called out by his brigade to help extinguish his handiwork, as he simply wanted to be involved. Johnson was so helpful, he would even contact police

---

117   Ibid-para 32.

118   Ibid-para 36.

and provide details about motor vehicles he observed in the vicinity of each fire. Such details, of course, being false.

He was subsequently diagnosed with depression and most likely suffering from a post-traumatic stress disorder (PTSD) possibly, with "tongue in cheek", related to his fire lighting escapades. Johnson was sentenced in 2016 to three years and four months jail, with a non-parole period of 20 months.

Volunteer firefighter, Blake William Banner, was not only good at putting out fires, but he also learnt a technique in how to start one. His claim to fame was adopting a clear plastic water container as a magnifying glass, which would then ignite the blaze. The Black Summer bushfires in late 2019 were difficult enough for local communities and certainly no thanks to Banner.

After police placed a listening device in his vehicle, he was arrested and charged with lighting seven fires in the months of October and November 2019 in the Bega Valley in the far south coast of NSW. It was alleged by police on one occasion, after lighting a fire in a dry riverbed on a total fire ban day, he panicked after trying to extinguish it and left hurriedly, later returning with his local RFS unit to help put it out.

Banner appeared before Justice Tupman in a judge alone trial in October 2020 on seven counts of cause fire and be reckless to its spread,[119] for which he pleaded not guilty. Her Honour acquitted Banner of six charges, but determined he was guilty on count seven, being the setting of the fire in a dry riverbed in late November 2019. Banner, with a history of mental illness and particularly PTSD after the death of his brother in a motor vehicle crash, had also now been diagnosed with borderline autism spectrum disorder. Banner, however,

---

119   *Crimes Act 1900* (NSW)-section 203E.

accepted and understood why his local community were very angry towards him and was very remorseful.

Taking into account his strict bail conditions for some 34 months while waiting for his trial, which included the condition he could not leave his house between the hours of 8pm and 6am, he was sentenced to a two-year intensive corrections order (ICO).[120] This also included a strict condition that he undergoes mental health treatment.[121]

A South Australian volunteer firefighter with over 30 years' service was arrested and convicted on seven counts of starting bushfires in the Adelaide Hills on a day of extreme fire risk in January 2021, which destroyed two homes and around 2,700 hectares of bushland, with 2000 firefighters and staff and around 400 appliances attending the blazes. Gregory McGannon steadfastly maintained his innocence, despite evidence by two police officers that they saw him light one of the fires, then fled the scene in his motor vehicle, which just happened to have defaced number plates, with police in hot pursuit.

On being pulled over, he had an alcohol reading of 0.145 which is a good drink, being nearly three times over the limit. Police also found two cigarette lighters, one in the boot of his vehicle. McGannon told police he had observed a person starting the fire and he then "tapped it out". The other problem, saying he had nothing to do with starting the fires, was CCTV footage of him in the Adelaide Hills region, together with mobile phone data tracing him from his home to the first fire.

Despite his defence counsel submitting it could not be

---

[120] *Crimes (Sentencing Procedure) Act 1999* (NSW)-section 7(1).

[121] *R v Banner* [2022] Unreported, NSWDC. Judge Tupman 7 July 2022.

proven beyond reasonable doubt the same person started all the fires, that didn't wash with the jury. They found him guilty in September 2023, after less than five hours deliberation on all seven counts, together with dangerous driving when he tried to avoid police when leaving the scene of one of the fires. McGannon, of course, could have chosen to give evidence before the jury in his defence, but on the advice of his lawyers, maintained his silence, which was his right. He let the prosecution prove its case, which they did.

Victim impact statements read out in court certainly brought home the reality of the personal devastation caused by the fires lit by McGannon. One such statement was on behalf of an elderly couple who lost their much-loved home of 40 years, together with all their personal possessions.

Another victim also said in respect of the aftermath:

…was only made worse by the denial of a man who was fully aware…deliberately driving from one location…starting fires and watching them take hold, light a match and drive away.

South Australia's Country Fire Service Chief, Brett Loughlin, in describing the actions of McGannon as abhorrent, also brought home the dangers faced by his fire crews:

Our people knew they were under considerable pressure to do whatever they could to prevent the next Ash Wednesday type impact from occurring…At times the fire behaviour was so intense it threatened to overrun firefighters on the ground who faced walls of flame and searing heat as they went about their duties…

He then went onto say that:

This trauma is only amplified when they know that multiple roadside ignition points means that the fires are not accidental… but instead, the wilful and deliberate actions of a criminal who wants to destroy local communities and put our firefighters at risk…

McGannon was subsequently sentenced in April 2024 to 13 years imprisonment in respect of the fires, together with a further 12 months for dangerous driving, with Judge Telfer unable to come to any conclusion for his motive. He will be eligible for parole in in January 2030.

One volunteer firefighter who escaped a lengthy prison sentence was Jude Craig Wright, setting a total of nine fires, one of which was on Boxing Day 2021 in Perth, WA. This particular fire, in the east of Perth, resulted in a house, farm buildings and machinery being totally destroyed with damage estimated to be in the order of $1 million. The 18-year-old Wright lit more bushfires over the summer period of December 2021 through to January 2022, by continually setting paper alight and throwing the burning package out of his vehicle, hoping it would set fire to roadside bushland.

Well, it certainly did, with one of his fires causing significant damage to the Perth to Kalgoorlie pipeline. When he was finally arrested in late January 2022, Wright told police, 'I done it, I just don't know why.'

On pleading guilty in the District Court of WA in February 2023, his defence counsel described his autistic client as having the 'mental age of a child'. Despite this though, he said further that Wright well knew he would be called on to attend the fires he lit and it would help him feel wanted and valued by the local community.

Despite the WA State Prosecutor submitting that an immediate term of imprisonment was applicable, District Court Judge Whitby who, at times in the sentencing remarks admonished Wright for his conduct, took into account the nine months he had already served whilst on remand, and that any further term of imprisonment would not be in his better interests. The court also accepted in mitigation that during his time in custody, he had been assaulted, being set on fire by other inmates and he was now suffering from PTSD.

It was also noted in his favour that when he was finally released on bail, after the nine months on remand, he had undertaken some degree of rehabilitation. In the circumstances and that in the learned judge's opinion, he did not pose any further risk to the community, a three-year jail sentence with two years wholly suspended was appropriate, providing he be under supervision and continued with his rehabilitation.

This meant, with time already served, Wright walked free from court supported by his family and friends. Support him they certainly did, with the audacity to abuse waiting media who simply wanted a comment from Wright on the court outcome. Never mind, of course, the havoc and destruction this "wanna-be" firefighter, turned firelighter, caused, including to one poor elderly woman who escaped the inferno of her house as it burnt to the ground, being left with nothing but the clothes on her back and luckily her vehicle.

Another now former volunteer firefighter who also walked free from court was Jack Hardidge, after being effectively let off with a light slap on the wrist. He was initially charged with a total of 15 offences, which included 13 of intentionally causing a fire and letting it spread recklessly. These grass fires, which didn't result in major property damage, were lit in the NSW Hunter region in July and August 2023, because Hardidge was apparently bored. He would then return to quell them as a part of his brigade duties with the RFS. Obviously, being very proud of his work, he would then take a few mates out to show them his handiwork, no doubt bragging how he put them out.

The only thing that probably saved him from some time inside, was a plea deal in that he would plead guilty to eight offences of lighting the fires on the basis that a further four on the same charge would be taken into consideration by the Cessnock Local Court in respect of sentencing. Hardidge has to perform 250 hours community work as part of a 12-month intensive corrections order. It's fair to say he won't be seen again wearing his RFS uniform.

The infamous conduct of these wannabee firefighters with their local brigades pales into insignificance when compared to the despicable efforts of some selective firefighter arsonists in the US. The first was a firefighter trainee who also just wanted to prove himself to his brigade colleagues that he was, in fact, quite competent and could fight "real fires".

William Celtruda, after a drinking session at his local fire station, drove a fire truck in his inebriated state and set fire to a home early one morning in July 2008 and then, of course, was one of the first responders. He was at it again on 12 August 2008. This time setting fire to two houses, one of which was set not long after the first fire because he had not been called out to attend that blaze. He was subsequently sentenced to a maximum of 14 years imprisonment and will serve at least 10 years, being the mandatory term in respect of first-degree arson. He was also sued civilly by the owner of the destroyed home regarding the first blaze.

Another rookie volunteer firefighter, Caleb Lacey, apparently became extremely frustrated after joining the Nassau County Lawrence-Cedarhurst Fire Brigade in October 2008. His frustration stemmed from the fact he was called to attend around 90 emergency calls, all of which were not fire related. Interesting though, he never attended any call outs between midnight and 7am until the fire he had set, which was only a short distance from where he lived.

He went quickly to his fire station, put on his firefighting uniform and equipment and then rushed to the fire. This fatal apartment fire, which had no fire escape, resulted in the deaths of a mother and three of her children. Fortunately, two other sons were able to escape the blaze through a rear window. Prosecutors led evidence that, in their view, the motivation of Lacey in lighting the fire was nothing but a 'twisted bid to become a hero again.'

He was subsequently found guilty after a jury trial in 2010 and convicted of four counts of murder and manslaughter involving arson and reckless endangerment, being sentenced to 25 years to life in prison. Lacey subsequently appealed the Nassau County Court judgment, still professing his innocence on the basis that the evidence did not support his conviction as sentenced. According to him, he was not properly cautioned on his right to silence, known in the US as the Miranda warning and often called "Miranda Rights".[122] Such warning as stated:

You have the right to remain silent. Anything you say can be used against you in court. You have the right to talk to a lawyer (attorney) for advice before we ask you any questions. You have the right to have a lawyer with you during questioning. If you

---

122 See the decision in *Miranda v Arizona* 384.U.S.436(1966).

cannot afford a lawyer, one will be appointed for you before any questioning if you wish. If you decide to answer questions now without a lawyer present, you have the right to stop answering at any time.

On Lacey's version of events, he was not told by interviewing police of his rights and, indeed, one allegedly said to him that he had 'major problems.' The Appeal Court had no issue in rejecting his appeal as it simply was without merit and that in any event, his guilt had been established beyond reasonable doubt.[123]

Suspects can waive their right to silence and such "Miranda Waiver" will allow investigating police to continue or resume questioning their suspect. However, as in all adversarial systems of justice, such waiver by a suspect must be voluntary and not subject to any coercion, as a court will closely monitor the defendant's choice to waive their rights and ensure they fully understood their right to silence and a lawyer. [124]

Obtaining a confession from a guilty person is, of course, the ultimate aim of any investigator when interviewing a suspect, as it certainly makes the task of proving guilt beyond reasonable doubt a certainty. Another tool that can assist to achieve that aim is not widely known or even used by investigators. It is called a computer voice stress analyser device (CVSA). Such device measures components of a human voice and determines signs of stress, to a degree, it is similar to a polygraph which measures and records rises in blood pressure and pulse, for example, except in a CVSA there are no wires attached.

---

123   *The People(respondent)v Lacey(appellant)* (2012).

124   Also see for further example-*Law Enforcement (Powers and Responsibilities) Act 2002* (NSW).

The use of a CVSA instrument brought to justice in Whites Crossing, Pennsylvania, volunteer fireman, Benjamin Christensen, who went about lighting multiple fires during February 2007 to March 2008, which caused in excess of $3 million in damage, destroying homes and businesses. Crime unit detectives, whilst interviewing Christensen over allegations of sexual assault, which he admitted to and was now facing a count of statutory rape as he was over 25 years of age, couldn't keep quiet and started telling detectives that he was indeed a volunteer firefighter who had attended many fires assisting in extinguishing them as part of his brigade duties. Police then put to him dates and times of certain suspicious fires they were in the throes of investigating and he inadvertently confirmed that he had indeed responded to some of these fires but denied, on further questioning, that he was in fact responsible.

Whilst, at this point in their investigation, his denials seemed to have merit, to make sure of his innocence, he was invited and accepted to undergo a CVSA interrogation in order to further exonerate him or perhaps put him in the spotlight as the arsonist. It's fair to say he didn't do very well as the algorithm chart indicated, quite clearly, ranges of stress in his voice when answering questions. This led to detectives questioning him further, showing him the results of the CVSA, which strengthened their view that he was very evasive, bordering on trying to cover up guilt.

When challenged further with the compelling evidence, he first confessed to lighting two fires, followed by a full confession, admitting to starting a total of seven fires. He was so upfront he even dobbed in a mate who had acted in concert with him. Christensen was sentenced to 10-20 years in prison, plus 20 years' probation, together with a restitution order in the sum of $3 million. The only consolation for him was his rape sentence was to be served concurrently with the arson convictions.

On sentencing, it was submitted that he had selected his building arson targets, knowing they were vacant, to make sure there were no victims. Psychological evidence confirmed he been in a number of psychiatric facilities and suffered from schizophrenia. His now not-so-friendly mate copped four to 16 years in prison. The use of CVSA technology has been recommended to, not only law enforcement as a tool to assist their investigations, but also to fire departments with applicant screening which, perhaps, the latter may have identified Christensen as not suitable as a firefighter.

Serial arsonist and former volunteer firefighter, Christopher Message, had 10 years in prison to reflect on his crimes, after setting fires during 2011 in three separate towns in Connecticut, US, resulting in massive damage. Message pleaded guilty to arson and reckless burning of 11 separate fires, brought on by a history of psychiatric issues, coupled with bouts of heavy drinking. Message, who appeared to be remorseful stating he had simply no excuses for his conduct, was also ordered on release to undertake 100 hours of community service and make restitution for the damage caused by his arson spree.

The firefighter son of one of the most respected brigade members in Montana, US, was convicted in February 2024 of two counts of felony arson, for lighting fires in July 2021 and found not guilty on a further two counts. Craig Allen McCrea was sentenced to a total of 60 years in prison with 30 years suspended and a non–parole period of 15 years. One of the fires in Boulder destroyed 31 homes and outbuildings, with over

2,600 acres being consumed and another eight homes damaged in the area of Flathead Lake.

Evidence was presented to the jury, which included fire investigators referring to the fires as "hot starts", meaning they were intentionally set with lighters or matches with no accelerant used. The girlfriend of McCrea was initially thought to be involved when under a Geofence warrant, data from her mobile phone determined she was in very close vicinity to three of the fires. Such warrant allows investigators to request from Google any and all data within a nominated area, followed by a separate warrant providing access to a mobile, also known as cellular phone data, which then pinpoints the exact location of such device at any given time.

On being interviewed by police, she initially denied any knowledge but then made admissions implicating McCrea, in that he would leave their vehicle to light a fire usually with a torch. To further assist police, she agreed to make a telephone call to him, which was recorded and later used in evidence, in which McCrea insisted she needed to deny any knowledge as the only evidence investigators would have, as far as he was concerned, was if she confessed to being present. Even a recorded call to the father of McCrea would have him telling her nearly the same, citing two cases in the past he knew of, when suspected arsonists were acquitted because no one actually saw them light the fires.

Her evidence at the trial in the Polson District Court was compelling, although she stated she did not see him light the fires after alighting from the vehicle, but the DNA of McCrea was located on a drinking straw left at one of the fires, together with a knife in a sheaf that his, now ex-girlfriend said belonged to McCrea. This potential piece of evidence may have been more useful to the prosecution, if one of the fire investigators had collected if from a fire crime scene wearing gloves, which he admitted he failed to do.

The father of McCrea, who had been involved in fighting fires for over 50 years, admitted in evidence that his son had questioned him on how hard it would be to detect and catch an arsonist and, when shown photos of a suspect seen near one of the fires, he admitted it was most likely his son. The defence argued, without success, that the fires were, in fact, lit by the girlfriend of the accused, based on her mobile phone that was detected in close proximity to each of the fires. In addition, they submitted she had only assisted the prosecution by giving such evidence, due to also facing unrelated criminal charges and on that basis, was hoping to receive some leniency on sentencing for her evidence against the accused.

McCrea, father of seven children, also had a lengthy criminal record, particularly for dealing in drugs and had already been on remand pending trial for a total of 730 days. At a pre-sentence hearing, his father asked the judge for some leniency stating, in his view, he didn't believe his son was responsible. His Honour, in a curt response, took that to task saying the jury also disagreed and that:

What do you think of a guy who goes out and deliberately starts a fire? The guy who has done millions of dollars' worth of damage, displaces dozens of people, shuts down a community for two weeks, costs the tribes over a million dollars in lost resources. And God knows how much more to firefighters…

The judge, on sentencing, made a somewhat unusual, but compelling comment when he said:

I must consider the seriousness of the offence and the criminal history that he's got and his behaviour over all these years… And now, the chicken's come home to roost and he's going to have to deal with it. And I'm sorry about that…

The chickens certainly came to roost for one of the worst of the worst, being disgruntled firefighter, Ray J Norton Jnr, whose criminal endeavours were supported by an air force fireman and some misguided US Boston police officers. They were all involved in a conspiracy that led to what was seen as the largest arson case in US history and sometimes referred to with the catch cry, 'Boston is on Fire.'

Such conspiracy, over a ten-month period in 1982 and 1983, led to around 264 separate fires to premises including factories, churches and even the Massachusetts Fire Academy, resulting in $22 million in damage and injuries, including to civilians and 270 firefighters with several permanently disabled. These string of fires were all over trying to convince Boston authorities to re-employ hundreds of firefighters and police who had been terminated, including the closure of several fire stations, due to budget cuts.

It seems, their faulty reasoning was that by lighting the fires, the city of Boston would have no choice but to re-employ those laid off due to the persistent crime wave, notably arson. In some way, it could be described as a terrorist act, with buildings on fire and the constant wailing of fire alarms from responding units, literally terrorising the city. Arson Squad investigators slowly and methodically found those responsible after seeing some television footage and mobile phone tracking, then finding some incriminating evidence following a search warrant.

One of the other perpetrators, Donald Francis Stackpole,

from a Boston security company, would even attend some of the fires in a red station wagon, posing as a fire chief. They also had a handwritten note from a "Mr Flare" put together in different fonts and sizes from newspapers which read:

I'm Mr Flare. You know me as the Friday firebug…I will continue till all deactivated police and fire equipment is brought back.

Investigators had also determined the fires were lit, using what was loosely described as a "La Bomba", which was an incendiary device put together in a plastic bag with a zip, filled with fuel and then placed in a paper bag with tissues before being lit. It was also sometimes placed in used car tyres. Mr Flare, alias former police officer, Gregg Bemis, together with Norton and seven other conspiracists, are now serving prison terms ranging from five to 60 years in prison.

Stackpole and Norton did appeal their convictions and sentences on the basis of alleged errors by the judge during their separate trials. Such objections were dismissed by the US Court of Appeals as these lacked any merit.[125]

It is quite obvious, however, that the worst convicted US serial arsonist was former fire investigator, John Leonard Orr, who during his reign of terror over seven years earned a number of nicknames such as "The Pillow Pyro" as he set fire to polyfoam type materials, "Frito Bandito" being an animated mascot and, for some reason, "The Coin-Tosser".

This tosser, for want of a better description, grew up in

---

125 *United States of America, Appellee, v Donald Francis Stackpole, Defendant, Appellant; United States of America, Appellee v Ray J Norton, Jr; Defendant, Appellant* 811 F2D 689(1st Cir.1987).

Los Angeles, California and first became a member of the US Air Force, where he perhaps initially gained an attraction to fires as a member of its firefighting school.

On leaving the military in 1971, due to a dislike for superior officers, he then attempted to first join the Los Angeles Police Department (LAPD) but was rejected after failing its entrance requirements. He was subsequently accepted into the Glendale Fire Department in 1974 and by studying the science of fire part time, he was promoted to the rank of captain and arson investigator.

Orr's fire lighting journey, coupled with investigating such fires, began in October 1984 with a blaze in a hardware store in South Pasadena, California, resulting in the death of four innocent victims, including a two-year-old child. Arson investigators initially determined the fire was started by faulty electrical writing, but in comes our hero, Orr as a follow up investigator and states quite empathetically, no it was definitely arson, knowing of course that it was, because he lit it.

For the next seven years, until 1991, Orr would go on an arson spree that simply had no comparison, causing literally tens of millions of property damage, using a lit cigarette wrapped up in paper and held together by a rubber band. In January 1987 in Bakersfield, California, a number of deliberately lit fires followed an arson investigators conference in nearby Fresno and attended by Orr. Crime scene investigators at this fire were able to locate a piece of paper, which was believed to be connected to an incendiary device, together with a fingerprint.

Suspicions that this fire was carried out by one of the arson investigators at Fresno, gained prominence following a number of further fires around the coast of California. Once again, a seminar for arson investigators was being held nearby, so putting together the list of attendees at both conferences, a number of possible suspects were highlighted and, you guessed it, one of which was Orr.

However, it was back to square one as the fingerprint found at the Bakersfield fire could not be matched to the short list of suspects. The possible perpetrators, including Orr, were cleared of any wrongdoing. In view of the senior position of Orr as a fire investigator, perhaps they felt their suspicions were not justified and maybe they needed to look elsewhere.

However, no one should be above suspicion and, thanks to fingerprint technology and the laziness of Orr, a further fingerprint, taken from a crime scene at one of a number of suspicious fires lit around Los Angeles during late 1990 and the beginning of 1991, this time matched our man. This was thanks to an LAPD fingerprint data base which included all previous applicants wanting to join, one of which was Orr. So, at this point, investigators had Orr firmly in their sights, but a sole matching fingerprint was not sufficient to tie Orr into the number of fires they believed were lit by him.

Orr, of course, could possibly use the excuse that one of his disgruntled colleagues had set him up. These co-workers had, in fact, seen Orr as a bit strange, as he would often pursue shoplifters and house burglars in his fire truck. But he was also considered very clever as he always knew how to extinguish the blaze, even knowing the location of the closest fire hydrant. He also seemed to have a gift in determining what caused the fire. He was blessed, somehow being the one who first responded to a fire, but he was never a suspect in their eyes.

Further dedicated surveillance techniques were then out in place to watch Orr's every move, including placing a tracking device in his vehicle, which he later uncovered but was told by police it was a hoax. However, unbeknown to Orr, a further tracking device was placed in his vehicle and this time there was no doubt as he was tracked to another suspicious fire. They finally had their suspect.

He was placed under arrest at his home and a thorough search, including of his vehicle, uncovered further incriminating evidence: in a black bag, components for his incendiary device with a matching fingerprint on a piece of paper, together with binoculars, rubber bands and two cigarette lighters, noting Orr didn't smoke.

The final nail in Orr's coffin was found in his home. It was a draft 350-page manuscript, written by him, the equivalent to a confession in a police record of interview regarding his fire lighting exploits, including specific details of the murder by arson at the South Pasadena hardware store. Details only Orr could have possibly known.

Orr, despite pleading his innocence, was initially convicted in July 1992 of three charges of arson and sentenced to 30 years jail. Subsequently, in 1998, he was further tried and convicted on four counts of murder and 21 charges of arson during his spree over seven years commencing in 1984. this included, what can only be described as, a firestorm in Glendale in 1990 which destroyed 67 homes. Orr will no doubt meet his maker from prison as he will never be released, serving concurrent terms of life in prison without the possibility of parole. In the US, a death penalty has to be a unanimous verdict by the jury and in Orr's case they were deadlocked at eight to four.

At sentencing for the 1984 hardware store murderous fire, the Superior Court Judge commented that his crimes showed:

...great violence and sophistication...the enormity of the

defendant's crimes should not be understated…he embarked on a campaign of setting arson fires that is remarkable in the number of fires he set and in the expert way he set them…[126]

This notorious serial arsonist is believed to have set in the vicinity of around 2,000 separate fires during his seven-year arson spree. Distinctly, he set such fires during daylight hours in unoccupied businesses and buildings and even grassland settings, by using his noted incendiary time delay device. His frequent and powerful desires certainly fit the category of a serial pyromaniac, as it was obvious he simply loved lighting fires. However, was there an underlying problem with Orr that was associated with his fire setting? An interview with one of his daughters, after he was convicted and tried, suggests there was more than an attraction to just lighting fires on a regular basis.

In an interview in June 2018 with Lori Orr Kovach, she said she and sister Carrie first saw their father as some type of hero, but that all changed after he was arrested and convicted. In making reference to her father's so called fiction novel "Points of Origin", which formed part of the evidence against him, she said:

It was disgusting to read his book, that was supposed to be fiction and having in the back of my mind that he wrote it about himself. It was horrible to think that's exactly what he was doing; watching something burn and doing those horrible sexual things.[127]

---

126 United States of America v John Leonard Orr 29F.3d 636(1998)- also see United States of America, *Plaintiff-appellee, v John Leonard Orr, Defendant- appellant*, 29 3d 636(9th Cir.1994).

127 True Crime Blog-My Firefighter Father John Orr Got Sexual Thrills from his Murderous Arson-interview with Maria Ricapito.

It is obvious, by Orr's own admission in his book, which he to this day argues was fiction, a very well chronicled exact enactment of the fire lighting deeds of a firefighter in Southern California, he suffers from pyrophilia as he appears to gain sexual arousal associated with fire. He even talks in the book, about stroking an erection while watching a fire. Orr still has illusory visions of self-grandeur as, while he serves life in prison, he has published a number of accounts of his time and exposure to prison life. In other words, real life accounts just like his unpublished book on arson.

Orr can certainly be elevated, for want of a better word, to one of the worst serial arsonists in modern times. Even perhaps to the notorious "worst of the worst" serial arsonists, but of course, there are many others who fit the same bill.

11
WORST OF THE WORST

Renowned, now retired, FBI special agent, John E Douglas, has written a number of books and not only his own autobiography, but true crime novels. The concept of serial arson and an appropriate definition can perhaps be attributed to him in which he described it:

Serial arson is an offence committed by fire setters who set three or more fires, but with a significant cooling off period between the fires.[128]

Other definitions state that a serial arsonist is someone who habitually and compulsively sets fires and can also fall under the pyromania category. In other words, an impulsive control type of disorder with a pathological desire to set fires.

The definition of serial arson may well be confused with

---

[128] Crime Classification Manual: A Standard System for Investigating and Classifying Violent Crimes-Douglas, Et Al, 1992.

a concept known as spree arson, which is normally attributed to an arsonist who lights two or three separate fires, usually one after the other with no cooling off period to gather their thoughts. Men certainly commit more arson than women, but they can also carry out such a crime, but generally less often. In any event, we have certainly witnessed, over time, many different types of arsonists or firebugs, whether they be considered in the spree category, serial or pyromaniac, with some of these miscreants placed in the category of the worst of the worst.

One serial arsonist, during his arson reign lighting, all up 21 separate fires in Michigan, US, during the period 1924 to 1926 was Grover Cleveland Pauter, with the only loss of life being some nesting hens. His spree included setting fire to businesses, a church, houses, a school and even his own home. Pauter was already known to police for minor assaults and battery, including belting his father-in-law and a breach of liquor licencing laws where he served 90 days in the Lenawee County lock up.

Police had absolutely no idea he was the local firebug, however, they soon formed the view, given the number of fires, there had to be a pyromaniac on the loose. His modus operandi was normally a combination of using oil and matches to set fire to paper and straw and, after setting his handiwork, would then quickly leave the scene. He even set fire to a barn and wheat silo and most probably encouraged after watching a fireworks display. Thankfully, this would be his last fire.

What followed was his arrest for one of his many assaults, this time being his second wife. He was sent again to the county jail for 14 days on remand, pending further enquiries. Pauter had obviously annoyed his now-divorced first wife and she went to police and told them about suggestive comments he had made to her, after reading in the local newspaper about the series of fire, which firmly put him in the frame that he knew a lot more and who was responsible. When police put to him the allegations, he finally confessed to all the fires after a night of heavy questioning, even suggesting his former and current wives had accompanied him on what he called "trips". Police later exonerated the women from having any involvement.

Pauter pleaded guilty in December 1926 to the 21 fires and was sentenced to 35 years, to be served at the Jackson Penitentiary. A subsequent Michigan State Trooper publication, in referring to the activities of Pauter, suggested his efforts consisted of 'one of the most amazing pyromania stories in the history of Michigan.'

He applied for parole in 1943 but was rejected on the ground that he was still a menace to society. This pyromaniac died in custody in 1963, aged 78.

Fast forward to the 1970s and suspected serial arsonist, Albert Zenner, also nicknamed "Fat Albert", based on the Bill Cosby 1970s comedy show titled, "Fat Albert and the Cosby Kids", was believed to be involved in the lighting of literally hundreds of fires around Chicago. He was arrested on a number of occasions for arson, some of which were reduced to the lesser charge of criminal damage to property.

It got to the stage, after Fat Albert would light a fire, responders often recognised his handiwork and, on some occasions, they would see him standing in the distance watching them battle the building on fire, as it burnt to the ground. His normal attire was to wear a leather jacket, tan shirt and trousers and he would travel around the city of Chicago, lighting his fires, targeting garages and empty buildings.

His motives were never quite clear, but he obviously

had an attraction to flames. After one fire he set in 1976, he telephoned the Chicago police bomb and arson unit. His voice was recognised from a similar previous call and he said to the watch commandeer:

there is a big fire in the back of my place. You better get your guys over here...it must be arson.

It was noted at the time, during the call, that Zenner was in an excited state, gasping and panting over the phone. He was subsequently convicted of one count of arson following this fire and sentenced to a term of imprisonment of two to six years. He appealed to the Appellate Court of Illinois on the basis it was not proved beyond reasonable doubt he was guilty, stating some pre-trial statements were improperly admitted into evidence.[129]

His appeal failed and in 2003 he passed away from natural causes, but his reputation was immortalised in the 1991 movie "Backdraft", the portrayal played by famous actor, Donald Sutherland, of a serial arsonist, very similar, would you believe, to Fat Albert.

Another serial arsonist, who also inspired a movie in 1995, portraying his prolific setting of more than 100 fires, was Paul Kenneth Keller, who terrorised the city of Seattle in the State of Washington, US. During his six-month arson spree in 1992-1993, he caused in excess of $30 million in damage and the loss of three lives. Keller was prematurely born in 1966 and would later be diagnosed with a number of behavioural issues, including hyperactivity. He was certainly extremely active when he set out on his murderous arson rampage.

---

[129] *People v Zenner* October 16, 1979-396 N.E 2d 1107.

In his upbringing and as he matured, so to speak, he was fascinated with firefighting and tried on two separate occasions to join his local brigade but was ultimately rejected. One must wonder why. Keller liked nothing better than being in the company of firefighters, including collecting fire memorabilia and listening to his two-way radio for emergency call outs. He would then attend the scene of the fire.

He initially worked in a variety of occupations, one of which was as a bookkeeper, but was terminated after he set his own work desk on fire. Accidentally, of course!! His initial successful employment with his father, as an advertising salesman, saw him fall into a state of despair, accompanied by fits of anger, probably not helped by his heavy drinking, drugs and a sex fetish.

In 1992, Keller was declared a bankrupt which then set off his six-month rage of lighting fires in and around Seattle, wherever he could, including local houses and business outlets, even his own church, amongst other churches. One of his efforts sadly resulted in the deaths of three residents, when he set fire to their retirement village. To make matters worse, he would send notes of sarcasm to local fire brigades as he listened to their attendance while putting out his deliberately lit fire excursions on a nightly basis.

An arson task force, with the operational name of "Sno-King", named after the two local counties of Snohomish and King and led by detectives from both the ATF and the Seattle Fire Department, was set up to identify the arsonist responsible. It was also given the name of "Spectre", as Keller was certainly a ghost at this particular point. They slowly and methodically collected credible pieces of evidence from the respective fire crime scenes, including a fingerprint, a urine sample and even footprints.

A suspect was starting to eventuate from a partial vehicle registration and witness reports, which led to a composite photo fit sketch drawn up by a police artist of a well-dressed male seen leaving the scene of a fire and driving a vehicle. Facial composites have, over time, proved very useful, particularly in unsolved crimes. Perhaps the most notable case, apart from eventually assisting in identifying Keller, was the one leading to the identity of the infamous Oklahoma City bomber, Timothy McVeigh, who was responsible for the 1995 Federal building explosion that killed 168 people, including 19 children.

The photo fit composite drawing of Keller was then circulated by task force investigators and two members of his family, including his father, on seeing the likeness to his son and reading the attached descriptive profile of the suspect's main features, started to feel very uneasy. After checking the petrol receipts of Keller, his suspicion was confirmed as a number of them matched Keller's purchasing petrol at various locations. They just happened to include the same locality where a number of arson attacks had occurred.

Keller's father had no hesitation in reporting his suspicions, that his son may be the Seattle serial arsonist, so investigators placed him under close surveillance. On checking his mobile phone records, their suspicions were confirmed as they also matched him in close proximity to many of the fires. They now had the perpetrator.

One investigative tool, which I admit I had never thought of, but I am sure many eagle eye detectives have done, is when arresting a suspect, make sure he knows why you have him firmly in your sights, even before he is formally interviewed. In the case of Keller, when arrested, he was quickly escorted to their police headquarters, with lights and sirens blaring away. They then walked him through their office, which had pinned up his name and description, identifying him as the culprit, alongside his facial photo fit drawing. It's fair to say, at this point, Keller must have known the game was up. This was further confirmed by his father, George, who was patiently waiting there for him.

Within minutes of being interviewed, after giving him the usual Miranda card rights warning, Keller readily confessed, but initially to only 76 of the total fires. He told police he would set each fire along areas he knew, when working in advertising with his father, using a cigarette lighter to ignite any flammable material, even corrugated car ports, whilst listening to communications on an emergency radio as the responses were co-ordinated by various police and fire authorities.

In 1993, Keller pleaded guilty to 32 counts of arson for which he received a prison sentence of 75 years. In 1994, he entered a further guilty plea to two charges of first-degree murder and an Alford plea to a third murder charge, related to the retirement village fire. He was sentenced to 99 years in prison to be served concurrently with his initial 75-year incarceration. An Alford plea is available in most Federal and State Courts in the US and is sometimes referred to as the Alford doctrine, which is defined in the Webster's New World dictionary as:

A guilty plea entered as part of a plea bargain by a criminal defendant who denies committing the crime or who does not actually admit his guilt…such plea may be accepted as long as there is evidence that the defendant is actually guilty.[130]

---

130   also see *North Carolina v Alford* U.S. 25 (1970).

In the case of Keller, the Alford plea to the third murder charge reduced it from first degree murder, which is an intentional murder being wilful and premeditated and with malice aforethought to kill or harm, to second degree murder. This is the lesser charge, which is still murder, but not premeditated or actually planned in advance of carrying out the crime but still results in a death. This, in effect, meant that Keller avoided the death penalty in the event he pleaded not guilty. It went to trial and he was found guilty of murder in the first degree.

Keller will not be eligible for parole until 2078, which means he would be 112 years old before any possibility of release, so there is more than a fair chance he will die in prison. But like Fat Albert, alias Albert Zenner, the Keller's exploits of arson and murder by arson were also the subject of the CBS movie called "Not our Son". His father, understandably, was left shattered, but to his credit gave the reward money he received to a local church, which was the one his disgraced son burnt down. The Sno-King Task Force was also recognised by the International Association of Arson Investigators, receiving the Outstanding Accomplishment Award for bringing Keller to justice.

Any fire, whether it be arson or accidental, can lead to a tragic outcome, including losing property destroyed by fire or the terrible loss of life. Bushfires, worldwide, are absolutely devastating and unfortunately occur without fail from year to year. Such conflagrations are also known as wildfires, particularly in the US and in 2003 one event was particularly confronting with a huge fire in Southern California. This was to become known as the "Old Fire" or the "Fire Siege of 2003", burning for nearly nine days over 91,000 acres of land, destroying nearly 1,000 homes but, luckily, only resulting in six deaths. The total damage bill was put at an extraordinary $1.2 billion.

In this case, there was never any doubt as to who caused the fire. It was lit by arsonist, Rickie Lee Fowler, who had a long criminal history, including rape and aggravated burglary. He started the blaze after supposedly being evicted from a family residence. However, a plea in mitigation went along the lines that he never intended or set out to cause any loss of life. One factor in his favour was, the five victims did not die as a result of burn injuries or smoke inhalation, but from heart attacks, no doubt caused by the ferocity of the fire enveloping their properties. Counsel for Fowler argued his client could not be blamed for the loss of life from such heart attacks, with one victim only dying some days after the fire, no doubt from the trauma of not only losing his house, but his business.

In the absence of prior intent to cause injury or death to a person, it begs the question whether it can be classified as murder or, more likely, involuntary manslaughter. Indeed, in 1982 the US Supreme Court found for reversing a death sentence regarding a person convicted of aiding and abetting a murder. In other words, in the absence of premeditated intent, murder cannot apply. Regardless of no intent and whether it was foreseeable the victims would suffer heart attacks, a jury convicted Fowler in 2012 of five counts of murder and two of arson, with a verdict imposing the death penalty.

This was further affirmed by the trial judge in 2013, so the question of "whodunnit" on this occasion was not an issue. As for Fowler, he currently remains on death row waiting his fate, noting his petition for habeas relief[131] was ultimately denied by the Ninth Circuit Court of Appeals.[132]

---

131   *Antiterrorism and Effective Death Penalty Act* 1996 (U.S.).

132   *Rickie Lee Fowler Petitioner-Appellant, v Ronald Davis, Warden. Respondent-Appellee* D.C. No 5:15-cv-02529-R.

In another serial arsonist case, a plea arrangement was entered into in which the defendant, Maurice Dews, agreed to plead guilty of eight counts of arson and four counts of aggravated assault, carried out over a three-year period, commencing in 2008. If accepted by the Washington Superior Court, it would see him serve 25 years imprisonment and a further five years on probation.

A statement of facts was agreed to between the US Attorney's office and Dews which set out the circumstances surrounding his offending, including lighting five fires in surrounding neighbourhoods in Washington DC and a further three fires in Maryland, about 60 kilometres from the capital. The aggravated assault charges stemmed from one fire that resulted in injuries to four firefighters, including one who suffered burns to 30 percent of his body.

Dews, after setting each fire, would normally call emergency 911 to report his handiwork and, on two separate occasions, even warned residents living adjacent to the building on fire, they were in danger. He would also be seen loitering near each fire, watching the buildings burn in the middle of the night and usually just after midnight which were estimated to have caused hundreds of thousands of dollars in damage. So serious were the fires that could have resulted in loss of life if the serial arsonist wasn't caught, local police were joined by the ATF, further supported by the Washington Fire Emergency Service Department and, thankfully, he was brought to justice.

Dews had already fallen onto their radar after making a false claim that he was a volunteer firefighter. The final nail in his coffin was when he telephoned one of the District of Columbia investigators, not long after his last arson, to supposedly provide details about that fire. On the court accepting the plea agreement with Dew to serve 25 years, the local fire chief on 13 March 2012 had the final say:

Mr Dews caused life-changing injuries to these firefighters and destroyed homes in densely populated neighbourhoods…this sentence won't heal the firefighters' injuries, but we hope that it will cause others to think twice before committing arson in the future.

The 1992 LA riots, following the acquittal of four LAPD officers charged with excessive force for the arrest and beating of Rodney King, resulted in, not only numerous deaths and thousands injured, but an estimated 3,600 fires started with around 1,100 buildings destroyed. This would remain the worst series of arson attacks in the city until along came Harry Burkhart in late December 2011. Burkhart went out on his own riot, allegedly motivated by his hatred of Americans. He set fire to dozens of homes, car ports, motor vehicles and garages under apartment buildings late at night, in his foray of rage to put as much fear into the local LA community as possible.

He would usually start each fire by placing the fire starter on top of a compressed wooden log, covered in wax, under a vehicle engine. After doing this to multiple parked cars, many of the fires spread to buildings and residences as he moved on to his next target. It all started on the night of 30 December 2011, after he appeared in court in support of his mother at her extradition hearing to Germany. When he came to the conclusion she would be sent back to face criminal charges, he left court, walking out with his distinctive limp, screaming, 'Fuck the United States.'

Over the next four days, under the cover of darkness, he

would carry out his reign of terror. He committed almost 50 arson attacks throughout Hollywood, West Hollywood and the San Fernando Valley.

Burkhart was recognised on a parking garage security video, thanks to his long ponytail and black clothing, not only by one of the special agents, watching a news program about the fires, who was also in court the day his mother was extradited, but also by a deputy sheriff who placed him under arrest after pulling over his blue minivan in the early morning hours on 2 January 2012. He certainly didn't cooperate with police and reportedly was even offered the option of a polygraph lie detector test. Police, of course, cannot force a suspect to undergo such a test, however, at trial they are only admissible if both the prosecution and defence agree to allow such results into evidence.

They certainly hit the jackpot, finding matching fire starter sticks in Burkhart's vehicle and would later obtain CCTV of him purchasing such fire starters from local shops. DNA would also bring him to justice, found on a propane canister and matchbox. This would connect Burkhart to two of the fires. It also became apparent he was deemed to be a suspect by German authorities for a 2011 fire that destroyed a home, owned by his family, with Burkhart then making an insurance claim.

After pleading not guilty to almost 100 counts of arson, with a total damage bill estimated in the order of $2 million, Burkhart was finally indicted by a grand jury in March 2015 on a total of 49 counts of arson of inhabited buildings, together with possession of flammable materials. His plea of not guilty by insanity initially fell on deaf ears in his trial in August 2016, being found guilty by a jury on all counts. However, this trial was declared a mistrial as eight members of the jury determined he was, in fact, insane and therefore unable to reach a unanimous verdict. Two forensic psychologists offered conflicting opinions on his level of sanity.

In March 2018, a new jury trial found he was indeed sane and, prior to being sentenced, he was offered a deal of 23 years in prison but after Burkhart rejected that, he was sentenced to 33 years and four months. At a subsequent appeal in August 2020, the California's District Court of Appeal ordered his conviction on 49 counts be conditionally reversed, due to his "mental illness", and his eligibility be considered for a mental diversion program.

If, in the event the trial court reached a conclusion he was, in fact, ineligible for such a diversion, or even exercised its direction not to grant diversion, then the court was at liberty to reinstate his convictions and sentence.[133]

This is what the trial court ordered as Burkhart was found not suitable for such diversion and currently remains in jail serving his lengthy prison term. His claim to fame, in all probability, is one of, if not the most dangerous arsonists in the archives of LA history.

Linda Gail Lee certainly didn't think twice over her Louisville, US serial arson attacks. She would have one drink too many, then go out on her escapades, setting dozens of fires in late 2013 and early 2014, leading to her being deemed the "wreath fire arsonist". Lee, after drowning her sorrows at a local bar, would then drive around adjacent neighbourhoods normally setting a wreath on fire, or an American flag left hanging outside the porches of unsuspecting residents.

---

[133] *People v Burkhart*–Court of Appeal of the State of California Second Appellate District No B2890699 Cal, Ct. App Aug 19, 2020.

She certainly didn't fit the usual profile of a serial arsonist but to their credit, arson investigators kept an open mind by not eliminating either a male or female as a suspect. Lee made two mistakes: the first, she was seen on CCTV set up outside one the houses and secondly, she stayed around after one fire to watch it burn.

This 48-year-old married woman with a teenage daughter was responsible for 43 separate fires and, surprisingly, in her first court appearance in June 2014 was given bail with a bond or surety of $25k and on the strict condition, she make no contact with any of her victims. Her selected arson targets were normally at random and after her heavy drinking, but Lee would also select other victims based on some sort of grudge she had against the house owner. On that basis, it was somewhat unusual, in her first arraignment before the court, bail was granted. Sentences for arson in the US vary depending on the degree and circumstances, but Lee was looking at a bare minimum of one year to a maximum of 20 years, regardless.

On sentencing, in mitigation it was disclosed that the motive for her offending was based on having relationship difficulties and Lee considered herself an under achiever and looked upon as somewhat unsuccessful. She was sentenced to a 20-year term in the state penitentiary for her crimes. Luckily, the majority of her fires only resulted in charred front porches but still caused well in excess of $100,000 in damage.

Like Lee, it paid not to get on the wrong side of former Maryland US Chief of Police, David Crawford, because if he was wronged, he was likely to come for payback. This is what happened with Crawford, after serving diligently for many years as a police officer and then as police chief for some four years until he was forced to resign in 2010, when he embarked on his arson endeavours.

His first victim in May 2011 just happened to be the deputy city administrator for nearby Laurel County, apparently because Crawford did not have a close working relationship with him when he was chief. Further fires were lit by Crawford over four years, from 2016 in which he went after his former police colleagues, including the one who replaced him when he resigned, two of his relatives and even a couple of his local medical practitioners, all because they somehow, unknowingly, got on his wrong side or had an argument with him.

Crawford put together a target list on his mobile phone and, once again here was a serial arsonist who, despite his training, unknowingly was assisting investigators in identifying him as the suspect. In Crawford's case, he would always wear the same clothes and drive his vehicle to each fire with a distinctive number plate, which was the same as the brand of petrol he used. Crawford also had a distinguishable gait while walking, carrying his petrol to light the fire and he was instantly recognisable.

He was arrested in March 2021 and held on remand without bail pending his jury trial in March 2023 in which he faced 12 charges, including arson that damaged or destroyed homes and cars, together with counts of attempted murder in the first and second degree, as his so-called enemies were home at the time he lit the fires.

The jury only deliberated for six hours before finding him guilty on all counts and totally rejected his not guilty plea. His defence counsel, in closing arguments, stated there was simply no pattern, no motive and basically no proof that could link him to the crimes as charged. Counsel also submitted before the jury that, given there was no DNA, no fingerprints and supposedly no facial recognition, how could they possibly find him guilty?

Crawford, also and most likely, on the advice of his lawyers chose not to give evidence and be subject to cross examination. Counsel did not call any witnesses, which is the right of any accused to simply remain silent and let the state prove its case. His counsel even called the fires just a "nuisance value" with hardly any damage. This was, however, rebutted by the prosecution who said that as soon as he lit each fire in an occupied building where the victims were asleep, he had committed attempted murder and it was, of course, lucky he was not facing murder charges.

Well, prove their case they did and his defence team obviously forgot about the target list on his mobile phone of those who had supposedly wronged him, which was found following a police search warrant which then linked him to each of the fires. Apart from CCTV footage identifying Crawford and his gait, there was also the further circumstantial, but incriminating, evidence that the preferred type of petrol, used by Crawford to start the fires, also happened to match his vanity, with the same name on his vehicle registration plate. It got worse for his defence team, as it was also demonstrated that after Crawford lit a fire, he would then telephone the victims seeking photos of the damage, again being linked to his revenge arson target list.

Electronic devices, including mobile phones, certainly assist investigators in identifying a suspect and, in the case of Crawford, there was evidence of Google map searches seeking the address of each of his victims. His Apple iPhone health data clearly set out his sleep patterns and, guess what, it showed he was, in fact, wide awake when he lit the fires, which was usually just before dawn. Funny enough, he even set himself on fire, which was captured on CCTV, leaving behind a burnt shoe and clothing. A subsequent check of his email account, investigators were to find evidence of a medical report Crawford made some two weeks after the same fire about a burn to his leg, which still clearly showed such a burn mark.

You would think Crawford, with all his police training and experience, would know that every contact leaves a trace and, in his case, despite his defence counsel saying there was nothing to connect him to any of the fires, he must have failed any investigation course that he would have attended. Crawford was sentenced to life in prison, plus a further 75 years and he will never be released.

Every contact leaves a trace would also lead to the eventual downfall of serial arsonist and burglar, 42-year-old Sarah Jane Ramey. It would not only be by leaving a casino card behind at one of the fires, but also stealing items from burgled premises, which would later be found in her possession. A total of 17 fires would be set by Ramey throughout the US Washington cities of Tacoma and Rushton. The first was one of three lit on 30 December 2021.

This was followed by a further burglary and arson the next night on New Year's Eve around 5.30pm in Tacoma, which sadly, resulted in the death of an elderly resident from smoke inhalation. Some two weeks later, fire investigators put this blaze down to an electrical fault, but thanks to accelerant sniffing arson detection dog used by the ATF, there was clearly evidence of an accelerant. In fact, the canine uncovered no less than 17 hits for possible accelerants and a further search by

ATF personnel would find red containers with evidence of petrol.

Ramey, still not satisfied with her efforts to date, would go on to commit further burglaries and cover her tracks by fire, or so she thought, with no less than 14 fires in homes, a garage and a vehicle from 19 January 2022 through to the night of 26 January, when she alone set a total of six separate fires. Her first act started around 12.04 am and she would continue setting more targets on fire until four hours later, no doubt thieving whatever was on offer. However, she was brought undone as Ramey left behind the identifying casino card at one of her fires, which police were able to trace and on 28 January 2022 she was taken into custody.

Under warrant, her mobile phone data was searched, which traced her to, not only the fatal house fire, but a number of other locations in the vicinity of the other blazes. An internet search was also damning as it revealed a suspicious browser history, which included Ramey asking questions about the Tacoma arsons, length of jail terms for misuse of a credit card and even how to set fires. A search of her home would uncover a cheque book belonging to the victim, taken from his home on New Years Eve, together with his late wife's credit cards and other victims' debit and credit cards. Ramey used these to purchase goods worth over just over $6,000, confirmed by surveillance footage of her from one shop in particular.

Police also located a very visible stolen jacket which, on examining CCTV footage, showed Ramey wearing it when walking to and away from some of the fires. Ramey was even recorded making a telephone call while under arrest, begging her mother to attend her home immediately to remove certain items of her clothing and keys, before police attended under warrant. Later, a witness would also come forward to tell police how she assisted Ramey to remove items from the deceased victim's now-destroyed home, stating she was told by Ramey she had permission to do so from the owner.

A probable cause hearing took place after she had originally been charged with eight arsons between January 23 and January 26 2022. Such a hearing is a pre-trial stage of criminal cases, also referred to as a preliminary hearing. In the event sufficient evidence is tendered by the prosecution, the case will proceed to trial. The additional evidence alleged that Ramey was responsible for the earlier arsons and, of course, the fatal fire on New Year's Eve. Ramey pleaded not guilty to all charges and her defence counsel could only hope, given the veracity of the evidence, that the jury would not convict her on all counts for the 17 fires, which also included first degree murder.

Following a trial over some three months in the Pierce County Superior Court, the jury, on 3 July 2024, after taking three days to consider their verdict, found Ramey guilty on all but three of the counts of arson. Such finding also included the count of first-degree murder in the course of committing an arson, or by engaging in conduct that showed extreme indifference to human life, counts of burglary, first–degree identity theft and theft of a motor vehicle. All up, a total of 23 criminal counts.

On 23 July 2024, Ramey appeared before Judge Angelica Williams for sentencing. The prosecution was seeking a sentence outside the normal range for such criminality, in that they wanted Ramey jailed for around 111 years. Her defence counsel submitted that a standard sentence of somewhere between 34 to 45 years would be appropriate, noting she was now 45 years old so she would most likely die in jail before being eligible for parole. The judge effectively sided with the state and took into account the suffering of the victim's family, losing their much-loved grandfather. She sentenced Ramey to a total of 81 year and six months.

I think it's fair to say, her defence lawyer was right, Ramey will never see the light of day and will die in jail.

The UK has also had its fair share of infamous serial arsonists, one being Peter George Dinsdale, also known under adopted name, Bruce George Lee, and later as Peter Tredget, so we will stick to Tredget. He started his murderous rampage at the ripe old age of nine when he allegedly set fire to a number of shops and a timberyard and later confessed to being responsible for the arson murder of 11 residents in a nursing home, despite it being inconclusively determined as accidental. Three years later in December 1972, he allegedly set fire to a classmate's house who, like Tredget, was physically handicapped, with our arsonist having a withered arm and walking with a limp.

He continued on his merry way, setting more fires for the next seven years, perhaps urged on by the constant referral to him as "daft Peter". He would hobble along, setting fire to various buildings in his suburb of Hull, but it all came crashing down following a fatal house fire on 4 December 1979. On this occasion, police determined that a container full of paraffin oil was lit and then placed in the letter box of the Selby Street house, resulting in the death of three young brothers. This family was widely known as a bunch of crooks, with their father in prison and also had a reputation for carrying out pay backs on whoever supposedly wronged them, so revenge gave police a possible motive.

How right they were, as when they questioned Tredget,

among a number of others suspects, he readily confessed to using the paraffin oil to get back at one of the boys who died in the fire, following his threat to dob Tredget in to police over some sort of sexual contact. The other motive for revenge, although he told police he never meant to kill anyone, was the teasing he was subjected to by that family after he supposedly fell in love with their daughter.

On further questioning, Tredget admitted to being responsible for another nine fires in the Hull area during his seven-year arson spree, which were initially determined as not suspicious, including the nursing home fire. He even accompanied police to various locations to show them where he had started each of the fires. Although revenge appeared to be a motive regarding the Selby Street fire, he did admit to starting most of the fires at will, because he loved setting the blaze and then watching it burn.

On 20 January 1981, he pleaded not guilty to 26 charges of murder, but guilty to manslaughter on each count on the basis that he had diminished responsibility due to his substantial physical and mental impairment,[134] of which eleven counts were quashed on appeal. In 2022, the Court of Appeal, being the highest court of the senior courts in England and Wales, acquitted him on a further three counts of manslaughter and two counts of arson, regarding two of the fires.[135]

Regardless, Tredget was believed to be responsible for around 30 fires, including non-fatal, however, to this day his lawyers continue to argue for his release citing his psychological and physical disabilities which, in their view, renders his confessions without merit. They say it would be all

---

134 *Homicide Act 1957* (UK)- section 2.

135 *Tredget and Regina* [2022] EWCA Crim 108.

but impossible for someone with such disabilities to first carry incendiary devices, then access buildings and light the fires. Despite such pleas alleging a total miscarriage of justice, he remains under tight security in a psychiatric hospital.

Englishman, Paul William Jones, has been included in the worst of the worst, not for the totality of his arson spree but the fact he was sentenced to an indefinite term of imprisonment. Jones carried out three separate arson attacks during the months of January and February 2012 in the West Midlands in the UK.

He first set fire to a vacant house, causing £275,000 in damage, followed by the torching of a fitness centre and his final effort was lighting a fire in an historic railway signal box, all in the town of Oswestry. Not satisfied with the arson attacks, he then terrified various businesses throughout the UK, calling his victims and telling them, 'There is a bomb on the premises, tick, tick, tick,' leading to the evacuation of many shopping centres.

Jones was sentenced to seven years imprisonment with a maximum of three years and six months, however, the sentencing judge stated that as, 'the public had every reason to be extremely worried,' he was not to be released from prison until such time the parole board was completely satisfied he was no longer a risk to the community. Let's hope he is not released from his indefinite jail sentence under that condition, noting Jones did have the final say when he said he wanted to remain in prison, 'for a long time.'

Serial arsonist, Thomas Ashcroft, had a passion for setting fire to public buildings and hospitals. In 2012, he received a 12-year sentence for committing arson at the Hilton Hotel in Sheffield, UK and the Midway Maritime Hospital in Kent. He was then released on licence, which is the same as parole with set conditions that must be adhered to. Well, he certainly didn't stick to his release conditions, when in June 2017 he first set a fire at the SeaCity Museum in Southampton, after stealing £200 in cash, despite the building being occupied with teachers and students, who luckily escaped.

Ashcroft then proceeded the following day to the Staffordshire University and set fire to its Beacon building and, still not satisfied, a few hours later torched the largest hospital in Staffordshire, namely the Royal Stoke University Hospital, setting the fire in the basement to bagged linen stored in a metal cage. He once again put the public, including vulnerable patients, at risk with the fire resulting in a mass evacuation. This fire caused nearly £450,000 in damage and it didn't take police all that long to figure out who they were looking for. In any event, his not so-called heroics were captured on the hospital's CCTV and it didn't take long before he was placed in handcuffs and remanded in custody.

In February 2018, he appeared for sentencing in the Stafford Crown Court after pleading guilty to three counts of arson and one of burglary. The crown prosecutor submitted that Ashcroft's modus operandi was to enter public buildings and set the fire alarm off, which would ensure the occupants were evacuated so he could then re-enter and steal money. He had a total of 66 prior convictions, which included his numerous arsons, many of which were hospitals. His defence counsel, with really not much to work with in mitigation, suggested that Ashcroft, although not having a fascination for fires, was under the influence of alcohol, but it was all part of his plan to steal money.

Ashcroft, now 40 years of age, received a maximum term of life imprisonment, but has the right to be released after serving a paltry minimum of seven years and six months, then being eligible for parole. Hopefully, he will never be released with a local detective-inspector saying he is a very dangerous risk to the public, shows complete disregard for public safety and the country is certainly a much safer place without Ashcroft on the streets. A truer word could not be better spoken.

I have included two further miscreants in this chapter for want, perhaps, of a better description, as members of the "Hall of Fame", of the worst of the worst. Not because of any serial arson offending, but the sheer damage one caused and the life sentence imposed on the other, noting he was also a school arsonist. Casey James Fury was a nuclear submarine shipyard worker and on the sunny afternoon of 23 May 2012, he decided he wanted the rest of the day off. The problem was he had no annual or sick leave credits.

What better way to get away early, but to set fire to the docked submarine USS Miami undergoing a total refurbishment as it sat idle in Kittery, Maine, US. Fury set alight a container filled with rags situated in the ship's stateroom, which set off a large inferno of flames taking over 12 hours to bring under control and injuring seven people.

The total damage bill was initially put in the order of US$450 million and it was fortunate it didn't burn along to the rear end of the vessel, which contained its nuclear components. The damage estimate would later be raised to around US$700 million because it was ultimately determined the nuclear submarine would have to be scrapped. It was initially thought the fire started accidentally due to a faulty industrial vacuum cleaner.

However, some weeks later, after setting another fire to the now badly damaged sub but only causing minor damage, Fury confessed, saying he had suffered another "anxiety attack" and again needed to leave early to go home. It was, of course, noted that his anxiety couldn't have been too bad as, during the first huge blaze, he sat on the pier and watched as firefighters tried to douse the flames.

In March 2013, Fury pleaded guilty to two counts of arson with his defence counsel submitting that he suffered from depression and anxiety and it was never his intention to cause any harm. The difficulty for Fury in that regard was, of course, he had started two fires and it was fortunate in the first blaze that a major catastrophic explosion did not occur, injuring more victims and perhaps causing death. Fury did acknowledge his remorse but has around to 15 to 19 years in prison to think about what he did, together with a US $400 million restitution order waiting for him on release.

He, however, did contend in 2015 that he made a false confession and he was not responsible. In addition, he didn't think the court properly took into account his mental health and drug addiction issues. Fury, now 33 years of age, followed up in 2021 and tried to argue for compassionate release, citing "extraordinary and compelling" reasons to warrant, at least, a reduction in his sentence, claiming the impact of the pandemic and again, citing his mental health issues. His appeal was rejected, with the court finding he would still pose a danger to the community if he was released, noting his earliest possible release date will be August 2027.[136]

Another one who must be included in the worst of the worst and not just because he set fire to a school, then again, perhaps that's why I have included him, was 19-year-old Aaron Foster. His first arson was in August 2020 when he set fire to

---

[136] *United States v Fury*-Docket No 2;12-cr-00186-GZS 31 March 2012.

a library in Mixenden, Halifax in the UK, causing £180,000 in damage. He was seen by a witness smashing a window, climbing into the building and setting it alight, but he would not be properly identified until he was caught after burning down a primary school. This fire in Ash Green, in the same township of Mixenden in February 2022, was again thanks to Foster, who was initially detected on CCTV first breaking into the school and then seen walking around outside with a lit cigarette before climbing back into the burning building.

Once again inside the school and obviously trying to deflect blame away for him, Foster telephoned 999 claiming he was trapped inside the burning building started by his mates. The total damage was later estimated in the order of a staggering £4.5 million completely devastating the local community and, of course, its students.

Foster denied being involved in both counts of arson but at a trial before a jury in July 2022, admitted forcibly entering the school with others to steal iPads and only went back inside to steal more items and make sure his so-called mates were all okay. The jury, after viewing the CCTV school footage, which also showed him going into classrooms and recording the moment when the first of three fires were started by Foster igniting objects, then listened to his version of events. He was cross examined by the crown prosecutor who put to him:

Mr Foster, you went back into the school because you decided to pretend that you had been trapped… This was you playing the victim in this situation. Pretending to be trapped when you weren't?…trying to create a drama…?

Foster denied this allegation saying:

Admittedly I could have got out, but my mind went blank...

The Bradford Crown Court jury also listened to the emergency services call with Foster saying:

...all I can see is flames...I'm in a hallway. All I can see is flames...

Foster was then advised by the control room responder to cover his mouth with a jacket and stay close to the floor. Foster then said he couldn't believe his mates had left him behind and that he failed to understand why they lit the fire.

Regarding the library fire, he also said it wasn't him as he had been home in bed until around 7.30am before leaving for work. However, a witness gave evidence that she, in fact, saw Foster smashing a library window and, after he climbed inside, saw flames coming out of the building. She further said that when alarms then went off, Foster came out laughing about his accomplishment.

On 18 October 2022, Foster was found guilty on both counts of arson and one of burglary and was sentenced to a maximum of life imprisonment, with a nine-year minimum. The sentencing judge stated:

The cost to these children, of them having their own work destroyed, their environment literally gutted and their peace of mind disturbed by the thought that somebody has come into their building and burned it down because it seemed a good idea at the time, is just incalculable.

It's best, for want of a better description, to leave one of, if not the worst of the worst, to last and Thomas Sweatt certainly fits into that category. He didn't appear, however, to fit the usual profile of a serial arsonist, being around 50 years old, no convictions and gainfully employed as a manager of a fast-food outlet. He did, however, have an attraction to young men in military uniform and, after following them home, this so-called attraction turned nasty when he set fire to his possible beau's home or car. While there were many fires occurring in and around Washington DC in the US, including one in 1985 resulting in the death of two people, Sweatt didn't come on to their radar until after a series of fires from 2002 through to 2004.

His fire lighting escapades even included setting fire to police vehicles by throwing a slow burning incendiary device, which was either a milk or soda bottle, capped off with a wick to prevent the petrol escaping. He also had an attraction to, not only setting vehicles on fire, but also to buildings and apartments which resulted in the deaths of two residents in separate fires in 2002 and 2003.

The murderous arsons started to unravel when a security camera detected his vehicle at one of the fires at a military barracks, followed by other fire crime scenes matching DNA evidence, which included a fingerprint and skin cells from pants left behind, further supported by a single hair strand. After police placed him under 24-hour surveillance, he agreed to a police request for his DNA, which matched the collated evidence.

Following his arrest in April 2005, Sweatt readily admitted his guilt to many other suspected fires, including the 1985 arson murder which police initially believed was accidental and caused by a cigarette butt. This particular fire was lit in a two-storey residence of a man he found attractive and apparently wanted to see him again. Unfortunately, the residents living on the second floor suffered the consequences with a husband and wife killed from burn injuries, whilst two others from the same family escaped unharmed.

His usual modus operandi was to light his incendiary device and then sometimes marvel at his handiwork while sitting in his motor vehicle as the fire burned. He was oblivious to the possibility of causing death and injury to his innocent victims. Investigators were also able to connect him to a 2002 fire in which an elderly resident died, finding at Sweatt's home a newspaper report of this incident. He had no hesitation in confessing to this crime and entered into a plea agreement regarding 33 separate fires and even accepted responsibility for another 12 fires, including an attempted arson.

The agreement was for him to serve life in prison with no possibility of parole on counts of felony murder, second degree murder and related charges of possession of destructive devices in the furtherance of a crime of violence and, of course, counts of destruction of buildings causing injury. Such fire damage was in the order of millions of dollars in damage.

During his sentence hearing, his public defence lawyer submitted to the court that Sweatt was under some sort of psychological compulsive disorder, even likening him to a Dr Jekyll: being, on the one hand, peaceful and then turning into a fire setting and murderous Mr Hyde. In other words, according to his counsel, there were two versions of his client: one being the good Mr Sweatt and the other and quite aptly put, the sick Mr Sweatt.

Her Honour, District Judge Deborah K Chasanow, was

having none of that, saying in June 2005, that Sweatt's mental health issues in no way justified his actions in terrorising the community, let alone taking the life of innocent victims. Sweatt, with cap in hand, did make a trite apology, which fell on deaf ears saying in open court to the victims' loved ones:

I'm very sorry for all the harm that I've caused you. To those who lost loved ones, I share your hurt and I share your pain every day...for those who can't forgive me...God replace the hate with understanding that time will heal...

Her Honour accepted the plea agreement, but to make sure Sweatt was never released, made an order of an additional 136 years on top of his life sentence. Sweatt currently languishes in the federal correctional prison in Hopewell, Virginia and he will, of course, never be released. There is absolutely no doubt that if Sweatt had not been arrested, he would have continued on his merry way lighting fires at will, resulting in not only more damage, but the loss of innocent lives.[137]

Unfortunately, Australia has also had its fair share of serial arsonists.

---

[137] also see *United States of America v Thomas Sweatt*-Criminal Case No DKC 05-0230 16 July 2021.

12
TOO CLOSE TO HOME

The making of movies depicting the unsavoury exploits of serial arsonists, such as Fat Albert Zenner and Paul Keller, may well have been the inspiration for the 2003 Australian crime film called "Razor Eaters", supposedly based on a well-known vigilante street gang responsible for a series of hedge fires over some 10 years from the late 1980s in Melbourne, Victoria.

The lighting of hedges can even be traced back as early as 1926 when a "incendiarist", as referred to then, set fire to 60 odd hedges around the suburb of St Kilda, including one poor woman's hedge that was set alight on three separate occasions. It was believed it was the work of one solitary male offender who was often seen loitering around after the fires were lit, but no one was ever charged.

Perhaps these types of hedge fires were the inspiration behind Gregory Anastasiou who, despite being jailed on two separate occasions, obviously didn't learn from these arson sprees, as he was at it again some years later. Anastasiou, or perhaps we should call him after his nickname, "Lucifer", was the leader of a disgruntled gang that for some reason wanted to terrorise the leafy eastern suburbs of Melbourne and obviously thought setting fire to hedges was the answer to whatever grieved them. Lucifer, of course, is the name given to the "bearer of light" or the "morning star" but was also known as Satan and in a more general sense as the Lucifer in Christianity.

With respect, Anastasiou was certainly no subservient to God and, with his fellow cohorts in tow, they set fire to 39 hedges from the late 1980s. Now you would think he would learn a salutary lesson, after being convicted and jailed in 1991 and sentenced to two years, six months. But alas, he was back at it again setting more fires on being released, but this time he added grassfires to his collection. For this foray, he copped another conviction in 1995 and you would like to think by this stage he would simply move onto better things in life.

But not Lucifer. Perhaps he was just a pyromaniac. After being released from his second stint in prison, he started again and was charged in November 2000 with setting fires including a hedge in the affluent leafy suburb of Balwyn, Victoria. At the time, his lawyer advised the Melbourne Magistrates Court that his client would vigorously defend this latest charge and would, in due course, make an application for bail.

I think, given the history of Anastasiou, he would have been lucky to get bail, as he was already on bail for four previous hedge fires, so this would now bring it to five charges of criminal damage by fire at the time of his arrest. In late 2001, he was off to jail for the third time. This time being sentenced to five years imprisonment, together with a restitution order of $30,000 regarding four of the hedge fires. At the time of his sentencing for this spate of hedge fires, another serial arsonist was still to be caught over 20 other hedge fires.

Not only did Anastasiou become synonymous with the title of Lucifer, but his hedge burning exploits even drew some comparison to a spate of tacks placed along the Yarra Boulevard to trap unsuspecting cyclists and puncture their tyres as they rode merrily along. I don't think the aptly titled "Boulie Tacker" was ever caught, despite a $50,000 reward on offer and it would also seem that unless I am mistaken, our Lucifer has also now ridden off into the distance.

Another serial arsonist with an extensive criminal history, elevated himself from perhaps hedge burning when he was sentenced in the Queensland District Court to 10 years in jail in 2011. Clayton Jay Ganzer, a 36-year-old male, first came to the attention of police in 1991 after setting fire to his own workplace a year later. He finished up with two pages of criminal convictions, including theft, breach of suspended sentences, breach of parole, breach of community orders and, of course, offences of arson.

Despite spending some time incarcerated, following three offences of arson in 2001 when he set fire to houses near where he lived. He caused at least $100,000 in damage over a period of 12 months from September 2006. He then went about causing further massive damage by fire in and around the northside of Brisbane. This time he set fire to a shopping complex at Boondall causing $2 million in damage to three shops, followed by another fire to his local neighbour's home but, thankfully, only causing minor damage.

Not satisfied at this point, he then turned his attention to a real estate agent's premises first stealing computers and then, possibly to cover his tracks, set the shop on fire resulting in around $300,000 in damage. Once again, this serial arsonist came undone when identified on CCTV at the shopping complex, carrying a full can of petrol to start the blaze. He was then linked to the scene of the real estate fire, leaving behind some DNA evidence. Ganzer spent three years on remand and was then sentenced to a total of 10 years in prison, but with a three-year parole minimum, meaning he was immediately eligible for parole.

This apparent lenient sentence was probably due to a submission by his defence counsel, no doubt supported by expert psychological evidence, that his client suffered from a degree of intellectual impairment and also mental health issues. It seems that Ganzer also had an impulsive control disorder, stemming from a brain injury suffered during birth. Ganzer, as far as can be determined, has since not come to the attention of police.

It was interesting to note in the sentencing of mother of three, Helen Judith White, that His Honour, Judge Michael Boylan, did not consider her to be a typical arsonist. It then begs the question why White has been included in this chapter of notable serial arsonists, given that description by His Honour. The reason is, White set a total of 21 fires in the Adelaide Hills of South Australia during the summer months of 2007.

White had an unusual method to ignite the fires as she used mosquito coils and matches to carry out her ill deeds. Thankfully, none of her fires caused any substantial damage. It's fair to say that White had some serious issues with her mental health and this may well explain why on one day in January 2027 she set six fires. Many months later on 5 December 2007, a further four fires and then during one evening over two days a week later, she set another 11.

It was only good luck that she didn't cause a major bushfire but as His Honour said:

It is, I think fair to say that, throughout parts of two fire seasons, you terrorised your community... Your neighbours were worried sick that they, their families and property might be victims of a major bushfire disaster. Every movement, every outing, even shopping expeditions, had to be planned against that possibility... We live in a country where fire can be our greatest and most dangerous enemy... People who start bushfires must be punished and punished severely so that others will be deterred from copying them.[138]

With White sobbing in the dock, she was indeed severely punished with His Honour imposing a maximum prison term of 13 years, with a non-parole period of nine years following her guilty plea. The Court of Appeal, however, did have some sympathy for her, reducing her non-parole period by two years and six months after her counsel successfully argued that the sentencing judge did not give enough weight to, not only her psychiatric issues, but her genuine remorse. This meant White became eligible for parole in 2014.[139]

An arson spree carried out by a husband-and-wife team was described by a sentencing judge as 'without precedent in Western Australia'. This duo was responsible for a series of fires in the Kalgoorlie–Boulder Goldfields region over nearly a 12-month period, commencing around November 2010. These arson attacks resulted in WA Police, under Operation Twain, conducting an intensive investigation over a nine-month period, resulting in the arrest in September 2011 of Alan Robert Sloane and his sometimes partner-in-crime, Rebecca

---

138   *R v White* [2009] Unreported, South Australia District Court, Judge Boyland, 7 April 2009.

139   *White v R* [2009] Unreported, SASCA, 14 August 2009.

Louise Sloane. Their wanton arson spree, usually not revenge motivated, would sometimes see Mrs Sloane drive her husband around Kalgoorlie and outer areas, usually on a late evening, seeing what could be set on fire.

The targets included houses occupied by residents, by setting curtains hanging out from open windows, on fire using a cigarette. Other vacant properties included the same location on three separate occasions, vehicles, including one he stole from his workplace, a caravan and, in one instance, a front-end loader causing damage in the order of $143,000, while their young twin daughters sat in the back of the vehicle. The total damage bill, thanks to the Sloanes, would later be estimated at nearly $1 million.

It was fortunate that no one was injured, given that Sloane would sometimes use a Molotov cocktail or some other sort of accelerant, including a bucket full of methanol, to start the fire. Sloane also had a penchant, on two occasions, to alert authorities and then helped to extinguish the blaze. Mrs Sloane was totally complicit in the action of Sloane, although not putting a match to any of the fires, the part she played was to drive hubby around looking for potential targets to ignite. No doubt, Mrs Sloane sitting in the front seat would have been encouraging him as he went about his business and then she would watch on with some glee.

Operation Twain was certainly assisted in identifying the Sloanes as they would use their own vehicles in the arson rampage and, following their arrest in September 2011, the lead detective in the record of interview got straight down to business and said to Sloane:

We believe that there's 24 fires okay. That we believe that you're

> *involved. Either been seen at, assisted fighting, contact FESA (fire emergency), your vehicle's been at, with either vehicle, your Magna or your Ford Ranger which you say that only you and Rebecca drive...let me know if there's anything you would like to tell us about those fires...*

The game was up for the Sloanes, who were later given the nickname "Mr and Mrs Arson", although he initially denied any involvement, but after talking with Mrs Sloane, who was also in custody, they both confessed. Sloane, on pleading guilty to 19 counts of criminal damage by fire, was sentenced to a total of nine years and nine months jail with a seven year and nine month no parole period. Mrs Sloane, who played a much lesser role, only received a total of 14 months imprisonment and can be freed on parole after only serving seven months, following her pleading guilty to even counts of arson involving motor vehicles.

It seems the only motive, apart for Sloane being habitually under the influence of alcohol, was to have a break away from their children, despite the fact they had them in the back seat of their vehicle on at least one occasion. [140]

Sloane subsequently appealed his conviction and sentence which, lucky for him, was reduced by two years, meaning he could be paroled after only five years and nine months. The Supreme Court of Appeal took into account the sentencing judge had erred in respect of the cost of the overall damage, resulting from the front-end loader fire.[141]

One crook who did come to the attention of police, time

---

[140] *State of Western Australia v. A. Sloane and R. Sloane*, Jenkins J, File No INS 199 of 2011-4 April 2012.

[141] *Sloane v The State of Western Australia* [2013] WASCA 53.

and time again, was Justin Andrew William Nona, who began his offending at the ripe young age of 12 years in 1998. By the time he reached the mature age of 23 years old, he had amassed a total of 84 convictions, including for stealing, aggravated unlawful entry, criminal damage, unlawful use of a motor vehicle and also assault. Nona was a recidivist offender having breached good behaviour bonds, suspended sentences and even offending while he was on parole. His first foray into arson was around late 2008, following the theft of a motor vehicle, then setting it on fire, for which he was jailed for 12 months, then released in April 2010.

Within three weeks of his release, he committed a further number of minor offences and then on 12 June 2010 he set out on his perilous arson spree around Darwin in the NT in a drunken and drug affected state. He first set fire to a tavern, causing minor damage in his bungled attempt to force entry. Unperturbed, he tried to forcibly enter two vehicles and then set them alight, destroying both. A boat in a driveway was the next casualty, followed by setting fire to a unit with a mother and two children inside asleep.

Sadly, one of the children perished in the fire from smoke inhalation. The mother suffered serious burns while trying to rescue her son from the blazing building, which was completely destroyed, along with a motor vehicle, resulting in damage all up in excess of $300,000. Despite the havoc he had already caused, he torched another vehicle on his way home, making a total of six fires deliberately lit.

Police immediately set up an investigation team consisting of 40 well-trained officers, with forensic crime scene specialists, carefully examining each fire to hopefully obtain evidence which might lead to the identity of those responsible. Nona was subsequently arrested by police on 29 July 2010, but only for the attempted arson committed at the tavern. He then made further limited admissions to the other fires he lit that night but vehemently denied the unit fire causing death and the fires to any of the vehicles and boat.

Nona was remanded in custody on the charges that he had admitted to and, in the interim, NT police offered a reward of $250,000 for information leading to the arrest of the person(s) responsible for the death of the young child. No doubt they must have suspected Nona given, his conduct on the night in question, but they did not have sufficient evidence to charge him.

He must have had an attack of the guilts as, just prior to his committal hearing in late February 2011, he first confessed to the arson causing death to a prison officer and then full admissions to police, even taking them on a tour of each of the fires he lit that night. His bumbled excuse was, 'I was too drunk…I was stoned…I was in that criminal mode,' even admitting he knew the unit was occupied when he set it alight.

Nona subsequently pleaded guilty in the NT Supreme Court in June 2011 to 11 charges, including criminal damage, unlawful entry, setting fire and the most serious charge, that of manslaughter. He was sentenced to a total concurrent term on all charges to 15 years imprisonment, with a non-parole period of 10 years. The sentencing judge, taking into account that Nona made full admissions some months after investigating police had reached an impasse in identifying him as the culprit, said further:

…you are entitled to credit for your plea…and the acceptance by you of responsibility for your actions…I also accept that the plea

> *indicates feelings of remorse on your part...You were told by the investigating officer that he did have sufficient evidence to charge you, but you went on to incriminate yourself by making appropriate admissions. That entitles you to an added element of leniency.*[142]

Despite this apparent lenient sentence, Nona lodged an appeal on the grounds of an excessive sentence and that he should have been given additional leniency for his voluntary disclosure of guilt. The Court of Appeal had no hesitation in dismissing the appeal.[143]

I would have thought that despite his voluntary admission of guilt and his degree to a point of so-called genuine remorse, he would be eligible to apply for parole after 10 years. This was indeed lenient to say the least, given that the poor young child lost in the fire didn't even make it to his 10th birthday, being only eight years old. I have no doubt the Darwin community were shocked to a point of outrage at the senseless and horrific crimes carried out by Nona and the sentence handed down.

The fact Nona caused a death by arson, yet only received a minimum of 10 years, noting manslaughter in Queensland has a maximum penalty of life imprisonment, perhaps at first glance, makes it a much reduced prison term when compared to the fire lighting efforts of Gary John Trestrail and another, by the name of Sean Douglas Broom, and their subsequent sentences.

Trestrail set a number of blazes when he targeted unsuspecting victims, which luckily did not result in death from intentionally lighting a total of 11 separate fires. These efforts

---

[142] *The Queen v Nona* File No CA 9 of 2011.

[143] *Nona v the Queen* [2012] NTCCA 03.

included seven counts of bushfires also resulting in damage to, not only a motor vehicle, but a home and two buildings in the southern fringe of Adelaide in early 2014. He obviously was not too happy with his Big Mac and fries as he also tried to set fire at a local McDonald's restaurant.

For this firebug spree, he was sentenced in December 2016 to 12 years imprisonment with a non-parole period of seven years, leading Justice Barry Beazley to say in the District Court of South Australia:

> *Fortunately, no one was physically injured. It is plain, however, that a large number of victims suffered and still suffer from various psychological issues as a consequence of your criminal conduct.*[144]

Unlike Nona, the conduct of Trestrail did not result in the loss of life and the same can be said for the exploits of Broom. He was certainly a serial arsonist and most likely a pyromaniac, even setting fires within days on being released from prison for previous arson convictions. His firebug past first started as far back as the late 1980s, when he set fire to a vacant house and scrubland, for which he was jailed.

He was then sentenced to a further term of imprisonment in a NSW jail for four years and nine months for arson, causing around $1 million in damage to a car and two industrial buildings. On being released in July 2008, he then travelled up to Brisbane, Queensland, probably much to the relief of the NSW community, as he wasted no time setting more fires within 24 hours of his release.

This time, Broom set fire to a motor vehicle followed by

144　　*R v Trestrail* [2016] Unreported, SADC, Judge Beazley.

two industrial bins. The very next day he was at it again when he crawled under a house and set it on fire whilst an elderly resident slept inside. The wooden structure becoming quickly engulfed in flames, causing $250,000 in damage. Fortunately, the owner of the now destroyed building was able to escape the inferno. It was our fire lighter, now turned fire hero, Broom, that saved the day as he rescued the elderly gentleman unhurt from his burning home.

This "wanna-be hero" even called Triple 0 and knocked on the doors of surrounding residents' homes to warn them of the imminent danger. He then assisted attending fire crews to quell the blaze. Obviously very satisfied with his efforts, Broom gleefully attended a local nightclub, telling all the patrons and anyone who would listen, of his heroism saving the resident from the burning flames. Of course, he forgot to tell them that it was in fact him that started the fire.

I think it is fair to say Broom was not all that smart as the night before the house fire, he made a call to emergency services about a pretend fire. It was then a simple matter for arson investigators to match his mobile phone number to that hoax call, leading to his arrest. He was still proclaiming to all and sundry he was a hero and even a volunteer firefighter who also drive a fire truck.

Broom pleaded guilty in November 2010 in the Queensland District Court to two counts of arson, together with charges of wilful damage and making a hoax emergency services call. He was sentenced to eight years imprisonment with a three-year non-parole period. With time already served, he became eligible for parole in June 2011 not that, given his history, parole would be granted in any event, so he served his full term.

Now, as they say, history repeats itself and that certainly was the case with Broom as, immediately on his release, he was at it again lighting fires in two inner suburbs of Brisbane. Within 24 hours of his release and, perhaps to celebrate his 50th birthday, he purchased a lighter from a shop and first set fire to some wooden pallets and then moved on to Highgate Hill, setting fires in two houses. Once again, he started one by crawling under the house, resulting in damage to the order of $285,000. Not satisfied with these fires, he then set alight a vehicle in a three-storey apartment carport, placing a number of residents in danger. Luckily, they escaped but the building was effectively destroyed.

Broom's movements were quickly uncovered when investigators examined the security footage from the store where he purchased the lighter prior to commencing his arson spree. I think that as soon as the investigators looked at the footage they probably said, 'Here we go again, Broom is back in town and up to his old tricks,' or words to that effect.

Now you would like to think that, given his 20-odd years of fire lighting activities, the court would have locked him up and thrown away the key, as any conviction for arson in that state allows a maximum penalty of up to life behind bars.[145] But alas, that was not the case as in February 2023, with the judge using his discretion, Broom was only sentenced to nine years jail with a minimum of two years and eight months, before being eligible for parole. The Queensland District Court sitting in Brisbane, took into account that Broom suffered from an intellectual disability and the loss of his family in a car accident in 1992, which he unfortunately came across when he attended the scene as a tow truck driver.

---

145   *Criminal Code Act* 1899(Qld)-Section 461.

His Honour, in sentencing Broom, noted he denied starting the fires due to any sort of arousal or immediate satisfaction, but he did not have the benefit of mental health treatment whilst in prison. Of course, it was revealed in the 2010 sentencing and, as aptly put by the court then, Broom had a strong desire to light fires where he seemed to gain some sort of psychological gratification being looked upon as a hero.

Regardless, with his latest arson foray, the learned judge went on to further say he failed to accept, let alone understand, how Broom did not fit the category of a pyromaniac:

I strongly suggest you get treatment for the problems you have…I agree with the prosecution, it is clear you are a recidivist offender and community protection is very relevant here…this was terror caused to Highgate Hill residents…you said you were wandering around and got bored…I accept you didn't deliberately come to Brisbane to light fires.

Now, with no disrespect to His Honour, I fail to understand his last comment, that Broom didn't just come to Brisbane to light fires. This was, in fact, his second stint of lighting fires in and around Brisbane. The first set of fires was in 2008, after being released from prison and then again in 2020, and yes, once again, straight after being released from prison. We, therefore, have two separate and distinct occasions with Broom deliberately lighting fires in and around Brisbane, yet the court seems to take a differing view, that Broom didn't purposefully come to Brisbane and set the suburbs on fire. On that basis, why did he then go to Brisbane? I don't think it was just to enjoy the nightlife.

It remains to be seen whether this recidivist arsonist was

released on parole from prison in late October 2024. If he was, which I very much doubt, or whenever he will be released back into the community, let's trust he doesn't go back to Brisbane and do it all over again. Hopefully, he may receive treatment for his mental health and pyromania issues.

A similar recidivist arsonist, despite having the benefit of regular contact with mental health services, had a similar track record like Broom. Once again, seemed to be treated with some indifference and leniency by the Victorian justice system. Andrew Morgan, prior to setting out lighting numerous fires, certainly had a rather chequered criminal history, including convictions for drink driving, reckless conduct endangering life, in which he drove a car at police, burglary and theft, possession of a firearm and setting fire to a hay shed.

Morgan was a habitual drug user and had been hospitalised in mental health institutions on a number of occasions. He turned his hand to further arson offending in December 2015, first setting fire to an abandoned roadside couch containing rubbish, followed by 11 separate fires in and around bushland in Labertouche in the Gippsland region of Victoria. His excuse at the time of torching the disused couch, was that he was under the misguided view he was, in fact, assisting the community by disposing of some rubbish left behind.

Morgan was charged with two counts of intentionally causing a bushfire and possessing a drug of dependence. On his plea of guilty, he was sentenced in the County Court of Victoria on 5 July 2016 to an aggregate term of imprisonment of 176 days, which he had already served by way of pre-detention. This meant he was automatically released back into the community, but had to undertake a CCO of 18 months, despite being determined to be unsuitable for such an order.

Given his extensive criminal history and the fact the CFA units took some hours to extinguish the bushfires, at first glance, his meagre sentence of six months jail did seem rather lenient.

However, His Honour, on sentencing, took into account that Morgan was suffering from mental issues which he was trying to address with medication, but was most likely not helped by his habitual use of drugs. Prior to his release and before he commenced the CCO, Morgan was the subject of an assessment order under the *Mental Health Act 2014* (Vic), meaning his mental health issues had to be further assessed and medically treated before he was released back into the community.

Morgan would also be the subject of judicial monitoring,[146] which meant he would be closely monitored appearing before the court on a regular six-monthly basis and further supported by a report from Corrections Victoria on his progress. His Honour, in addressing Morgan, where the court needed to monitor his dangerous behaviour said:

So, Mr Morgan, I hope you have taken all that in, because if you have and if you do the sort of things I have been outlining to you, we probably will not see you again. [147]

Morgan made some gratuitous comment about his young age and he hoped he could still do something with his life, noting he was advised by the court if it had not been for his guilty plea, under section 6AAA of the Sentencing Act, he would have been sentenced to a maximum term of three years imprisonment, with a minimum of 18 months, before being

---

[146] *Sentencing Act 1991* (Vic)- section 48K.

[147] *DPP v Andrew Morgan* [2016] VCC 939-para 77.

eligible for parole. Unfortunately, this young man, now aged 28, didn't listen to the sentencing judge and, you guessed it, the court would see him again within just six months, when he appeared before the Bairnsdale Magistrates Court on 18 January 2017, charged with arson.

Morgan was lucky that this indictable offence was able to be heard summarily under the jurisdiction of the lower court and both the prosecution and defence agreed to it being determined that way. Despite his previous offending, luck was once again on Morgan's side and he was sentenced to a further CCO, regardless of his history of breaching every such order.

It would only be a matter of time before Morgan was up to his old tricks and lighting more bushfires, which he did in early January 2019. Once again, he pleaded guilty to eight charges of intentionally causing a bushfire,[148] which carries a maximum penalty of 15 years jail for each offence. Morgan was sleeping rough on a mattress near the East Gippsland town of Nowa Nowa, north of Lakes Entrance, Victoria. It just so happened that eight fires were lit by Morgan over two days in January 2019 around the town and outer lying areas requiring, not only the attendance of the CFA ground crews, but also water bombing aircraft.

Morgan had previously been seen by police camping at the local recreation reserve and, on a second welfare check, had disappeared. He was then observed sitting on a log on 3 January 2019 in the area of the latest fire, where he told a Department of Sustainability and Environment (DSE) officer that he had in fact lit a fire the previous evening, because he was cold and wanted to get warm, noting the fire did a 'great job', obviously warming him up.

---

[148] *Crimes Act 1958* (Vic)-section 201A.

He then went onto say further that he had also lit the other fires the day before, as the surrounding bush area needed some attention with cleaning up. The DSE officer suggested to Morgan that it was not really the right time to be lighting fires in the bush. Morgan, and not with tongue in cheek, replied:

If it's ready to burn, then it's the right time of year.

He subsequently appeared in the County Court of Victoria on 27 July 2020, for sentencing on his guilty plea to the eight charges, but luckily before a different judge that made the 2016 comment about probably not seeing him again. This time, the court had no hesitation in sentencing Morgan as a serious arson offender under section 6B of the Sentencing Act, given his previous convictions for a similar type of arson offending.

Morgan had by now spent some 571 days in custody, being held at the Thomas Embling Hospital on a secure treatment order. This hospital is a high security forensic mental facility and is situated in Fairfield, Victoria, under the auspices of the Victorian Institute of Mental Health, commonly referred to as Forensicare.

His Honour was mindful of the long-standing mental history of Morgan, which was supported by Forensicare psychiatric reports, however, his offending on this occasion did not appear to be related to his habitual use of drugs. Despite evidence of active psychotic disorders, including paranoid schizophrenia, Morgan was still considered fit to plead guilty before the court. In any event, he would still need to continue with treatment and not just at Thomas Embling, but on conditional release at an appropriate in-patient psychiatric facility.

On sentencing Morgan to a total of three years imprisonment, with a minimum of two years before being eligible for parole, His Honour declined to impose any CCO on release, understandably on the basis that he had previously breached three such orders. In respect of sentencing Morgan as a serious arson offender, His Honour noted that:

> *The law says that where an offender is sentenced as a "serious offender", the court must regard protection of the community as the principal sentencing purpose, despite the existence of a mental impairment or illness. But, as always, although comity protection may be a key sentencing consideration, a court should not focus on one consideration to the exclusion of other relevant factors... on archiving the appropriate balance in the sentencing process.[149]*

It was obvious Morgan was not a well man and had a number of mental health challenges that, quite rightly, the court took into account in imposing, once again, a lenient sentence, given the tenure of his recidivist offending. Despite being classified as a serious arson offender, it still begs the question, is the community adequately protected once he is released? Only time will tell.

CCOs were certainly the flavour of the month in 2007, despite three recalcitrant offenders causing in excess of $500,000 damage to Bendigo's Historic St Aiden's Orphanage, with firefighters taking some 90 minutes to extinguish the blaze. The orphanage was built in 1905 and, at the time, was the sole Good Shepherd Convent in Australia, looking after boys up to 11 years old and girls up to 16 years of age.

---

[149] *DPP v Andrew Morgan* [2020] VCC 1113-para 68.

It continued as a residential facility until 1984 and has since been converted to a very attractive set of apartments. Unfortunately, the building also suffered from other fires, the first in 1909 which saw the loss of life of a young orphan girl, who suffered horrendous injuries dying in hospital. The fire was later determined to be accidental following a magisterial inquiry and not requiring any further investigation.

The fire in August 2006 was certainly not accidental with two brothers, Scott Hagley, 22 years of age and Justin Hagley, two years older, together with a mate by the name of Scott Allen, conspired and set fire to the old orphanage, first by using sparklers, which obviously didn't do the damage they had hoped for. They then returned the next night by pouring kerosene into the laundry and, after lighting it, left the scene to change their clothes, only to then return to look at their efforts.

This was not to be the last of their adventures as the two brothers later set fire to a disused school building, with one of them lighting a further fire at a football club room. This was then followed by a damaging fire lit in the tennis clubrooms at a sports oval named after Harry Trott, a famous Australian test cricketer who also formed the Bendigo Cricket Association in 1903. Their final claim to fame was when Justin Hagley set fire to a haystack situated in Golden Square, damaging a building site causing $105,0000 in damage.

Taking into account the Hagley brothers both suffered from intellectual disabilities, Judge Chettle, in the County Court of Victoria in October 2007, certainly had some sympathy for them on their guilty plea. His Honour noted they both came from a broken family and their grandmother had died only a week before they started out on their fire rampage, with His Honour stating that they obviously expressed their grief by lighting fires. In respect of Allan, it was noted he too was under a significant amount of stress having already been a victim of crime, so perhaps that also was an excuse for his fire lighting escapades, not that the court made that comment.

The Hagley brothers were sentenced to 250 and 200 hours of community work under a CCO, whilst Allen got off even lighter, being ordered to undertake a paltry 100 hours. His Honour did order they also undertake a juvenile fire awareness and intervention program, a support program about fire risk behaviour in a child or young person.

The court also ordered the three convicted offenders pay restitution of nearly $600,000 with a defence lawyer for one of the brothers and Allen making a gratuitous comment to His Honour. This was to the effect they were not opposing the order but, 'the practicality of it is that both my clients will never, ever, have the ability to repay,' which was also supported by his lawyer colleague also acting in the matter, which led the judge to comment, 'Not unless they win the Tatts.' His Honour then went on to say:

You've got to understand you cannot light fires and you cannot damage property in this way. Do you understand?...You don't want to see me again.

Despite the trio pleading guilty at the first opportunity and having no previous convictions until now, further expressing untold remorse for their actions in lighting the fires, the brothers were, obviously like some others, not listening to the learned judge. Once again joining forces, they carried on with their dirty work in late November 2019, but this time with another tenpin bowling mate by the name of Andrew

Valli. These soon-to-be serial arsonists went on a fire lighting rampage, totalling in the order of nearly 50 fires with some destroying farm fencing and 180 acres of farmland, including a hay shed.

Many of the fires were set by the use of, believe it or not, sparklers on a late Friday afternoon and evening along roadsides from November 2019 through to late March 2020, while travelling between Bendigo and Shepparton on their way to play tenpin bowls. They obviously knew that a sparkler, being a handheld type of firework that burnt sparks slowly and, given their previous success in lighting fires, this would again be their weapon of choice.

The tenpin bowling fanatics were now known with the moniker of the "Three Terrors" firebug gang, possibly named, not only after their bowling team, but the Heckle and Jeckle terry toons cartoon the "Ten Pin Terrors". No doubt, young children loved watching these cartoon antics downing breakfast cereal of Weet-Bix, but this trio quickly became the subject of an intense investigation by the Bendigo Criminal Investigation Unit (CIU).

Whilst they had a number of persons of interest under the radar, it wasn't until 24 January 2020 when dedicated CIU members carrying out a patrol along one of back roads, where a previous fire had occurred some days earlier, they observed a Mazda utility with three heads on board just before midnight, which was only the second car seen that evening.

They pulled the vehicle over and, after introducing themselves and the reason they were in the area due to incidents of arson, it's fair to say the CIU detectives suddenly became very interested when the trio told them they always travel on the same road on a Friday evening after tenpin bowling. Their interest became further heightened when, after checking licence details, they ascertained that the Hagley brothers were indeed known to police with convictions for the 2006 arson fires. However, there was still more work to do on these now very firm suspects, waving them on their way after taking their details.

The usual mobile phone location scans of the trio confirmed and reinforced that these individuals were now firmly in police sights, with the data matching the times and locations for a number of the fires. Still needing more evidence to charge them and prove their guilt beyond reasonable doubt, CIU detectives placed both a tracking and listening device in their Mazda vehicle after more fires were started along their usual route of choice to and from Shepparton. As tenpin bowling had been cancelled due to the COVID pandemic, the three miscreants, unaware their conversations and whereabouts were being closely monitored, drove to Melbourne and back on 27 March 2020.

They would stop along the way to buy, not only ice-creams, but also their favourite fire starters, being sparklers, which they would later use by throwing the slow burning item out of the car window, hoping it would ignite fires along the roadway. On listening to their conversations as the suspects left Melbourne and were returning to Bendigo, police put out an alert to 'any units in the vicinity of' to be aware of the possibility of fires starting along the route.

This warning was prompted by the following incriminating and worrying conversation police had tapped into, with Valli saying to the Hagley brothers:

Not interested in talking about ice creams now. I'm more interested in a fire, alright?

This was followed by a further discussion as it seems the fire sparklers were not working properly:

Starting to get fucking frustrated. Been driving nearly two hours and not one fire has been lit. That's why we're going out here.

It was quite obvious they were hell bent on lighting fires and even went on chattering about setting alight a vacant house, followed by bragging to each other of their previous Friday night sparkler escapades, as they happily continued to light fires on the way back to Bendigo. Prior to being intercepted by police and, even on seeing an unmarked police car as they drove past, they were not perturbed and simply continued lighting the fires, throwing sparklers out of their vehicle. Finally, they were pulled over and, of course, their conversations were still being recorded. Probably in a panic, not that it sounded like it, one of the Hagley brothers said to his cohorts:

They can't say that we lit them because…they can't prove that we lit them…

Their forlorn hope that the police had no proof soon became apparent to them, as these very competent investigators had a plethora of incriminating evidence they had painstakingly put together. When faced with this, the trio pleaded guilty to 49 separate fires from early November 2019 to late March 2020, but this time there was no hope of a CCO.

Each were sentenced to a total of six years and four months in prison, without being eligible for parole until they had served at least four years behind bars. Given their history of serial arson offending, they may well struggle to be released until they have served their full term and will most likely be fitted with a tracking device on release.

However, the final word needs to be given to Detective Leading Senior Constable Heazlewood of Bendigo CIU for his team's outstanding work for which they should be congratulated. He said:

It was one of the best jobs because we were able to get evidence so good that there was just no fight by the defence…I'm pretty happy I solved it because the alternative was that these three guys didn't get caught and were free to light another series of fires in the summer of 2020/21.[150]

Bendigo police certainly must be applauded for another diligent investigation, bringing to justice two other serial arsonists, who caused mayhem and havoc throughout the Bendigo region in early 2016. Corey Devereaux and Ricky Mackay, both in their early 20s, set out on their arson adventures during January and February 2016 lighting over 20 fires, mainly in Eaglehawk and Kangaroo Flat, situated about 13 kilometres from the main town centre. They set fire to a bookstore, portable classrooms and put struggling sports clubs to suffer the loss or damage to clubrooms, critical equipment and sporting memorabilia. The total damage bill, thanks to their heroics, was in the order of $825,000 and saw three firefighters injured trying to extinguish the fires.

They first came to the attention of Bendigo detectives when they allegedly witnessed a gang of youths setting fire to

---

[150] *Stopping a fire starter* - from Police Life Autumn/Winter 2022 - Victoria Police, editorial by Jesse Wray McCann.

a portable classroom in early February 2016. They were still at the scene when local CFA units arrived and willingly provided their details for what they said they had witnessed, followed by similar witness statements to police. This was all a load of rubbish as they were the ones responsible for setting the fire, which police had already determined. They would both be later charged with attempting to pervert the course of justice under section 320 of the Crimes Act, which carries a maximum penalty of 25 years imprisonment for misleading investigators on what had transpired.

Police now placed them both under close surveillance and on 19 February 2016 they were known to be in the vicinity of a rubbish bin fire, moments before it went up in flames. This was then followed by their next and last fires the day after. One was at a sports oval destroying the scorer's box and goal posts and the other in their usual Cleanaway rubbish bin. When arrested the following morning on Sunday, 21 February 2016, police found in their possession a backpack full of a number of firelighters and other items connecting them to the fires.

Mackay pleaded guilty to 13 charges of arson and the one of perverting the course of justice, while Devereaux also entered a guilty plea to 11 charges and the pervert justice charge. They also pleaded guilty to a number of lesser charges under section 11 of the *Summary Offences Act 1966*(Vic) of lighting fires in the open air, which carries a maximum punishment of 120 penalty units, 12 months' imprisonment or both.

Her Honour, on sentencing both offenders in the County Court of Victoria on 13 October 2016, referring to a number of victim impact statements, said:

It was apparent from these victim impact statements just how

> *far reaching the consequences of your actions were. In lighting these fires, you not only caused financial damage, but also considerable emotional distress and despair to members of the community that were affected by the fires.[151]*

In material tendered to the court by defence counsel, by way of mitigation, it was submitted that Mackay demonstrated a vulnerability to social influence and had a manipulation borderline personality disorder, according to the psychological report. This meant, having such a low cognitive ability, he was most likely not the instigator in carrying out these crimes.

However, counsel for Devereaux, also supported by a psychological report, suggested that it wasn't his client but the instigator was Mackay, so they were both blaming each other. This was despite it suggested that Devereaux apparently had no motive for his offending, but on balance he had good prospects for rehabilitation. In the end it was agreed and supported by Her Honour that both offenders were equally complicit in the offending.

The court, on sentencing, took into account their early guilty pleas, their apparent remorse and that they were both young offenders with no prior convictions. Her Honour, in weighing up all these factors, said further:

> *…even allowing for the mitigating factors…this case presented a difficult sentencing exercise with respect to you both. This is because of the serious nature of your offending and the effects it had on the community. While no lives were lost, the community lost educational and sporting facilities…In the case of the portable classroom…they gave young people who had fallen*

---

151   *DPP v Corey Devereaux & Anor* [2016] VCC 1528-para 21.

through the gaps an extra chance at an education. The loss of the sporting club…has taken away a valuable recreational facility. Fire crews had to extinguish all the fires you lit over that summer period.[152]

The court then laid down what is one of the basic principles in our criminal justice system:

The administration of justice depends upon the system operating so that people who commit crimes are pursued and brought to court and are punished, and those who take part in trying to interfere with that system commit a grave injustice insofar as the community is concerned.[153]

Devereaux and Mackay were both sentenced as serious arson offenders and to serve a maximum of five years with a longer than normal parole period of three years. This took into account the 236 days already served on remand, but that the protection of the community was forefront when imposing such a sentence. The usual 6AAA of the Sentencing Act was also referred to, if not for their plea of guilty, the head sentence would have been seven years with a bottom non-parole period of four years and eight months.

This was the second serious case of arson offending to be brought before the County Court in the week beginning 10 October 2023, with Nicholas Archer being sentenced to 14 years in prison, despite not sentenced as a serious arson offender. Crime Stoppers Victoria (CSV) emphasised to the community, following both court cases, it was important for

---

152 Ibid-para 59.

153 Ibid-para 61.

the public to be aware of what was happening around them and to report any suspicious activity which may assist crime investigators.

Crime Stoppers has been a leading campaigner in Victoria, established in 1987 thanks to Geoff Wilkinson who, at the time was director of media for Victoria Police. It certainly raised awareness in the community regarding arson and other offending, enlisting the assistance of the public in solving crime by identifying the perpetrators responsible.

The County Court of Victoria was certainly kept busy in the latter half of 2016 and on this occasion, they had the pleasure, or perhaps not, of the self-represented Brendan Davies, found guilty of five counts of arson by a jury on 25 November 2016, with two of the verdicts by way of majority and the remaining three unanimous. A majority verdict of 11 out of 12 jurors can be accepted on the direction of a judge in situations where a unanimous verdict cannot be reached, despite lengthy deliberations.

Being self-represented, of course, poses a number of problems and, as the saying goes, Davies had a fool for a client, namely himself. He was certainly not only a fool but a very argumentative one at that, continually interrupting proceedings and vigorously cross-examining witnesses for the prosecution. He would also make spurious objections that simply had no proper basis and, believe it or not, repeatedly interjected and argued with the presiding judge who, at one stage, became very tired of his behaviour, telling Davies basically to shut up. The trial lasted 61 days.

Davies even thought he could plead guilty to some of the charges as laid, but to the others, it had to be on his terms and conditions, which was totally unacceptable to the court. The jury was obviously glad this circus of a trial was over and, after handing down the guilty verdicts, some jurors expressed their utter frustration, even crying and cheering with relief.

Davies first came to the attention of police when he was only 18 years of age in 1997 and, in the Magistrates Court's view, he was a low-level offender, placing him in an adjourned undertaking of 12 months without conviction. This was despite Davies being charged with what could be considered serious offences: stalking, assaults, unlawfully on premises and criminal damage. In 2004 and with further convictions, including possession of weapons, he also set out lighting his first fire and this was to his family home. Fortunately, his mother and two brothers escaped unharmed. All this offending resulted in him serving custodial sentences right through, up to and including 2006.

He didn't help himself of course regarding the arson conviction as, when police searched his backpack they found firelighters, sparklers and numerous boxes of matches. Of course, Davies denied they were used to set the house fire, claiming they were for purposes of camping, but a jury certainly rejected that defence finding him guilty. On that occasion, he was sentenced to a maximum of three years with only 15 months of non-parole, which saw him released from custody in 2006, but surprisingly, without any supervision while on parole.

His next foray into offending took place in February 2009 for which he was bailed. This again was questionable seeing he was charged with serious offending, including being armed with a knife, allegedly so he could kidnap a sex worker in order to remove her teeth and fingernails.

Despite a set of onerous bail conditions, which included a night curfew, he set out on an arson spree in January and

February 2011. Davies set fire to the unoccupied Mt Waverley Police Station and two churches, using firelighters and petrol causing minor damage, noting one of the churches was occupied by an unsuspecting priest who was asleep at the time, but luckily, he was not injured. He then set two more large fires using accelerant, one in late January 2011 to a bakery shop in Mount Waverley, followed by a further fire, again using accelerant to a childcare centre, some days later in February. These two fires alone caused significant damage to both premises with losses estimated in the order of $800,000.

Davies was certainly a strange but disturbed and dangerous felon. This was obviously demonstrated by his creativity, setting up a website page in which he blatantly displayed his disgust and hatred for society. He called and disguised himself as a seer, obviously based on some sort of Greek mythology, with a range of powers, including seeing things obscured to others. Under the disguised moniker of "Seer Travis Truman" on his website, wearing a balaclava and sunglasses, he put together YouTube videos and excerpts. He not only spoke about random arson events, but what he intended to do in similar attacks on society.

All this would come back to haunt him as they would later be used in evidence by the prosecution of him preaching to anyone that would listen, what he would go on to commit.

In one of the videos, he said:

I hope that has been instructive, whether or not you are an arsonist...I am making this video for my benefit, for my reasons...as my final word is that society brings these attacks on itself. It absolutely deserves them...These individuals who undertake these actions have got every right to do so...

Davies, being motivated by his website antics, obviously didn't realise he would be the subject of both surveillance and a tracking device installed in his vehicle. It was put in place by the State Surveillance Unit of Victoria Police under "Operation Navarre", as they monitored his whereabouts, placing him at the scene of the bakery shop fire. The dedicated surveillance team of detectives then followed him back to his home in Rowville, noting they still didn't think they had enough on him at this stage to effect an arrest.

His final fire at the childcare centre was his undoing, with separate police surveillance teams observing him parking his vehicle in a nearby street and setting off towards the centre on foot via a laneway. Some minutes later, he was seen running back to his car and then driving off. Even with these officers quickly reporting the building on fire, it was still destroyed, but they would now arrest Davies as there was no doubt what he had been up to.

It took some use of capsicum spray to put him in handcuffs and this wanna-be lawyer, acting on his own legal advice, then made a "no comment" record of interview. A subsequent search warrant on his vehicle and his room in his mother's home, found further compelling evidence in both physical and digital form, adding further weight to the prosecution's case.

This fool for a client lawyer, now defendant, after being found guilty in November 2016, appeared before the County Court of Victoria on 10 April 2017 for sentencing on five counts of arson but still proclaimed his innocence. This was despite the abundance of incriminating evidence, including his website antics and videos, not to mention the close covert surveillance, CCTV footage from his home, tracking undertaken by Victoria Police and DNA taken from a bottle linking him to one of the church fires, resulting in conviction on all counts.

Davies, now 38 years of age, with an extensive criminal history, including previous periods of incarceration, was sentenced to a total of 14 years, six months imprisonment as a serious arson offender, with a fixed non-parole period of 12 years and six months with 1,123 days already served while on remand awaiting trial. Davies, in his usual aggressive and argumentative fashion, was even carrying on about the jurors being in court when he was sentenced, which the judge dismissed as they had every right to be present.

His Honour noted Davies had never been employed and was the recipient of a disability pension, when not in jail, since he was 18 years old. Davies suggested in his lengthy submissions that, due to his early childhood, he suffered from post-traumatic stress disorder and anxiety, coupled with autism spectrum disorder and possibly Aspergers Syndrome, or impaired mental functioning, being accepted to a degree by the court.

It was noted, however, that Davies refused to cooperate with an expert Forensicare evaluation, including for eminent psychologist, Mr Tim Watson-Munro, to speak with Davies' still-supportive mother.

His Honour, in trying to put Davies submissions into some sort of sentencing context of his moral culpability, noted there was no evidence that Davies had any useful insight to his offending whatsoever and said:

…your moral culpability remains very high and is not, in my view, to be seen as diminished by reason of any aspect of your impaired mental functioning…You knew precisely what you were doing by committing each of the arsons and that it amounted to what you intended, which is a deliberate attack

on our community. It was a considered, deliberate campaign all planned and executed by you...[154]

His Honour, based on the evidence and coupled with all relevant matters before him, then said further:

...it is clear in my view that you are an ongoing danger to the community. The likelihood of you reoffending in the future is very high. On any realistic analysis, your prospects for reform and rehabilitation are very slim at best and most likely non-existent...[155]*...I make it clear that you are not punished for pleading not guilty and running a trial. Nor that you represented yourself...*[156]*...there is a total absence of remorse...*[157]

It was, indeed, abundantly clear that Davies was a dangerous recidivist offender, even to a degree that the prosecution team in the 2016 trial and sentencing, preferred to be only known as Mr Prosecutor, obviously concerned for their safety and not wanting to reveal their identity to this much maligned sociopath. But Davies, with all his "experience" in self-representation, including previous numerous interlocutory applications to a higher court, still appealed his sentence to the Supreme Court of Victoria Court of Appeal. This was determined on 29 March 2019, with Davies, once again representing himself, and now a Madam Prosecutor for the Office of the DPP.

The court's exhaustive 129-page judgment addressed a

---

154   *DPP v Brendan Davies* [2017] VCC 1101-para 90.
155   Ibid-para 95.
156   Ibid-para 105.
157   Ibid-para 106.

total of 12 grounds of appeal, including and, not limited to, that the sentence was manifestly excessive, admissibility of evidence, such as internet exhibits and videos, the DNA sample and also that the judge was biased and may have erred in applying the Verdins principle. Davies was ultimately right for once and was resentenced to 12 years and three months imprisonment with a non-parole period of 10 years, three months.

The Court of Appeal, in using their discretion further, took into account his autism spectrum disorder reducing his culpability, whether the delay in prosecution was a limited mitigating factor and, would you believe, a deduction of two days as the pre detention figure of 1,123 days on remand was incorrect. Well, I suspect Davies would be satisfied to a point, as at least he received a deduction on top of the sentence and parole by some two years.[158]

One violent offender, who was also sentenced as a serious arson offender, was Joshua Tormey. At the time of sentencing in the County Court of Victoria in January 2023, Tormey was 32 years of age but had a criminal history as far back as 2010, when at the age of 19 years, in company with his younger brother, set fire to a Melbourne school resulting in millions of dollars damage, burning it to the ground. He subsequently was sentenced to a total of three years imprisonment with a non-parole period of only 12 months.

He went back for a short stint in jail in 2015 for making threats to kill, but obviously didn't learn his lesson, pleading guilty to a further charge of criminal damage by fire and again making threats to kill. This time he threatened to kill his mother and her sister, then set a fire, not to a school this time, but the family home. Tormey went back to prison as a serial

---

158 *Davies v The Queen* {2019} VSCA 66.

arson offender for the school and house fire, for a total of 34 months with a non-parole period of 20 months.[159]

As part of my role in the prevention and detection of school crime for the Victorian Ministry of Education, I had the unfortunate pleasure of going after a number of school arsonists over nearly 20 years from 1974 through to 1993. One school serial arsonist, or perhaps I should elevate him to a pyromaniac, not that he was in the same level of some serial arson offenders I have referred to so far, was a scoundrel by the name of Raymond James Saville. He had 20 previous arson convictions, including his foray into trying to burn down Shepparton Technical School in January 1975. His previous arson convictions stemmed from four court appearances as far back as 1973, with two substantial terms of imprisonment of four years in 1976 and five years from 1983.

Saville had a penchant for lighting fires in stormy weather and even being found in bed after one such fire in wet pyjamas, telling investigators he just had a shower at home, obviously fully clothed. In October 1989, he couldn't help himself, setting fire to a church, followed by a school in Eltham, causing damage in the order of $250,000. Needing to witness his handiwork once again, he returned to the scene of his crimes where he would watch the buildings burn and also where he was arrested.

In August 1990, Saville appeared before His Honour, Judge Cash, and the learned judge commented that Saville had chosen the crime of arson as his criminal speciality. He went on to say that Saville was a menace to society with an appalling history of lighting fires, particularly in schools. His modus operandi was to search a building looking for money and, in the case of the Eltham Christian Church and School where he

---

[159] *DPP v Tormey* [2023] VCC 28.

only found three dollars, he became so annoyed that he set the fires which almost gutted each building.

The judge noted Saville had poor social skills and, on release, he needed to get help for his pyromania, but at the same time he could not be seen as someone who did not know what he was doing. On that basis and, given his prior convictions, he was jailed for 10 years and six months. Another not so likeable rogue out of action for some time.

On my only sojourn to Pentridge, I visited Saville, our well credentialed rogue school arsonist. I arrived one sunny afternoon to serve him with some papers, putting him on notice that the Ministry of Education would be seeking restitution against him by court order and if that failed, they would sue him civilly if he was ultimately convicted of his latest school fire. To put it bluntly, he told me to, 'Fuck off,' which I did.

The number of Victorian school fires, unfortunately, were to escalate during the period 1990-1992, to a degree where I finally came to the conclusion that the task of preventing and detecting school crime and, despite our hard-earned efforts, school arson was simply out of control. Since 1985, fires, burglary and vandalism were averaging around $5 million a year in costs to the ministry, of which half could be attributed to arson.

By the end of the financial year in 1992, we would unfortunately experience 136 school fires over a two-year period at an estimated cost of around $5 million alone. This was despite arson only accounting for one in every 50 offences involving school property crime.

The ministry, however, was not the only education body being subjected to school fires, noting a fire at Wesley College in Prahran in the early morning hours on Sunday, 19 November

1989. Damage was estimated to be, at the very least, around $3 million. Being one of Australia's most famous and private schools, it had past students of some note, including former prime ministers, Sir Robert Menzies and Harold Holt. The fire not only destroyed the school library, but a collection of rare Greek and Roman antiques and a valuable collection of Australian books.

It was also noted at the time that school fires in the UK had increased from $18 million in 1987 to $55 million by 1990. In due course, they would introduce an amendment to their *Criminal Justice Act 1967* (UK), which would hold parents liable to pay compensation for their child's acts of vandalism. This was certainly a new approach but, despite us making inroads in seeking compensation restitution against the actual offender, suing parents was another level and I was not convinced of the success they would have with this approach.

At common law, the general principle is that a juvenile cannot be held liable in the absence of any statutory provisions, which then extends to parents and the question of vicarious liability. There clearly would have to be a distinct set of circumstances to make a parent liable. It would also raise the issue of whether the parent had in fact been negligent and, therefore, directly liable for the actions of their child.

Our detection and arrest of school arsonists was, however, foremost on our agenda and one distinct example of such untiring and dedicated efforts was clearly demonstrated in the Frankston High School fires, bringing the firebugs to justice.

13

CATCHING THE FIREBUGS

On Monday, 2 July 1990 at 2141 hours, Frankston High School, situated around 55 kilometres from the Melbourne CBD, was set on fire causing damage to its north wing in the order of $1 million. Unfortunately, fires lit by the same two offenders at this school on another five occasions would take place over the next 12 months. The school was a large multi campus co–educational facility situated in Foot Street, Frankston.

Occupying two interacting sites and built in 1924, it offered education for years 7-10 and senior years 11 and 12. It was considered to be a very proud school, not only in providing academic excellence, but with strong parental support and had formed close links with the local community. The school's principal, Ken Rowe, was ably supported by a diverse range of excellent teachers, but they were soon to have their spirits lowered by a spate of deliberately lit fires.

Following the first fire on Monday, 2 July 1990, effectively destroying the school's north wing, the firm policy of the

Ministry of Education, implemented by our security officers, was to place any school, that had suffered a fire, under patrol for a number of weeks and also to install a silent alarm system. Frankston High School was already alarmed and the first notifications to our control room was the fire itself as it had been started from outside the building. The close surveillance given to the school seemed to be successful as nothing more happened until January 1991 when two fires were lit: the first at 0015 hours on Wednesday, 2 January 1991, followed by another only seven days later at 2302 hours on 9 January 1991.

Like the fire in July 1990, we only received alarm notifications at 0015 hours when the actual fire was burning and certainly not as a result of any forced entry. The second fire was clearly due to a forced entry and it appeared the arsonist(s), using an accelerant, had set the fire in a stack of papers. The fire on 2 January 1991 had occurred in the junior block of the school with damage estimated at $175,000. The fire on 9 January1991 was in the senior administration block causing damage in the order of $100,000.

Following a meeting with Detective Inspector Laurie Ratz, officer in charge of Frankston Criminal Investigation Branch (CIB), we decided the school needed to be placed under better surveillance by the use of close circuit television cameras, as well as our patrols. This type of video surveillance would allow video cameras to transmit a signal to our control room by the school telephone line. In view of two of the fires being lit without any forced entry into the building, the thinking at the time was we could observe any activity that was taking place after hours.

Such surveillance methods were not uncommon, as in 1968, New York became the first city in the United States to install video cameras as a means of fighting crime, particularly street crime. Similar initiatives had been tried in the United Kingdom and a number of businesses, prone to burglary, had also implemented this form of surveillance. It was also hoped that by installing CCTV around the school it would serve as a form of deterrence to any would-be offenders.

A problem we had though, was achieving real time pictures back to our control room. We were receiving the images but there was a time delay of 45 to 60 minutes. The technology we were effectively experimenting with meant that while the CCTV was recording around 25 frames a second, once it was being fed into a telephone line, it was in a time lapse. This meant one to three frames every second were being fed to a telephone line, as in the example of a fax machine. Another issue we also faced was that too much data was being transmitted, resulting in the data banking up while waiting to gain access before being received by our control room. We tried this form of surveillance but technically it had its issues and therefore the idea was soon shelved. Back to square one.

At around 2336 hours on Wednesday, 20 March 1991, a Molotov cocktail was thrown through a window setting fire, once again, to the senior block, but this time the staffroom was affected. The damage was only minor, but it was obvious that after the fourth fire at the same school, it had to be placed under covert surveillance until such time we were able to effect an arrest. Following a further meeting with Laurie and members of the Frankston CIB, our under-cover surveillance team were given the task to coordinate after hours covert surveillance inside the senior and junior blocks of the school buildings. It was determined this would provide a good view of the main areas being targeted and hopefully, at some point in time, the offender(s) would attempt further mayhem.

As part of our planning, we had to determine what hours we would sit inside the school. Given that the four fires, apart from the first one on 2 July 1990, had been set late at night with one occurring after midnight, we decided the covert surveillance would commence around 2200 hrs until 0300 hours, seven days a week. Part of our thinking was that a five-hour shift would not be as tiring on our operatives but in the event it became too tedious, we could replace them with other security officers. In addition, the school was equipped with a silent intruder detection system so if the offender(s) gained entry to any of the buildings, prior to the covert surveillance, at least we would be notified. Although, this type of surveillance had not worked very well to date.

We clearly made an error in determining the hours of the covert surveillance, as on Sunday, 5 May 1991 at 2142 hours, a multi section break alarm activation was received by our control room from the school's administration building. One of our undercover team was only a few minutes away from the school as his covert surveillance was to commence at 2200 hours. Unfortunately, not only did we once again fail to arrest the offender(s), but the fire had quickly gained control. On arrival a few minutes after receiving the alarm notifications, he radioed in that the school was once again on fire.

This was now the fifth fire in the space of 10 months and the impact this was having on the school community, in particular staff and students, was totally devastating. Although our security staff were also very disappointed and frustrated at our lack of success, we were not going to let the culprit(s) continue with such acts of arson. We believed it was only a matter of time before an arrest would be made.

Unfortunately, our positive thinking received another

setback as around 2051 hours on Thursday, 8 August 1991, a fire causing around $100,000 damage, was set inside a portable classroom after being started with an accelerant. This now meant a total of six fires, with damage in excess of $1.5 million and, despite our undercover surveillance now in its fifth month, we were still no closer in identifying any suspects.

Laurie and his team of investigators, now working in close liaison with the Police Arson Squad, led by Detective Sergeant Neville Taylor, were also at their wits end trying to determine who was responsible. They had convened a task force named "Operation Firebug" after the fifth fire, to try to bring this mayhem to an end. Finally, at around 2315 hours on the night of Monday, 12 August 1991, the nightmare was to come to its final conclusion.

A very urgent radio transmission from one of our surveillance operatives was received by our control room notifying us of "offenders on" and requesting immediate back up. Hiding under a table in the senior school administration wing, he very quietly whispered that two offenders were actually right above him on the school roof. He could hear them talking while, at the same time, they appeared to be drilling a hole in the building's roof, obviously to place an accelerant before setting the fire.

After being notified and driving to the school, which was 45 minutes from home, I directed that all units switch over to channel B on our radio network as our undercover operative needed to have direct radio communication without any interference from other users on channel A. Our control room had notified Police D24 Communications of "offenders on" and, it's fair to say, the Dog Squad and police units from all directions were on their way to the school, including Police Air 490.

The offenders continued drilling directly above our officer, placing him in danger so a decision was made to try and effect an arrest before they could place their accelerant and light a fire. By this stage, we had a number of police officers virtually surrounding the school, so he was able to safely leave the building. When finally seeing the police, the two offenders took off but were quickly arrested, handcuffed and placed separately into police divisional vans.

An examination of the building's roof left us in no doubt that we had finally arrested the offenders for the Frankston High School fires. We found an incendiary type of bomb device with more than 30 rifle cartridges, a bag of tools and a portable drill. No doubt, we would have the pleasure of seeing the offenders in "the dock" in due course.

I had the pleasure of unbolting the police divisional van rear doors to introduce myself to each offender, wishing them well and trusting they would enjoy prison. I also had a vivid memory of drunken spectators, escorted from the cricket ground with the crowd cheering and singing the Painters and Dockers song, 'You're going home in the back of a divvy van.'

In the County Court dock before Judge John Nixon in June 1992, were Evan Rees Williams, 19 years of age and Jonathan Cleveland Loftes, 17 years, both now former students at Frankston High School. They were sentenced for arson in respect to the four fires they lit between 9 January 1990 and 8 August 1991, and also the attempted arson on 12 August 1991. However, they were not charged in respect to the major blaze on 2 July 1990 and for the fire on 2 January 1991. I have no doubt that these two miscreants were most likely responsible for those two fires as well.

Regarding the fire on 9 January 1991, they were equipped

with a green army-type carrier bag which contained, not only tools, but two containers of a mixture of kerosene, turpentine and petrol. They cut a hole in the school roof, climbed down into the administration area and set fire to a stack of papers. Their modus operandi on 20 March 1991 was courtesy of a Molotov cocktail and while Loftes held the bottle, it was lit by Williams and then thrown through a smashed window.

On 5 May 1991, a similar accelerant was used which Loftes poured around inside before setting it alight and leaving to walk home with Williams to Cecil Street, Frankston. As we suspected, the portable classroom fire on 8 August 1991 was started by pouring petrol down a drilled hole into the classroom after Williams had passed up the necessary tools and equipment.

Prosecutor, James Bowen, submitted to the court that the raids were somewhat sophisticated, but gave examples of the type of arson committed on public buildings, in particular, schools. He also noted that these two offenders placed responding fire units in grave danger if the incendiary devices left behind had detonated, while the fires were being extinguished.

Loftes was represented by barrister, Peter Cash, who provided the court with a variety of reasons why his client set the fires, including wanting days off from school and not wanting to sit exams or complete assignments. Counsel further submitted, his client had not considered the amount of damage that would be inflicted on the buildings but also saw himself as some sort of modern-day Batman by scaling school walls and climbing onto the roof of various buildings. Cash also blamed the other offender's parents who appeared to have no control over their son, Williams. He also said it was rather extraordinary that Loftes carried out this type of offending because of his loyalty to Williams.

In the case of Williams, barrister, Ron Clark, noted the fires were an aberration for his client as he was a dedicated member of the Church of Jesus Christ of Latter-Day Saints in Frankston, in addition to his work in the community. Overall, it was admitted that he was equally involved in the offending with Loftes. His excuse was, he had a grudge against teachers and in some way, 'wanted to get back at those who crossed his path.'

His Honour was not impressed and, on remanding both in custody, pending pre-sentence reports, noted that it would be practically impossible for either counsel to submit they should be freed. Williams was subsequently sentenced to two and a half years in a Youth Training Centre (YTC) and noting Loftes had previously been "inadequately" sentenced by a learned magistrate in an earlier Children's Court sentence for only six months, the judge gave him 18 months. Williams was also ordered to make restitution to the Ministry of Education to the sum of $527,427, with Loftes receiving a lesser amount of $156,736 for reasons unknown to me.

Overall, those involved in this lengthy time-consuming investigation were extremely disappointed with the meagre sentences of only two and half years for Williams and a lesser sentence of only 18 months for Loftes. I say this on the basis that there are two arsonists who caused absolute mayhem, setting fire to Frankston High School on four separate occasions, but were not charged for two other fires, noting one of the fires was only seven days prior to the fire on 9 January 1991. They were also ordered to pay a piddling restitution amount of $680,000, yet the total fire damage bill was well over $1 million. Of course, such compensation would never have been recovered in any event.

What was also not taken into account, the effect these fires had on the school community. In the words of principal, Ken Rowe, who gave a victim impact statement before the court, 'The impact on the morale of pupils and staff was devastating, it caused untold concern and anxiety.'

The school lost, not only buildings, but furniture, equipment, including computers, irreplaceable school records and memorabilia. In addition, after two of the fires, over 700 students were sent home for two days before they and the staff could be subsequently relocated.

To again quote Lord Chief Justice Gordon Hewart, when he set down the often quoted maxim:

Justice should not only be done but should manifestly and undoubtedly be seen to be done.[160]

In the case of the Frankston High School arsonists, on this occasion, those principles were in no way given such relevance, given the lenient sentences imposed on these two serial arsonists. However, for our covert surveillance team and Frankston CIB, it was certainly one well deserved and satisfying outcome.

---

160   *R v Sussex Justices, ex parte McCarthy* [1924] 1KB56 [1923] All ER Rep 233.

14
NURSING HOME TRAGEDY

Unfortunately, many arsonists, whether they be serial, spree or simply even a one-off fire lighter, perhaps don't realise, then again, some probably do, their planned or spontaneous acts in setting fires to buildings or even scrub land, such as we have seen in many sad instances, can and often will, result in death and injury to unsuspecting victims.

Nursing home fires have also seen a sad outcome for many elderly and infirm residents resulting in the loss of life. Such was the case in the Wincrest Nursing Home fire in Chicago, US on 30 January 1976. Despite the building only suffering minor heat and smoke damage, 23 elderly residents perished. The fire started in a third-floor room and was first reported by a nursing aid notifying the local fire department and, pending their arrival, which was only a matter of minutes, staff attended to the evacuation of many of the residents. Unfortunately, there were other residents trapped in their wheelchairs on the third floor, including one employee, later dying from smoke inhalation.

Chicago Police subsequently arrested and charged a nursing home housekeeper who was indicted on 47 counts, including murder and arson, but she was acquitted on all charges by a jury in 1977. The aftermath of the fire did, however, see a positive outcome with the city of Chicago and its Board of Health updating their fire regulations for nursing homes. This included the installation of sprinkler systems in all new and existing type facilities, together with many other safety improvements and proper emergency training for all nursing home employees.

Following a nursing home fire at a facility known as the Greenwood Health Center in Connecticut, US in February 2003, a woman by the name of Leslie Ardino, was described by some as, 'the worst mass murderer in Connecticut's history.'

Ardino, who was also a resident of the nursing home, was responsible for setting the building on fire in the early hours of the morning by obtaining a lighter and then setting fire to some bed linen, resulting in the death of not only her roommate, but 15 other mostly bedridden residents. The firefighters, who responded to the inferno, later said it was one of the worst fires they had ever attended and sadly, many of the victims were just your typical grandpa and grandma, who were made to suffer through no fault of their own.

Ardino was a drug addict and had been subject, throughout her young life of only 23 years, to not only a poor upbringing, but repeated physical, emotional and sexual abuse. It was also reported that she suffered from multiple sclerosis and all these afflictions supposedly culminated in a final outburst of the lighting of the fire, but which she would later describe as an accident. She was charged with 16 counts of murder and arson, but it was determined she was not competent to stand trial due to her mental health condition.

This meant Ardino was deemed to be mentally unfit and, in the US, by denying the defendant the right to a fair trial, this would violate their constitutional rights. It is important, though, to note that any incompetency assessment is not a complete defence to the crime as charged, because if it is later determined the defendant is now competent, the criminal proceedings can continue. A sitting judge will then evaluate competency on a case-to-case basis, usually based on expert psychological reports and they can even order the defendant to take recommended medication that would at some point render them competent.[161].

Ardino remains in a state psychiatric hospital and this severely disabled woman most likely will never regain her competency to stand trial.

Similar "unfit to plead" circumstances applied in the 1981 Pacific Heights Nursing Home fire in Sylvania Heights, situated south of Sydney, NSW. Sadly, 16 elderly residents perished from carbon monoxide fumes and a further 51 were injured, many of which will continue to suffer for the rest of their lives. Responding fire and ambulance crews were met with an horrific scene witnessing the dead and injured lying defenceless throughout the building, with some residents literally hanging on to their bed frozen in disbelief at what was happening. One fire responder even said to the media after the fire:

We had to pry them away from their beds to get them out.

The nursing home was not required in those days to have fire sprinklers installed under NSW regulations but was fitted out with internal fire doors and also the obligatory smoke detectors and, of course, numerous fire extinguishers. However,

---
161   *Sell v United States* 539 US 166(2003).

the resident nurses on duty would have had no time to put them to any use. One elderly resident, Harry Hatton, who survived the tragedy was later charged with murder and arson, but at 88 years old and probably not of sound mind, there would not be much the justice system could do, other than place him in a secure mental health institution for the rest of his days.

Fire sprinklers have since become compulsory in residential aged care facilities from 1 January 2013, following the tragic but deliberate fire in the Quakers Hill Nursing Home in the early hours of 18 November 2011. Quakers Hill is situated about 40 kilometres from Sydney, NSW and is considered a family-orientated part of the southern suburbs with a number of both public and private schools.

The aged care facility accounted for up to 100 full-time residents needing daily high care, with the building complex divided into two wings and normally requiring access by the use of a security code. The facility was also protected by both internal and external CCTV. On the night shift commencing 16 November through to 18 November 2011, the nurse in charge was one misfit by the name of Roger Dean.

At some stage during the night shift of 17 November 2011, pain medication drugs were removed from a secured treatment room and not for the purpose of treating any of the residents. The theft was discovered by other nursing staff that morning, following an audit by the facility manager showing proper drug book protocols had not been followed. It was then reported to local police who attended the home with Dean as supervisor also being advised of the theft, not that he was considered, at this point, to be a suspect.

A subsequent review of the internal CCTV footage by the manager, revealed that Dean had, in fact, entered the drug treatment room by himself on a number of occasions during the course of his shifts. Perhaps it was due to his normal duties in ministering the medication, but that required Dean, as the night shift registered nurse, to have any drug to be dispensed signed off, not only by him but the assistant nurse on duty.

In the early hours of the morning of 18 November 2011, Dean, now possibly fearing he was a suspect regarding the stolen drugs obviously tried to cover his tracks. At approximately 0451 hours in the morning, fire detectors activated an alarm both internally and by way of notification to the fire brigade. Units responded within eight minutes and, on arrival, the fire was then extinguished, before it could cause any major damage. Little did they know at the time but a second fire in the other wing had been started by Dean, again using a cigarette lighter and then disposing of it in a sanitary bin. This fire had been burning for over 10 minutes, for which two residents were unable to escape as they were both bedridden. Dean, at this point, stopped a patient who was trying to get these residents out, telling her not to worry as others would look after them, as he ushered her out of the building.

Dean then assisted in helping other residents to be moved out of danger but conveniently forgot to tell the fire crew responders of the second fire, which by this time had spread further up into the roof, with residents calling for help. Dean, despite being instructed to move away from the entrance to the building, tried to enter on three separate occasions, each time being told by both fire responders and police to get out. Eventually, he was allowed into the building on his insistence, as he said he needed to retrieve the drug books from a locked cabinet in the treatment room as, according to Dean, they were desperately needed to be kept intact.

With the drug books now in his safe keeping, Dean further assisted firefighters in unlocking a stubborn door, even though he complained of being an asthmatic and needed to get home to retrieve his Ventolin. Prior to leaving the now disastrous scene, Dean, being the hero he was, even commented to media crew cameramen in a relaxed and coherent manner and said:

Hi, I'm Roger, I am one of the nurses,…there was fire and I just quickly…did what I can get everyone out and the smoke it is…overwhelming, but we got a lot of people out so that's the main thing.

After disposing of the shredded drug books by placing then in a wastepaper bin, he then returned to the nursing home and was later sent by ambulance to a local hospital. He was supposedly distressed and suffering from the effects of the fire with soot covering his face and clothes, obviously hoping he would be later recognised for his fire rescue efforts. However, police had Dean firmly in their suspicions, particularly as he was the night shift supervisor and they were aware of a possible theft of drugs from the locked treatment room, not that Dean would have thought, at this stage, he was a possible suspect.

He was interviewed on the afternoon of 18 November 2011, in order that police could get some idea of his movements over the shift. They were particularly keen to hear his version of events around the two separate fires, for which Dean detailed to police but, of course, left out any admissions.

Police then, by way of a warrant, listened to his phone calls and intercepted his text messages while he was still at their station, when he told an acquaintance he was now a suspect. Two of his friends, on his request, attended the police station where he also told them he had been lighting the fires, but apparently offered no explanation why. Over the next few hours, in a police record of interview, Dean made full admissions to police, waiving his right to silence.

His pathetic excuse for lighting the fires was, according to him, due to a mental condition and suffering from depression, having nightmares and that "Satan" made him do it. He meekly explained that he didn't believe the fires would cause any damage, let alone burn out of control. It was noted he made no bona fide attempt to try and extinguish them. He did admit to destroying the drug books, insisting to the firefighters that they were desperately needed but, of course, the fire was some sort of evasive distraction to cover his tracks of his illicit use of the drug medication, albeit a tragic one.

Dean, now aged 37 and with no previous criminal convictions, eventually pleaded guilty to 11 counts of murder[162] of the residents who were aged between 73 to 97 years and to eight counts of recklessly causing grievous bodily harm,[163] for the eight residents who suffered serious burn injuries and smoke inhalation. He had earlier offered a guilty plea but to manslaughter only which, not surprisingly, was rejected outright by the Crown.

Prior to Dean being sentenced to life imprisonment with no possibility of parole, his defence counsel submitted to the court that his client's many years of drug use in some way explained his bizarre version of events. Indeed, according to his learned counsel, he was only trying to cover up the theft of the drugs by way of some sort of a distraction, in setting, what his client described as, a small fire.

---

162   *Crimes Act 1900* (NSW)-section 18.

163   Ibid-section 35(2).

Judge Latham was having none of that and said:

I am unable to accept that the offender has been entirely honest and reliable in his account of the offences, partly because that account offends common sense...[164]

Her Honour then went onto say:

In my view, the murders and s.35(2) offences fall into the worst category... the murders were committed by way of reckless indifference to human life...[165]

Regarding Dean's drug use, it was accepted that he was indeed a drug addict with 43 different types of prescription drugs found at his home. It was also accepted by the court that Dean did suffer from a personality disorder, but with no doubt, narcissistic traits. However, an expert psychiatric report, as tendered to the court, considered that such drug addiction in no way reduced his capacity to foresee the possibility of death, when he intentionally lit the fires.

This was accepted by the court with Justice Latham noting the expert report which said:

There is no evidence, in my opinion, to substantiate a view that the [offender] had impaired capacity to foresee the probability of death when he lit the fires... The thought processes... revealed when describing his fire lighting and intentions, demonstrates

---

164   *R v Dean* [2013] NSWSC 1027-para 66.
165   Ibid-para 69.

that there was no impairment of capacity to think through the intention and consequence of his plan.[166]

It was with some relief for the victims' families, some of whom didn't get to say goodbye to their loved ones, that at long last our court system handed down an appropriate life sentence without parole to a murderous arsonist. Dean, of course, lodged an appeal, largely based on whether the sentencing judge erred by coming to the conclusion that it was not at all adequately possible to consider in respect of the culpability of Dean, any lesser sentence than the one imposed.

The NSW Court of Appeal had no hesitation in dismissing the appeal as, in their view, no doubt applauded by all and sundry, that a life sentence without parole was not in any way manifestly excessive.[167].

Dean certainly, and with proper justification, was held totally responsible for the 11 counts of murder and sentenced appropriately. However, it was later revealed, following a coronial inquest in 2015, that he had a history of being drug affected in his previous employment, taken off a night shift due to concerns raised by residents and even suspended and terminated by previous employers for misconduct. Unfortunately, he was employed by the Quakers Hill Nursing Home without any proper reference checks being carried out.

It, of course, begs the question that if a proper and diligent background and reference checks had been undertaken, the tragedy may never have occurred. The coroner, in making recommendations, said not only should fire safety be improved in nursing homes, but a proper healthcare employee data

---

166   Ibid-para 95.

167   *Dean v R* [2015] NSWCCA 307.

base needed to be established. This would then ensure proper background information was readily available and that nursing staff need to be better trained in order to recognise illicit drug abuse by other nursing employees.[168]

At least Dean will never be released which, unfortunately, provides little comfort to the victims' and survivors' loved ones, who must continue to live with the effects of this tragedy for the rest of their lives.

---

[168] *Quakers Hill Nursing Home; Inquest into the deaths and fire*...2011/391175[2015] NSW Cor C 14 9 March 2015.

15
NIGHTCLUB AND BACKPACKER HOSTEL FIRES

Nursing homes, taking care of the elderly and infirm, were not on their own as subjects to attacks by arsonists. It was also not uncommon for nightclubs and backpacker hostels to be set on fire for a variety of reasons. One of the deadliest fires took place at the Boston Cocoanut Grove nightclub in the US, around 10.15pm on 28 November 1942.

The club patrons were celebrating Thanksgiving and most likely time out from the Second World War, when a former lawyer, then owner, who seemed to have a blatant disregard for building code and safety regulations, asked one of his employees to change a lightbulb situated above fake palm trees, which contained flammable type material. This young 16-year-old high school student did as he was told, standing on top of a chair in a darkened corner of the club, then lit a match so he could see, while replacing and tightening the bulb.

A fire suddenly erupted, engulfing the satin canopies above the trees as frightened patrons tried to escape. The problem was, exit doors had been secured, allegedly to prevent non-paying patrons from entering, so they then tried to get out via the front revolving door. Due to the massive number trying their best to survive, this exit door became blocked and a plate glass window, which would have been an escape route, was boarded up. When firefighters arrived, they found many dead revellers stacked near this door on top of each other. Once inside the nightclub, it would become more horrific, with several dead bodies being found sitting up against the club bar, still holding their drinks.

A total of 492 people would die as a result with many from, not just being burnt to death, but also dying from what is now believed to be a faulty air conditioning system pumping out flammable and toxic fumes. This death toll was nearly as high as the Chicago Iroquois Theatre fire of 1903 which saw 602 moviegoers perish, all due to a broken arc lamp igniting flammable curtains. This exceeded the Brooklyn Theatre fire in 1876, with the death toll reaching nearly 300, apparently caused by a similar scenario with painted scenery coming into contact with gas lamps on the stage.

It soon came to light that despite the Cocoanut Grove nightclub given a good fire rating a week before, its owner had consistently turned a blind eye to obtaining proper licensing permits. This included poor and incomplete electrical wiring with unlocked doors only opening inwards, meaning the patrons could not escape via these doors as they would not open outwards. The young lad was initially held responsible but would later be cleared of any wrongdoing. As for the nightclub owner, he would be convicted on 19 counts of involuntary manslaughter as a consequence of his complete disregard for proper building and licensing permits.

He would only serve around four years before he received a governor's pardon, supposedly on medical grounds. Interesting though, the governor who pardoned him just happened to be enjoying free drinks at the nightclub at the time of the fire, obviously escaping, along with almost another 350 patrons who survived. The only positive outcome for this disaster was the enacting of new regulations for public buildings, which included that emergency exits must be clearly marked at all times, remain unlocked and able to open both ways, with flammable decorations also banned. Visitors to Boston can see a memorial consisting of 492 granite bricks with the names of all the victims, which has been erected in Statler Park.

Montreal's downtown Blue Bird Café and the Wagon Wheel nightclub was known as a popular country and western nightspot for Canadians and their visitors, where they would happily dance into the early hours of the morning enjoying the odd drink or three. However, such a revelling night of joy on 1 September 1972, all came to a sudden and fatal end when three drunken louts became upset because they were denied entry to the upstairs bar area. They decided, as payback, to use an accelerant to set fire to the only entry come exit staircase, resulting in the death of 37 patrons.

This was the second largest nightclub fire in the history of Canada, the other being the 1927 Laurier Palace Theatre, also in Montreal, in which 77 mainly young people did not survive, with the majority dying from smoke inhalation, but some crushed to death trying to escape. Although the Palace Theatre owner was held criminally responsible for negligence, the fire was believed to have been started by a discarded cigarette butt. However, there were some suggestions that children were seen lighting fires under seats.

This was certainly not the case at Blue Bird as the three perpetrators: Gilles Eccles, James O'Brien and Jean-Marc Boutin, were subsequently convicted, two for second degree murder and the other for manslaughter. Their sentence, however, was a measly 10 years and all were paroled within that time. One of the problems faced by those trapped inside, in trying to escape the advancing flames and smoke, was the lack of fire exits, thanks to inconsistent building fire code regulations.

Responders with some wearing breathing apparatus, took many hours to bring the fire under control and what they discovered, would no doubt forever remain entrenched in their memory. Many of the victims were found huddled together and crammed in a corner of the bar, as there was simply no way out. For those who ever visit the City of Montreal, they will find a memorial plaque near the renovated site of the nightclub, commemorating the victims who perished. The only positive outcome from this tragedy was the fire regulations in Canada were vastly upgraded, to ensure more fire exits in these types of buildings.

Gulliver's nightclub in Port Chester, New York, went up in flames nearly two years after the Blue Bird disaster, when in the early hours of 30 June 1974, 24 people were killed, with many patrons injured, as well as firefighters, who attended the scene, also suffering from burns and smoke inhalation. This fire didn't actually start in the nightclub, but the bowling club next door and was lit by one of its patrons, 22-year-old Peter Leonard.

It seems he wanted to cover up a burglary he had carried out after the club had closed, apparently forcing entry into cigarette vending machines. Many of the nightclub victims could only be identified from dental records due to their badly charred bodies. Subsequent autopsies revealed their primary cause of death was from smoke inhalation, before being badly burnt, as there was only one possible, but crowded, exit when trying to escape the flames.

Leonard pleaded guilty to 28 charges of which 24 were counts of murder, with the remainder being for arson, burglary and larceny(theft). On sentencing him to 15 years to life in prison, the judge commented that he had performed:

> ...*stupid actions in attempting to cover up a third-rate burglary by arson, resulting in...worst tragedy...You're certainly not an all-American boy, but you're not a vicious killer either...*

However, it must have been Leonard's lucky day. It certainly wasn't for the 24 victims, as in March 1986, after a successful appeal, he was now allowed to plead guilty to second degree manslaughter, as his original guilty verdict was thrown out on appeal after he made self-incriminating statements to investigators, without his lawyer being present. In other words, he wasn't properly "mirandized" for his right to silence and, as a consequence, was sentenced to 15 years in prison, but was released due to good behaviour after only serving 10 years.[169]

The only possible saving grace of comfort for the victims' families were a number of civil lawsuits alleging negligence and careless conduct against the Village of Port Chester and

---

169   also see *People v Leonard* 59 A.D. 2d 1(18 July 1977) and *People v Leonard* 113A.D.2d 258 16 December 1985.

Greenwich County. They were the responsible entities not carrying out proper and sufficient building and fire inspections, for both the bowling alley and the nightclub.

Once again, an argument with a bartender and being thrown out of the premises was apparently the motive for setting fire to an unlicenced nightclub on 16 August 1980. The Denmark Place Bar fire situated near Tin Pan Alley in Central London in the UK, was thanks to a Scotsman, known to police, by the name of John Thompson. After being ejected from the premises for arguing with a bartender over the cost of his yet to be consumed drink, Thompson returned with some vengeance and poured accelerant into the front door letter box and then set it alight.

His actions resulted in the death of 37 patrons, with another 43 injured and some suffering from serious burns. Given the nightclub was not licenced, it didn't adhere to any building regulations. It was difficult for the 150 or so revellers inside the premises to escape the inferno, as many doors and windows were securely locked. In fact, to gain entry to the building, you first had to yell out from the street below that you needed a drink and the club key would be tossed down to you.

Escaping from the building also wasn't helped with the front door and wooden staircase on fire and when firefighters attended, they were able to rescue some of the attendees by smashing in a window and a door. What they would later find inside the bar were many patrons, who died, like at the Cocoanut Grove, still sitting on chairs and around tables, clenching half consumed drinks. One distressed fire responder would later comment:

I have seen worse fires, but I have never seen dead bodies packed together like that before.

Thompson was convicted in May 1981 and sentenced to life imprisonment for a solitary specimen charge of murder by arson, for one of the victims. A specimen criminal charge, under the UK legal system, is a simple way, in the interest of efficient justice, of laying just one charge, as against 37 individual charges, for the total number of victims.

Arson perpetrators come up with a variety of excuses behind their intent for lighting fires, but bartenders certainly need to learn a salutary lesson in 'don't argue with your patrons or then throw them out of the club'. I do say that, of course, very much with "tongue in cheek".

The motive behind the unlicenced Happy Land Social Club fire in March 1990 in the Bronx, New York City, certainly reached similar heights, whilst the unsuspecting Honduran victims celebrated.

On this occasion, an unemployed Cuban refugee, by the name of Julio Gonzalez, first had a verbal spat over his rejection by his ex–girlfriend. Then, and here we go again, when thrown out of the nightclub, he made threats he would be back as he left, to the degree where he said he was going to 'shut this place down.'

Well, he certainly did close the Happy Land club because on 27 March 1990, he set fire to it after spreading petrol at the bottom of a staircase, resulting in 87 patrons dying, with only a few surviving after punching a hole through a wall in their bid to escape. Investigators, on becoming aware of the argument and the threats he made, arrested him and had no doubt of his involvement as they found his petrol-soaked clothes lying by his bedside.

This was followed by his admissions, after being properly advised of his right to silence. Gonzalez, after being charged with 174 counts of murder, that is two counts for each victim and I have no idea of the legal science behind that, then pleaded guilty based on an insanity defence to 87 counts of murder, one for each of the victims. Gonzalez was sentenced to 25 years to life imprisonment on each count, but to be served concurrently.[170]

Gonzalez made a feeble attempt to be paroled in 2015 which, rightly was refused. He died of a heart attack the following year at the age of 61 years. He certainly lived a lot longer than his young victims and, like the Blue Bird memorial, the victims are well-remembered with a street adjacent to the club renamed, "The Plaza of the Eighty–Seven", with all the victims' names inscribed on a memorial plaque. The tragic fire was written into songs such as the 'Sin of the City' by Duran Duran and 'Happyland' by Joe Jackson, which will ensure they will not be forgotten.

The pathetic motive, of having an argument with your former girlfriend, was certainly not behind the Sweden, Gothenburg Disco fire in October 1998, which killed 63 nightclub patrons, mainly of school age, with over 200 injured. It was, however, still an argument, this time not over being ejected, but refused entry to the club. Four very annoyed teenage youths then decided to simply burn it down, no doubt to ruin the enjoyment for everyone else.

However, given their young age, three of them between 17 to 19 years, Swedish law allowed then to get off lightly only sentenced to a maximum of six to eight years in prison. The other offender was even luckier, given he was under 15 years old at the time of setting the fire and sentenced to three years

---

[170] also see *People v Gonzalez* 163 Misc 2d 950(10 February 1995)- *People v Gonzalez* 228 A.D. 2d 340 20 June 1996.

in juvenile detention. The victims are remembered with their names permanently etched in gold and polished granite on a plaque near the fire scene.

The 2003 fire at the Station Nightclub in Rhode Island, US resulted in the death of 100 patrons, including four employees of the owners of the building. The fire started following the negligent or perhaps accidental, ignition of acoustic foam used in a pyrotechnic display, during a hard rock concert watched by over 400 revellers. Involuntary manslaughter charges were laid, but against the person who actually ignited the display. Daniel Biechele was sentenced to 15 years imprisonment, but he only served around four years as he was released in 2008.[171]

The owners of the nightclub were also charged, with one receiving a similar sentence to Biechele and the other only 500 hours of community service. Monetary settlements followed in the order of $115 million against a number of defendants, with the owners also fined $1 million for failure to maintain any employee workers compensation insurance. One positive outcome was the fire code regulations for Rhode Island were amended to ensure all nightclubs, within excess of 150 patrons, were required to have mandatory fire sprinklers.

Similar charges followed the loss of 194 lives in the República Cromanon nightclub fire in the late evening of 30 December 2004. The club, situated in Buenos Aires, Argentina, was hosting a rock concert enjoyed by around 4,000 revellers, when the ceiling was ignited, this time by a pyrotechnic flare discharged in the audience. The problem for the concert organiser and owner of the nightclub was, they had secured a number of entry doors, which happened to also be fire exits, leaving only two possible escape routes, all over making sure

---

[171] also see *State v Biechele* K1-03-653A (2005).

everyone paid and that there was no free entry. The other issue for the owner was the nightclub was not equipped to host that many in attendance, resulting in the venue being hopelessly overcrowded.

The victims, which included a number of teenagers, perished mainly from smoke inhalation and it was later determined to be cyanide poisoning, helped along by combustible materials inside the building, effectively creating a gas chamber. Some of the victims also included young children, found dead inside a makeshift nursery so their parents could watch the concert.

It was later revealed the nightclub, not only did not have a fire safety licence, but was also deficient without any sort of capable fire prevention devices, including a number of unworkable fire extinguishers. The band members were originally held not criminally responsible, until it was later revealed at a retrial in 2011, they had, in fact, encouraged their adoring audience to light the flares. Along with the criminally negligent owner and manager of the nightclub and two city officials for neglecting to carry out building proper inspections, all received varying jail sentences.

Australia is often referred to as the "lucky country", given its abundance of natural resources, apart from its politicians, with excellent weather, not including the state of Victoria, which can have four seasons in one day. We are so lucky, even to the degree that Australia geographically distances itself from world problems. Succinctly put, "The Tyranny of Distance", by noted academic and author, Professor Geoffrey Blainey, in his acclaimed novel. Our lucky country was certainly not on its own suffering from disastrous nightclub and hostel fires and, once again, varying motives came to the fore.

Well known crook, John Andrew Stuart, on being released

from prison in 1972 after serving time for attempted murder, started making threats against Brisbane nightclubs, unless they paid extortion money, they may not know what might happen. It didn't take long for this gangland identity's threats to come to reality when a vacant nightclub, named "Torinos", was burnt to the ground in February 1973, not that Stuart was supposedly involved. It was, however, later determined this fire might have, in fact, been an insurance job, following admissions by another unassuming identity, although the owner was never charged.

It didn't take long, however, for Stuart to bring his threats to reality when at 2.08 am on 8 March 1973, the Whiskey Au Go Go nightclub went up in flames in the suburb of Fortitude Valley, located on the inner fringe of Brisbane's CBD. This suburb is often known by its local inhabitants as "The Valley" and is certainly well-credentialled for fine dining and its vibrant nightlife. Well, the drinking and dancing came to an abrupt end and the firebombing of the nightclub was not a surprise to anyone, let alone local police. They had been specifically warned that Stuart was on a rampage and had this particular nightclub in his sights.

His threats were even written up in a local newspaper, all to no avail, for reasons only known to police, as they never took the warning seriously. This was probably why the then Chief Commissioner of Police, Ray Whitrod, who was certainly not a fan of the then Queensland Premier, Joh Bjelke-Petersen, belatedly set up a crime intelligence course for their detectives.

Stuart ignited a drum full of petrol and the nightclub, described by some as a death trap, due to a lack of fire exits, with one only escape path being strewn with empty beer bottles and other fine consumed beverages, went up in flames, killing 15 nightclubbers. Many of the other patrons were lucky to escape by jumping out of windows and falling on to hard ground below but saved by an awning blind. Stuart was now firmly on the radar of Brisbane detectives and, despite supposedly having a firm alibi, he was arrested along with his good mate, James "Jim" Finch.

They both continually maintained their innocence and that they were "verballed" by police for their supposed confessions, as well as being beaten up. To be verballed by police is perhaps better described as police writing up a so-called confession, without the suspect's knowledge. In other words, they made up the guilty evidence and submitted a supposedly signed confession before a jury to secure a conviction.

Alleged police corruption in Queensland some years later became the focus under the Government Committee of Inquiry known as the "Lucas Inquiry". This was to particularly look at the planting of evidence and the use of false confessions by police. One of its main recommendations was to bring in the use of tape recording of police interviewing suspects, which was not put in place until 1989, also followed by other states.[172] Of course, the covert recording of suspects was not unusual and was used on a discretionary basis, for example, by the Victoria Police Homicide Squad as early as 1966.

The pleas of innocence by Stuart and Finch fell on deaf ears with both convicted in October 1973 of murder and sentenced to life in prison. The jury accepted their motive as a planned extortion terror threat campaign against the owners of the nightclubs. Stuart certainly wasn't having a good day as he was sentenced, in his absence, while in hospital suffering from self-inflicted injuries.

Trial in absentia in some countries is a common practice

---

172   also see Fitgerald Inquiry 1987-89.

for a variety of reasons. One example from days gone by was in respect of Charles the 1st, King of England, who on trial for treason was sentenced, in absentia, due to his constant court disruptions and was given a death penalty by beheading, which was carried out in 1649. Finch, on the other hand, went one better than Stuart as, during the committal stage of the trial proceedings, he severed one of his fingers.

These self-harm antics continued in prison with Stuart even sewing his lips together, all while protesting innocence, followed by Court of Criminal appeals, even as far as the Privy Council in the UK and then its Judicial Committal, after the High Court of Australia dismissed an earlier appeal. The Privy Council certainly had a powerful influence, at the time, over Australian law as it could hear appeals, not only from the High Court but even from State Supreme Courts.

Such an appeal process came to an end, however, with the passing of the *Australia Act 1986*(Cth), leaving the High Court as the sole arbitrary body regarding appeals. Such appeals were all to no avail as they were dismissed and Stuart died in prison in 1979 following a hunger strike, although there was some suggestion this violent criminal may have met his fate at the hands of other prisoners.

Finch, on the other hand, finally won his release in 1988, but only after serving nearly 15 years and was considered to be a model prisoner during his incarceration. He was immediately deported back to the UK, then made full admissions describing in detail his involvement in the firebombing, using two full drums of accelerant spread over the doorway of the nightclub.

Despite this confession, he still insisted he was verballed by police but he had to be careful in what he said, because he failed to remember he had only ever been charged with one murder and waiting for him on extradition could be the other 14 murder charges. A coronial inquest into the nightclub fire was again ordered in 2017 by the Queensland Government, but Finch did not appear and died in his homeland around 2021.

Backpackers visiting Australia on the odd occasion seem to be followed around by arsonists. In September 1989, the Downunder Hostel in Kings Cross, Sydney, NSW was set on fire in which five unlucky tourists died, including an Austrian and a Swedish national. The perpetrator was Gregory Allan Brown, who suffered from a mental illness and was also a habitual drug abuser, helped along by excessive alcohol consumption.

Brown, on confessing to the fire, was sentenced to 18 years imprisonment, sentenced for manslaughter and not murder, based on his partial defence of diminished responsibility. Such partial defence requires that an accused be able to demonstrate a substantial form of mental impairment when differentiating between right and wrong, therefore reducing their criminal liability.[173]

There were some doubts whether Brown was, in fact, the actual fire setter, with a suggestion he had an alibi being in another state at the time, supported by banking and medical records, with the latter being a day after the fire. The only evidence he was convicted on was his confession before a judge, sitting alone without a jury. He served the maximum term of 19 years and was released in 2009 after not applying for parole.

The only positive aspect to come out of the Downunder fire was legislation introduced by local governments, with special enforcement powers for buildings that pose a fire risk, together with a number of recommendations following a

---

[173] see section 23A of the *Crimes Act 1900* (NSW).

coronial inquest. This included the use of sprinkler systems and proper fire exits, ensuring they were clearly identified.

Brown also admitted to setting some of the 1983 Ash Wednesday fires and allegedly told police he set more than 200 fires in both Melbourne and Sydney during 1989 and 1990. Such was the concern for his recidivist offending, on his release in 2009, an application was made to the Victorian Civil and Administrative Tribunal (VCAT) for a guardianship order but was refused leaving him free to roam at will.

He subsequently moved to Tasmania with convictions for, not only arson, but theft, property damage and assault and was, of course, back again before the court. This time, Brown, now 60 years of age, was charged and convicted of one count of child exploitation,[174] being sentenced to 12 months imprisonment wholly suspended.[175] Only time will tell if and when we will next see Brown up to his old tricks.

The Childers Palace Backpackers Hostel fire brought Queensland back into the arson homicide foray once again. On 23 June 2000, Robert Paul Long, evicted some months earlier from the hostel, set it on fire in the early hours of the morning, killing 15 innocent guests, with 12 all from overseas hoping to enjoy the lucky country. The remaining 70-odd guests were lucky to escape with some only suffering minor injuries and smoke inhalation. It certainly wasn't their fault, but Long apparently had a dislike for these types of backpackers. It was also not the first time he had threatened to burn the hostel to the ground.

A coronial inquest into the fire and deaths subsequently

---

174 *Criminal Code Act 1924* (Tas)- sections 130 and 299.

175 *State of Tasmania v Gregory Allan Brown*–comments on passing sentence-2 December 2022-Estcourt J.

determined the hostel owners had disconnected malfunctioning fire alarms some weeks prior and the first floor of the building was only equipped with one solitary fire extinguisher. Despite these damning findings, no criminal charges for negligence were ever laid. No doubt, the families of the victims would give serious consideration to a civil action for their loss.

With respect to Long, his arrest was not without incident and after stabbing a police officer and their detection dog, he was shot and wounded before being taken into custody by police. He was convicted of two counts of murder and one of arson, despite there being 15 victims as, apparently, this was to make sure the trial didn't last for months. He was sentenced to life imprisonment in 2002 and not eligible for parole until at least 2020.

It begs the question, of course, that if he had been acquitted of the one charge, would he have been charged with the further counts of murder by arson. If, in effect, the evidence was sufficient to reach a verdict of not guilty, that does not mean a jury in any further trial would automatically also bring in a not guilty verdict.

In 2002, both Long and the State of Queensland lodged appeals. Long's appeal was firstly on his conviction for murder and arson where he alleged it to be a miscarriage of justice from the pre-trial publicity, believing he could not get a fair trial. Long also appealed that his trial was held in what was known as a "Banco" ceremonial type of court. Whatever that had to do with the guilty verdict, I have no idea, other than perhaps he thought it was a show trial.

He also alleged his confession was not voluntary as he made it in extenuating circumstances, after he had been shot by police and it should have been excluded. The trial judge declared it was a dying declaration and, therefore, made voluntarily. The concept of a dying declaration originated from a decision in the UK, where the English court ruled:

A dying declaration is admitted in evidence because it its presumed no person, who is inevitably going into the presence of his Maker, will do so with a lie on his lips.[176]

Hearsay evidence is generally inadmissible in a court of law, but a dying declaration is an exception to this rule. In the case of Long, his appeal on the ground that it was not made voluntarily, whether or not he was about to meet his maker, was questionable and was dismissed, as were all his other grounds of appeal.

The Attorney General of Queensland didn't do any better as his appeal, on the ground of manifestly inadequate sentencing of a minimum of 20 years, was also dismissed.[177]

Long became eligible for parole in 2020, which was denied, as it was again 12 months later. No doubt, he will continue to apply for parole and the victims' and survivors' families will continue to petition the Queensland Parole Board, that quite rightly, he should never be released. It remains to be seen, of course, whether Long will see the light of day, but the fact he was only sentenced to a minimum of 20 years and only charged with two counts of murder and one of arson, suggests his sentence was clearly in the lower end range, given that his actions resulted in the deaths of 15 innocent backpackers. The hostel site was later redeveloped and is now known as the Palace Memorial Building, with a portrait of those who were lost in the fire, in recognition of the sad outcome.

The question of inadequate sentencing also raised its ugly

---

176 *R v Osman* (1881) 15 Cox CC 1.

177 *R v Long; ex parte A-G* (Qld) [2003] QCA 77.

head, this time in Launceston, Tasmania when, in the early hours of 31 December 2004, the night manager of the Metro Backpackers Hostel set it on fire to cover up his theft of money. Tony Laurence McLennan, a New Zealander, after a night of heavy drinking and to help his pokie addiction stole, on two separate occasions, cash from the hostel's night safe. He then hatched a plan that he needed to conceal his brazen thieving by setting fire to the hostel stairwell. Who cares about the sleeping backpackers? A young Scottish tourist lost his life in the inferno, while around 60 other residents fled the building with only six treated for minor injuries. This wasn't the first fire at the hostel as one occurred some two weeks earlier on 14 December 2004, with 78 residents evacuated.

McLennan was charged with murder, arson and two counts of theft. The latter charge he pleaded guilty to, but not the more serious ones, noting if convicted of murder in Tasmania, the sentence was life imprisonment. A jury of his peers deliberated for eight hours and, as they were not unanimous on the murder charge, they only returned a guilty manslaughter verdict by way of a majority and, of course, also guilty in respect of arson.

It was McLennan's lucky day as he was only sentenced all up to nine years jail, with a non-parole period of just six years. On sentencing, the learned judge said:

> *devoid of credibility… inept plan that was fraught with danger to destroy (his) evidence of theft… While I accept that following the fire the defendant was extremely distressed, I place little weight on this as a mitigatory indication of remorse as, it seems plain from his failure to acknowledge lighting the fire that his predetermined concern was for himself and not for others…*[178]

---

[178] *R v McLennan* Unreported, Supreme Court of Tasmania, Justice Evans, 6 September 2006

He had a prior conviction for arson in New Zealand in which he set five separate fires over five months, again at his workplace for which he was convicted and placed on probation. Although the judge was scathing in his comments in respect of the hostel arson, McLennan somehow escaped a heavier sentence and was released in 2011 after serving just under seven years. The parole board stated that McLennan regretted his conduct and was a model prisoner during his time behind bars.

They did impose certain conditions on his release, which included a ban on drinking alcohol, entering any licensed club premises and he must undertake counselling regarding his attraction to setting fires. One must wonder though, that once again we see a lenient sentence imposed on a culprit who took the life of another. Lee was facing a maximum sentence of life for murder, but got away with the manslaughter verdict, which carried a maximum prison sentence of 25 years and 21 years for arson, yet he is out in seven.

As an aside, McLennan returned to New Zealand and was most likely deported on his release. Suddenly, in late 2014 and early 2015, as reported by New Zealand's Whanganui Chronicle, his house went up in flames on two separate occasions, with the first fire set in his vehicle in the carport before badly damaging the house. McLennan reported, although he lost most of his possessions, at least his house was covered by insurance. Prior to the house being repaired, it once again suffered at the hands of an arsonist, or maybe it was from an accidental cause, when this time the fire was successful, with his house completely destroyed.

I am not saying for one moment that McLennan was responsible, noting he vehemently denied any involvement, nor am I suggesting that the fires were connected to his prior history. Police, as they should, were keeping an "open mind" of who may have set the fires. It certainly raised the same question in a number of other arson cases, as to guilty as charged or not guilty.

16
GUILTY OR NOT GUILTY?

Louis Taylor was only 16 years of age when he was accused of setting fire to the Pioneer Hotel around midnight on 20 December 1970. The hotel was situated in Tucson, Arizona in the US and was considered to be the social highlight for local business clientele after a busy week. As for the young African-American Taylor, he was at the hotel in order to see what free food and drinks he was lucky enough to obtain from revellers at a local Christmas party. Unbeknown to those guests imbibing in the celebrations and others who lived at the hotel, a fire would engulf the building, resulting in the deaths of 29 people, which included one victim dying from smoke inhalation many months later.

Taylor was initially seen as some sort of a hero, alerting the party goers and hotel guests and residents of the impending blaze, also assisting emergency responders, placing some of the injured on stretchers. As the hotel was built in 1929, it still had not been upgraded with sprinkler systems and, what was deemed for security reasons, a number of padlocked fire exits could not be used by those trapped inside. In trying to escape, many of the victims used tied bedsheets to climb down, while others threw mattresses out of the hotel windows and then jumped but died when trying to safely land on them.

Police focused their attention on Taylor as he was alleged to have been seen near where the fire started and when he voluntarily attended at the local station to make a statement as a witness, he was subjected to a lengthy record of interview. Despite his age, which probably explained his evasiveness at their line of questioning, he was not allowed access to a lawyer or even a guardian while he was being interviewed.

When investigators found matches on him, as far as they were concerned, he was the perpetrator whose motive was to set the fire as a distraction and then carry out room thefts. This was despite a number of previous suspicious fires at the hotel and a well-known arsonist being questioned by Tucson police just days earlier.

Following the arrest of Taylor, one fire investigator would confirm it was definitely arson, saying an accelerant had been found on the hotel debris, despite this finding not being supported by forensic laboratory testing. Another fire investigator profiler came up with what could only be described now as some sort of systemic racial prejudice theory, noting at the time there was race related unrest in Tucson. In his learned view, the arsonist was young and probably around 18 years of age, of black origin and that their use of fire for financial gain was not uncommon.

Prosecutors would then rely on what they considered to be these crucial pieces of evidence, albeit circumstantial. There was no taping of the police record of interview being led as evidence, because it wasn't ever recorded; no police interview file notes were produced as, most likely, none were taken and stone silence on the exculpatory laboratory tests of no trace of accelerants.

Somehow, he was convicted in 1972 by an all-white Pheonix jury on 28 counts of felony murder. Taylor continued to profess his innocence and was lucky to escape the death penalty, but was now facing life in prison and would serve some 42 years before justice prevailed. The Arizona Justice Project, a non-profit legal team of volunteer lawyers, would eventually represent Taylor and, along with other clients' tenuous arson convictions, would bring into question the credibility that multiple and different points of a fire's origin were definite proof of arson. Not only would they closely examine the questionable and bias testimony of the two prosecution's so-called experts, but they would also use the services of a number of fire experts to re-examine the evidence and witness testimony.

One of these experts, acting on a pro–bono basis, was the renowned John Lentini, certified to conduct both fire scene investigations and debris analysis. He probably holds the record for investigating fires with some 2,000 to date, appearing as an expert witness in over 200 cases. He was also a member of the National Fire Protection Association (NFPA) Technical Committee on Fire Investigations and, in 1992, it recommended new guidelines be adopted by fire investigators, later to be known as NFPA 921. This encouraged more rigorous forensic science applications to properly determine the cause of a fire, as against largely untested and circumstantial possible causes.

Further editions put out by the NFPA, also provided additional scientific principles that should be adopted in any analysis to assist fire investigators of the origin and cause. In particular, what became relevant was what was deemed a "'flashover-fire" which, to a degree, was a largely unknown phenomenon around 1982 and only started to become credible around 1985. According to forensic fire experts, this occurs when hot gases at the beginning of a fire, combine, causing the heat to build up as high as ceiling level and, on reaching 1,100 degrees Fahrenheit, which is the equivalent of 533.33 Celsius, explodes into a ball of flames. It can, however, mimic a fire started deliberately by the use of accelerants with similar post-burn fire patterns, meaning the fire was most likely accidental and not arson.

The stated origin and cause of the Pioneer Hotel fire was closely examined by Lentini and he came to the view that the evidence presented by the prosecution against Taylor, could, in no way, support the cause as arson. As far as he was concerned, noting the laboratory testing of the hotel debris found no traces of accelerant, the cause of the fire had to be listed as undetermined.

This meant, in the absence of proof of arson, there could be no conviction for murder. The report by Lentini was then handed to the Pina County prosecutor and the court, petitioning for the murder convictions of Taylor to be set aside and there be a retrial. At the request of the prosecution, the Tucson Fire Department then carried out their own reinvestigation, which supported the finding of Lentini as an undetermined cause. Taylor was now looking at his pending release.

However, Pina County prosecutors were not so convinced, notwithstanding the cause was now considered as undetermined, taking the view that this did not rule out arson. The only offer they were prepared to put on the table was for

Taylor to agree to enter a plea of no contest to the arson and murder charges and, on that basis, with time served, he would be released.

A no contest plea, or "nolo contendere", is an interesting legal concept, as the accused person on making such a plea does not admit or deny the crimes as charged. In other words, it is an alternative to a plea of guilty or not guilty, accepting the punishment imposed as if guilty, despite not admitting guilt.

In the case of Taylor and, in order that he could be immediately released from prison at 58 years of age, a no contest plea with a time served sentence, was really the only viable option, meaning his convictions would be set aside with him resentenced to time served. The prosecution, on the other hand, still considered him to be guilty, but their chances of gaining a new trial, given the evidence now before the court, was remote, given the charges were now vacated. This meant Taylor would have, in any event, most likely have been released on bail, pending a new trial on a further presentment of charges.

On Tuesday, 2 April 2013, Taylor walked out of the state prison a free but desolate man, having lost most of his family members while he served time, which also saw him stabbed by another inmate. Given that Taylor, in effect, did not contest the charges, he is effectively prevented from commencing civil proceedings for wrongful incarceration as, in a legal sense, he is still considered guilty as convicted regarding the murders. This was confirmed by the Ninth Circuit US Court of Appeals in 2019, ruling that he was barred from seeking incarceration-related damages.[179]

However, he ultimately did commence a further action against the County of Pima and the City of Tucson, alleging

---

179   *Taylor v City of Pima* 913 F.3d 930, 936(9th Cir 2019.

wrongful imprisonment and prosecutorial misconduct.[180] This civil proceeding would see the defendants, of course, file a response relying on what is known as the "Heck Bar defence", which can prevent the plaintiff, in this case Taylor, from seeking criminal damages from a government body.

The Heck Bar emanated as a legal precedent in a US Supreme Court case,[181] in which the court ruled that a person convicted of a crime would be barred from filing civil proceedings, if the claim as filed implied that their conviction was invalid. This meant that Taylor would first need to have his convictions overturned, before he could seek any relief by way of damages for wrongful conviction.

That civil trial was, therefore, vacated in July 2024 and we will need to wait on a decision in a separate legal challenge by Taylor for post-conviction relief, in which he seeks to expunge the 2013 no contest plea deal. If this results in the 2013 convictions being overturned, there will be no bar to prevent him seeking financial compensation by way of damages for the 42 years he spent incarcerated. It will be interesting to see what the final outcome is for Taylor.

John Henry Knapp was only 48 hours away from knocking on death's door in 1985 and not by losing his life in a suspicious fire, but by execution. Knapp was convicted by a jury in November 1974 of two counts of first-degree murder, that resulted in the death of his two young daughters, aged three and two, from a fire allegedly set by him in their Mesa home in Arizona, US. There must have been some doubt from the outset because he was only convicted following a second trial, after his first trial in August 1974 resulted in a hung jury.

---

180 *Louis Taylor v County of Pima*, et al, No 23-15110(9th Cir.2024).

181 *Heck v Humphrey*, 512 U.S 477(1994.

He would spend a number of years on death row at the Arizona State Prison and, despite a number of legal appeals that failed,[182] it would not be until 1985 that things started to turn in his favour. In 1992, he agreed to a no contest plea in exchange for time served. But let's first take a look at what led to his conviction and sentence of death on the counts of murder and the sequence of events that followed.

Knapp was a returned Vietnam veteran and following his marriage to his wife, Linda, it's fair to say, they were not managing all that well, both financially and with Linda's health as she suffered from depression. They were blessed with their two young daughters and lived in what was later described as a squalid home, cooking on a portable stove as their gas and electricity had been disconnected due to their failure to pay the bills. The fatal fire started around 8am on the morning of 16 November 1973 and rapidly consumed but was confined to the children's bedroom. Their bodies were later found badly burnt.

When the fire was responded to by firefighters, they observed what was later described as some sort of oily substance in the bedroom. They would also find fuel containers with smudged, but no identifiable fingerprints, which Knapp would later say, such containers were used for the portable stove and also for a lantern as they had no power to the house.

Investigators would also find evidence of smaller but previous fires throughout, but determined they were unrelated to the fatal fire. They were believed to have been set by their young children when playing with matches, which were also found throughout the household. Given there was evidence of an intense floor level fire with burn patterns, it was quickly determined the fire was deliberately lit and by the use of an accelerant.

---

182   see for example *State v Knapp* 114 Ariz.531(1977).

Police clearly had both Knapp and Linda as suspects and interviewed them three days after the fire. Knapp stated he was asleep in the lounge room and woke up to his wife screaming and the children crying, with their bedroom consumed by flames and smoke. He had grabbed Linda and taken her outside and then went back in to try and rescue the children and put the flames out. All to no avail. Linda's version of events was mostly consistent with that of her husband and the day after being interviewed, she left to reside in Nebraska with her father.

Knapp was basically left to fight on his own and, in a bid to protect Linda from suspicion, fearing she may try and commit suicide, he not only said she wasn't in anyway involved but purportedly confessed he was, in fact, the arsonist. He would recant this alleged confession but at his first two trials, the presiding judge determined, with appropriate instructions to the jury, Knapp had been properly advised of his rights and the confession was made knowingly and voluntarily.

Many years later though, it was revealed that after allegedly confessing, he was allowed to telephone Linda and the conversation was covertly taped by police. This revealed, during the call to her, he maintained he was innocent, that he only said he was the perpetrator in order to protect her, fearing she would harm herself and his confession was allegedly based on what police told him to say.

Now on death row, with his execution set five times but, thankfully for him, delayed,[183] he continued to fight to clear his name and a number of further interesting developments would come to light. It seemed after being divorced by Linda, she

---

[183] *John Henry Knapp, Prison Inmate No 33659 et al v. Harold Cardwell, et al* 667 F.2d 1253(9th Cir.1982).

remarried and had a son who, at the age of six years old, almost died following a fire in his bedroom.

But it didn't stop there, as her second, but now divorced, husband involved in a custody battle with Linda, allegedly told a private investigator, hired by lawyers who had taken on Knapp's case pro bono, that his former wife had confessed to setting fire to the deceased children's bedroom. Despite this apparent incriminating evidence, it still wasn't sufficient to grant a new trial, with a judge saying, notwithstanding it in some way implicated Linda, it still wasn't enough to exonerate Knapp.

In 1985, along comes fire consultants, Marshall Smyth and Richard Custer. This could now be the turning point, noting Custer would later be the author of the "Field Guide for Fire Investigators". It certainly would be a pivotal moment as they reconstructed the events and produced videotapes. This further demonstrated the scientific concept of "flashover", with the tapes once again showing two rooms spontaneously igniting from one small open flame, meaning it was indistinguishable from a fire believed to have started by the use of an accelerant. Based now on the possibility of an accidental fire, thanks to the flashover argument, Superior Court Judge, Stephen Gerst, in 1987 dismissed the case without prejudice, meaning the prosecution could still refile the case at a later date after correcting any issues.

They certainly did. After Knapp was released from custody, only to be rearrested in October 1990, he faced a jury of his peers. Due to the earlier claims of Knapp regarding his so-called confession that was only made so he could protect Linda, the prosecution now added to his indictment of felony murder, an alternative charge where he is an accessory with the co-conspirator, Linda. She was, of course, never charged with any crime and was never named in any indictment.

However, in 1991, there was another hung jury as they could not reach a unanimous verdict, despite the credible flashover argument, meaning the fire could have been started by Knapp's daughters playing with matches, or then again, there was the possibility it was lit by Linda. However, in view of the compelling new scientific evidence, the prosecution was obviously not convinced of the successful outcome of another trial.

In 1992, Knapp agreed to their offer of a no contest plea to second degree murder, meaning he would be sentenced to time served of 13 years and was released, to try and resume some sort of normal life. The final word in summing up this case was left to Supreme Court Justice Stanley Feldman, when he said:

In light of the evidence and proceedings in this case, we do not know if Knapp was guilty... We do know that his execution would have been a miscarriage of justice.

Failed and inaccurate arson forensics would, once again, come to light in the sad case of Davey Reedy, convicted for the deaths of his two young children, who died in a house fire in the US state of Virginia in August 1987. They died from smoke inhalation, despite the efforts of Reedy trying to save them. He would also suffer from smoke inhalation, with severe burns and lacerations to his hands. A cursory examination of the fire scene by the local fire department came to the conclusion that the fire started on the back porch and kitchen area of the house, finding the presence of an accelerant that had been poured, causing burn patterns.

An examination of the clothes, namely his t-shirt and

underwear, Reedy was wearing also had traces of the same petrol, later confirmed by a gas chromatography test, as a match. A medical report also stated that the burn marks on various parts of the body of Reidy were irregular and, on that basis, must have been caused by a direct flame.

The conduct of Reedy, leading up to the early hours of the morning when the fire occurred, was also brought into question. He had been drinking and after an argument with his girlfriend, she left the home taking her belongings. Reedy was initially a bit confused at the location of the children when the fire erupted at first, saying they were not in the house, but later from his hospital bed confirmed that they had been. There was also some suggestion, some months prior, he had allegedly said if he ever lost his children in a custody battle with his ex-wife, then the home would go up in smoke.

All this alleged suspicious conduct would stack up against Reedy and, despite professing his innocence, he would be found guilty in February 1988 on two counts of first-degree murder and arson, with the jury not accepting he should be convicted for capital murder, which meant he would have been sentenced to death. In any event, he was sentenced to two life terms plus a further 10 years and it would take another 21 years before he would be granted parole and released in 2009 at the age of 61.

The question, of course, was always "guilty or not guilty" and, based on the turn of events that would transpire, he was deemed wrongly convicted and granted an absolute pardon by the Governor of Virginia in late December 2015. However, according to the prosecution, at the time of this decision by the governor, they were somewhat dismayed about not being consulted. As far as they were concerned, he was guilty of arson and murder, even without the evidence of an accelerant.

In looking at what transpired in support of the innocence of Reedy, there is a strong argument he was wrongly convicted. This is on the basis that in a media article published in 1999,[184] it attracted the interest of a former public defender who, ably assisted by a number of other crusaders for justice on a pro bono basis, would fight for his release. It would take a number of years.

A number of appeals during the period 2000 to 2003 would fail, which included a petition for a Writ of Habeas Corpus being filed on his behalf. Such writ seeks a court order to bring the jailed person before a judge and requires the prosecution to lawfully demonstrate why that person should remain incarcerated. In the case of Reedy, the petition set out a number of grounds that he was not only legally incompetent to face the accusations on mental health grounds and further, that his bewildered and disoriented state after the fire was from smoke inhalation.

The Appeals Court denied the writ saying there was no factual basis to support his innocence. As a result and, pending the outcome of a petition for clemency filed with the governor in 2003, it was time for his legal team to reassess the prosecution's forensic scientific evidence.

The first report, obtained in 2005, from a science and combustion company discredited the initial laboratory report. They supported the now credible flashover concept, where the same burn patterns and destroyed debris could also occur without the help of an accelerant. They were not alone in reaching such conclusions, with even agreement from the ATF after conducting tests in 2005 and 2007. These tests also

---

184 *Did Davey Reedy Really Do It?* Roanoke Times, 28 March 1999.

confirmed that burn patterns were in no way conclusive when determining the origin of a fire.

As to the alleged accelerant on the clothes of Reedy, our man Lentini would bring that into some doubt, saying there was no such evidence on his t-shirt and underwear and also the laboratory tests were indeed suspect regarding the presence of any sort of accelerant at the crime scene.

Finally, the state agreed that, in fact, Reedy had been convicted on outdated and inaccurate arson forensics and he was granted parole and released in April 2009. He would remain on parole for almost another seven years, still being considered guilty as charged, by not only the state, but the general public. The Governor of Virginia obviously thought otherwise, having the power to grant an absolute pardon in his own right, noting there were some US states that had pardon boards with the authority to grant them independently.

A pardon is not uncommon in many countries including, for example, in Chile where it is known as the institution of pardon (indulto), which under its 1874 Criminal Code can be granted as a remission or commutation of a sentence. In Canada, clemency can be ordered by its governor-general or the governor in council can grant a royal prerogative of mercy, which is also similar to an executive power in Australia. Such prerogative is vested in the king and can be exercised by the governor-general, including a state governor for clemency in rare and exceptional circumstances.

In 2014, the Governor of Virginia received a further independent report which, after reviewing the initial laboratory tests and file notes, supported the contrary findings of the experts, such as the well-respected Lentini. On 21 December 2015, Reedy was granted a rare and absolute pardon erasing his conviction as it was clear to all and sundry, he was not guilty, other than, of course, the original prosecution team who maintained he was guilty as originally charged and convicted.

However, it didn't matter, as the now discredited fire evidence which convicted him at trial, had no proper basis for the presence of any accelerant and, in any event, his alleged conduct before the fire meant nothing in such absence.

Following his pardon, two claims in 2016 and 2017 for compensation to be paid to Reedy would proceed in the General Assembly for the State of Virginia, but both bills failed.[185] If, however, they are eventually passed, Reedy should receive in the order of $1.1 million to compensate him for his wrongful conviction and for the 21 years he spent incarcerated.

Federal pardons can also be granted in the US which, under its constitution allows the president to grant a reprieve or a pardon regarding only a federal crime and usually following a referral from its Department of Justice. An example of full pardons under an Executive Grant of Clemency, were those issued by President Trump in July 2018 to an Oregon father and son Dwight and Steven Hammond.

They were tried and convicted in 2012 of intentionally setting a fire in September 2001 and again in August 2006, that leaked onto public land they leased for grazing purposes. As ranchers, they had been in protracted disputes with various government bureaus over land management for a number of years.

They did not have any permit or waiver to light the fires, despite saying they carried out such acts to protect their land from wildfires and invasive plants. They, however, reached a plea agreement not to challenge the partial guilty jury verdicts

---

185   *Claims; Davey Reedy.* (SB 649 and SB 1337).

so far reached in their trial. Both were sentenced to only a few months in jail as part of the plea bargain, rather than face, what was described by the trial judge as, grossly disproportionate given the tacit nature of their offending, the mandatory five-year term of imprisonment for arson.

After serving the much lesser terms, they were both released, only in 2015, to be again resentenced to the mandatory minimum of five years, less time served. This was as a consequence of an appeal by the Department of Justice to the US Court of Appeals for the Ninth Circuit, which vacated their original sentences on the grounds they were illegal,[186] resulting in the District Court applying the mandatory minimum term of 5 years imprisonment and three years' supervised release.

With the Hammonds now back in jail and also ordered to pay $400,000 in restitution to the US, their supporters, consisting of other ranchers and militia groups, held a number of peaceful protests. In addition to a fund being established to assist the Hammonds with their legal fees, a petition seeking clemency was made to the then US President, Barack Obama. Finally, on 10 July 2018, US President, Donald Trump, granted them a full pardon after both had served between three and four years respectively, with a White House Press release stating:

... The evidence at trial, regarding the Hammonds responsibility for the fire(sic) was conflicting... The Hammonds are devoted family men, respected contributors to their local community and have widespread support from their neighbours, local law enforcement and farmers and ranchers across the West. Justice is overdue... both of whom are entirely deserving of these Grants of Executive Clemency.

---

[186] *United States v Hammond* 742 F.3d 880(9th Circ 2014).

A similar presidential pardon also brought some relief for Syrita Steib-Martin, particularly not having to now pay almost $2 million in restitution. She was sentenced to 10 years imprisonment, followed by a three-year supervised release order in July 2000, at 19 years of age, after pleading guilty to carrying out an act of burglary and arson in which a Texas motor vehicle dealership went up in flames. Steib was released in 2009 after serving nine years but still faced the consequences as a convicted person.

To her credit, she has turned her life around and is now a nationally certified clinical laboratory scientist and has also established Operation Restoration, as an advocate for criminal justice reform for women. Steib was also responsible for the drafting and passing of the *Louisiana Act 276*, which would prevent post-secondary institutions, such as universities, from asking questions regarding criminal history which, prior to the act, denied admission to convicted applicants.

Although granted a full pardon by President Trump in January 2021, it does not apply to her convictions in Texas under state law for the same crimes. Steib is, therefore, still considered a convicted person in Texas, until such time she also receives a full pardon from the state governor, but at least she has been relieved from paying back compensation.

Despite the advanced findings of Lentini and other recognised fire experts with the flashover argument, Cameron Todd Willingham would not be so lucky, executed as a guilty man in February 2004, when he may well have died by lethal injection, being not guilty. Two days before Christmas on 23 December 1991, the Willingham family home was destroyed by fire. Willingham's three daughters, the oldest aged two and twins, only one-year-old, would perish.

One died due to smoke inhalation and the other two with

their bodies burnt beyond recognition. Their mother was not at home at the time as she was shopping for Christmas presents for her children and Willingham. He was woken up and escaped from the inferno in bare feet, with only minor burns.

The police investigation went down the usual path, finding the so-called typical indicators of arson by the use of an accelerant with multiple pour patterns. The burn marks and charred wood on the floor suggested three different points of fire origin: the floors, the exterior threshold between the front door and floor and the front concrete porch. What they did not take into account, however, were eyewitness reports of flames exploding out of the house windows which, is another clear indicator of a flashover fire. However, on testing an area around the front door, it come up positive for an accelerant.

Prosecutors would later suggest at his subsequent trial in August 1992, the motive of Willingham was to dispose of his unwanted children and that he abused his wife, noting he did have an extensive criminal record for violence, convicted of a number of felonies and misdemeanours. One expert for the prosecution labelled Willingham a violent sociopath with complete disregard for property and life, not that there was any credible prior history to support this.

Their case was further strengthened, along with the forensic expert evidence, by a jailhouse snitch giving testimony, most likely in exchange for a sentence reduction, that Willingham had supposedly confessed to him he had set the fire, allegedly to cover up an injury to one of his children. Neighbours would also give evidence of seeing him crouching down in the front yard as the house burned, refusing to make any attempt to rescue the children. He seemed more concerned about moving his car, so it would not be damaged by the advancing flames.

Despite Willingham pleading his innocence and supported by his wife, who testified they had a very happy marriage and he was not a domestic violence abuser of either her or the children, he was found guilty of murder. During the course of the trial and prior to being sentenced to death, he was offered, but rejected, a plea deal of life imprisonment if he pleaded guilty. This plea rejection was against the advice of his defence counsel but to his credit, Willingham was reported as saying, he refused to plead guilty to a crime he never committed.

Prior to his execution on 17 February 2004, Willingham would spend a number of years appealing his conviction and sentence, all to no avail.[187] This was even despite a report submitted by esteemed fire investigator and scientist, Dr Gerald Hurst, some days before the execution, who was adamant that after reviewing the evidence, he could only conclude the fire was accidental.

Indeed, as far as he was concerned, the conclusion reached, that it was arson, was simply "junk science" and if the now accepted new standards, which originated from around 1992, had been considered, Willingham would have never been convicted.

The Hurst report was ignored, despite being sent to the governor on the day of execution as Willingham waited in the Texas death chamber, with his petition for clemency denied by the Texas Board of Pardons and Paroles. Even as he was about to receive the lethal injection and asked if had anything to say, Willingham still professing his innocence:

The only statement I want to make is that I am an innocent man

---

[187] see for example *Willingham v The State of Texas*-Court of Criminal Appeals 897 S.W.2d (1995).

convicted of a crime I did not commit. I have been persecuted for twelve years for something I did not do. From God's dust I came and to dust I will return, so the Earth shall become my throne.

Well, God may well have been looking over him, but some months after the execution, his death certificate stated the cause of all things was "Homicide". Following a media report that suggested an innocent man had been executed, a New York-based advocacy organisation, known as the Innocence Project, had a closer look at what appeared to be a wrongful conviction. The Innocence Project was becoming well known for providing free investigative and legal services to those convicted of crimes, for which they maintained they did not commit.

They would engage the services of five well known and creditable fire scientists and investigators, which included, of course, the well credentialed Lentini and also a combustion science engineer. They provided a 48-page report on two Texas arson convictions of possible, if not probable, innocent men, namely Willingham and Ernest Ray Willis.

They all, effectively, came to the same conclusion what was set out in the Hurst report, that the conviction and execution of Willingham was certainly a result of what could only be described as flawed arson evidence. In their Arson Review Committee executive summary,[188] after considering not only all the evidence as presented in the trial of Willingham, but also the witness testimony trial transcripts, they said:

The artifacts examined and relied upon by the fire investigators

---

[188] Report of the Peer Review of the Expert Testimony in cases of State of Texas v Cameron Todd Willingham and State of Texas v Ernest Ray Willis– Arson Review Committee-March 2006.

[in both cases] are the kind of artifacts routinely created by accidental fires that progress beyond flashover...the State's expert witnesses [in both cases] relied on interpretations of "indicators" that they were taught constituted evidence of arson...each and every one of the indicators relied upon have since been scientifically proven to be invalid.[189]

As to the questionable capabilities of the Texas fire investigators, they were also put on notice:

To the extent that there are still investigators in Texas [and elsewhere], who interpret low burning, irregular fire patterns and collapsed furniture springs as indicators of incendiary fires, there will continue to be serious miscarriages of justice.

They didn't stop there. With courts and the state of Texas being made aware, by further reiterating:

In the cases of individuals already convicted using what is now known to be bad science (or no science), the courts should treat the 'new' knowledge as 'newly discovered evidence'. It was resistance to this concept that allowed the state to execute Mr Willingham, even though it was known that the evidence used to convict him was invalid.

The report was then referred in 2007 to the recently established Texas Forensic Science Commission. It would, however, take them another two years before they determined the Willingham case needed further scrutiny. This state agency is authorised under Texas legislation to investigate any

---

189   Ibid-page 3.

substantive allegations of forensic analysis negligence and even misconduct and make recommendations to correct any flawed findings.

With regard to Willingham, the commission, in January 2009, engaged the services of renowned fire expert, Craig Beyler, to investigate whether the deceased had been sent to the death chamber as an innocent man, based on what may have been flawed evidence for arson. Beyler came to the inevitable conclusion that it was indeed scientific evidence that could not be sustained and, in all probability, Willingham died by lethal injection, most likely as an innocent man.

To that effect, Beyler said in his August 2009 report, later confirmed by his testimony before the commission in early January 2011, that the murder conviction of Willingham:

> *...could not be sustained either by modern science or by the standards of the day...the basics of (this) investigation is such that you could not come to the conclusion that there were arsons, they are undetermined...By their acknowledgement, child fire setting, somebody else coming in and setting the fire, are things they acknowledged were not ruled out...and in this case, they shovelled out the bedroom...before examining the electrical evidence, so you can't rule this out as a cause.*

The well-considered opinion of Lentini was also corroborated before the commission by arson expert, John DeHaan, who also co-authored a number of editions of "Forensic Fire Reconstruction", as well as the notable book titled "Kirks Fire Investigation". This book, thanks to its original authors, was considered to be one of, if not the "Bible" in respect of fire and arson investigation. DeHaan was also a member of the NFPA 921 Technical Committee and the UK's Forensic Fire Society. His valued work also led to the solving of the 1913 mystery Californian fire, known as the Jack London's Wolf House.

Although arson was not ruled out in that fire, which largely gutted the home interior, DeHaan, along with other experts, determined it was caused by linseed oil-based cabinet stains self-heating. His report tendered to the commission, in the case of Willingham, agreed with Lentini in that he was convicted on unreliable evidence, which he further pointed out was largely used and typical of fire investigations around the time of the 1991 fire.

In April 2011 in its final report, the commission, although agreeing the science adopted in the case of Willingham was indeed flawed, considered there was overall insufficient evidence to determine whether he was convicted and executed as an innocent man. It was interesting though that, despite the commission motto being "Justice Through Science", they did not conclude the fire marshals were in anyway negligent, but did make recommendations that the now accepted national standards should be adopted. This included that fire investigators needed better training and education of the science to be used in fire investigation.

Another interesting development took place when relatives of Willingham, in October 2012, presented a petition to the Texas Board of Pardons and Paroles, seeking a posthumous exoneration. This largely came about on hearing that a Texas State District judge some months earlier, after reviewing the now discredited evidence and recanted testimony from the jailhouse snitch, was proposing to consider such exoneration.

The plot had obviously thickened around Willingham's

innocence, when the inmate who originally testified the defendant had confessed to him he was responsible, now alleged he only said that when promised the robbery charges he was facing would be withdrawn in return. It was also revealed this wasn't the first time the snitch had recanted his testimony. A media report suggested he had filed a motion some 12 years earlier saying he had lied. However, such motion was withdrawn as it never came to any fruition, let alone placed in the court file or a copy provided to the lawyers for Willingham.

The petition for a posthumous exoneration, however, was not supported by the ex-wife of Willingham and mother of their deceased children, who had now changed her view about him being innocent, saying she was convinced of his guilt. The Texas Board of Pardons and Paroles must have also not been convinced of his innocence and wrongful execution, as in March 2014, Willingham was denied a full posthumous pardon.

One confronting article worthy of mention titled, "Trial By Fire" was also penned by David Grann, a staff writer with the New Yorker, who over 16,000 words meticulously looked at the Willingham case and the evidence relied on to send him to the death chamber. To his credit, Grann let his readers form their own view whether an innocent man was executed. Subsequently, in 2018, a biographical drama movie was released.

The bottom line was, even in the face of the failed, unreliable arson science, supported by a number of renowned experts, it was not enough to come to the conclusion he was not guilty of the murder by arson of his three children. Willingham went to his grave as a guilty man, but a successful question of innocence thankfully would be raised in a number of other cases.

17
A QUESTION OF INNOCENCE

In late May 1982, a jury in Arizona in the US handed down a guilty verdict for first degree murder and arson. The convicted felon was Ray Girdler Jnr, who was sentenced to two life terms plus 21 years with a minimum of 64 years, in respect to the death of his wife and child.

In sentencing Girdler, Yavapai County Superior Court Judge Sult could not hold back his absolute disgust for the crimes committed by the man, saying in no uncertain terms:

> *Your killing of Jennifer Anne Girdler constitutes the most vile betrayal of the highest trust which is placed on a human being…An analysis of the murder would surely establish that no mitigating circumstances exist and I would then be in a position to sentence you to a death you so richly deserve…I have not sentenced you to death in the gas chamber…I have,*

> *however, sentenced you to a death of sorts, perhaps even a crueller and more lingering death. You are now 36 years of age. When you complete these sentences, you will 100 years old… You will be deprived of freedom… the memory of these freedoms will remain and you will never entirely forget them…*

Little did Judge Sult know at the time, those crushing words would come back to haunt him some eight years later. Let's first turn the clock back and look at what took place on that fateful early morning on 20 November 1981. The unemployed Girdler, his wife, Sherry, and their three-year-old daughter, Jennifer, lived in a 50-foot-long mobile trailer home situated in the hillside of Prescott, some three miles from Arizona. The family were in a financial struggle and in jeopardy of losing the power to the home, with their phone already cut off due to not paying the account.

After consuming a few beers and watching television alone, with his family already snuggled up sleeping, Girdler also went to bed only to be woken around 2.45am with the mobile trailer on fire. Girdler escaped from the burning home to retrieve a car fire extinguisher, thinking his wife, who was also now awake, would go and save the child. He then tried to re-enter through a rear door, but the blaze was too intense. All Girdler and a neighbour, who had arrived on the scene, could do was watch the inferno with Girdler repeatedly saying, 'They're gone, they're gone.'

After firefighters arrived at 3.08am, Girdler walked away from the burning home, apparently according to a neighbour, appearing to be very disinterested. Then again, he may well have been in a state of shock, as the fire was slowly brought under control. The bodies of his wife and daughter would later be found together in the child's bedroom, with an autopsy revealing they both died of carbon monoxide poisoning.

A cursory examination of the fire scene the following morning, which only took a couple of hours, by the chief deputy fire officer and another investigator, who were both considered to be the best of best, determined the fire showed signs of abnormal burning as in some areas the floor was completely gutted, with multiple points of ignition. They both formed the very strong view that the fire was started by use of a liquid accelerant and there was no likelihood the fire could have been started by any intruder, as the fuel vapours would have resulted in what they termed an "instant holocaust". Girdler was arrested some four days later to plead his innocence before a jury.

At Girdler's trial in April 1982, in the Yavapai County Superior Court, the prosecution was adamant it could have only been started by him, even suggesting his financial issues were also connected to his motive where he could collect a $6,400 insurance payment. The expert evidence to the massive blaze also suggested there was no possibility Girdler, being asleep at the time, would have had any chance of escaping from the instant inferno. In addition, evidence led to an alleged conversation Girdler had with a fellow inmate while on remand, in which he admitted he killed his child.

The only witness for Girdler was a local minister who said, the day after the fire Girdler attended his church in a complete desolate state, breaking down over the loss of his family. His defence counsel's argument that fire was accidental and most likely caused by either a lit cigarette or an electrical fault, was all to no avail, with Girdler being found guilty. After being belittled by the sentencing judge, he was led away in handcuffs to begin effectively what was a life sentence.

Time, most likely, didn't pass quickly for Girdler as he sat in prison and his first appeal for a rehearing was denied in January 1984.[190] However, in February 1988, his lawyers filed a further petition, known as Post-Conviction Relief, in other words, another appeal challenging his conviction and sentence. The new grounds in support of this appeal were based on what his defence would argue he was wrongly convicted. Again, their argument was not arson, but the accidental origin "flashover-fire", a largely unknown phenomenon around 1982.

The Girdler defence team, supported by expert forensic evidence, were adamant the flashover fire was not started by the use of an accelerant, but was due to a smouldering cigarette or, alternatively, a faulty homemade electrical appliance and was certainly not arson. Interesting that at this hearing before sentencing Judge James Sult, one of the leading prosecution witnesses, a well renowned fire investigator who examined the deadly blaze, said that he knew of the so called new "flashover phenomenon" as far back as the original trial for Girdler. However, he completely ruled out any such possibility, saying, in his expert opinion, it was arson caused by the use of an accelerant.

A number of hearings took place over 11 days during June to August 1990, in which the jailhouse snitch also now admitted he gave false evidence. Girdler also reiterated to the court that he steadfastly maintained his innocence, reminding His Honour of what he said to him prior to being sentenced in 1982:

I stand before you tried, convicted and about to be sentenced

---

[190] *State of Arizona, Appellee v Ray Girdler, Jr; Appellant* 675 P.2d 1301,138 Ariz.482.

for a crime I did not commit. It may be that this sentence may result in my death by one means or another. My death will not eliminate nor change the truth of what occurred on the evening of November 20. Therefore, I simply want to state, I personally do not feel that justice has been served in this case. Furthermore, I do not feel that anyone in Yavapai County has anything to be proud of over this case.

Not only was *'justice done, but was seen to be done'*, with Judge Sult coming to a decision that if a new trial was held, Girdler would most likely be found innocent, based on the flashover argument, saying:

This newly discovered evidence, had it been introduced at trial in this matter, would probably have changed the verdict of the jury.

On that basis, on 21 November 1990, the judge set aside the guilty verdict as it was clear Girdler had been unjustly convicted and ordered a new trial, which never eventuated. The Superior Court in December 1991 dismissed all charges against Girdler and he was now a free man. The Wrongly Convicted Database Record, compiled as a joint project by the Universities of California and Michigan, stated he was released by judicial exoneration and that the conviction had been due to:

Prosecutorial misconduct of presenting false "scientific" evidence that flammable liquids caused the fatal fire...

It didn't come to an end there though, as in September 1993, Girdler filed a complaint in the US District Court in

Arizona against Deputy State Fire Marshal David Dale and others. Dale was one of the fire investigators who concluded that the fire was started by arson and, more specifically, by the use of accelerants. In the statement of claim filed by lawyers for Girdler as plaintiff, they stated:

Prior to Ray Girdler's arrest and at the time he testified at Mr Girdler's trial, Mr Dale was aware of a fire phenomenon called "flashover". When he testified at trial, Mr Dale knew that as a result of flashover, a fire of accidental origin could result in post-fire burn patterns resembling those resulting from arson fires resulting from liquid accelerants. In spite of that knowledge, Mr Dale knowingly withheld critical exculpatory evidence regarding flashover from the prosecutor, judge and jury.[191]

The defendant's legal team, however, filed for dismissal, on the basis of a statute of limitations argument and further, that Dale was in any event entitled to absolute and qualified immunity. According to a media release by the National Registry of Exonerations, a civil rights lawsuit, taken out by Girdler, was settled for $150,000, which in today's terms equates to $335,000 or, effectively, around $42,000 for each year spent in prison.

The flashover defence argument was also thanks to John Lentini, certified to conduct both fire scene investigations and debris analysis.

Lentini credits his expertise in what he referred to as a "life changing moment" in fire investigations, resulting in charges being withdrawn against Gerald Lewis, for was known as the "Lime Street fire". A total of six people, including his

---

[191] *Girdler v Dale*, 859 F. Supp.1279 D.Ariz.1994.

wife, her pregnant sister and her four infant children died in a Jackson, Florida house blaze in the early hours of 16 October 1990, with fire investigators deeming it suspicious due to the so called "floor pour patterns" analysis.

Lewis, who escaped the inferno intact with his young son, told police the fire started on a couch and it was accidental, with the home going up in flames in a matter of minutes. Not convinced, police charged Lewis with first degree murder and arson and he was facing a death sentence. Lentini was asked to review the arson chemist's fire report for gasoline found in some of the debris and, at first glance, he disagreed with the findings. Although other experts agreed with a further fire inspection report, that the fire was deliberately lit, Lentini still wasn't convinced nor, as it would eventuate, were the Florida County prosecutors.

At their request, Lentini conducted a recreation of the fire using a similar style house two doors down from the fatal blaze, with the same floor plan, carpet and furniture, including the exact same couch. Along with his colleagues, they set fire to the couch without using an accelerant and if a flashover was to occur, it would take around 15-20 minutes for the whole room to go up in flames.

However, much to their surprise, the room was engulfed in flames in just over four minutes, leaving behind floor pour patterns which basically confirmed what had transpired, according to the events told by Lewis. All charges were withdrawn and the Lime Street fire investigation is now lauded as the seminal case in modern fire investigations analysis.

This evolving fire science included, once again, our man John Lentini, which would also be a turning point in the lives of two convicted arsonists, who spent almost 33 years in prison before being exonerated. In February 1980, a Brooklyn townhouse exploded into flames, killing a mother and her five children living on the third floor. The owner of the townhouse nominated three men who she alleged had argued with her over a batch of drugs. These men were Raymond Mora, Amaury Villalobos and William Vasquez. According to her version of events, it was clearly arson because she saw then walking away from the building before it suddenly caught on fire, going up in a massive inferno.

Arson it was, according to a state marshall fire investigator as, in his opinion, the fire had ignited in two separate areas on the first floor and, on that basis, it must have been set deliberately by the use of an accelerant. In addition, he found pour patterns on the floor tiles in the form of puddle shapes, with the floorboards burnt to the ground.

Despite the wives of two of the men providing an alibi and, with no help from their defence lawyers in not challenging the fact laboratory tests found no trace of an accelerant, they were convicted by a jury in November 1981 for murder and arson. They appealed their 25 years to life sentence and Mora would pass away in prison some eight years later. Villalobos, and Vasquez, blind after losing his sight to a medical condition, would both finally be released in 2012 on parole after serving almost 33 years.

Both men knew they were always innocent and, on release, requested the New York Law School's Post Conviction Innocence Clinic, to take up their fight to prove they were indeed not guilty. They took up the cause with some gusto and were initially denied complete discovery of documents from the New York City Fire Department, as they were heavily redacted.

In 2015, the Appellate Division of the Supreme Court

of the State of New York determined, after inspecting the documents as discovered, that the fire department must provide all documents completely legible and unredacted and pay the costs of Villalobos.[192]

The unredacted documents would subsequently be thoroughly examined by John Lentini and the now credible flashover argument would discredit the original fire analysis, in that there were two separate fires and the pour patterns relied on had no basis that an accelerant was used. Lentini stated in his findings:

...interpretation of the fire damage was consistent with what was believed about fire behaviour in 1980, but today's knowledge of fire behaviour would dictate a different interpretation... the errors caused by this particular misinterpretations... have resulted in numerous wrongful prosecutions...If today's standards and knowledge of fire dynamics were applied to this investigation, the results would have been significantly different...

What would also come into play, thanks to the Innocence Clinic submitting the Lentini report to the Brooklyn District Attorney, was the questionable witness testimony of the now deceased townhouse owner. Their Conviction Review Unit, concerned that three men had been wrongfully convicted, interviewed her relatives, who said that their family member had been a chronic liar and alcoholic.

They also said she admitted to them, just before passing away, of having lied on the witness box in saying she saw the three accused walking away from the building just before it went

---

[192] *Matter of Villalobos v New York City Fire Dept*.06249 22 July 2015.

up in flames. They also stated, not only did she lie about their perceived involvement, but had, in fact, been the beneficiary of an insurance payment from her insurer for the loss of the townhouse, noting that was also denied by her under cross-examination at the original trial.

The convictions of all three men were vacated and the charges dismissed in the Kings County Supreme Court on 16 December 2016. The National Registry of Exonerations listed the contributing factors to not only the false or misleading forensic evidence, but an act of perjury and false accusation as a consequence of the now discredited witness testimony of the deceased landlord. Mention was also made of the inadequate defence by their legal representatives, in failing to submit as evidence the laboratory tests, which found no trace of an accelerant.

It was probably and understandably of no comfort to the family of the late Mora to receive in 2017 a total of $1.4 million in compensation for the eight years he spent in prison, but never to see the light of day. Villalobos and Vasquez would each receive $9.7 million from the City of New York and a further $5.75 million from the state for their 33 years behind bars and the unjust prosecution.

A multi-million dollar settlement in 2023 was also paid to the now 63-year-old Victor Rosario, who was wrongly convicted of arson and eight counts of murder following a 1982 apartment fire in Lowell, Massachusetts. Unfortunately for him, he happened to witness the fire and tried desperately to rescue the five children who would perish in the blaze, by smashing a window. Somehow, he came to the attention of police who were only interested in bringing anyone they could before the court.

Rosario supposedly signed a confession, following an all-night interrogation, which fitted the police narrative in that it was definitely arson caused by him and two other males, throwing a Molotov cocktail into the building, setting it on fire. In 1983, he was convicted on all counts and sentenced to eight consecutive life terms of imprisonment. This was despite absolutely no evidence of any sort of incendiary device, such as a Molotov cocktail, being used, let alone any forensic evidence of an accelerant.

Rosario always maintained his innocence and would serve a total of 32 years behind bars until, in July 2014, his convictions were vacated and he was released on bond by the Middlesex County Superior Court pending a new trial. As early as 2006, fighters for justice, such as lawyer Andrea Petersen, fire engineer, Craig Beyler, and, of course, John Lentini, had initially led the charge to have Rosario finally declared innocent.

Indeed, the 28-page affidavit, filed by Lentini, makes for fascinating reading in respect of the allegations and misunderstanding of fire behaviour when Lentini said:

The Commonwealth alleged that the defendant and two other men threw a Molotov cocktail into the residence where the fire occurred. In my opinion, based on my education, training and experience, this is a very unlikely scenario because no remains of Molotov cocktails were recovered, nor were any of the samples collected, positive for the presence of gasoline.[193]

Lentini would then go on to say that if Molotov cocktails were in fact used, physical evidence of such use would be leaving

[193] *Commonwealth of Massachusetts v Victor Rosario* Middlesex Superior Court No 82-2399-2407 (2010)-para 123.

behind, not only the bottle, but also portions of the wick, together with its ignitable liquid residue. He would also provide an explanation of what he called "variations in ventilation" and, more importantly, not from separate fire origins.

To that effect he also said:

In the early stages of a fire, it grows as it involves additional fuel. The fire at this stage is called a "fuel-controlled" fire. Once all the fuel has become involved, the fire grows as it mixes with more air. This is called a "ventilation-controlled" fire. Fully involved or post flashover compartments contain ventilation-controlled fires.[194]

On that basis and due to his observations of the 1982 apartment fire, he followed up with:

I am of the opinion that there can be no doubt that the fires in the kitchen, living room and hallway were all ventilation controlled. As such, the fire damage would have been mainly influenced by ventilation, not by the duration of burning in a particular room...[195]

With regards to the tardy and, sadly, lacking investigation that followed after the blaze was extinguished, he would leave some scathing comments saying:

All of the misinterpretation made by the Commonwealth's experts in this matter have been shown repeatedly to be invalid long after the case was tried...Because of their having been

---

194   Ibid-para 30.

195   Ibid-para 31.

> *misled by faulty "indicators" of arson, the Commonwealth's investigators did not even consider the possibility of an accidental cause.[196]*

Lentini was also clearly of view that in his professional opinion:

> *...the Commonwealth's investigators failed to produce any valid or reliable evidence that this fire had more than one point of origin or that liquid accelerants were used to start the fire.[197]*

Beyler also would provide telling evidence that a Molotov cocktail, when thrown onto a wooden floor, could not in any way start a fire of such magnitude that occurred in the 1982 Lowell apartment fire, as the accelerant in the bottle would simply burn itself out after about 10 seconds. This proven theory was known to prosecutors at the time of his trial, but was ignored, as was the evidence from a witness who had not seen Rosario carry out any such act.

As to the false confession and, despite Rosario breaking down during the interrogation over the children who perished, the learned judge still allowed it into evidence in his 1983 trial. Lawyer Petersen, however, would obtain an affidavit from a translator who was present at the police interview, who would say Rosario was so psychotic at the time he would have admitted to anything put to him.

The prosecution's case was in tatters and, when presented with the evidence from six experts, including Lentini and Beyler, also assisted by two medical practitioners, a new trial

---

196   Ibid-para 32.
197   Ibid-para 34.

was affirmed in May 2017.[198] This was confirmed after his lawyers filed an amicus brief requesting that the 2014 decision for a new trial be upheld. Such brief was filed in appeal cases by a third party known as "Friends of the Court" (amicus curiae), in which additional evidence and arguments are provided to further assist the court.

In this case, the friends of Rosario included the New England Innocence Project and the Boston College Law School Innocence Program, which was sufficient to finally bring this long drawn-out chapter in his life to an end, with the prosecution, some months later, withdrawing all charges. The City of Lowell subsequently exonerated Rosario paying him a compensation settlement in the sum of $13 million for wrongful incarceration.

An intriguing point was later raised by Petersen in a publication titled, "*A Quest for Justice; The Story Behind the exoneration of Victor Rosario*". After taking on the case for Rosario, she requested the curriculum head for the US Department of Homeland Security explain the errors found in this case. Apparently, he advised her that he could not assist the defence, obviously due to a conflict of interest.

However, some months later, she received a course outline aptly titled, "Myth and Legends in Fire Investigation", to be used by the department in training their fire investigators. Much to her amazement and probably frustration, such course was a replica of the 1982 apartment fire, emphasising that the evidence of arson put forward by the investigators, in respect of the case of Rosario, was indeed a myth.

The term of imprisonment experienced by Rosario before

---

[198]   *Commonwealth v Victor Rosario* 477 Mass.69 November 8, 2016-May 11, 2017.

being exonerated can also be compared to the plight of Harold Staten, who was incarcerated for almost 40 years, before he was deemed innocent and released. Once again, the arson mimicking but the now credible flashover argument would come to the fore in concluding that the fire should have been classified as undetermined. The fire started in the early hours of the morning of 30 October 1984 in a Glenwood neighbourhood in north Philadelphia, Pennsylvania, US, resulting in four victims sleeping upstairs passing away in hospital, with one later succumbing to his burn injuries

After the fire was extinguished, a local fire department marshal commenced an investigation of how the fire may have started. Surprisingly, local firefighters had in place a practice where they would immediately carry out an "overhaul'" of a fire-damaged property, removing items such as furniture and rugs before the possible crime scene could be carefully examined. You could understand such a process if it was to ensure there was nothing else left burning that had not been doused, but it seemed that was not the case.

However, unperturbed, the keen fire marshal examined the fire scene even why the removal process was underway. He determined that the fire was caused by an open flame being applied to an accelerant but would later testify he couldn't smell any flammable liquid. Regardless, firefighters did say they detected a gasoline odour when attempting to bring the blaze under control. The following day, the Philadelphia Police Criminalistics Laboratory (PPCL) determined there was no evidence from the samples provided of any accelerant being used.

Regardless, the fire was deemed arson and detectives quickly determined Staten as a possible suspect, all over an argument he had with one of the victims about payment of one of his accounts. Other witnesses would also say that when the account wasn't paid, he mumbled something about burning the house down, with one young woman also telling detectives she saw Staten near a door of the targeted house around 3am, holding a bag in his hand and then saw smoke about 10 minutes later.

The fire marshal submitted his crime scene examination report in February 1985, adamant after his exhaustive analysis that it was a deliberately lit fire. In his opinion, there was clearly a flammable liquid used, but somehow, he overlooked the findings of the PPCL of no trace of any such accelerant. Rumours throughout the neighbourhood ran amok that Staten was involved and on 26 March 1984, he was charged with second degree murder, arson and other related offences.

This also included a felony charge of risking a catastrophe under the *2010 Pennsylvania Code Crimes and Offenses* as per section 3302.[199]

During a preliminary examination hearing, which is similar to a committal hearing in Australia, evidence was given by the fire marshal of an accelerant used, ignited by an open flame. His testimony somehow covered up the laboratory report finding of no accelerant, saying such chemical vapours were consumed in the fire.

The Philadelphia Court of Common Pleas had no hesitation in sending Staten for trial, which commenced in early October 1986, before Judge Richette sitting alone in a bench trial without a jury, which was Staten's preference. The accelerant argument was again put forward from the so-called

---

[199] This charge is similar for example to section 197(2) of the *Crimes Act 1958* (Vic) in respect of a fire that endangers the life of another person.

expert witness, again completely disregarding such evidence to the contrary contained in the laboratory report.

The "eyewitness", being the young woman, also gave varying and conflicting accounts of her seeing Staten near the door of the house around the time of the fire, holding a can or hose in his hand. This evidence was, however, different to her boyfriend's, who stated that they were home around 2.15 am and were in bed when they saw smoke coming from the house on fire.

Evidence was heard from both Staten and his grandmother who said he was home with a woman that night at her house, although she was vague to the exact time. For some reason, his defence counsel did not call the woman who was with Staten during the fateful night, including other witnesses who may well have given exculpatory evidence for Staten not being the alleged perpetrator. Regardless, Judge Richette, although troubled by some of the conflicting evidence, obviously took into account one witness testifying to the verbal threat by Staten to set the house on fire, found him guilty on all counts on 7 October 1986.

Following various appeals to set aside the verdict with witness statements, which now completely contradicted the previous witness testimony, a sentence of life imprisonment was confirmed in February 1989, without the possibility of parole. This was despite Judge Richette saying in one appeal hearing in February 1988 that she thought a new trial was warranted. This was in view of the evidence that the young woman, who allegedly saw Staten near the house door just prior to the fire, was hopelessly drunk that night and had to be put to bed by her roommates. So much for the credibility of this alleged eyewitness.

The only thing that was going to save Staten now, was an independent forensic review of the testimony into the cause of the fatal blaze. This was because, despite the young woman recanting her original statement in 1996, with another withdrawing the so-called admission by Staten threatening to burn the house down, a petition for a new trial was still refused in 1997.

This was regardless of the new recommended guidelines in 1992 to be adopted by fire investigators, namely NFPA 921 which, as we know now, encouraged more rigorous forensic science applications to properly determine the cause of a fire, as against largely untested and circumstantial possible causes. In particular, a 1980 book put out by the then US National Bureau of Standards, titled, "Fire Investigation Handbook", largely relied on myths of fire pattern assessments, put together by untrained chemists into the origin and cause of fire.

Further editions, subsequently released by the NFPA, not only debunked many of these uneducated myths, but also provided additional scientific principles that now should be adopted in any analysis to assist fire investigators into the origin and cause.

Finally in 2020, while Staten counted the days away in jail while still professing his innocence, a private investigator from New Jersey reviewed the crime scene reports and findings. He determined, by applying the recognised NFPA scientific standards, the only conclusion that could be reached to the cause of the fire was "undetermined".

His report was indeed scathing regarding the initial investigation and conclusion, as determined by the fire marshal. Without any evidence and only based on what firefighters told him about smelling an accelerant, he simply ignored the absence of any such contamination in the floor samples. In the investigator's view, the fire marshal had "tunnel vision". In other words, he was wearing figurative blinkers at the time and simply ignored other possible causes, being strictly focused on a case of arson.

This expert report was also supported by a retired special agent and fire investigator with the ATF, once again referring to the flashover concept stating:

Failure to understand the distorting impact ventilation and flashover can have on fire effects can result in misinterpretation of those effects, leading to erroneous origin and cause determination.

The Philadelphia District Attorney's Conviction Integrity Unit, in further consideration of the claim by Staten and his lawyers that he was wrongly convicted, agreed a new trial was indeed justified, based on the now credible expert forensic reviews. After spending nearly 40 years in prison, Staten was released on 5 February 2024 after the Court of Common Pleas agreed that a new trial was warranted but also delivered a further motion in dismissing all charges as there was no reasonable prospect of a conviction.

Although Pennsylvania, like some other states in the US, does not provide a legal process for compensation to any person wrongfully convicted, that doesn't mean Staten could not commence legal proceedings by way of a federal civil rights lawsuit. That is exactly what Staten did, filing such writ on 3 April 2024 against the city of Philadelphia and others and we certainly wait with much interest for the outcome.[200]

---

[200] *Staten v The City of Philadelphia et al,* US District Court for the Eastern District of Pennsylvania 2.2024 cv01380.

No doubt, such civil proceeding, in its statement of claim, will rely on what was aptly summarised as contributing factors by the National Registry of Exonerations citing:

false or misleading forensic evidence, perjury or false accusation, official misconduct and inadequate legal defence.

The flashover argument and misleading forensic evidence was again rapidly gaining credibility and it came to the fore to save David Lee Gavitt from spending the rest of his life in prison. However, it was almost 26 years before his plea of innocence over responsibility for the fire, which killed his wife and two daughters, would be believed by fire experts and, finally, the court.

It was certainly a sad day for Gavitt when around 10 pm on 9 March 1985, after being woken by his dog scratching on the bedroom door, he would discover his Ionia house in Michigan on fire. Despite his best efforts to save his wife and two young daughters, which included smashing a window to try and extract them from the blaze, it was all to no avail. When firefighters arrived, the house was completely engulfed in flames and they would later discover the three victims had all died from carbon monoxide poisoning, with Gavitt taken to hospital with severe burns over his body and a lacerated arm.

A potential crime scene was then examined by fire investigators who determined that it had been started deliberately. This was decided after tracing the path of the fire and finding the usual irregular floor burn patterns, where, no doubt, an accelerant had been used. Police would interview Gavitt a number of times and, despite his plea of innocence, even providing in dramatic detail his efforts to save his family, he was charged with three counts of murder, three counts of felony murder, arson and arson on an insured property.

In June 1985, at a preliminary examination hearing, the District Court found probable cause existed on all charges, except the insurance fraud count, which was dismissed. In February 1986, before the Ionia County Circuit Court, a trial by jury took place and, despite the prosecution not providing evidence of any possible motive of the accused for killing his family, Gavitt was found guilty on all charges. The prosecution simply relied on corroborative expert evidence from three fire investigators, which included a laboratory technician from Michigan State Police.

He stated that after analysing 17 house debris samples and using a gas chromatography technique to detect the presence of chemicals, the only conclusion that could be reached from two samples was, an accelerant had been used. In addition, the technician also told the jury that after conducting "flame tests" on undamaged carpet from the Gavitt home, he found the only way he could be burnt was by use of an accelerant. Little did he know at the time, many years later, this testimony would come back to haunt him.

With no disrespect to the learned counsel for Gavitt, but his defence was sadly lacking, as they should have at least called their own expert evidence to the probable accidental cause of the fire and certainly challenged the arson claim. All they did, in what could only be seen as accepting the fire was indeed deliberately lit, was to call Gavitt to give evidence of what he said had actually happened.

This testimony was further supported by neighbours, who gave a chilling account of the efforts of Gavitt trying to save his family. Gavitt, who was a clean skin with no criminal record and certainly no history, let alone any evidence offered by the prosecution, of family violence being a possible motive, was found guilty and sentenced to life in prison without the possibility of parole.

Despite two appeals to conviction and sentence in 1988 and again in 1989, such leave to appeal was refused. This meant Gavitt was left to bide his time in prison, maintaining his innocence and trying to avoid being bashed by other inmates that saw him as a "child killer". During his period of incarceration, he would also lose his parents, who had financed his defence, with both passing away. However, he never gave up and in 2010 the University of Michigan Law School's Innocence Clinic took up the fight to prove he was an innocent man.

They engaged the services of a number of arson experts, once again with the esteemed John Lentini, who concluded, with support from another expert, that the so-called chromatogram test was wrongly interpreted. Namely, it should have read that no accelerant had been detected on carpet samples, also the flashover cause was now top of the list of culprits. Around the time of this fire, such concept was largely unknown, but it was now conclusive this is what had occurred. It had reached a point when it simply exploded, completely enveloping the living room, which was also corroborated by another expert witness now engaged by the prosecution.

In his affidavit, Lentini got straight to the point and said the original fire forensic experts simply put together what he described as "bundled myths" and further that:

> *In light of modern science, there is not simply one shred of credible evidence that the fire... was intentionally set...*

It was now obvious the prosecution's case was in tatters, because it had simply relied totally on the evidence of the fire experts. This meant, based on the now adopted modern forensic standards of fire investigation to origin and cause, no rational jury could find Gavitt guilty, as there were simply no grounds to reach the conclusion that the fire was caused by arson.

On 5 June 2012, the Ionia County Circuit Court agreed and, by way of a joint request from both lawyers for Gavitt and the prosecution, his conviction was dismissed with Gavitt being released from prison. Sadly, his first port of call, as a free man, was the graveside where his wife and daughters were buried.

In June 2014, Gavitt sued Ionia County naming its police and prosecutors as defendants for compensation by way of monetary damages, but it was dismissed on the grounds that the defendants had absolute immunity and the claim for injunctive relief failed to state a claim.[201]

Gavitt, unperturbed by this set back, then turned to the *Michigan Wrongful Imprisonment Act*, also known as Act 343 of 2016. This legislation provides compensation to any individual for being wrongfully convicted and sent to prison for a crime they did not commit. Gavitt, now 61 years old, certainly qualified to make a claim, being awarded in 2019 the sum of $1.3 million by way of compensation from the State of Michigan. I don't think that really comforts him though for not only spending nearly 26 years in prison as an innocent man, but also for the loss of his much-loved family.

Biding his time on death row for 17 years was the fate that now waited 39-year-old Ernest Willis, after he was convicted of murder by arson, following a fire in his West Texas home

---

[201] *Gavitt v Ionia Cnty, et al*, United States District Court Easten District of Michigan Southern Division, 67 F.Supp.3d 838 (E.D. Mich 2014).

in June 1986. Once again, the pour patterns argument would be his undoing with the floor left charred. On that basis, fire investigators had no doubt an accelerant had been used.

Willis was considered the only suspect as he was not injured and, after being woken up around 4.00 am, along with his cousin, they escaped from the blaze, while two innocent women, they had only just met, died in the inferno. Willis had tried valiantly to wake them up, all to no avail, before escaping the flames and becoming overwhelmed by the smoke, after smashing windows to assist the other occupants.

His other conduct at the time of the fire would raise suspicions, although it could hardly be considered damning. As the fire responders extinguished the blaze, Willis watched on, smoking a cigarette and it appeared he had not suffered from any smoke inhalation. Police were also of the view that his feet should have been burnt, but that was not the case. Although they could not determine any sort of motive and no physical evidence linked him to the fire, it must have been him using an accelerant, evidenced by the pour patterns.

He did have a minor criminal record, mainly three driving convictions and, of all things, a naked visit to a drive-through restaurant, probably McDonald's, but that was it. Willis was a heavy drinker and had consumed a large amount of alcohol the night before the fire. He had also been married six times. He admitted to police during a record of interview that he had passed out on the fateful night and was first woken up around 3.30am to smell something burning but went back to sleep.

He failed a polygraph test and, based on purely circumstantial evidence, he was indicted on a charge of capital murder. Whilst waiting in jail on remand, he was doped up with, not only pain medication for a chronic back ailment but, for reasons unknown and without his apparent knowledge, anti-psychotic drugs.

By the time he got to trial in August 1987, it's fair to say he was in somewhat of a dazed and expressionless zombie-type state, which was seized on by the prosecution. They labelled him a cold-hearted murderer and "Satan in disguise" which, for some reason, his somewhat young and inexperienced defence counsel did not object to, nor did he call any character evidence on behalf of his client.

The jury only took one hour to find him guilty and he was sentenced to wait his pending execution, being housed in a five-by-nine foot cell for the next 17 odd years on death row. His lawyers would subsequently file an appeal in the Texas Court of Criminal Appeals in 1989 on six grounds, which included a lack of evidence proving he was responsible for the arson.

The appeal also included improper testimony regarding the polygraph examination, the admissions he allegedly made to another prisoner while in custody on remand and that there was no evidence he was a danger to society. This appeal ground was on the basis that if he was assessed as posing no danger, then a sentence of death would not have been handed down meaning, even with a sentence of life imprisonment, he may have had a possibility of parole.

One other ground of appeal was in respect of his failure to testify, which was his right but on the advice of his lawyers he chose not to. The closing argument of the prosecutor to the jury was strongly objected to on the grounds it was "so egregious" when it was said:

With his cold fisheyes on everybody and everything that has come in here, and he just merely stared and watched very impassively, very coldheartedly, much like he probably did that morning outside the fire when he watched and listened.

However, the Court of Appeal upheld his conviction with a rehearing being denied on 17 January 1990.[202] A subsequent Writ of Certiorari to the Supreme Court, seeking an order for his case to be judicially reviewed from the lower court by the higher court, was also refused.

Thankfully, the US multinational law firm, Latham & Watkins, established as far back as 1934 in Los Angeles, California, took up the fight for Willis. This law firm is believed to be the second biggest team of lawyers in the world, on the basis of client revenue it brings in each year, reportedly paying each partner around $6 million per financial year, generated from its profits.

In the case of Willis, one of their clients, grateful for the compassion shown by Willis to her mentally ill son, who was imprisoned alongside him, recommended they take a look at the case. They agreed to act pro-bono. They focused their attention, not only on their client being subjected to the anti-psychotic drugs before trial, but also on a confession by another inmate on death row, that he was, in fact, the arsonist. This particular individual, David Martin Long, happened to be a cohort of Willis' cousin and both were involved in crime.

Long was about to be put to death by lethal injection, after being sentenced to the death penalty for murdering three women, but he not only confessed to a 1983 mobile home arson, that resulted in the death of his former employer but also provided details on how he set the Willis house alight. According to his taped three-hour confession, he had an

---

[202] *Willis v State* 785 S.W.2d 378 Tex.Crim App 1990.

immense dislike for Willis' cousin and this was why he set the West Texas home on fire. His apparent confession went nowhere though, with Long executed in 1999, but it at least created further doubt to Willis' guilt.

In 2004, the pro-bono lawyers for Willis, now further encouraged by the doubt over his conviction, filed a federal habeas corpus petition (Writ) in the US District Court challenging the conviction and death sentence. Such a petition was on the basis that the arrest, conviction and sentence violated US constitutional law and it followed that any imprisonment was unlawful.

It was no surprise that the District Court agreed the constitution had, in fact, been violated and granted the petition specifically on the following grounds:

1) Willis' due process rights were violated by the state's administration of medically inappropriate antipsychotic drugs without Willis's consent; 2) the state suppressed evidence favourable and material to the sentencing determination; 3) Willis received infective assistance of counsel at the guilt-innocence phase and 4) Willis received ineffective assistance of counsel at the sentencing phase...[203]

As a consequence of this ruling, the Pecos County District Attorney reviewed the circumstances and all the aspects surrounding the Willis case, in particular, the cause and origin of the fire. Indeed, experts would now find there was no evidence of arson, even to a degree that it may have started from electrical issues within the house.

---

203 *Willis v Cockrell*-United States District Court, W. D. Texas, Pecos Division Aug 9 2004–paras 3-4.

Given the case was now undetermined and, in view of the habeas corpus ruling, Willis, now aged 59, was finally released from prison on 5 October 2004. He was subsequently compensated by the state of Texas in 2005, being awarded $429,000 and a monthly annuity of $9,965 for the loss of 17 years of his life, which also included coming within 48 hours of death by lethal injection.

Interest in this case and that of Cameron Todd Willingham, then caught the attention of the Innocence Project and they would engage the services of five well known and creditable fire scientists and investigators as part of an Arson Review Committee. They would provide a 48-page report in March 2006, after reviewing, not only all the evidence as presented in the trial of Willis but also, the witness testimony trial transcripts.

The committee experts which unsurprisingly, included the much-heralded John Lentini and fire scientist, Douglas Carpenter, again highlighted in their report one of the many myths without any scientific basis from the NBS 1980 "Fire Investigation Handbook" and said:

Floors seldom receive damage to that of ceilings, even in the case of total burnout, as the heat of the fire will be concentrated at the ceiling. In addition, as ceiling materials are damaged and fall, these materials protect the floor below. If, on the other hand, a large area of floor is extensively damaged, the use of accelerants may be indicated.[204]

---

[204] Report on the Peer Review of the Expert Testimony in cases of State of Texas v Cameron Todd Willingham and State of Texas v Ernest Ray Willis–Arson Review Committee-page 39.

After reviewing the witness testimony of the state's investigators, the report was further particularly scathing in respect of the 1986 Willis fire scene examination, stating:

...the state investigators...relied on their alleged ability to visually interpret the significance of irregular patterns on the floor in a fully involved compartment fire...in 1987 such interpretations, although wrong, were common. It is now well known that in post-flashover compartment fires, irregular patterns on flooring are commonly observed. [205].

They also said further regarding another questionable testimony of one of the fire investigators that:

...he believed, because of the extent of damage on the couch in the Willis residence, someone must have poured liquid accelerant on it. Again, this was never validated by a positive laboratory analysis.[206]

The committee then made a number of recommendations in order to avoid further wrongful convictions and it was of no surprise when they pointed out:

...first and foremost, individuals conducting investigations of fire incident must be provided with fundamental scientific knowledge of the physics and chemistry of fire as a perquisite with the practical application of fire dynamics within the context of the Scientific Method... The significant lack of understanding of the behaviour of fire, as evidenced by the expert opinions in

---

[205] Ibid- page 24.
[206] Ibid.

[both cases], can and does result in significant misinterpretations of fire evidence, unreliable determinations...with respect to the crime of arson...[207].

In a parting statement the committee also said:

To the extent that there are still investigators in Texas and elsewhere, who interpret low burning, irregular fire patterns and collapsed furniture springs as indicators of incendiary fires, there will continue to be serious miscarriages of justice. The authors sincerely hope that this report will help undo similar miscarriages and help prevent further ones from occurring.[208]

Willis would certainly hope that no other prisoner suffered such a miscarriage of justice as he did, but sadly, his body failed him and in early January 2021 he died from natural causes, as stated on his death certificate. Then again, given he spent 17 years pacing up and down on death row, it's hard to imagine what he must have gone through, so perhaps his death, aged 75, was premature.

Sonia Cacy certainly didn't spend as much time in prison as Willis as she only served five years, but it would take almost 23 years before her 1993 conviction for murder was vacated on the basis of actual innocence. Cacy was charged with the murder of her stepfather, who died in an early morning house fire in November 1991 in Fort Stockdale in the Pecos County of Texas in the US, with arson investigators supposedly finding traces of accelerant on the clothing of the deceased.

Cacy, who lived at the home, happened to be a beneficiary

---

207   Ibid-page 40.

208   Ibid-pages 42-43.

in the last Will and Testament of her stepdad. The fact she was able to escape from the burning inferno, despite trying to get back when most likely trying to save him, determined in their eyes that Cacy had a motive and was the culprit. This questionable evidence was also coupled with the fact that there had previously been a number of suspicious fires at the home, so there was, indeed, patterns of behaviour, again pointing to Cacy.

At Cacy's trial in February 1993, the prosecution led evidence of an accelerant being poured over the victim while he was asleep and then set on fire. The testimony from a laboratory toxicologist, who analysed the clothing from the fire, left no doubt in the mind of the jury that gasoline was used in a deliberately-lit fire. The prosecution also alleged that Cacy had been drinking on the evening prior to the fire and her palm print was found on his will in a book drawer. The defence, on the other hand, presented evidence of the previous fires, which caused only minor damage saying they were lit by her now deceased stepfather.

As to Cacy being a beneficiary of his estate, they said he didn't really leave her much, other than a now destroyed home, but overlooked presenting any evidence from medical and arson experts. Sadly for Cacy, a jury reached a unanimous verdict of guilty and she was sentenced to a term of 55 years imprisonment.

In 1995, her conviction for murder was upheld by the Appeals Court, but they vacated her sentence and ordered a new sentence hearing. This was on the basis of the prosecution making irregular comments to the jury about the fact that Cacy had elected not to give evidence at her trial which, of course, was her right.[209]

At a resentence hearing in 1996, Cambridge graduate,

---

[209] Cacy v State, 08-93-00085-CR Tex. App-El Paso May 11, 1995.

Dr Gerald Hurst, one of the leading pioneers of arson investigation, after examining all the evidence, formed a very strong view and gave testimony to the court that there was absolutely no evidence of arson. This was to the degree that the lab analysis had, in fact, been misinterpreted and it was burning plastic residue from mattresses and furniture, which once again resembled the aftermath from an accelerant-induced fire.

Another experienced Texas fire investigator, Ken Gibson, detailed for the defence how the fire had started from a burning cigarette near the bed of the deceased. This then set the bed sheets on fire, with the victim dying, not from burns but, from a heart attack trying to escape from the burning home with a damaged window crank handle found in his hand. Cacy, this time, testified in the witness box, telling the court she was innocent and that there was no financial motive as she had everything she ever needed.

To that effect, Cacy also said her stepfather would have given her anything she ever wanted, so there was absolutely no reason to set him on fire. Despite all the exculpatory evidence now pointing to a question of innocence, Cacy copped a further 44 years to her sentence, which meant she was now facing 99 years in prison, which would later be affirmed.[210]

This crushing sentence, however, only encouraged her legal team to continue the fight for her innocence, ably assisted by medical specialists and fire experts, such as Hurst. All acting pro bono, they appeared before the Texas Board of Pardons and Parole Board in 1998. Regarding the medical submissions, they argued the deceased died from a heart attack and the burns were only a subsequent result, but did not cause his death.

Hurst would again make a lengthy assessment into the

---

210   Cacy v State, 08-96-00239-CR Tex App-El Paso March 19, 1998.

cause of the fire, believing the lab finding of accelerant on the victim's clothing was erroneous. The parole board concurred and on 28 November 1998, Cacy was released on parole after serving five years for a crime she didn't commit.

It didn't stop there though, as the Innocence Project Team of Texas filed a Writ of Habeas Corpus in 2012 in the Court of Criminal Appeals for relief as to her innocence. This was now supported with evidence from the Texas State Fire Marshall's Office which concurred with Hurst's findings that there was no evidence of arson.

It went as far as to say, the original analysis had been contaminated in the laboratory with accelerant-based residue, although the forensic scientist who carried out the initial analysis, still maintained his findings were correct. This opinion, however, was quickly called into question when further sworn evidence was submitted by a former toxicologist at the lab, that no accelerant had ever been detected on the clothing of the deceased.

Following the two-day evidentiary hearing in 2014, finally the judge recommended to the Appeals Court that relief be granted by way of exoneration, accepting the victim did not die by an accelerant-based arson and that it was a sudden cardiac arrest death. The court was also quite scathing of the defence team for Cacy in her initial trial in that they failed to call any testimony from experts, challenging the cause of fire and subsequent death.

This recommendation was accepted and, in early November 2016, the Texas Court of Criminal Appeals declared Cacy, now in her 60s and suffering from ill-health, was entitled to relief on the basis of actual innocence.[211]

---

211   Ex Parte Sonia Cacy- Applicant- On Application for a Writ of Habeas Corpus-Cause No P-2037-B-83-CR in the 83rd District Court from Pecos County-2 November 2016.

Finally, some 19 years after Cacy was released on parole, the charge of murder was dismissed by the prosecution in 2017, which meant at long last she had no criminal record and it was no longer a question of innocence. It would be remiss not to applaud the assistance once again provided by the legal team from the Texas Innocence Project, however, the earlier comment by journalist, Brantley Hargrove, in the Texas Monthly in June 2014, really summed up the dedicated effort of Dr Hurst when he said:

If there was a moment when fire investigation began to emerge out of the dark age of hunches, untested hand-me-down arson indicators and wives' tales, it occurred when Hurst turned his attention to Cacy's case.

While a question of innocence was the final determination in these cases, there were others where the jury is still out, but worthy of mention.

18
THE JURY IS STILL OUT

Most criminal matters in Japan are first tried by a panel of three District Court judges with the right of appeal to the High Court. Any criminal appeal to the Supreme Court is restricted to constitutional questions or in situations of conflicting precedents. There is also, what is known as, a lay judge judicial panel to hear more serious cases being introduced in 2009, with six citizens randomly chosen and overseen by three judges. The role of the District Court judges, similar to what we know a trial by judge alone, is to hear the evidence, question witnesses, have an independent role in calling for further evidence and then play the part of the jury before passing sentence.

Regarding 88-year-old grandpa, Iwao Hakamanda, not only is he known as the world's longest serving prisoner on death row, but the jury, being the District Court, is once again out considering its verdict following a retrial. The problem was going to be, as he waited his fate sitting in his lounge chair at home with serious health issues after being freed in 2014, he may well have passed away before such verdict was handed down.

The lingering question would be whether his health would get in first, would he be exonerated or was he to be found once again guilty. If again deemed guilty, it would be back to death row for Iwao as the prosecutors again seek the death penalty in his retrial. All up, he spent 46 years on death row, which was indeed a record being recognised in the Guiness Book of World records. Iwao was convicted back in 1968 of stabbing four people to death in June 1966, which included two children. He then set fire to their home, incinerating their bodies.

For some reason, he was not held in high regard, being a former professional boxer and after becoming ill, he retired around 1961, was now working in a factory and also had been employed in a local bar. He was divorced and when police found he was an employee of the now deceased factory owner, Iwao was brought in for questioning four days after the fire.

He was initially released due to lack of evidence, but one month later they took him back into custody and for the next 20 days put him under what can only be described as a 240-hour horrendous interrogation. Japan is rather unique in that regard. Not only can police interview a suspect without the presence of a lawyer, but they can detain that person for up to 23 days without laying charges and, if they can find any new allegations, detention can be extended further, time and time again.

Clearly, they were after a confession from Iwao and that's what they got, well sort of, even though he had a right to remain silent. Not only was there no taped recording of any such admissions, with mandatory video recording only in respect of serious cases being introduced in 2016, but at trial, prosecutors presented to the three-judge panel 45 different confession statements, with the learned judges only accepting one. One interesting aspect of this is, according to leading Asia academic, David T. Johnson, in his paper,[212] such confessions have underpinned the criminal justice system in Japan.

Although the "confession" by Iwao would be ruled inadmissible in other democratic jurisdictions, it wasn't in Japan. Iwao pleaded not guilty and repeatedly stated that his confession was fabricated and it was only made after he was beaten and threatened by police. All to no good though with the prosecution producing a set of blood- stained clothes suggesting that his motive was robbery.

Iwao was convicted and sentenced to death in his 1968 trial in a majority decision, with one judge dissenting. That one particular judge actually resigned some six months later and stepped away from the judiciary, obviously totally disenchanted with what had taken place.

Iwao's death sentence was confirmed by the Supreme Court of Japan in 1980 and he would now wait on death row for his execution by hanging, still continuing to maintain his innocence. His cry of not guilty and letters of innocence from him to anyone who would read them, for some time fell on deaf ears. This was despite a DNA test in 2004 which revealed it was not his blood group on the five pieces of clothing found at the fire. It also didn't match any of the deceased victims.

Wait he did and it was not until 2014 that his calls for justice finally prevailed. He was released after a retrial was ordered by the District Court of Shizuoka, on the basis that police may have planted evidence against Iwao. His release was

---

[212] Wrongful Convictions and the Culture of Denial in Japanese Criminal Justice-2015.

only agreed to because if his age and fragile mental state after years in solitary confinement. He nearly went back in though, when the Tokyo High Court, some four years later, overruled the earlier 2014 finding of the lower court, without providing any reason for such decision.

This resulted in further appeals by lawyers for Iwao with the Supreme Court now ordering the High Court, of all things, to reconsider their decision. They did just that, in favour of a retrial, obviously persuaded by Amnesty International and the former boxing association of Iwao, who organised a number of protests on the front doors of Japan's Parliament. Back to the Shizuoka District Court we go in October 2023, with Japanese prosecutors again seeking the death penalty of 88-year-old Iwao.

This was on the basis there was sufficient evidence he was guilty, based on the very dark red blood stains on the clothing and, no doubt, his retracted so-called confession. His defence lawyers were relatively confident of his final acquittal, given the very tenuous clothing evidence, stating they did not fit him, given they were found some 12 months after the fire. On that basis, why were they not discoloured if they were simply left behind in a barrel?

The problem faced by Iwao is that 99 per cent of criminal cases tried in a Japanese court resulted in a conviction. Although he was one of only a few inmates on death row able to gain a retrial, his fate was still not in his hands. A jury of his peers, being once again three judges, were left to decide his fate and if found guilty, he would certainly retain the Guiness record as the longest-serving death row inmate.

Japan is now one of only 55 countries that still retain the death penalty, which also includes the US, China and North

Korea. Amnesty International featured Iwao in its campaign to abolish the death penalty in Japan, to join more than 140 members of the European Union who have now outlawed such a penalty.

Finally, on 25 September 2024, the district judges ruled he was not guilty, recognising the so-called evidence against Iwao simply didn't stack up. His case of innocence had finally been acknowledged but the problem sadly was, the jury was still out in the mind of Iwao.

He has a number of mental issues and continues to suffer from post-incarceration syndrome. According to his family, he lives in his own world and simply has no idea he has, at long last, once and for all been acquitted. However, when a Japanese police chief bowed and apologised to him for the wrongful conviction, Iwao did mutter that police need to act with integrity and certainly not misuse their power. Maybe the jury, to a degree, is not out in his mind.

A similar problem was faced by James "Jimmy" Carver, to prove he was wrongly convicted and entitled to a fresh trial. This was based on new scientific evidence, but it would be almost 35 years before such a motion would be heard as he remained behind bars. The other issue Carver faced, in respect of a Beverely, Massachusetts, US rooming house fire in 1984, he had confessed to a female friend that he was responsible. The fire had started around 4 am on the morning of 4 July 1984 and it was described in a number of media reports to be one of, if not the worst, mass murder by fire in the state's history.

A total of 15 people would be killed with many only identified from dental and x-ray records, as the fire would simply engulf the 30-room building, reaching the second and top floor even before the fire alarm had been activated. The loss of life was unavoidable, even though the Beverely Fire Department responded within a matter of minutes on receiving the alarm notification. The following day, investigators determined the fire was set deliberately, ignited by pouring gasoline over a bundle of newspapers near the front entrance to the building.

Carver, a part-time cook and taxi driver, became a suspect when in late 1987, police were advised of his so-called confession and how he had set the fire. Following his arrest in May 1988, they conducted a line up with one witness identifying Carver as being close to the building just before the fire. The Essex County District Attorney's Office (DA), subsequently indicted Carver on 15 counts of second-degree murder, assault and battery with intent to murder and one count of arson.

At his first trial in March 1989, with Carver maintaining his innocence and refusing to accept a guilty plea offer, the prosecution failed to hand over, by way of discovery to his defence counsel, one of the incriminating witness statements, until the trial had started. Quite rightly, the presiding judge declared a mistrial and in November 1989 at his second trial, Carver, at the age of 25, was found guilty on all counts. He was sentenced to 15 consecutive life terms but eligible for parole after 30 years.

His conviction was based on his confession to the female friend and also included another witness, who was a co-worker of Carver, that he had admitted he had set the fire by pouring a liquid accelerant over newspapers and then lighting them with a match. As to motive, the prosecution led evidence that Carver was very angry over an ex-girlfriend dating a man who lived at the rooming house.

In respect of the fire being deliberate, an investigator testified there was "alligator charring" on the walls near the front doorway, meaning it looked like reptile blisters or scaly skin similar to burn marks and, therefore, the only explanation was that petrol had been used. This was despite evidence from a chemist, attached to the state laboratory, saying their forensic tests found no evidence of any flammable liquid, either on the newspapers or debris removed from where the bundle of papers was located.

One interesting aspect from his 1989 trial and conviction was that his defence counsel, who was later disbarred for misconduct issues and has since passed away, never challenged the forensic evidence of arson, preferring to rely on an alibi argument. The misleading cause of the fire would eventually become a point of contention at his petition for a new trial.

Fast forward to 2018 when Carver became eligible for parole but he dug in, refusing to accept such release on the basis he was not guilty. In 2020, he did make application to the State Commissioner of Corrections for release on a number of medical grounds, which included cardiovascular disease as he was now confined to a wheelchair. This was denied and later confirmed by the Massachusetts Supreme Judicial Court, despite such debilitating health, he was still considered a danger to the community if released.[213]

Thankfully for Carver, his plea of innocence would be taken up by, not only the State's Public Defender's office but also, the Boston College Innocence Program. In 2022, they filed a motion for a new trial and, not only did they contend he had inadequate legal representation at his 1989 trial, but for the first time argued there was no scientific evidence to support his conviction. In response to the motion, the office of the DA

---

213   *James Carver vs. Commissioner of Correction & Anor* (Massachusetts Supreme Judicial Court-SJC 13247 September 9, 2022-April 3, 2023.

in agreeing that even if there was a lack of proper scientific and physical evidence of a liquid accelerant, including ambiguous evidence from the arson investigator, there was still sufficient evidence to a proper finding of guilt.

This was most likely on the purported confession made by Carver and on that basis, he should not be granted a new trial. The other issue, given the length of time that had now passed, was a memory blank, leaving gaps in evidence and even a problem where some of the witnesses may have passed away.

In April 2024, with Carver now aged 60 and having served, to date, almost 35 years in prison, he was wheeled into the Essex County Superior Court presided over by Judge Jeffery Karp for an evidentiary hearing on the motion. Famed arson expert, Craig Beyler, appeared on behalf of Carver, having prepared a prior written report and testified after reviewing all the trial transcripts, witness statements and testimony, and, of course, what was submitted on behalf of the prosecution of the alleged crime scene evidence. In his learned opinion, testifying over three days, it was virtually nigh on impossible for a batch of newspapers to start a fire with such ferocity that resulted in engulfing the whole of the building.

Regarding the concept of alligator charring, this was a myth that now failed any scientific basis as proof that an accelerant had been used, but Beyler agreed it was certainly a common point of reference around the 1980s. On that basis and, given the laboratory tests had found no evidence of any accelerant, the fire had to be concluded as undetermined and not based on mere speculation. In respect of a possible cause, Beyler did not rule out an electrical fault, noting the fire investigator, who had since died, had not carried out any sort of examination of the wiring and the electrical system installed in the building.

The DA relied on expert evidence from a retired Massachusetts State Police arson investigator, who reviewed all the same material as Beyler, noting he was not at any time one of the officers involved in the investigation and examination of the fire damaged building. In his view, it was entirely possible the fire was started by an accelerant and the laboratory tests found no trace, as it was most likely washed away when fire responders extinguished the blaze. However, he conceded, it was indeed also likely there was no accelerant used but dismissed Beyler's theory that the fire could not have started such a ferocious blaze by the mere lighting of newspapers.

This was in direct contradiction of evidence given at the 1989 trial by one of the state's arson investigators, who said, using the expression then, of trying to 'light wood on fire', without using a flammable liquid. As to an electrical fault, he would concede it was indeed conceivable, but in likelihood that did not occur.

To the other point of contention, the supposed confession of Carver, counsel submitted on his behalf that the new scientific evidence, discounting arson by use of an accelerant, was sufficient to order a new trial. In any event, counsel was of the view that the confession lacked credibility as the witness was allegedly told by Carver in 1984 that he set fire to the newspapers using a liquid accelerant, but it would not be for another three years before police were advised.

Further, it was a matter of record at the first trial that Carver had been drinking at the time, was extremely upset and most likely looking for sympathy. Judge Karp would make a relevant point though as to why Carver would confess, after 15 people had died, just to try and gain any sympathy. In his learned view, this would be a moot point that any jury in a new trial might have some difficulty with.

The judge was now left with the task of determining if a new trial should be granted, on the basis of new evidence, that there was an argument of how the fire started. It was noted by counsel for Carver that the prosecution, courtesy of the DA, had now changed their steadfast position, agreeing that it was possible the fire started without an accelerant, which is in marked contrast to what was put at the 1989 trial. Indeed, counsel for Carver put to Judge Karp, in closing remarks, it was always the contention of the prosecution which resulted in his conviction that it was arson started by an accelerant.

However, we now have a situation where there is a large question mark over how the fire started. It really needs to be put to a new jury, regardless of the question of his confession. The judge reserved his decision, so we now wait to see whether the motion for a new trial will be granted. Pending that ruling, the jury is still out, which it may well be in the future, if Carver once again faces a jury of his peers.

Any suspect who makes a false confession is going to be faced with a difficult task trying to overturn a subsequent conviction, regardless of the lack of any other compelling evidence to proof of guilt. Case in point was the arrest, interrogation and subsequent conviction of 23-year-old Michael L. Ledford for first degree murder and arson of an occupied dwelling. This followed an October 1999 Virginia apartment fire in the US that resulted in the death of his young son Zach and with critical injuries to his wife, Elise.

Two fire investigators subsequently determined the fire was arson and police turned their attention to Ledford, despite having no physical evidence connecting him to the fire. After learning he was not a well-liked member of the local community and just happened to be a volunteer fire fighter who, lo and behold, left home some 20 minutes earlier to go to the fire station, then returned to the scene of the fatal fire.

They would subject him to what can only be described as a brutal interrogation over five hours without a lawyer present. Effectively, by the time they finished using what is known as the "Reid Technique", he would have even admitted to being Father Christmas. Such method of interviewing suspects was first developed in the US by John E Reid around the 1950s. Reid was a former Chicago police officer with expertise in polygraph tests.

The whole idea, after first forming the view that a suspect is guilty regardless, is to place the person being interviewed under immense pressure of their guilt, intertwined with sympathy and kind offers of assistance, the latter only on the basis of making a confession and if you do, the police will be your friend. In some way, it assists police in using such a technique to breakdown tough and ruthless criminals but was never designed to extract confessions from suspects more vulnerable.

Ledford was indeed in that category, being autistic and diagnosed as suffering from a severe nonverbal learning disorder. He lived in his own shell, to a degree, being a social recluse and struggled to show any emotions, which was evident when he attended the scene of the fire and reportedly didn't try hard enough in any attempt to save his child, let alone display any grief. In his taped record of interview shown to the jury in his 2000 trial, it was obvious he was totally exhausted and in shock, making totally irrelevant comments but continuing to maintain his innocence. After some persistent prodding by police, even telling him of possible motives why he did it and that he had supposedly failed a polygraph test, which was incorrect, he gave in.

No doubt, in a confused state of mind and with his hand shaking, he signed the following statement:

Around 8.00 pm we put Zach to bed then Elise went to bed at 8.30 pm. I told Elise that I was going to put gas in the car and put my name on the EVAC sheet at the firehouse...then go to bed. Before I left, I lit a candle and threw it in the chair. I never wanted to hurt my family. I was tired of trying to live up to Elise's parents' standards. I now wish I took my mom's advice and moved back to Pennsylvania. I agree I need help and willing to get help. I just hope my family and friends and God can forgive me.

Based on that confession, police then literally rewrote the fire investigation report, so it matched the confession details with the candle and cushion, despite not having any pertinent physical evidence to support this. Unfortunately for Ledford, he was not forgiven with Elise divorcing him after he was found guilty and sentenced to 45 years for the murder of Zach and five years for the arson. As to motive, the jury heard his relationship with his wife was, at best, somewhat testy and he was not liked by her family. Coupled with this, Ledford had a $75,000 death insurance policy on both her and his young child, Zach.

He was now facing life in prison without the possibility of any parole, as such an early release does not exist in Virginia. His convictions were upheld in 2001 by the Virginia Court of Appeals, which was then confirmed by the Supreme Court. In November 2005, his petition, for a Writ of habeas corpus to determine if his convictions were lawful, was refused.[214]

---

214 *Ledford v Commonwealth of Virginia*-United States District Court, W.D. Virginia, Roanoke Division, Civil Action No 7:05CV00600 Nov 3, 2005.

A further petition for a writ of actual innocence was then filed on behalf of Ledford by the Mid-Atlantic Innocence Project and global law firm Baker Boots, based in Houston, Texas and was heard before a trial court in an evidentiary hearing in July and November 2021. Such petition set out two main points of contention, namely, new scientific evidence and the timeline surrounding the fire meant Ledford was wrongfully convicted. As to Ledford confessing, he had thrown a candle onto the seat of a chair, this was determined to be scientifically incorrect. His defence lawyers arranged for two thermodynamic scientists to critically examine his confession to how the fire supposedly started and they carried out a similar scenario at a Novia Scotia test laboratory.

What they found was, in fact, the burn patterns on the wall would show the fire could not have started from the cushion and chair but emanated from the rear and base of the chair and certainly not the cushion, meaning an accidental cause could not be ruled out. This meant it was physically impossible to have been started by placing or throwing a candle on the seat of the chair, which effectively ruled out his confession, not to mention, of course, how it was obtained by police.

In respect of his confession, in any event, when taking into account the amount of time taken for the chair to burn and then reported to Triple 0, his lawyers argued it was nigh on impossible that he set the fire. This was on the basis, allegedly after setting the fire, then leaving the apartment, filling his car up with petrol, the emergency call came in some 20 minutes after he had arrived at the fire station.

Based on the new expert findings and testimony, with the presiding judge aware of the much-criticised confession obtained by police being the only evidence that tied Ledford to the fire, the evidentiary court accepted the truth of the legal arguments submitted on behalf of Ledford. He was now looking at being a free man after spending 23 years in prison.

This, however, was not the case, as in April 2022 the Virginia Court of Appeals denied the writ of actual innocence and 12 months later in April 2023, the Virginia Supreme Court refused to hear the case. This means he is now facing another 27 years in jail, despite the new scientific evidence invalidating his confession and that he was wrongfully convicted. His only hope now is for the Governor of Virginia to effectively step into the shoes of a jury, to consider any appeal for clemency by way of a pardon.

The jury is still out in that regard.

EPILOGUE

I never thought for one moment, when I first started writing a book on arson, that I would uncover what can only be described as long, drawn out and dramatic history. Not just with cases of arson, but the media attention that it would be given. It's fair to say that most countries, not just Australia, have suffered at the hands of arsonists, or perhaps I should just call them plain villains. This includes, of course, fires that remain unsolved as to cause. Or were they simply an act of nature, such as lighting strikes, but many with horrific consequences?

Then again, I digress as, given my previous background as Head of School Security, Victorian school fires were not just spontaneous combustion as put down by some, but clearly acts of arson, unless proved otherwise. It, of course, raises the question to this day, whatever possessed me to go into law? Maybe I thought I would get to represent some of these school arsonists, but lucky for them, apart from acting in many other criminal matters for clients, a good old arsonist never joined the list. Perhaps if one did, then my learned submission as to sentence would not have upheld the ethics of the legal profession.

You may well have also noticed that in various parts of this book, I have challenged or, in some way, made what appears to be disparaging comments of other legal practitioners and judicial court hierarchy. These remarks were in no way meant to be disrespectful and were made only in my, shall we say, learned opinion, noting I was admitted to practice on April Fool's Day in 1996. So, who am I to talk?

What, of course, did become readily apparent to me in my research for this book, was there are a high number of fires that are acts of arson and connected to varying types of motives. This book has looked at a few select motives but really has only scratched the surface. As you have read so far, I have touched on a few obvious motives and have named under, what I loosely describe as a "Rogues Gallery", a list of 125 miscreants.

Naming these rascals, as you will note, is also supported by over 100 cases in respect of conviction and sentence, mainly thanks to the Australian Legal Information Institute (AustLii). This online resource is operated as a joint initiative by the University of Technology Sydney and the University of New South Wales and provides such access to not only decisions by courts and tribunals, but other legal information, such as legislation, law reform reports and those of royal commissions. I am truly indebted to this valuable resource tool.

As a former or, perhaps I should now say, retired lawyer, I have also included a couple of chapters, trying to give some balance, not just to arson committed by perpetrators with motive, but those that raised a question mark of their guilt and where they were indeed not guilty. Some, of course, never escaped the jaws of justice and with one in particular, as you have read, being sent to meet his maker from death row.

As to motive, terrorism arson, whether it be due to some

political objective or based on unexplained psychological factors, is very much an issue. Organised crime groups helped along perhaps by outlaw motorcycle gangs, seem to be attracting much publicity, particularly in respect of the recent spate of "chop chop" arsons in Victoria, Australia. We still, of course, have acts of arson that are carried out by some misguided individuals, purely based on revenge, fuelled by anger and hatred.

There are other areas of acts of arson for profit, thanks to cases of insurance fraud and, in some instances, other acts carried out to simply eliminate a competitor in order to line their pockets. The list is endless and this epilogue does not bring any closure, nor does this book, as these and a number of other arson motives and cases still need to be addressed. This then begs the question of "Another Question of Arson", but for the time being, the defence rests Your Honour.

However, before I rest my case, there is also a question of thanks in particular to those very close to me. If it was not for the ongoing support from my wife Michelle, I don't think I would even get to finish one book, let alone three, to date. Of course, whether I finally test her patience once again in book four, remains to be seen. Thanks also to my two boys, Hayden and Patrick, for their love and support and, of course, our much-loved retired greyhound, Sandy, the most spoilt dog in history.

Finally, my untold thanks again to Alana Lambert of Book Burrow for her publishing skills, Samantha Elley for her editing expertise and to Melinda Childs for her imaginative front cover design.

GLOSSARY

NOTE: Words may include, in some cases, both legal and ordinary meaning.

A

Accelerant A substance, such as petrol, which is used to ignite and aid the spread of fire.

Acquit An accused is discharged after being deemed not guilty, for example, following a jury trial.

Actus Reus A guilty act. In criminal law one of the elements required to prove a crime has been carried out by voluntary actions or omissions. It can also be either a positive or failure to act. Also requires mens rea as the other essential element.

Adjourn Court matter is suspended to another specified date, postponed, or stood down. Also known as *sine die*.

Adversarial System The legal system of justice in common law countries where the opposing parties present and argue their case or position before an impartial third party, such as an arbitrator, judge, magistrate or jury to make a decision. The main aim is to ensure fairness between both the prosecution and defence throughout the trial process.

Affidavit A written document setting out evidence or statement of facts voluntarily made by a person known as the deponent and sworn on oath or by way of an affirmation before a person authorised as a witness, such as a lawyer.

Age of Criminal Responsibility The minimum age a juvenile can be arrested, charged or jailed. For example, the Victorian Government plans to raise such minimum age from 10 to 12 in late 2024. Also see Doli Incapax.

Aggravated Burglary A criminal offence that involves the use of a weapon to commit another crime when illegally entering occupied premises in order to steal or cause damage.

Alford Plea A guilty plea in the United States of America criminal jurisdiction where a defendant does not admit to the criminal act and continues to assert innocence.

Alibi Defence A statement or claim by a person under suspicion for a crime that they were in a different place or elsewhere when the alleged crime was committed.

Alleged A fact that has been stated but has not yet been proven to be true.

Alligator Charring A now debunked theory that suggested burn marks that look like reptile blisters or scaly skin meant an accelerant must have been used.

Amicus Brief Legal brief that may be filed with an Appeal Court by a party not involved with the current case, but in support of the legal issue in question.

Amicus Curiae Not a party to a legal case but is permitted to assist the court. Known as "friend of the court".

Appeal To review a decision from a lower court or tribunal before a higher court.

Appellant A person who appeals a decision from a lower court or tribunal to a higher court.

Apprehended Domestic Violence Order A court order introduced in New South Wales that is made to protect a person in a domestic relationship by restricting and prohibiting certain types of conduct by the other person.

Arrest Taken into custody and usually in order to bring the person under arrest before a court.

Arson In its simplest term, it is an act of willfully and deliberately setting fire to property.

At Large A person may be deemed to be at large if they have committed a criminal offence or escaped from custody, have not been arrested and remain "at large".

B

Bail A person accused of a crime may be granted bail with certain conditions, which may include payment of money, or on their own undertaking, to return to court on the adjourned date to answer the charge(s) as laid.

Balance of Probabilities More probable than not that the evidence presented in a civil proceeding is true. Compare this to a criminal trial in which the standard of proof is beyond reasonable doubt. In sentencing for a crime, all factors submitted in favour of the accused are accepted on such balance.

Barrister A legal professional called to the Bar specialising in courtroom advocacy and client representation. Usually, they take instructions from solicitors. Also referred to, for example in the US, as an Attorney at Law.

Bench Trial Trial by judge sitting alone as opposed to a trial by judge and jury.

Beyond Reasonable Doubt The highest standard of proof in a criminal trial that the prosecution must meet in order to prove the guilt of an accused before a judge or jury. In the event of any doubt must be deemed to be not guilty. Compare to the civil proceeding standard of proof of a balance of probabilities.

Blood Alcohol Content Amount of alcohol in a person's bloodstream for which police may test, for example, by way of a roadside random breath test.

Brief of Evidence Prepared by police for prosecution in which they intend to rely, setting out the charges, a summary of the evidence and documents such as witness statements and may also include a list of any previous criminal or traffic convictions. Also known as Police Brief.

Brain Wave To have a sudden and clever thought or idea.

Bonehead In this context being a course for students lacking in any sort of fundamental skills.

Burden of Proof The requirement in a criminal case for the prosecution to successfully prove beyond reasonable doubt the guilt of the accused. The defence is not required to prove anything and can simply maintain innocence, unless a particular defence is raised, meaning the burden then reverses.

C

Cap in Hand To humbly ask for a favour.

Case Law Also known as common law or judicial precedent and refers to decisions of judges in previous cases. Can be a binding or persuasive precedent from a higher court.

Cathartic Psychological relief through an open expression of strong emotions.

Character Reference A written statement that sets out an accused's good character, behaviour and reputation. Such a reference should be addressed appropriately, for example, "The Presiding Magistrates" or "Your Honour" and be typed, dated and signed and no longer than one A4 page.

Character Witness A person who provides character testimony in court, in person, on behalf of the accused.

Charge Formal criminal accusation made against a person. Can also be a judge's direction to a jury, a fee for service or a financial burden, such as a lien or encumbrance.

Clean- Skin A person with no criminal convictions and has previously not come to the attention of law enforcement.

Closed-circuit television Video surveillance by the use of cameras, often just referred to as CCTV.

Coercive Control A pattern to establish and maintain control over another person, particularly in domestic relationships.

Committal Hearing held in a Magistrates Court to determine whether there is sufficient evidence to commit an accused to trial in the jurisdiction of a higher court. Sometimes also called a preliminary hearing.

Committal Mention Second stage of the committal process following a filing hearing. Areas of disagreement are discussed and the magistrate is advised how the matter should proceed.

Common Law The component of English Law traditionally derived from common custom and judicial unwritten law.

Community Corrections Order (CCO) A flexible sentencing order with conditions that an offender serves in the community. Most orders will require unpaid work in the community under supervision.

Compensation Order Requires a person, convicted of a criminal offence, to pay a monetary amount to the victim of that offence as determined by the court. Will not apply if the accused does not have sufficient financial means or ability to pay the compensation.

Contest Mention Hearing Allows the Magistrates Court in criminal proceedings to efficiently manage the matter in the first instance and provides for any issues in dispute to be resolved between the parties. Applies to summary offences and indictable offences triable summarily in the lower court.

Conviction A determination by a court of law that a defendant is guilty of a criminal offence. Despite a guilty finding, a court may exercise its discretion not to record a conviction.

Criminal Culpability In criminal law an accused is held responsible for a criminal act or negligence when found to be at fault and liable for their conduct. Also see Actus Reus and Mens Rea.

CVSA Device Computer Voice Stress Analyser which measures components of a human voice and determines any signs of stress. Similar to a polygraph but in a CVSA, there are no wires attached.

Culpable Driving In Victoria, the crime of culpable driving causing death can occur when a person driving a vehicle causes another person's death due to driving recklessly or negligently under the influence or affected by alcohol or drugs to a degree, they could not control their vehicle.

Cumulative Sentence Prison sentence served, one after the other. Compare it to a concurrent sentence where all sentences are served together.

Custodial sentence Term of imprisonment imposed by a court to prison or some other secure facility.

Custody Legal detention over a person when arrested or sentenced. Also denotes legal rights or a duty of care of someone, such as a child, following parent separation. Also see remanded in custody.

D

Defendant A person or entity where the party is accused of committing a crime or named in a civil action where a remedy is sought.

Diminished Responsibility In criminal law a defendant may argue, as a potential defence or in mitigation that, although they committed a crime they should not be held fully accountable and criminally liable as their mental function was impaired or diminished. Also, can be referred to as diminished capacity.

Diversion Order A diversion plan is typically run in the Magistrates Court in Victoria where an order is made to allow the matter to be dealt with out of the court system and allow the defendant to avoid a conviction, providing a plea of guilty is entered. A magistrate must agree that the offender is eligible for a diversion plan which will include certain conditions that must be adhered to. In the United States of America commonly referred to as deferred adjudication.

DNA Evidence A tool used by crime scene investigators to collect and identify a suspect to a crime from blood, semen, saliva, hair follicles and even bone and teeth.

Doli Incapax The common law principle that a child between the ages of 10 to 14 years is presumed incapable of forming criminal intent unless rebutted by the prosecution that such child knew their conduct was morally wrong. Emanated from the Latin phrase "incapable of evil".

Duty Lawyer A legal professional who provides free advice and assistance to a person attending a court or tribunal hearing who is not represented by another lawyer.

Dying Declaration An exception to hearsay evidence and can be admitted into evidence in the belief of impending or certain death.

E

Emphasis Added A phrase commonly used in legal writing to indicate that certain words have been highlighted or emphasised in order to draw attention to a specific text or meaning.

Entrapment May provide a defence to a criminal charge when it is alleged a law enforcement officer induced the person charged to commit a crime they would otherwise not have committed. Must be demonstrated that the person was persuaded or coerced.

Evidence The information used in a court of law to either support or disprove the truth or existence of a fact. Usually obtained from witness testimony, documentary evidence and exhibits, such as weapons and clothing.

Exhibit Refers to a piece of evidence or a document presented during a trial, hearing, or other legal proceedings. Can take many forms, for example, such as emails, contracts, CCTV footage, photographs etc.

F

Family Violence Intervention Order A court order designed to protect individuals, their children and property from harmful behaviour by another family member, partner, or ex-partner. Also see Apprehended Domestic Violence Order and Personal Safety Intervention Order.

Family Violence Safety Notice Taken out by Victoria Police to provide immediate protection for individuals facing family violence.

Filing Hearing First court appearance in a criminal matter where a timetable is set on how the matter will proceed.

Firebug An arsonist or pyromaniac. A penchant for lighting fires.

Flashover A fire-related event which can mimic a deliberately lit fire when all the combustible materials in a room or building reach an ignition temperature at the same time. Can leave similar arson burn patterns.

Forensic Genetic Genealogy Also known as investigative genetic genealogy which uses genetic relative matching information from select companies such as Ancestry DNA in order to identify suspects or victims in criminal cases.

G

Geo-Fence Warrant A search warrant issued by a court to allow law enforcement to conduct a digital database search.

Good Behaviour Bond A defendant is ordered by the court to be of 'good behaviour' for a designated period of time in lieu of other applicable penalties. A breach of the bond can result in a further and more stringent penalty being applied.

Grand Jury A legal body comprising citizens that determine whether to indict a person in a criminal matter based on the evidence put before it by the prosecution. Commonly used in the United States of America.

H

Habeas Corpus Petition A petition filed with the court when a prisoner wishes to contest the legality of their imprisonment.

Hand-Up Brief A brief of evidence tendered by the prosecution in a committal hearing in which they intend to rely, setting out the charges, a summary of the evidence and documents such as witness statements and may also include a list of any previous criminal or traffic convictions. Also known as Police Brief.

Hearsay Evidence An unverified statement based on what a witness has allegedly heard from another person, for which the witness has no personal knowledge or experience and is offering in court as the truth. Hearsay evidence is normally inadmissible in a court proceeding unless an exception applies to the hearsay rule.

Hero Syndrome A psychological issue which causes a person to seek recognition as some sort of hero.

Hot Starts A term sometimes used by fire investigators when referring to a fire that was intentionally lit using matches or lighters but with no accelerant.

Hung Jury A jury that cannot agree upon a verdict of guilty or not guilty after an extended deliberation and is unable to reach the required unanimous or majority verdict. Can lead to a retrial.

Hydroclimatic Whiplash Also known as hydroclimatic volatility being a climatic phenomenon, influenced by global warming, identified by an abrupt alternation between intense rainfall followed by severe drought.

I

Inadmissible Evidence that cannot be used in court to prove or disprove a fact in a case. For example, it could be irrelevant or obtained illegally.

Indictable Offence A more serious criminal offence than a summary offence and generally heard before a judge and jury. Some indictable offences can be triable summarily in a lower court such as before a magistrate.

Infant A person who has not yet reached the age where they are legally considered an adult. Specified age can vary depending on the jurisdiction but is generally under the age of 18 years. Such legal term can also be known as juvenile and is referred to in criminal law, family law and civil proceedings.

Informant Individual who provides privileged information about a person or organisation to an agency such as a law enforcement body. Also, can be referred to as a confidential human source. In criminal matters, an informant is the person who lays the charge and includes a police officer, council officer or other government official.

Injunction A specified court order that compels or directs a party to do a specific act or thing or refrain from doing so. It is an equitable remedy depending on the discretion and fairness of the court. Can be interim or may continue indefinitely. If breached can lead to a criminal or civil sanction and can be seen as contempt of court.

Innocence Project. A nonprofit legal organisation in the United States of America who provide investigative and legal services to persons who maintain they were wrongfully convicted of a crime.

Intensive Corrections Order A form of custodial sentence that allows an offender to serve a sentence in the community but under strict requirements and conditions.

Inter Alia A Latin term commonly used in legal matters meaning, "amongst other things". More than one issue but only referring to one particular issue.

Intervention Order A court order that prohibits a person (the respondent) from behaving in particular matters such as physical, verbal or emotional abuse towards another person (the protected person). See Apprehended Domestic Violence Order, Family Violence Interim Order, Family Violence Safety Notice and Personal Safety Intervention Order.

Inquisitorial System A process of justice in a legal system in which the court, through active judge participation, investigates the facts of the case.

J

Jewish Stocktake A slang term (somewhat racist though) given to a process in which a shop owner allegedly destroys their business by fire in order to claim insurance.

Judicial Monitoring A sentencing option available to judges and magistrates that allows the court to actively manage and monitor compliance with sentencing requirements and conditions and can include a number of appearances before the sentencing judicial officer.

Judicial Officer Includes judges, associate judges, registrars, magistrates and justices of the peace.

Judicial Registrar Generally involved in directions and interlocutory hearings and the management of criminal, civil and family law matters, issue various procedural and case management orders and also can participate in resolution conferences such as pre-hearing conferences in the Magistrates Court.

Judicial Review Review by a court for an executive, legislative or administrative action taken by a public body. Also see Review on the Merits.

Jurisdiction Legal authority given to a court of law to determine a matter before it. Can also relate to mean the geographical boundary in which a court order can be enforced.

Juror Someone who is a member of a jury. In a criminal trial the number of jurors is typically 12 but can vary based on the jurisdiction and specified legal system. Civil trial jurors can also vary from six to 12 jurors but in most jurisdictions, it is normally six.

Jury A sworn body of people (jurors) from the general public convened to hear evidence in order to reach a verdict in a criminal trial based on the evidence presented and determined beyond reasonable doubt of the guilt or innocence of an accused and in civil cases, if proven on a balance of probabilities, the amount to be awarded in damages.

Jury Charge Legal guidelines and explanation by the presiding judge to the jury to assist in their deliberations and a summary of the evidence presented to determine whether an accused is guilty or not guilty.

Justifiable Homicide Absolves a person of any criminal liability who killed another, such as in self-defence. Can also be in situations where a police officer acting, not just in self-defence but, in situations to prevent a very serious crime being committed by a person.

Juvenile Police Caution Police may issue an informal caution meaning that no formal action will be taken and it will not be listed on the young offender's record. If the matter is more serious, a formal caution will apply but under similar criteria but not serious enough to justify a criminal charge to bring the juvenile before the Children's Court.

L

La Bomba Device An incendiary device placed in a plastic bag with a zip, with fuel and then put in a paper bag filled with tissues before being lit.

Law Enforcement Assistance Program (LEAP) The online database used by Victoria Police that details their interactions with persons of alleged crimes, incidents of family violence and also missing person reports.

Lawyers Picnic A somewhat colorful expression used by others and even lawyers to describe situations where lawyers are perceived to benefit excessively or overcharging for a particular legal matter.

Legal Aid Provision of free assistance from public monies for persons unable to afford their own legal representation.

Legal Eagle Not only referred to in jest but can also describe a very skilled lawyer or clever student of the law. Also legal practitioner, such as a solicitor, barrister or attorney (US).

Legal Professional Privilege Protects confidential communications and documents between a lawyer and client and can only be disclosed with client permission. It is a cornerstone of the legal system to ensure clients can obtain legal advice and guidance without fear of compromising their rights.

Legislation Also known as Statutes or Acts of Parliament being the written law created by Parliament or delegated bodies.

Local Laws Laws and regulations enacted and enforced by local councils.

M

Magistrate A judicial officer who administers the law and presides over court matters that deal with, normally, less serious criminal matters and conducts preliminary hearings, such as a committal in more serious indictable criminal charges. Also presides over civil matters, including victims of crime applications.

Mandatory Imprisonment A fixed sentence legislated by lawmakers, such as a parliament, regarding certain serous criminal offences which do not allow any judicial discretion.

Manifestly Excessive Appeal of the sentence in a criminal matter that is considered too harsh or severe and can occur by way of example where a sentence is imposed for a number of different offences at the same time but, overall, a lack of consideration has been given of the collective effect of all of the sentences together.

Manifestly Inadequate The prosecution may appeal a sentence in a criminal matter on the basis that it is considered too lenient. A Court of Appeal would then consider the merits of the appeal and whether there has been a substantial injustice with the original sentence.

Manslaughter A legal term for homicide but considered at law as less culpable than murder. Can also be classified as voluntary, meaning, for example, with intent on extreme provocation or involuntary, resulting in death caused by criminal negligence or an unlawful and dangerous act. Also see Cambridge Dictionary definition.

McKenzie Friend A person who assists a self-represented party in a legal proceeding with leave of the court. Such a friend cannot, however, give legal advice or address the court on behalf of that person.

Men's Behavioral Change Program A court ordered, approved counselling program to assist and support a male in order to address violent and other problematic behaviour arising from a relationship.

Mens Rea The intention or knowledge of wrongdoing required to constitute a criminal act. It is the mental element of the state of mind of the accused which can vary from intent to recklessness or even dishonesty and malice. Most crimes committed require proof of both mens rea and actus reus.

Mention Date In the Magistrates Court it is the first date in which a criminal matter is listed and for the court to provide further directions to progress the matter. A plea of guilty can sometimes proceed on the first mention date.

Miranda Rights Also referred to in the United States of America as a Miranda warning which is a notification by law enforcement to a criminal suspect of their right to remain silent and anything said may be used against the suspect, who also has a right to a lawyer.

Mitigation in Sentencing Factors that may reduce a defendant's sentence, such as no prior criminal record, mental issues, remorse, cooperation with police and minor role played in the commission of the crime.

Modus Operandi In criminal investigations, a modus operandi or MO refers to a criminal's specific method of carrying out a crime. Such patterns of behaviour becomes so evident and distinctive it can actually assist law enforcement in linking and identifying the perpetrator to a spate of similar but separate crimes.

Molotov cocktail A glass bottle containing a flammable substance such as petrol and equipped with a fuse or wick. In some ways it is really a crude type of bomb.

N

Napalm An incendiary mixture of a gelling agent and a volatile petrochemical, normally petrol or diesel fuel.

No Contest Plea Used in criminal proceedings in the United States of America as an alternative to a guilty or not guilty plea, in which the defendant neither admits or disputes the crime. Also known as "nolo contendere" meaning, 'I do not wish to contend'.

Nolo Contendere Type of legal plea used in the US. Also known as a plea of no contest or no defence.

Notice of Appearance Legal practitioners normally use a prescribed court form to file an appearance on behalf of a party they are representing, such as an accused in a criminal matter. Can also be given in person in court, such as, 'I appear Your Honour on behalf of…'

O

Oath A sworn declaration of evidence to be given, such as the person will swear to 'tell the truth, the whole truth and nothing but the truth,' in a court of law. Can be given with one hand on a religious text, such as the Bible, or by way of affirmation if a person does not want to swear such evidence on a religious text.

Offence Can be either a summary offence (minor) or an indictable offence being a more serious offence in breach of Commonwealth or State Laws. Some serious indictable offences are triable summarily in a lower court such as the Magistrates Court.

Offender A person or entity who commits an illegal act.

Outlaw Motorcycle Gang (OMCG) Also known as bikies, being a motorcycle club subculture where its members use their status and affiliation with the club as a means to conduct criminal activities.

P

Pardon A government decision to absolve a person for a criminal conviction. Can be absolute or conditional. In the United States of America can also be a Presidential or State Governor pardon.

Parole The conditional release of a prisoner before completion of a sentence, subject to set conditions under a parole order. Such person would have first served a fixed non- parole period as determined at sentencing.

Parsimony in Sentencing Any sentence imposed should not be more severe than necessary to achieve their overall purpose and proportionate to the gravity of the offending.

Perpetrator A person suspected of or who has committed a criminal offence. Also referred to as the offender or suspect. Often referred to by law enforcement as "the perp".

Personal Safety Intervention Order A court order put in place to protect an individual, their family members and property by another person who is not a family member.

Plea Agreement Also known as a plea bargain or plea deal where the prosecution in a criminal matter offers a defendant sentence concession in exchange for a plea of guilty or no contest.

Police Brief The brief of evidence in which police prepare and serve on a person charged with a criminal offence, which will be relied on in a court of law by the prosecution to prove the guilt of the accused.

Police Caution Given to a person under arrest where they have the right to remain silent and seek legal advice and anything they do say may well be used in evidence against them.

Polygraph A device which measures psychological indicators, such as blood pressure and pulse, of a suspect when questions are put by law enforcement. Also referred to as a "lie detector or polygraph test".

Post-Conviction Relief A series of motions that can be filed in court to challenge a conviction or sentence.

Posthumous Pardon Refers to the pardoning of a crime after the death of the person convicted. Once granted, court and law enforcement records change to such as innocent.

Precedent Principle, rule or doctrine established in a prior legal case which courts are obliged to follow when hearing and making decisions in similar cases. Established from the reasoning given by judges when making decisions and can be either binding or persuasive.

Preliminary Brief Provides sworn early disclosure of the prosecution case and it may not contain a copy of all the witness statements but will detail the alleged facts and evidence that support the charges as laid.

Preliminary Hearing. Such a hearing or examination in the US is similar to a committal hearing where the prosecution leads enough probable evidence for the matter to proceed to trial.

Premeditated A crime carried out deliberately and planned in advance.

Pre-Sentence Hearing Procedures vary in each jurisdiction regarding sentencing for a crime but, generally, once a defendant is found guilty a pre-sentencing hearing is held. Expert reports can be submitted, detailing any medical issues that should be taken into account in mitigation. Both the prosecution and defence can present arguments and evidence concerning an appropriate sentence and victim impact statements can also be taken into account for consideration by the presiding judge or magistrate.

Presiding Magistrate The judicial officer (Magistrate) who presides over proceedings in a Magistrates Court.

Presumption of Innocence The legal principle that any person accused of a crime is considered to have such a presumption until proven guilty in a court of law.

Prima Facie A Latin expression meaning at first sight or based on the face of it, such as a first impression.

Prima Facie Case A case that has sufficient evidence to prove the facts of the matter as opposed to only speculation.

Prima Facie Evidence Evidence that exists which, unless disproven, is sufficient to prove a certain fact or circumstance and in criminal matters, a conviction beyond reasonable doubt.

Primary Victim A person who is injured or dies as a result of a violent crime. Compare to secondary and related victim.

Prisoners Compensation Quarantine Fund Initiated by a procedure that allows prisoners to seek compensation for alleged injuries or loss of property that occurred while serving a term of imprisonment. If awarded, it is held in the fund for initially 12 months. In some cases, their victims can make an application to be compensated for the monies held for damages alleged to have been suffered.

Probable Cause Hearing Generally the defendant's first court appearance in the United States of America after being arrested and for the judge to determine whether there is sufficient evidence to support the arrest and charge(s) laid. In the event of probable cause, the case can then proceed to trial. Can also be referred to as a preliminary hearing.

Pro-Bono Specialist services provided by a professional free of charge to an individual or community. The term usually refers to the provision of legal services free of charge.

Prosecution The party conducting a prosecution and presenting evidence against a person charged with a criminal offence.

Proviso A term used in Australian Court of Appeal jurisdictions to dismiss an appeal if it considers, even in situations where there has been some sort of error, there has been no substantial miscarriage of justice.

Provocation Conduct or speech used deliberately to make a person angry or afraid.

Pyromania An impulse control disorder in which a person referred to as a pyromaniac has an obsessive desire to set fires in order to release tension or for some sort of gratification. Also see the definition for pyrophilia, being gratification of a sexual nature.

R

Random Breath Test (RBT) A procedure whereby a member of the police force may breath test a vehicle driver at random to detect and measure any alcohol in the driver's system.

Rap Over the Knuckles Speak officially to an individual in such a way that shows disapproval of their actions and conduct.

Recidivist Offender A convicted person who engages in repeated criminal offending.

Reid Technique. A form of interrogation used by law enforcement when interviewing a suspect, mixed with immense pressure as to their guilt but intertwined with offers of sympathy and assistance.

Regulation A law or rule made by a government department or statutory body as enshrined by an applicable act of parliament.

Related Victim A person who at the time of a violent crime being committed where a person has died was a close family member or in a personal relationship with the deceased primary victim. Also see Secondary Victim.

Released on Licence Released from prison early but under a strict set of rules. Also see Parole.

Remanded in Custody A person charged with a criminal offence is held on remand in custody in prison or another facility until the matter is heard in a court of law. Also referred to as pre-sentence detention and is deducted as time served from the overall sentence when handed down.

Respondent A person named in a legal matter of whom a case or appeal is brought against. Can also apply by way of a summons.

Restraining Order In family law, an order issued by a court to protect a person applying for the order, from acts of domestic violence.

Reverse Onus Test Burden of proof shifts from the prosecution to the accused in criminal matters to show compelling reasons or exceptional circumstances in order to be released on bail.

Review on the Merits A review or re-hearing of a decision or ruling made by the primary decision-maker in order to reconsider the facts and the law to determine where it was a just and right decision in the first instance.

Right of Reinstatement A case or matter that has been struck out may be reopened in certain circumstances. For example, it was struck out but with a right of reinstatement.

Right to Silence Legal principle that provides a guarantee that an accused person has a right not to answer any questions put to them by law enforcement or judicial officers. Can also be on the basis of legal advice to say, 'On legal advice I make no comment.' Such a right to silence cannot be used as any inference of guilt or associated in some way with a crime under investigation.

Rogues Gallery Often referred to as mug shots or other images of criminal suspects kept by police for purposes of identification. Can also be used in the vernacular as a likable rogue, villain or miscreant.

Royal Commission An independent public inquiry conducted in Australia to investigate and make recommendations in matters of particular public importance with specific terms of reference. Generally, only established in rare and exceptional circumstances by the issuing of Letters Patent by the Governor–General. Commonwealth Royal Commissions can only be conducted regarding matters that relate to the responsibilities of the Commonwealth of Australia.

S

Saiban-in panel Japanese court system in which six people are chosen at random from an electoral roll to sit with a panel of three judges to listen to the facts, determine guilt and an applicable sentence.

Self Defence The defence of one's person or interests, which can include the use of physical force but only at a level or degree of response to the criminal act to remove the threat. By way of example, often used as a defence to a charge of assault or even murder on the basis of acting in self defence.

Self-Incrimination A privilege with certain limitations of not making a statement or doing anything that may lead to a criminal prosecution or used in evidence against that person.

Self-Representation To appear in person in a court of law without legal representation.

Sentencing Order The sentence imposed by a court of law following a defendant being found guilty in a criminal matter.

Serial Arson An offence committed by a fire setter who starts three or more fires.

Serial Arsonist A person who sets multiple fires in different locations and generally with the same or similar targets.

Serious Indictable Offence A severe crime, such as murder, manslaughter, arson, sexual assault or robbery and usually punishable by more than five years in prison. Also see Indictable Offence.

Show Cause An accused in this situation must show cause and demonstrate why their continued detention is not justified. The prosecution does not have the onus of showing that the person charged poses an unacceptable risk if granted and released on bail. The onus rests with the defendant to demonstrate why bail is justified.

SMS Abbreviation for a short message service from internet or mobile phone.

Spent Conviction Legislation allows the criminal record of the offender to be amended by the removal of certain offences after a period of time, without re-offending and usually those that are minor. In other words, they will no longer exist and can be spent by way of an application and if removed, need not be disclosed to any person or entity.

Spontaneous Combustion A fire without any apparent cause, perhaps started by self–heating from a substance with a low ignition temperature.

Social Justice Justice in relation to a fair balance in the distribution of wealth, opportunities and privileges in a society where individual rights are recognised and protected.

Solicitor A legally qualified practitioner who can deal in most legal matters and appear on behalf of clients in a court of law and tribunals. Also provides written instructions to barristers by way of a brief.

Standard of Proof The designated level of certainty supported by the evidence to establish proof in a court of law. For criminal matters, it is beyond reasonable doubt and for civil matters based on a balance of probabilities.

Strict Liability In criminal law a strict liability offence means a defendant can be held liable for committing an act against public policy without requiring proof of intent or mental state (Mens Rea).

Subpoena A subpoena or witness summons is a form of Writ issued by a court of law compelling a witness to attend at court on a certain day and time, in order to give evidence or produce documents.

Summary Case Conference A meeting between the prosecution and the accused and usually with their legal representative, to discuss the charges as laid, the evidence and issues in dispute with a view to progressing the matter before the designated court appearance. Also seen as Pre-trial Disclosure.

Summary Offence A minor offence that can be determined in the Magistrates Court without the need for a trial by judge and jury. Typical sentences can include a fine, good behaviour bond or community corrections order.

Summons A legal document issued by a court to a named person requiring their attendance at court on a specific date and time.

Surety A promise by a person as guarantor that financial obligations will be met if a party defaults, normally paid into the court by the person providing the surety and, in the event of default, the money paid will be forfeited. Often seen in bail being granted with surety.

Suspended Sentence A prison sentence on conviction for a criminal offence that will only be served if the convicted person defaults by committing further offences. Can be wholly suspended or a combined custody and treatment order.

Sworn Evidence Given when a person first takes an oath or affirmation before providing such evidence.

T

Thinking Outside the Square An idiom that means to think differently, or from a new and unconventional perspective. Also known as thinking outside the box.

Tower Dump Enables law enforcement, by way of warrant, to identify mobile phone data of a suspect's location and movements from a mobile phone tower.

Trafficking In criminal law, to deal or trade in something that is illegal, such as drugs or humans.

Treatment Order A court order that provides for compulsory mental health treatment in a psychiatric hospital for a person suffering from a mental disorder instead of prison when convicted of a criminal offence.

Triable Summarily Indictable offences that are less serious and can be listed before a magistrate for a hearing.

Tunnel Vision The tendency to focus exclusively on a single or limited point of view.

U

Utilitarian Sentence Discount A sentencing judge has a board of discretion in imposing a sentence for the utilitarian value of a guilty plea and any other factor which contributes to the efficiency of the criminal justice system.

Unanimous Verdict A verdict handed down at the end of a trial by a jury or judge as to the guilt or innocence of a defendant. If reached by a jury, it means they all agreed the defendant was either guilty or not guilty.

Unredacted Text that has not been censored or blanked out for legal or security reasons.

V

Voir Dire Common law legal term for a procedure before or during trial for a presiding judge or magistrate to determine a particular issue as raised by either the prosecution or defence. Also applies to prospective jurors on impartiality and fairness,

Victim Impact Statement A written statement provided to the court by a victim of crime, setting out the details of their injury, loss or damage as a consequence of the crime.

Visual Audio Recording Evidence (VARE) A formal statement in a criminal matter made by a juvenile to police, either by way of an audio or video recording where a suitably trained police officer will ask the child relevant questions.

W

Waive Refrain from or give up a legal right or claim, relinquished voluntarily.

Warrant A legal document issued by a court authorising an officer, such as a police member, to take certain action, which can include arresting a person to bring before the court or to search premises.

Wilful Blindness A term to describe a situation where a person seeks to avoid civil or criminal liability in respect of a wrongful act by intentionally and deliberately avoiding those facts that would implicate them. Often seen as 'turning a blind eye'.

Without Prejudice In a criminal matter a case could be dismissed without prejudice, meaning a prosecuting body has an option to correct any issues and could then refile the charges and case at a later date. If a case was dismissed with prejudice, that means it is finalised and no further case can be filed against the accused. Is also a term used in a legal letter or other form of communication in order to invoke legal privilege in a genuine attempt to resolve a matter or dispute and such communication cannot be used against the communicating party in any future court proceedings.

Witness A person who saw or heard an event and can provide such evidence or knowledge in respect of any fact or issue arising from it.

Writ A formal written order issued by a higher court, such as the Supreme or County Court, and has attached a statement of claim as part of the first step in a legal proceeding.

Writ of Certiorari A writ or order in a court process by which a higher court reviews a case tried by a lower court, "an order of certiorari".

Writ of Habeas Corpus A writ requiring a person under detention to be brought before a court to secure the person's release, unless it can be shown the detention was lawful.

Y

Youthful Offender System (USA) A specialised corrections program designed to apply to young offenders with the main aim of rehabilitation.

LIST OF CASES

Brown v DPP (NSW) [2018] NSWCCA 94 -Interest of justice for judge alone trials	38
Hricko v State of Maryland 134 Md. App. 218 (2000)-Court held evidence was sufficient to sustain convictions	49
Medich v R [2021] NSWCCA 36- Appeal against sentence	67
Commonwealth of Pennsylvania v Daniel Dougherty[J-39-2003] – Appeal from death sentence - dismissed	72
The Queen and Shahid Mohammed – In the Court of Appeal (Criminal Division) [2020] FWCA Crim 766)-Appeal against conviction and sentence	76
R v Hopkins [2011] VSC 517 – Plea of Guilty-conviction and sentence	78
Hopkins v The Queen [2015] VSCA 174 - Appeal against sentence- refused	79
R v Craig Anthony Leonard QSCPR 4; [2012] QSC 425 - Judicial discretion to Admit or exclude evidence	81
R v Evans; R v Rawlinson; R v Proud [2014] NSWSC 979 – Conviction and sentence	86
R v Spicer [2015] NSWSC 519 - Conviction and sentence	91
R v Stone [2019] VSC 452- Conviction and sentence	98
Stone v The Queen [2021] VSCA 186 - Application for leave to appeal- refused	99
DPP v Darren Clover [2019] VSC 123 - Conviction and sentence	103
R v Golightly 17 WAR 401 – Admissibility of dying declaration	106
R v Stone [2020] NSWSC 1485 - Conviction and sentence	108

Case	Page
R v McCosker [2020] NSWSC 1822 - Conviction and sentence	108
People v Seymour Oct 16, 2023, CO 53(Colo 2023) - Review and show cause Hearing- rejected	114
Regina v Jamie Edwin Barrow - In the Crown Court at Nottingham, 7 July 2023-Sentencing	116
R v Brian Earl Johnston [2024] QSC 36- Conviction and sentence	120
Bugmy v The Queen [2013] HCA 37- Criminal law appeal	124
R v Verdins & Ors [2007] VSCA 102; (2007) 16 VR 269)-Criminal law appeal	125
DPP v O'Neill [2015] VSCA 325- Criminal law appeal	125
Regina v Olig [2000] NSWSC 1246 - Conviction and sentence	129
R v Olig [2002] NSWCCA 249- Appeal against sentence – dismissed	129
R v Huynh [2006] NSWSC 1066- Conviction and sentence	131
R v Soon [2008] NSWSC 622- Conviction and sentence	135
The Queen v Angela Surtees [2022] VSC 124- Conviction and sentence	141
DPP v Borce Ristevski [2019] VSCA 287- Appeal against sentence	143
Angela Surtees v The King [2023] VSCA- Appeal against sentence	143
R v Hay [2021] NSWDC 669- Conviction and sentence	146
R v Chambers [2003] VSC 506 - Conviction and sentence	148
R v Chambers [2005] VSCA 34- Appeal against sentence	148
DPP v Bennett [2004] VSC 207- Conviction and sentence	152
DPP v Hayes [2022] VSC 679- Conviction and sentence	159
R v Watson [2009] VSC 261- Conviction and sentence	164
R v Barton [2007] NSWSC 651- Conviction and sentence	168
Barton v Regina [2009] NSWCCA 164- Appeal against sentence	168

The Queen v Vlahos [2013] VSC 171- Conviction and sentence	169
DPP v O'Neill [2015] VSC 25- Conviction and sentence	176
DPP v Thomas [2016] VSC 8- Conviction and sentence	178
The Queen v McKnight [2017] VSC 782-Conviction and sentence	186
R v Sokaluk [2012] VSC 167– Conviction and sentence	211, 217
DPP v Brendan James Sokaluk [2013] VSCA 48- Appeal against conviction and sentence	215, 219
DPP v Nicholas Archer [2016] VCC 1522- Conviction and sentence	232
DPP v Andrew Robert Briggs [2016] VCC 1557- Conviction and sentence	234
DPP v Keegan Danielz [2015] VCC 1506- Conviction and sentence	237
R v Banner [2022] Unreported, NSWDC. Judge Tupman 7 July 2022-Conviction and sentence	240
Miranda v Arizona 384.U.S.436 (1966)- Warning as to constitutional rights	245
The People(respondent)v Lacey(appellant) (2012)- Appeal as to breach of Rights	246
United States of America, Appellee, v Donald Francis Stackpole, Defendant, Appellant; United States of America, Appellee v Ray J Norton, Jr; Defendant, Appellant 811 F2D 689(1st Cir.1987)-Appeals following convictions	252
United States of America v John Leonard Orr 29 F.3d 636(1998)-Conviction and sentence	256
United States of America, Plaintiff- appellee, v John Leonard Orr, Defendant-appellant, 29 F.3d 636(9th Cir.1994). Appeal against conviction and restitution order	256
People v Zenner October 16, 1979-396 N.E 2d 1107-Appeal from conviction	261
North Carolina v Alford U.S. 25 (1970) -Acceptance of plea of denial	264

Rickie Lee Fowler Petitioner-Appellant, v Ronald Davis, Warden. Respondent- Appellee D.C. No 5:15-cv-02529-R-Petition for habeas relief	266
People v Burkhart–Court of Appeal of the State of California Second Appellate District No B2890699 Cal, Ct. App Aug 19, 2020- Appeal from conviction	270
Tredget and Regina [2022] EWCA Crim 108-Appeal from conviction	278
United States v Fury-Docket No 2;12-cr-00186-GZS 31 March 2012- Appeal on compassionate release grounds	282
United States of America v Thomas Sweatt Criminal Case No DKC 05-0230 16 July 2021-Motion to vacate convictions	287
R v White [2009] Unreported, South Australia District Court, Judge Boyland 7 April 2009-Conviction and sentence	292
White v R [2009] Unreported SASCA 14 August 2009-Appeal against conviction and sentence	292
State of Western Australia v. A. Sloane and R. Sloane, Jenkins J, File No INS 199 of 2011-4 April 2012-Conviction and sentence	294
Sloane v The State of Western Australia [2013] WASCA 53-Appeal against sentence	294
The Queen v Nona File No CA 9 of 2011-Conviction and sentence	297
Nona v the Queen [2012] NTCCA 03- Appeal against sentence	297
R v Trestrail [2016] Unreported SADC Judge Beazley-Conviction and sentence	298
DPP v Andrew Morgan [2016] VCC 939- Conviction and sentence	303
DPP v Andrew Morgan [2020] VCC 1113- Conviction and sentence	306
DPP v Corey Devereaux & Anor [2016] VCC 1528-Conviction and sentence	314
DPP v Brendan Davies [2017] VCC 1101-Conviction and sentence	321

Davies v The Queen [2019] VSCA 66-Appeal against conviction and sentence	322
DPP v Tormey [2023] VCC 28- Conviction and sentence	323
R v Sussex Justices, ex parte McCarthy [1924] 1KB56 [1923] All ER Rep 233- Impartiality and recusal of judges-Quoted maxim	334
Sell v United States 539 US 166(2003-Limits imposed on a lower court concerning use of anti-psychotic medication	337
R v Dean [2013] NSWSC 1027- Conviction and sentence	342
Dean v R [2015] NSWCCA 307- Appeal against sentence	343
People v Leonard 59 A.D. 2d 1(18 July 1977) -Appeal against sentence	349
People v Leonard 113A.D.2d 258(16 December 1985)- Further appeal	349
People v Gonzalez 163 Misc 2d 950(10 February 1995)- Appeal against conviction	352
People v Gonzalez 228 A.D. 2d 340 (20 June 1996)- Further appeal on grounds of denied fair trial	352
State v Biechele K1-03-653A (2005)- Motion to dismiss grand jury indictment	353
State of Tasmania v Gregory Allan Brown–comments on passing sentence-2 December 2022- Estcourt J)	359
R v Osman (1881) 15 Cox CC 1-Dying declaration to be admitted into evidence	361
R v Long; ex parte A-G (Qld) [2003] QCA 77- Appeal against sentence	361
R v McLennan Unreported, Supreme Court of Tasmania, Justice Evans, 6 September 2006 -Conviction and sentence	362
Taylor v City of Pima 913 F.3d 930, 936(9th Cir 2019)- Ruling on violation of constitutional rights	369
Louis Taylor v County of Pima, et al, No 23-15110(9th Cir.2024)- Action alleging wrongful imprisonment and prosecutorial misconduct	370
Heck v Humphrey, 512 U.S 477(1994)- Ruling on ability of convicted person to issue civil proceedings	370

State v Knapp 114 Ariz.531(1977)- Review of judgment and sentence	371
John Henry Knapp, Prison Inmate No 33659 et al v. Harold Cardwell, et al 667 F.2d 1253(9th Cir.1982)- Challenge death penalty on grounds of unconstitutional	372
Davey Reedy. (SB 649 and SB 1337)- Bill for compensation	378
United States v Hammond 742 F.3d 880(9th Circ 2014)- Appeal as to original sentence	379
Willingham v The State of Texas -Court of Criminal Appeals 897 S.W.2d (1995)- Appeal against conviction and sentence	382
State of Arizona, Appellee v Ray Girdler, Jr; Appellant 675 P.2d 1301, 138 Ariz.482 – Appeal for Rehearing	391
Girdler v Dale, 859 F. Supp.1279(D.Ariz.1994- Civil proceeding	393
Matter of Villalobos v New York City Fire Dept. 06249 22 July 2015- Civil proceeding	396
Commonwealth of Massachusetts v Victor Rosario Middlesex Superior Court No 82-2399-2407 (2010— Appeal against conviction and sentence	398
Commonwealth v Victor Rosario 477 Mass.69 November 8, 2016-May 11, 2017- Appeal- new trial affirmed	401
Staten v The City of Philadelphia et al, US District Court for the Eastern District of Pennsylvania 2.2024 cv01380- Civil proceeding	406
Gavitt v Ionia Cnty, et al, United States District Court Easten District of Michigan Southern Division, 67 F.Supp.3d 838 E.D. Mich 2014 - Civil proceeding	410
Willis v State 785 S.W.2d 378 Tex. Crim App 1990- Appeal for rehearing	413
Willis v Cockrell-United States District Court, W. D. Texas, Pecos Division Aug 9 2004- Habeas corpus petition	414
Cacy v State, 08-93-00085-CR (Tex. App-El Paso May 11, 1995- Appeal against conviction	418

Cacy v State, 08- 96 -00239 – CRTex App- El Paso March 19 1998- Affirmed sentence	419
Ex Parte Sonia Cacy- Applicant- On Application for a Writ of Habeas Corpus- Cause no P -2037 – B-83-CR in the 83rd District Court from Pecos County- 2 November 2016	420
James Carver vs. Commissioner of Correction & Anor Massachusetts Supreme Judicial Court -SJC 13247 September 9, 2022- April 3, 2023)-Appeal for release on medical grounds	428
Ledford v Commonwealth of Virginia–United States District Court, W.D. Virginia, Roanoke Division, Civil Action No 7:05CV00600 Nov 3, 2005 -Writ of habeas corpus	433

POLICE TASK FORCES/OPERATIONS

Operation Nomad- South Australia Police	25
Strike Force Tronto- New South Wales Police	221
Arson Task Force 'Sno-King', Federal Bureau of Alcohol, Tobacco and Firearms (ATF) and the Seattle Fire Department	262
Operation Twain-West Australia Police	292-293
Operation Navarre-Victoria Police	319
Operation Firebug-Victoria Police	330

ROGUES GALLERY

Gary Stephen Maynard	22	Joseph James De Angelo	26
Kimberley Hricko	48	Joseph Gill	52
Ella Hicksh	52	Roger Lyttle	58
Mike Lee Smith	60	Kevin Stralow	64
Daniel Dougherty	71	Shahid Mohammed	74
Shahid Iqbal	75	Shakiel Shazard	75
Nazar Hussain	75	David Warwick Hopkins	76
Craig Anthony Leonard	79	Rowan Baxter	81
Bradley Max Rawlinson	83	Wendy Anne Evans	84
Michelle Sharon Proud	84	Bernard Justin Spicer	84
Lynne Maree Martin	91	Kate Marie Stone	95
Darren Clover	99	Ashley Martin	103
Troy Lee McCosker	104	Shako Asahara	110
Shinji Aoba	110	Kevin Bui	113
Gavin Seymour	113	Dillon Siebert	113
Jamie Edwin Barrow	115	Hakeem Kigundi	116
David Clarke	117	Brian Earl Johnston	119
Shane Eugene Olig	127	Duan Tich Huynh	130
Grace Soon	132	Mick Philpott	136
Mairead Duffy	136	Paul Mosley	136
Angela Surtees	139	Jennifer Louise Hay	143
Luthanuel A J Chambers	147	John Robert Bennett	149
David John Campbell	154	Jenny Hayes	157
Richard James Watson	162	James Harry Barton	166
Con Vlahos	168	Lindy Yvonne Williams	170
Michael Anthony O'Neill	173	Colin Orman Thomas	176
Thomas Nick	180	Stuart Matthew McKnight	182

Brendan James Sokaluk	210	Brendan Hokin	225
Peter Burgess	226	Jarred Brewer	227
Nicholas Archer	229, 315	Andrew Robert Briggs	232
Alex Gordon Noble	235	Keegan Danielz	236
Stephen K Johnson	238	Blake William Banner	239
Gregory McGannon	240	Jude Craig Wright	242
Jack Hardidge	243	William Celtruda	244
Caleb Lacey	245	Benjamin Christensen	247
Christopher Message	248	Craig Allen McCrea	248
Ray J Norton Jnr	251	Donald Francis Stackpole	251
Gregg Bemis	252	John Leonard Orr	252
Grover Cleveland Pauter	259	Albert 'Fat Albert' Zenner	260
Paul Kenneth Keller	261	Timothy McVeigh	263
Rickie Lee Fowler	266	Maurice Dews	267
Harry Burkhart	268	Linda Gail Lee	270
David Crawford	271	Sarah Jane Ramey	274
Peter George Tredget (Dinsdale)	277	Paul William Jones	279
Thomas Ashcroft	279	Casey James Fury	281
Aaron Foster	282	Thomas Sweatt	284
Greg Anastasiou	288	Clayton Jay Ganzer	290
Helen Judith White	291	Alan Robert Sloane	292
Rebecca Louise Sloane	292	Justin Andrew W Nona	295
Gary John Trestrail	297	Sean Douglas Broom	297
Andrew Morgan	302	Scott Hagley	307
Justin Hagley	307	Scott Allen	307
Andrew Valli	308	Corey Devereaux	312
Ricky MacKay	312	Brendan Davies	316
Joshua Tormey	322	Raymond James Saville	323
Evan Rees Williams	331	Jonathan Cleveland Loftes	331

Leslie Ardino	336	Roger Dean	338
Gilles Eccles	348	James O'Brien	348
Jean-Marc Boutin	348	Peter Leonard	348
John Thompson	350	Julio Gonzalez	351
Daniel Biechele	353	John Andrew Stuart	354
James 'Jim' Finch	356	Gregory Allan Brown	358
Robert Paul Long	359	Tony Laurence McLennan	362

LIST OF LEGISLATION

Commonwealth

Australia Act 1986	357
Crimes Act 1914	139
Criminal Code Act 1995	31
Evidence Act 1995	42

Australian Capital Territory

Crimes Act 1900	32
Criminal Code 2002	32
Emergencies Act 2004	199

New South Wales

Crimes Act 1900	32, 53, 143, 239, 341, 358
Criminal Procedure Act 1986	38
Crimes (Sentencing Procedure) Act 1999	145, 240
Jury Act 1977	43
Law Enforcement (Powers and Responsibilities) Act 2002 (NSW)	246
Rural Fires Act 1997	33

Northern Territory

Criminal Code Act 1983	32

Queensland

Corrective Services Act 2006	172
Criminal Code Act 1899	32, 300

| Domestic and Family Violence Protection Act 2012 | 81 |
| Domestic and Family Violence Protection (Combating Coercive Control) and Other Legislation Amendment Act 2023 | 82 |

South Australia

Criminal Law Consolidation Act 1935	33
Criminal Procedure Act 1921	33
Sentencing Act 2017	33

Tasmania

| Criminal Code Act 1924 | 32, 359 |

Victoria

Coroners Act 2008	62
Corrections Act 1986	34
Country Fire Authority Act 1958	7
Crimes Act 1958	34, 40, 122, 123, 146, 148, 151, 153, 186, 304, 313, 403
Crimes Amendment (Manslaughter and Related Offences Act 2020	123
Crimes (Criminal Damage) Act 1978	34
Crimes (Mental Impairment and Unfitness to be Tried) Act 1997	45
Criminal Procedure Act 2009	35-37, 45
Mental Health Act 2014	303
Sentencing Act 1991	34-35, 44, 103, 156, 186, 189, 303, 315, 322
Summary Offences Act 1966	7, 313

Western Australia

Arson Legislation Amendment Act 2009	33
Bush Fires Act 1954	33-34
Criminal Code Compilation Act 1913	33

International

Act on Criminal Trials with the Participation of Saiban-in-Act No 63 2004 (Japan)	38
Antiterrorism and Effective Death Penalty Act 1996 (U.S.)	266
Louisiana Act 276 (U.S.)	380
Pennsylvania Code Crimes and Offenses 2010	403
Michigan Wrongful Imprisonment Act 2016	410
Criminal Damage Act 1971 (UK)	31
Criminal Justice Act 1967 (UK)	325
Homicide Act 1957 (UK)	278
Swiss Criminal Code 1942	180
International Covenant on Civil and Political Rights (adopted 1966)	39

REFERENCES

CHAPTER 1: DEFINING ARSON

- *The Crime of Arson*, Paul Jr Sadler Journal of Criminal Law and Criminology, 1950
- *Arson: Exploring Motives and Possible Solutions,* Richard N Kocsis, Australian Institute of Criminology, 2002
- *The arsonist's mind: part 2-pyromania*, Australian Institute of Criminology, 2005
- *The Changing Meaning of Arson in Australia*, Bushfire Arson Bulletin, no 57. Canberra: Australian Institute of Criminology, 2009
- *The Mind of a Pyromaniac is a Locked Box*, The Daily Beast, 10 February 2009
- *Burn after reading: a short history of arson*, Gemma Clark, UNSW 5 December 2014
- *Arson-associated homicide in Australia: A five year follow up*, Fergson et al 2015
- *Emergency Planning "Is Arson on the Threat Landscape for your Business?* Phill Cribb, Crisis Management, 2 April 2015
- *Unmasking the Many Faces of a Criminal Arsonist*, Gimbel et al, 22 December 2015
- *Why Do People Call Arson 'Jewish Lighting'-And Is It Anti-Semitic?* Aviya Kushner, May 2017
- *Australian arsonists: an analysis of trends between 1990 and 2015*, Therese Ellis – Smith et al Psychiatry Psychology and Law Natural Library of Medicine, 2019
- *Arson, mischief and recklessness: 87 per cent of fires are man-made*, Paul Read, Sydney Morning Herald, 18 November 2019
- *The Great Fire of London*, Ben Johnson, Historic UK July 2020

- *World Health Organization's International Classification of Diseases*, 11th Revision-ICD-11, 2022
- *Revenge, excitement, or profit: why do people commit arson?* The Conversation, 30 May 2023

CHAPTER 2: ARSON INVESTIGATION

- *Bushfire Arson Investigation*, Australian Institute of Criminology, 2006
- *A Guide for Investigating Fire and Arson*, National Institute of Justice, 31 May 2009
- *Arsonists to be monitored with GPS Tracking*, LiveView GPS May 2013
- *The Six Motives for Firesetting*, Robert Disbrow, 13 December 2013
- *Bushfires: GPS tracking for arsonists while hundreds of suspects on close watch*, Farah Tomazin, The Age, 19 December 2015
- *Cops use pacemaker data to charge homeowner with arson, insurance fraud*, CSO Online, 30 January 2017
- *Kirk's Fire Investigation*, David J. Icove and Gerald Haynes, Pearson 8th Edition 2017
- *Scientific Protocols for Fire Investigation*, John J. Lentini, Third Edition, CRC Press 2018
- *Vallejo man whose book on fire/arson investigation is most studied, to retire*, Rachel Raskin- Zrihen, Vallejo Times-Herald, 29 August 2018
- *College Professor Charged With Setting California Wildfire*, NBC, 12 August 2021
- *DNA tool that caught Golden State Killer could soon track Australian Criminals*, Mark Saunokonoko, Channel Nine News, 11 October 2021
- *Man charged with cold case murder of 13yo Arthur Haines in Waterloo hose fire*, Ursula Malone, ABC News 19 August 2022

- *Arson Dogs:5 facts about accelerant- detection canines*, Fire Rescue, 11 May 2023
- *The Process of Investigating Arson*, Stevenson University Online, 2024
- *Ex- Professor Gets More Than 5 years in Prison for California 'Arson Spree'*, The New York Times, 30 May 2024
- *Arson in Australia: 8 Things You Need to Know*, Walker Pender Group, 2024
- *The Signs of a Bushfire Arsonist*, Crime Stoppers South Australia 2024

CHAPTER 3: LEGISLATION AND PROCEDURE

- *Arson legislation in Australia*, Australian Institute of Criminology, 2004
- *Offending and reoffending patterns of arsonists and bushfire arsonists in New South Wales*, Damon A Muller, Australian Institute of Criminology, 2008
- *Outline of Criminal Justice in Japan, Annual Report of Statistics on Prosecution*, Ministry of Justice, 2014
- *Crime and Punishment in Japan: A Holistic Perspective*, Kawai Mikio, 3 June 2020
- *The Law Handbooks, Your Practical Guide to the Law In Victoria*, Fitzroy Legal Service, 2017-2022.

CHAPTER 4: A QUESTION OF 'WHO OR WHAT DUNNIT'

- *18 Die, 21 Hurt as Fames Sweep Missouri Nursing Home for Aged*, The New York Times, 1 November 1952
- *Arsonist and Murderer? Or Innocent Wife?* John McLemore, Justice Denied Magazine, March 2000
- *Gone. St Kilda kiosk, after 99 years on the sea*, The Age, 12 September 2003

- *St Kilda Pier arsonist jailed*, ABC News, 5 November 2004
- *Jail term for Kiosk arsonist*, The Age, 5 November 2004
- *$250,000 reward offered over the deaths of 5 people in Ipswich fire*, Minister for Police, Corrective Services and Sport, Queensland Government, 13 May 2008
- *A whodunnit for the rich and famous*, The Sydney Morning Herald, 24 August 2009
- *Iconic Stokehouse restaurant burns down*, Alana Schetzer, The Age, 18 January 2014
- *10 Mysterious Cases of Arson That Will Horrify You*, Robin Warder, Crime, 19 February 2014
- *Tale of St Kilda's 'fiery Curse' reignites after Donovans blaze*, Dana McCauley, Herald Sun, 1 September 2014
- *Some of the deadliest nursing home fires in the US*, Associated Press, 4 October 2014
- *Bayside Melbourne's history of mysterious fires*, Rania Spooner, the Age, 5 October 2015
- *Throwback Thursday: Arson Fire At The Barrel*, Eltham District Historical Society Inc, 24 August 2017
- *Ron Medich jailed 39 years for Michael Mc Gurk murder*, Kelly Forder, Nine News, 21 June 2018
- *Mystery Of A Massive Library Fire Remains Unsolved After More Than 30 Years*, Scott Simon, NPR, 13 October 2018
- *Who started the 1986 fire at the Los Angeles Library? Susan Orlean investigates in her new book,* Carlolyn Kellogg, Los Angeles Times, 21 October 2018
- *The Library Book*, Susan Orlean, Simon & Schuster, 2018
- *Unsolved murders: Eight people perish in 1929 Himatangi farmhouse fire,* Sam Kilmister, National Crime, 31 August 2019
- *Mystery Caller may hold clue to solving decades-old restaurant fire case*, Rebecca Masters, Nine News, 13 October 2019

- *A Case of Arson, Investigating the Fire at the Steiglitz Coffee Palace in September 1895*, Public Record Office Victoria, 27 March 2020
- *Former NSW police officers claim Sydney underworld figure Abe Saffron orchestrated the Luna Park Ghost Train fire*, Caro Meldrum-Hanna et al, ABC News, 30 March 2021
- *Naked City podcast: Abe Saffron and Sydney's corrupt cops*, Jonh Silvester, The Age, 28 July 2021
- *Ghost Ship building owner files bankruptcy, must pay $12M*, KTVU Fox, 2 September 2021
- *72 Katie Jane residents die in "15-minute holocaust" in nation's worst nursing home fire*, WCHS, 22 August 2022
- *07 Dec On This Day In History: 76 Years Ago 119 People Perished in Deadliest Hotel Fire in U.S. History*, Terp Consulting, 7 December 2022
- *The mystery of the vanished Sodder children has never been solved, but the cold case has haunted this small town for decades*, Lucia Stein and Rebecca Armitage, ABC News, 25 December 2023

CHAPTER 5: MURDER ARSON

- *Daniel Dougherty: third trial, Defrosting cold cases*, Research websites by Alice De Sturler
- *The use of fire in homicide*, Australian Institute of Criminology, 21 August 2007
- *Arsonist Craig Anthony Leonard sentenced to life for murders of Nicholas Spohn and Jennifer Bachmann*, Rose Brennan, news.com.au, 19 February 2013
- *Man jailed for life over Qld house fire*, Miranda Forster, AAP, 19 February 2013
- *Kelly Wilkinson murder: Family of young woman doused in petrol and burnt alive by her US Marine husband Brian Johnson, furious at his meagre sentence- as new disturbing twist in the case emerges*, Rex Martinich for AAP and Freddy Pawle for Daily Mail Australia, 14 March 2014

- *Wollongong lawyer Katie Foreman's killers jailed for fire murder*, Claire Aird, ABC News, 28 July 2014
- *Contract killer sentenced to 24 years' jail for arson murder of Wollongong lawyer Katie Foreman*, Mazoe Ford, ABC News, 15 May 2015
- *Darren Clover handed 30 years in jail for murdering ex-lover, her daughter and new boyfriend in factory fire*, Benjamin Ansell, AAP, 25 February 2019
- *Man convicted for 3rd time of murder, arson in 1985 fire*, Jeannette Reyes, Action News, 9 April 2019
- *Woman gets 34 years in jail for setting partner on fire*, Beth Gibson and Natalie Kerr, ABC News, 12 July 2019
- *Victorian woman Kate Stone sentenced to 34 years for burning her partner alive*, Benjamin Ansell, 9 News, 12 July 2019
- *Huddersfield house fire: Murder accused seen 'running away'*. BBC, 12 July 2019
- *Jilted boyfriend, 32, set ex-girlfriend's house on fire in blaze that killed her along with her new lover and himself, inquest hears*, Martin Robinson, Daily Mail Australia, 25 September 2019
- *Revenge arsonist who murdered eight in a house fire is jailed longer*, GOV.UK, 11 June 2020
- *Troy Mc Cosker jailed for burning Wade Still alive in 'brazen act of extreme violence*, Giselle Wakatama, ABC News, 16 December 2020
- *Bendigo woman Kate Stone refused leave to appeal her murder conviction, sentence*, Tara Cosoleto, Bendigo Advertiser, 27 June 2021
- *The Implications Of "Digital Dragnets" For Digital Rights*, Mayowa Oluwasanmi, Human Rights Pulse, 11 January 2023
- *Teen sentenced to 7 years for role in deadly Denver fire, awaiting juvenile sentencing*, CBS News Colorado, 1 February 2023
- *Man jailed for arson murder of neighbour and her two children*, Jessica Murray, Midlands correspondent, 8 July 2023

- *Lynne Martin: Guilty verdict in arson murder case,* Marty Sharpe, RNZ News, 22 November 2023
- *Killer found guilty in New Zealand arson murder after hidden devices record her watching her own cold case on TV,* Sky News, 22 November 2023
- *Arson killer Lynne Martin found dead in Gisborne Police Station cell day after guilty verdict,* RNZ News, 23 November 2023
- *'No sorrow': Arsonist's brother emotionless after death in police cell,* News National, 23 November 2023
- *Japan court sentences arsonist to death for deadly attack on Kyoto Animation studio,* Francesca Annio and Jessie Yeung, CNN 25 January 2024
- *Man sentenced to death for arson attack at Japanese anime studio that killed 36,* ABC News, 25 January 2024
- *Churchgoing man of 80 jailed for life for murdering 77-year-old wife in car fire,* Alex Ross, Independent News, 9 February 2024
- *Helen Clarke: Husband, 80, jailed for murder after attacking wife of 50 years with hammer and setting car on fire,* Sky News, 10 February 2024
- *Kelly Wilkinson's estranged husband pleads guilty to her murder on the Gold Coast,* Talissa Signato, ABC News, 14 February 2024
- *Kelly Wilkinson's murder to be investigated for 'systematic flaws' after ex-husband's guilty plea,* Bern Young et al, ABC News, 17 February 2024
- *Judge sentences teen to maximum for arson that killed 5 family members,* Janet Oravetz, 9 News, 15 March 2024
- *Dead-eyed Colorado teenager is jailed for 40 years for burning baby, toddler and three adults alive in their home in horrific case of mistaken identity- with dad who lost wife and kids insisting quadruple killer should be EXCECUTED,* Kamal Sultan, Daily Mail Australia, 17 March 2024

- *Final suspect formally sentenced to 60 years in prison for fire that killed 5 family members,* Janet Oravetz, 9 News 2 July 2024
- *Bradely Bell acquitted of murder of Gold Coast woman Kelly Wilkinson,* Talissa Siganto, ABC News, 13 September 2024
- *Dramatic jury verdict after Gold Coast mum Kelly Wilkinson was stabbed and set on fire by her ex-husband,* Blake Antobus, Daily Mail Australia, 13 September 2024

CHAPTER 6: MANSLAUGHTER OR ARSON CAUSING DEATH

- *Sale man fronts court over fatal hotel blaze,* ABC News, 17 November 2003
- *Grace Soon pleads guilty to manslaughter of Stephen Chin,* The Sunday Telegraph, 14 April 2008
- *Arsonist: I'm sorry for deaths,* Ballarat Courier, 5 November 2012
- *Mick Philpott will stay in prison until he is at least 71 over blaze deaths of six of his children,* The Standard, 5 April 2013
- *Vic man admits starting fatal house fire,* 9 News, 3 February 2015
- *Jealous fatal arsonist jailed in Vic,* SBS News, 1 May 2015
- *Bennett, John Robert Parole Board Decision,* Tasmanian Government, 15 January 2021
- *Sentencing Snapshot 249: Sentencing Trends for Manslaughter in the Higher Courts of Victoria 2015-16 to 2019-20,* Sentencing Advisory Council 3 March 2021
- *Court hears how Wagga Wagga woman Jennifer Louise Hay started a deadly house fire,* Shannon Corvo, ABC News, 12 November 2021
- *Woman jailed for fatal home fire 'revenge',* Shepparton News, 13 December 2021
- *Geelong woman jailed for 12 years for manslaughter after setting husband alight,* Dana Morse, ABC News 11 March 2022
- *Derby fire deaths; Killer Paul Mosley returned to prison,* Greig Watson, BBC News, 23 July 2022

- *Melbourne family of three killed 19 days after daughter born*, Karen Sweeney, AAP, 7 November 2022
- *"No justice": Arsonist who killed baby Ivy could walk free in six years*, Erin Person and Ashliegh Mc Millan, The Age, 11 November 2022
- *Angela Surtees; Sentence reduced for Victorian woman who killed husband in fire,* Liam Beatty, news.com.au, 7 March 2023
- *John Robert Bennett jailed over crime spree at Bunnings*, Nick Clark, The Examiner, 1 July 2023

CHAPTER 7: ARSON TO CONCEAL MURDER

- *Arson To Conceal Other Crimes*, Office of Justice Programs, U.S. Department of Justice, 1983
- *Murder suspected in Albury house fire*, ABC News, 8 September 2004
- *Murder suspect claims self-defence*, ABC News, 14 September 2004
- *Wife Killer verdict*, Bendigo Advertiser 6 April 2009
- *Victorian jailed for drug-fuelled murder,* 9 News, 12 April 2013
- *Man jailed for violent murder of mother-of-six,* The Age, 12 April 2013
- *Vic man who killed partner 'damaged goods',* SBS News, 16 December 2014
- *Stuart Rattle's family shattered at 18-year sentence for his killer,* AAP, 11 February 2015
- *Vic garage fire murder accused guilty*, 9 News, 16 October 2015
- *Man jailed for killing neighbour in Vic,* 9 News, 22 December 2017
- *Murder victim George Gerbic had affairs and was abusive, ex-wife tells the court,* Warren Barnsley, news.com.au, 18 July 2018
- *Lindy Williams sentenced to life for murder of George Gerbic,* 9 News, 27 July 2018
- *Australian woman guilty of murder in headless torso case,* BBC, 27 July 2018

- *Caught in a lie: The moment bumbling murderer who killed her boyfriend before dumping his decapacitated body by the roadside is caught lying to police in awkward crime scene video*, Kylie Stevens for Dail Mail Australia and AAP, 31 July 2018
- *Switzerland's leniency on criminal, explained*, Sibilla Bondolfi, Life and Aging, 11 January 2019
- *A deadly California wildfire was set to cover up a woman's murder, authorities say*, Stella Chan and David Willaims, CNN 29 April 2021
- *How a dating app meetup led to alleged murder*, Aron and 2 more deaths, Emily Shapiro, ABC News, 1 May 2021
- *Court date reshuffled for Vaca man, 29, charged with three murders, arson*, Richard Bammer, Vacaville Reporter, 15 November 2021
- *Woman who chopped up partner seeks parole*, The West Australian, 13 October 2022
- *No Body No Parole Hearing-Lindy Yvonne Willams*, Parole Board Queensland, 13 October 2022
- *DA continues to build murder case against Serriteno*, Richard M Bammer, The Reporter. 3 August 2024

CHAPTER 8: AUSTRALIA'S BUSHFIRES

- *'The Causes and Measures Taken to Prevent the Bush Fires of Jnauary,1939 and to Protect Life and Property', AND The Measures to be Taken to Prevent Bush Fires in Victoria and to Protect Life and Property in the Event of Future Bush Fires*, Report of the Royal Commission 1939
- *A Study Of Civilian Deaths In the 1983 Ash Wednesday Bushfires Victoria, Australia,* N. Krusel & S N Petris, CFA Occasional Paper No 1, Fire Management Quarterly, Country Fire Authority, 16 December 1992
- *Deliberately lit vegetations fires in Australia,* Australian Institute of Criminology, February 2008

- *Policeman recalls Ash Wednesday horror,* Andrea O Petrie and Jamie Duncan, The Age, 19 February 2008
- *Police track arsonist responsible for Victoria Bushfires,* Rowan Callick and Pia Akerman, The Australian, 10 February 2009
- *Arson suspects arrested,* Robyn Grace, The Age, 12 February 2009
- *Final Report 2009 Victorian Bushfires Royal Commission,* July 2010.
- *Teens in Black Saturday arson case let off,* Michelle Henderson, The Sydney Morning Herald, 7 November 2011
- *Firebugs: Australia's dangerous summer arsonist,* Nick Bryant, BBC, 18 January 2013
- *Australian Firefighters Battle Brushfires and Serial Arsonists,* Rena Golden, The Weather Channel, 21 March 2013
- *The Beaumaris Bushfires of 1944,* Leo Gamble, Kington Local History, City of Kingston, 27 July 2018
- *Bushfires versus wildfires: What's the difference?* Shelley Lloyd, ABC News, 22 August 2018
- *Arson, mischief and recklessness: 87 per cent of fires are man-made,* Paul Read, The Sydney Morning Herald, 18 November 2019
- *This is how most bushfires in Australia start and how we know,* Nick Kilvert, ABC News, 20 November 2019
- *How do most bushfires start in Australia?* QBE, 26 November 2019
- *We don't just haver a bushfire crisis. We have an arson crisis, too,* Arthur Chrenkoff, 4 January 2020
- *Disinformation and lies spreading faster than Australia's bushfires,* Christopher Knaus, The Guardian, 12 January 2020
- *Setting the Record Straight on Climate Change and Arson in Australia's Bushfires,* Saranac Hale Spencer, FactCheck.org, 17 January 2020
- *The truth about Australia's fires-arsonists aren't responsible for many this season,* Kevin Nguyen et al, ABC News, 18 January 2020
- *2019-20 Australian bushfires-frequently asked questions: a quick guide,* Lisa Richards et al Foreign Affairs, Defence & Security, 2 March 2020

- *Royal Commission into National Natural Disaster Arrangements Report*-28 October 2020
- *Major Bushfires in Australian History. The 1974 and 1975 Australian Bushfires,* John O'Donnell, 26 October 2021
- *More cultural burns needed ahead of bushfire season, Indigenous practitioner warns,* Declan Bowring, ABC News, 10 October 2023
- *NSW Coroner calls for overhaul of firefighting systems after black summer bushfires,* Catie McLeod, and AAP, The Guardian, 27 March 2024
- *Inquests and Inquiries into the 2019/2020 NSW Bushfire Season-Volume 2*–Decision of State Coroner O'Sullivan, March 2024.
- *Hydroclimatic whiplash: The new phenomenon unleashing deadly fires on our cities,* Angus Dalton & Nick O'Malley, The Sydney Morning Herald, 11 January 2025
- *The dangerous combination fuelling the L.A. fires: Exceptional dryness and strong winds,* Denise Chow, NBC News, 11 January 2025
- *Owner of 'last house standing' in Malibu reveals how his $9 million mansion survived Los Angles wildfires,* Arya Vaishnavi, Hindustan Times, 11 January 2025
- *The decades-long drying trend that increased fire risk in the US,* Caitlin Fitzsimmons, The Sydney Morning Herald, 14 January 2025

CHAPTER 9: THE CHURCHILL ARSONIST

- *Black Saturday arsonist jailed for almost 18 years,* Sarah Farnsworth, ABC News, 27 April 2012
- *Court rejects bid to increase arsonist's sentence,* ABC News, 7 March 2013
- *Black Saturday arsonist sued for compensation,* Mark Russell, The Age, 31 July 2013
- *Is Black Saturday arsonist Brendan Sokaluk a misfit or monster?* Paul Anderson, Herald Sun, 5 February 2014
- *The Arsonist,* Chloe Hooper, Penguin Books, 2018

- *On the arsonist's trail: inside Australia's worst bushfire catastrophe*, Chloe Hooper, 24 May 2019
- *Black Saturday arsonist's evil toll: Bullied fire big whose blaze killed 11 in Australia's worst-ever bushfires is now estranged from the dad who stood by him- after his crime ended his parent's marriage*, Josh Hanrahan, Daily Mail Australia, 1 January 2021
- *Black Saturday arsonist Brendan Sokaluk eligible for parole in June*, Allanah Sciberras, 9 News, 7 February 2023
- *Bushfire killer out of prison*, Jon Kalla, Herald Sun, 1 May 2024

CHAPTER 10: FIREFIGHTER OR FIRELIGHTER

- *A former Boston policeman was sentenced Friday...*, UPI Archives, 6 July 1984
- *Firefighter's arson trial begins*, UPI Archives 21 January 1985
- *Ex-Fire Investigator Gets Life Term in Fatal Arson*, Andrew Blankstein, Los Angeles Times, 18 September 1998
- *Man who 'craved to be a hero' jailed for Sydney fires*, Kathy Marks, Independent News, 5 June 2002
- *Prison for Drifter who sought fame in bushfire flames*, Kathy Marks, The New Zealand Herald, 5 June 2002
- *Bushfire may have been 'cry for help'*, ABC News, 3 October 2003
- *Detective denies RFS started fatal fire*, ABC News, 13 October 2008
- *CFA volunteer charged with lighting fires*, Ben Doherty, The Canberra Times, 6 February 2009
- *Australian Bushfires: inside the mind of an arsonist*, Philip Sherwell and Bonnie Malkin, The Telegraph, 14 February 2009
- *Pa. Firefighter Sentenced for Arsons*, Firehouse, 18 November 2009
- *Firefighter Arsonists-Stopping the Problem at the Door of the firehouse*, John K Murphy and Beth I Murphy, Fire Engineering, 4 July 2010
- *Police ignored Black Saturday evidence*, Michael Bachelard and Cameron Houston, The Age, 3 July 2011

- *Serial Arsonist Gets 10 Years in Prison*, Justin Reynolds, Patch Staff, 22 June 2012
- *Former RFS volunteer Alex Noble, jailed for two years*, ABC News, 8 October 2014
- *Firefighter turned pyromaniac Alex Gordon Noble will serve two years in prison after pleading guilty to lighting 15 fires*, Nelson Groom, Daily Mail Australia, 9 October 2014
- *Volunteer firefighter Keegan Danielz sentenced to youth detention for lighting fires during 'brain fart'*, Karen Percy, ABC News, 16 December 2015
- *'Brain Fart' led CFA Keegan Danielz to start bushfires*, Jacqueline Le, The Age, 16 December 2015
- *Report on the Firefighter Arson Problem: Context, Considerations, and Best Practices*, National Volunteer Fire Council (United States of America), February 2016
- *Self-confessed firebug and volunteer firefighter sentenced to a maximum of eight years in jail*, Dan Cox, ABC News, 11 April 2016
- *Firefighters who start fires: a look at the phenomenon of 'firefighter arson'*, Canadian Press, 3 May 2016
- *Donnybrook man jailed for lighting three summer bushfires*, Andrew Elstermann, Bunbury Mail, 24 June 2016
- *CFA volunteer Nicholas Archer faces 14 years jail for arson, criminal damage*, Jane Lee, The Age, 11 October 2016
- *$4m firebug sentenced to 14 years in Vic*, 9 News, 11 October 2016
- *Volunteer firefighter jailed after lighting fires as payback to CFA*, Adam Cooper, The Age, 19 October 2016
- *True Crime Blog-My Firefighter Father John Orr Got Sexual Thrills from his Murderous Arson*-interview with Maria Ricapito, June 2018
- *Burn Boston Burn- The Largest Arson Case in the History of the Country*, Wayne M Miller, Amazon 2019
- *Alleged Bega arsonist pleads not guilty*, Ian Campbell, About Regional, 17 December 2019

- *Alleged arsonist faces court charged with lighting Adelaide Hills bushfire*, Meagan Dillon, ABC News, 25 January 2021
- *Volunteer firefighter was drunk when he started Adelaide Hills bushfire, court told*, Claire Campbell, ABC News, 14 May 2021
- *RFS volunteer Blake Banner guilty of starting fire in Bega Valley in 2019, acquitted on other charge,* Adriane Reardon, ABC News 4 August 2021
- *Former RFS firefighter Blake Willaim Banner sentenced for intentionally lighting a 2019 fire,* Keita Proust and Alasdair Mc Donald, ABC News, 7 July 2022
- *Volunteer firefighter who lit Wooroloo bushfire and eight other blazes gets suspended jail term,* Joanna Menagh, ABC News, 3 February 2023
- *Volunteer firefighter tuned arsonist deemed too 'vulnerable' for prison,* Anthony Anderson, NCA NewsWire, 3 February 2023
- *'I done it, I just don't know why': Volunteer firefighter walks after arson conviction,* Rebecca Peppiatt, WA today, 3 February 2023
- *Volunteer firefighter charged over string of fires in Hunter region in July and August,* Rhiannon Lewin, 7 News, 31 August 2023
- *Jury finds former volunteer firefighter guilty of lighting several bushfires in the Adelaide Hills that destroyed two homes,* Shari Hams, ABC News, 27 September 2023
- *Cherry Gardens Bushfire Arsonist Found Guilty,* Jennie Lenman, Local News, 28 September 2023
- *CFS chief condemns volunteer firebug Gregory Mc Gannon, who deliberately lit Cherry Gardens bushfire*, Bethanie Alderson, ABC News, 27 February 2024
- *Former CFS volunteer Gregory Mc Gannon jailed for more than a decade for Cherry Gardens bushfires,* Olivia Mason, ABC News, 15 April 2024
- *McCrea sentenced to 60 years on arson charges*, Jeff Smith & Kristi Niemeyer, Lake County Leader, 16 May 2024

CHAPTER 11: WORST OF THE WORST

- *American Criminal Justice System The Defendant's Perspective*, Jonathon D Casper, Prentice Hill, 1972
- *'Backdraft'*, 1991 Universal Pictures motion picture starring Kurt Russell & Donald Sutherland
- *Crime Classification Manual: A Standard System for Investigating and Classifying Violent Crimes-* John E. Douglas, Ann W Burgess, Allen G Burgess, Robert K. Ressler, Lexington Books 1992
- *Sno-King Arson Task force Honored*, The Seattle Times, 12 September 1994
- *'Not Our Son'*, 1995 CBS motion picture starring Neil Patrick Harris
- *Thomas Sweatt Pleads Guity to 45 Residential Arsons in Maryland, District of Columbia and Viginia including Two Homicides*, Press Release, US Department of Justice, 6 June 2005
- *"Serial Arsonist" Thomas Sweat Sentenced to Life in Prison for Setting 45 Residential Fires in Maryland, District of Columbia and Virginia*, Press Release, US Department of Justice, 12 September 2005
- *District Man Pleads Guity to Series of Arsons in Densely Populated City Neighbourhoods- Several Firefighters Were Hurt in One of the Blazes; Fires Caused Hundreds of Thousands of Dollars in Damages*, Press Release U.S Department of Justice, 4 November 2011
- *6 Infamous Arsonists and How They Got Caught*, Meghan Holohan, Mental Floss, 3 January 2012
- *Accused L.A. Arsonist recognised by State Department Agent*, ABC News, 3 January 2012
- *Arsonist hoaxer asked blaze victim to drop charge*, The Leader, 5 August 2012
- *Shipyard worker who set fire to nuclear submarine sentenced to 17 years jail*, Associated Press, 16 March 2013
- *Infamous Arsonist Albert Zenner Passes*, John Agosti, Agosti Fire Investigations, 2 April 2013

- *Serial arsonist linked to 40 front door fires*, Wave 3News, 21 March 2014
- *Man convicted in 2012 USS Miami fire proclaims innocence,* The Associated Press, 18 May 2015
- *Investigators: Suspected seral arsonist would drink before lighting fires,* Wave 3News, 14 August 2015
- *Serial arsonist linked to 43 fires gets 20-year prison sentence,* Laurel Malloy, Wave 3News, 14 August 2015
- *Mistrial Declared After Deadlock Over Whether Notorious Convicted Arsonist is Sane,* Merrit Kennedy, NPR, 17 September 2016
- *Royal Stoke arsonist jailed for life after starting 'extremely dangerous' hospital fire,* Phil Corrigan, Stoke On Trent Live, 24 February 2018
- *'As with most sociopaths, he likes to brag': An Investigator recalls D.C.'s deadly serial arsonist,* Peter Hermann, The Washington Post, 9 March 2018
- *Arsonist who wanted to 'roast America' and set fires across L.A. as revenge for mother's arrest gets 33 years,* Richard Winton, Los Angeles Times, 23 March 2018
- *Former Maryland police chief facing dozens of attempted murder charges in alleged arsons,* Mark Osborne, ABC News, 6 March 2021
- *Judge Rule Against Convicted Arsonist,* City News Service, 7 April 2021
- *Grover Cleveland Pauter accused 'firebug' in Lenawee County, set ablaze 21 fires,* Dan Cherry, Daily Telegram, 19 January 2022
- *Lenawee County arsonist burned businesses, school, church, houses, barns from 1924-26,* Dan Cherry, Daily Telegram, 19 January 2022
- *History; Lenawee County 'firebug' spent remainder of his life in prison,* Dan Cherry, Daily Telegram, 25 January 2022
- *Serial arsonist 'Bruce Lee' loses appeal over 1970s fatal fire spree in Hull,* ITVX, 9 February 2022
- *Jury shown moment teen accused of setting fire to school with cigarette 'broke into Ash Green Primary School',* John Davies & Connor Teale, West Yorkshire News, 21 July 2022

- *Halifax school arson accused played the victim–prosecutor*, BBC, 22 July 2022
- *Arsonist Aaron Foster set fire to Halifax school then called 999 and said he was 'trapped'-now he has a life sentence,* Sophie Corcoran, West Yorkshire News, 12 October 2022
- *Halifax: Man jailed for life over devastating primary school fire,* Halifax Courier, 12 October 2022
- *Moment arsonist who set fire to school is given extremely calm treatment by 999 operator,* Connor Teale, Yorkshire Live, 13 October 2022
- *Tacoma serial arsons: Woman charged with murder and 17 counts of arson,* FOX 13 Seattle, 28 November 2022
- *Worker who wanted to get out of work early caused more than $580 million worth of damage,* Katherine Sidnell, LAD Bible, 9 March 2023
- *Howard County jury convicts David Crawford on all felony counts in arson trial,* WBAL TV, 9 March 2023
- *Former Laurel Police Chief turned serial arsonist gets life in prison,* Ryan Dickstein, ABC Baltimore, 27 June 2023
- *Ex-Maryland Police Chief Set 12 'Revenge Fires', Gest Multiple Life Sentences,* Emily Palmer, People, 28 June 2023
- *A police chief who became a serial arsonist is sentenced to life, plus 75 years,* Bill Chappell, NPR, 28 June 2023
- *Probable Cause and Probable Cause Hearings in Criminal Law Cases,* Justia, October 2023
- *Tacoma woman found guilty of murder, arson following deadly 2021 fire,* King5.com, 3 July 2024
- *Pierce County jury finds woman guilty of murder, more than a dozen counts of arson,* Peter Talbot, The News Tribune, 4 July 2024
- *Tacoma woman convicted of murder, arson sentenced to more than 80 years in prison,* Helen Smith, King5.com, 23 July 2024

CHAPTER 12: TOO CLOSE TO HOME

- *Fatalities and Accidents. Orphan girl burned to death. A sad case,* Bendigo Advertiser, 2 December 1909
- *Hedge-Burner Again,* The Argus Melbourne, 20 December 1926
- *Suspected Hedge–Burner,* The Argus Melbourne, 30 November 1927
- *Arsonist Gets 10 Years, Canberra Times,* 28 August 1990
- *Three years' jail for hedge burner,* Courier Mail 24 November 2001
- Power, sex may fuel arson behind fires, Belinda Goldsmith, IOL, 3 January 2002
- *Vic: 31-year-old man to contest hedge arson charges,* AAP General News (Australia), 12 November 2000
- *Hedge burner gets five years,* Courier Mail, 23 November 2001
- *Arson suspected in early morning hedge fires,* The Age, 6 May 2004
- *Fire causes $300,000 damage at old orphanage,* ABC News, 31 August 2006
- *Arsonist sentenced,* Bendigo Advertiser, 26 October 2007
- *Alleged Hills arsonist pleads not guilty,* ABC News, 23 June 2008
- *Proper treatment urged for Hills arsonist,* ABC News, 24 March 2009
- *Woman who lit 21 fires gets 13 years,* Tim Dornin, The Sydney Morning Herald, 7 April 2009
- *Arsonist shocked by 13-year term,* Rebecca Brice, ABC News, 7 April 2009
- *Non-parole cut for hills arsonist,* ABC News, 14 August 2014
- *Police suspect arson behind fire that killed 8yo boy,* ABC News, 14 June 2010
- *$250k reward to catch NT arsonist,* news.com.au, 25 August 2010
- *Arsonist wanted to be a firefighting hero,* Amelia Bentley, Brisbane Times. 3 November 2010
- *Serial arsonist who set fires dating back to 1992 has been jailed for 10 years,* Mark Oberhardt, Courier Mail, 28 January 2011

- *Serial firebug jailed, but set to walk free*, Christine Flatley, Brisbane Times, 28 January 2011
- *Mr and Mrs Arson*, Sam Tomlin and Usman Azad, Kalgoorlie Miner, 10 November 2011
- *Alan and Rebecca Sloane's arson spree 'unprecedented'*, Keith Robertson, PerthNow, 4 April 2012
- *Arsonist couple wanted 'break from kids'*, 9 News, 4 April 2012
- *Fired away*, Usman Azad, Kalgoorlie Miner, 5 April 2012
- *Arson couple sent to jail*, Belle Taylor, The West Australian, 4 April 2012
- *Arsonist's jail term reduced*, Usman Azad, Kalgoorlie Miner, 14 March 2013
- *SA court told alleged firebug Garry John Trestrail tried to burn down McDonald's during arson spree*, Sean Fewster, The Advertiser, 18 August 2014
- *Who is the Boulie Tacker? Two years on and no clues as cyclists hunt 'obsessive' culprit*, Tom Cowie and Liam Mannix, The Age, 15 December 2015
- *Men admit to carrying out Bendigo arson spree*, Peter Lenaghan, ABC News, 22 June 2016
- *Arsonists Ricky Mackay and Corey Devereaux jailed for summer arson spree in Bendigo*, Peter Lenaghan and David Sparkes, ABC News, 13 October 2016
- *Bushfire arsonist Garry Trestrail jailed for 12 years over blazes which threatened neighbours*, Candice Prosser, ABC News, 16 December 2016
- *'You will not speak now': 62 days in, judge tires of argumentative arsonist*, The Age, 16 March 2017
- *Vengeful Vic arsonist jailed for 12 years*, 9 News, 10 April 2017
- *Arsonist jailed for 14 years, trial exposed vulnerability in justice system*, The Age, 10 April 2017

- *Disturbed, dangerous and deluded: the arsonist who won't be deterred,* John Silvester, The Age, 16 September 2017
- *Serial firebug jailed over Vic bushfires,* Caroline Schelle, 7 News, 27 July 2020
- *Bendigo arsonists front the County Court for plea hearing,* Tara Cosoleto and Peter Lenaghan, Bendigo Advertiser, 25 May 2021
- *Bendigo arsonists jailed for series of fires between November 2019 to March 2020,* Tara Cosoleto, Bendigo Advertiser, 2 July 2021
- *Stopping a fire starter,* Police Life, Victoria Police editorial by Jesse Wray McCann, Autum/Winter 2022
- *Serial arsonist jailed for night of 'terror' in Brisbane suburb one day after jail release,* Rex Martinich, 7 News, 27 February 2023
- *Arsonist jailed for 'terrorising' apartment building,* Rex Martinich, Brisbane Times, 27 February 2023

CHAPTER 13: CATCHING THE FIREBUGS

- *Fire Deliberately Lit,* The Canberra Times, 4 July 1990.
- *Students Lit Fires,* Young Arcade, 16 June 1992.
- *Sentence for School Burners,* The Age, 26 June 1992.
- *From Vietnam Nasho to Catching School Crooks,* Colin O'Neill, Australia, 2024.

CHAPTER 14: NURSING HOME TRAGEDY

- *Woman indicted in Chicago Blaze,* The New York Times, 4 February 1976
- *Nursing Home Fire Kills 6 in Illinois,* The New York Times, 5 February 1976
- *23 fire deaths ruled murders,* The Vidette Digital Archives, 28 April 1976
- *Jury clears Nursing Home Aide,* The New York Times, 6 November 1977

- *Man, 88, charged in nursing home fire*, UPI Archives, 30 April 1981
- *Fire sweeps Through Nursing Home in Hartford, Killing 10*, Anthony Depalma and Alan Feuer, The New York Times, 26 February 2003.
- *DPP rejects alleged Quakers Hill nursing home arsonist's manslaughter plea*, Amy Dale, The Daily Telegraph, 13 October 2012
- *Woman who set Nursing Home Fire Will Stay In Conn*, NBC Connecticut, 2 October 2013
- *Quakers Hill Nursing Home fire inquest: Roger Dean 'stalked' former colleague*, Jamelle Wells, ABC News, 30 September 2014
- *Quakers Hill nursing home fire inquest: Owners should be held accountable, friends and relatives say*, ABC News, 9 March 2015
- *Quakers Hill Nursing Home; Inquest into the deaths and fire…2011/391175 [2015] NSW Coroners Court*, 9 March 2015
- *Killer Quakers Hill nurse Roger Dean hired without any reference checks before 14 residents died in aged care fire*, Rebecca Gredley, The West Australian, 7 March 2018
- *Woman Charged With Setting Deadly Nursing Home Fire Incompetent: Judge*, NBC Connecticut, 2 March 2019
- *Hell Hath No Fury Like a Nursing Home on Fire*, Donna R. Gore

CHAPTER 15: NIGHTCLUB AND BACKPACKER HOSTEL FIRES

- *Eighteen young fruit pickers killed in Australian hostel fire*, Richard Phillips, World Socialist Web Site, 24 June 2000
- *Man guilty over fatal hostel fire in Tas*, The Sydney Morning Herald, 23 August 2006
- *NZ man gets nine years jail for Tasmania hostel fire*, NZ Herald, 7 September 2006
- *Argentinian band convicted over nightclub fire*, Rory Carroll, Latin America correspondent, 21 April 2011

- *Five jailed over fatal Buenos Aires nightclub fire,* Associated Press, 20 August 2009
- *Backpacker arsonist on parole,* ABC News, 20 May 2011
- *Arsonist's home is destroyed by fire in Wanganui,* Whanganui Chronicle, 16 January 2015
- *Julio Gonzalez Who Killed 97 at New York Club in'90, Dies at 61,* Sam Roberts, The New York Times, 14 September 2016
- *The Tragic Story of America's Deadliest Nightclub fire,* Erin Blakemore, History Classics, 27 November 2017
- *John Andrew Stuart & Jim Finch: Double Trouble,* Inside Boggo Road, 20 June 2018
- *'They belonged somewhere': the forgotten victims of one of London's deadliest fire,* Simon Usborne, The Guardian–UK, 23 November 2022
- *You don't know about the Denmark Place fire because its 37 victims didn't count,* Simon Usborne, The Guardian–UK, 24 November 2022

CHAPTER 16: GUILTY OR NOT GUILTY

- *New Arson Tools Could Reverse Arizona Murder Convictions,* David Ferrell, The Los Angeles Times, 14 November 1990
- *Wrongful execution almost happened,* Howard Fischer, Capital Media Services, 17 July 2001
- *Field Guide for Fire Investigators,* Richard L.P. Custer, Jones and Bartlett 2003
- *Report on the Peer Review of the Expert Testimony in cases of State of Texas v Cameron Todd Willingham and State of Texas v Ernest Ray Willis*–Arson Review Committee, March 2006
- *Trial By Fire,* David Grann, The New Yorker, 31 August 2009
- *Report Documents the Execution of an Innocent Man in Texas,* Equal Justice Initiative, 2 September 2009
- *Background: Texas Forensic Science Commission's work,* Innocence Project, 11 September 2009

- *Cameron Todd Willingham: Improper Or Wrongful Conviction*, John T Floyd, 29 July 2010
- *Cameron Todd Willingham: Wrongfully Convicted and Executed in Texas*, Innocence Project, 13 September 2010
- *Spark of Truth: Can Science Bring Justice to Arson Trials?* Douglas Starr, 24 October 2011
- *Two Virginia Men Fight Arson Convictions*, Innocence Project, 7 August 2012
- *'The Pioneer Hotel Fire'*, Steve Kroft et al, 60 Minutes, 31 March 2013
- *Innocence Project Deploy Troubled By Plea of Wrongly Convicted Arizona Man*, Innocence Project, 2 April 2013
- *'Welcome back, Mr Taylor': new evidence frees man 42 years after deadly hotel fire*, The Sydney Morning Herald, 5 April 2013
- *The Prosecutor and the Snitch, Did Texas execute and innocent man*, Maurice Possley, The Marshall Project, 3 August 2013
- *Other Disputed Arson Cases*, Innocence Project, 10 October 2014
- *Davey Reedy Granted Full Pardon in 1987 Fatal Arson*, Gentry Locke Attorneys, 23 December 2015
- *Citing flawed forensics, Va. Governor pardons man who spent years in prison in deadly arson*, Rachael Weiner, The Washington Post, 24 December 2015
- *Davey Reedy*, The National Registry of Exonerations, 31 December 2015
- *Debunking Arson Indicators*, Sue Russell, Pacific Standard, 3 May 2017
- *Louis Taylor freed after 42 Years in prison for Deadly Tucson hotel fire, arrested again*, Megan Cassidy, The Republic, 14 July 2017
- *Kirk's Fire Investigation*, David J. Icove and Gerald Haynes, Pearson 8th Edition 2017
- *Statement from the Press Secretary Regarding Executive Clemency for Dwight and Steven Hammond*, The White House, 10 July 2018

- *Executive Grant of Clemency, Dwight Hammond Jnr & Steven Dwight Hammond*, Donald J Trump, President of the United States of America, 10 July 2018
- *What Trump's latest pardon means for the future of the American West*, PBS News, 15 July 2018
- *She, The People: Syrita Steid-Martin, Operation Restoration and Changing The System of Mass Incarceration One Woman At a Time*, Essence, 13 May 2019
- *When justice Fails- Wrongful Convictions in Australia*, Pheobe Meeton, Linked In, 2 October 2020
- *Executive Grant of Clemency, Syrita Steib-Martin*, Donald J Trump, President of the United States of America, 20 January 2021
- *Syrita Steib-Martin gets full pardon from President Trump on final morning of Presidency*, Shore News Network, 20 January 2021
- *New Orleans woman jailed at 19 stunned, elated by pardon from Trump*, Erika Ferrando, Nation World, 20 January 2021
- *Trump pardons local activist Syrita Steib-Martin*, Tiffany Baptiste, Operation Restoration, 21 January 2021
- *Operation Restoration Addresses Unique, Often Overlooked Reintegration Challenges Faced by Women*, Arnold Ventures, 26 April 2022
- *Kathleen Folbigg is free. But people pardoned and exonerated of crimes face unique challenges when released from prison*, Hayley Cullen & Celine van Golde, ABC News, 7 June 2023
- *N4T Investigators: Things heating up between attorney as Louis Taylor civil lawsuit nears trial*, Chorus Nylander, News 4 Tucson, 14 May 2024
- *Trial cancelled in case seeking damages in deadly Tucson hotel fire*, Charles Borla, Tucson News, 19 June 2024

CHAPTER 17: A QUESTION OF INNOCENCE

- *Down in Flames Judge Tosses Out Murder Conviction in 1981 Prescott Arson Case*, J. W. Casserly, New Times, 19 September 1990

- *Column One: New clues in trial by fire: What looked like arson in the past wasn't necessarily so, scientists find. The discoveries may affect the convictions of two men in Arizona*, David Ferrell, Los Angeles Times, 13 November 1990
- *New Arson Tools Could Reverse Arizona Murder Conviction*, David Ferrell, Los Angeles Times, 14 November 1990
- *Trial by Fire: Junk Science Sent Dad to Prison for killing wife, kids*, Hannah Rappleye et al, NBC News, 20 June 2014
- *Amaury Villalobos*, The National Registry of Exonerations, Maurice Possley, 18 December 2015
- *William Vasquez*, The National Registry of Exonerations, Maurice Possley, 18 December 2015
- *Raymond Mora*, The National Registry of Exonerations, Maurice Possley, 18 December 2015
- *Texas woman, wrongly convicted and severely ill, declared innocent in 1993 murder*, Terri Langford and Brandi Grissom, The Dallas Morning News, 2 November 2016
- *Sonia Cacy*, The National Registry of Exonerations, Maurice Possley, 13 February 2017
- *2 Men Wrongfully Convicted in 1980 Fire Will Receive $31 Million*, Alan Feuer, The New York Times, 6 March 2017
- *Ray Girdler*, The National Registry of Exonerations, Maurice Possley, 14 March 2017
- *Scientific Protocols for Fire Investigation, Third Edition*, John J Lentini, CRC Press, 25 October 2018
- *David Lee Gavitt*, The National Registry of Exonerations, Maurice Possley, 6 August 2019
- *Wrongly convicted Ionia man awarded $1.3M from state*, AP News, 15 August 2019
- *The State of Texas Tried to Kill Ernest Willis. But he Still Had a Lot of Living to Do*, Michael Hall, Texas Monthly, 20 October 2021

- *Ernest Ray Willis,* The National Registry of Exonerations, Maurice Possley, 21 October 2021
- *Claude Garrett 65, wrongly jailed for 30 years dis just months after being released,* Tim Hanlon, News Reporter, 3 November 2022
- *Wrongfully Convicted Massachusetts Man Gets $13M Settlement,* Bianca Beltran, NBC 10 Boston News, 3 May 2023
- *A Quest for Justice: The Story Behind the Exoneration of Victor Rosario,* Andrea Petersen, New England Innocence Project, May 2023
- *Philadelphia man exonerated after spending nearly 40 years in prison in deadly fire,* David Chang and Karen Hue, NBC News, 5 February 2024
- *Philadelphia man exonerated after nearly 40 years in prison,* Tesfays Negussie, ABC News, 7 February 2024
- *Man freed after nearly 40 years in prison after murder conviction in 1984 fire is reversed,* U.S. News, 7 February 2024
- *Harold Staten,* The National Registry of Exonerations, Ken Otterbourg, 14 February 2024
- *Philadelphia death row inmate was never in the photo lineup that helped convict*

CHAPTER 18: THE JURY IS STILL OUT

- *The Sceptical Juror Michael Ledford: An Overview, Stuarts Draft, Virginia,* The Sceptical Juror, October/ November 1999
- *'Wrongful Convictions and the Culture of Denial in Japanese Criminal Justice',* David Taylor 2015
- *2 convicted of arsons in Va. Seek to clear names,* Washington Examiner, 6 August 2012
- *This Japanese man spent almost five decades on death row. He could go back,* Emiko Jozuka and Yoko Wakatsuki, CNN, 21 March 2020
- *Court of Appeal hearing for Stuarts Draft man convicted for first-degree murder and arson,* Ayaano Nagaishi, News Leader, 16 July 2021

- *How Police Interrogation Techniques Fail People with Autism,* Dina Nayeri, Time, 4 May 2023
- *Interrogating a Suspect With an Intellectual Disability Using the Reid Technique: Recipe for a False Confession,* Jo Ellen Nott, Criminal Legal News, 1 September 2023
- *Science Proves Man Convicted of "Worst Mass Murer in Massachusetts History 'Is Innocent, Lawyers Argue,* Andrew Quemere, Redditt, 7 April 2024
- *Trial ruling date for man accused of 1966 murder set for September,* Kanako Takahara, thejapantimes, 22 May 2024
- *Japan Prosecutors Seek Death Penalty For World's Longest-Serving Death Row Inmate,* World News, 22 May 2024
- *Expert Witnesses Debate Cause of Deadly Fire That led to Man's Life Sentence,* Andrew Quemere, Redditt, 17 June 2024
- *Judge Hears Arguments About Whether to Overturn Man's 34-Year-Old Murder Convictions,* Andrew Quemere, Redditt, 24 June 2024
- *Man who spent 45 years on death row in Japan hopes for chance to clear his name,* Justin McCurry, The Observer, 7 July 2024
- *Verdict due in retrial of 88-yr-old man over 1966 quadruple murder,* The Mainichi, 21 September 2024
- *He's the world's longest-serving death row inmate. A court ruling may soon clear his name,* Lex Harvey, et al, CNN, 26 September 2024
- *Japanese court acquits a former boxer in 1966 murder retrial after decades on death row,* Mari Yamaguchi, World News, 26 September 2024
- *World's longest-serving death row inmate, 88, is ACQUITTED 56 years after he was sentenced to be hanged for murder in Japan,* Chris Matthews, Daily Mail Australia, 26 September 2024
- *Japanese police chief bows to wrongfully convicted man who spent 45 years on death row,* Michelle De Pacina, Yahoo News, 24 October 2024

PRINCIPAL REFERENCE WEBSITES

- www.abc.net.au
- www.afsa.gov.au
- www.asic.gov.au
- www.ato.gov.au
- www.austlii.edu.au
- www.childrenscourt.vic.gov.au
- www.countycourt.vic.gov.au
- www.fitzroy-legal.org.au
- www.legalaid.vic.gov.au
- www.magistratescourt.vic.gov.au
- www.supremecourt.vic.gov.au
- www.vcat.gov.au
- www.vocat.vic.gov.au
- www.1800respect.org.au
- www.wikipedia.org
- www.trove.nla.gov.au

ABOUT THE AUTHOR

Colin served in Vietnam as a National conscript during 1968-69. On his discharge from the Army, he resumed working for the Victoria Police Department as an unsworn member. In 1974, Colin was appointed Head of School Security for the Victorian Education Department in the prevention and detection of school crime.

He then entered the legal profession, being admitted to practice in 1996 as a Barrister and Solicitor mainly practicing in the areas of crime, family violence and industrial relations. He retired in 2022 and lives on the Mornington Peninsula in Victoria with his wife, Michelle.

www.ingramcontent.com/pod-product-compliance
Lightning Source LLC
Chambersburg PA
CBHW071226070526
44583CB00017B/2068